The Astrology of I Ching

The Astrology of I Ching

Translated from the 'Ho Map Lo Map
Rational Number' Manuscript
by W. K. Chu, Ph.D.

Edited, and commentaries added
by W. A. Sherrill, M.A.
Fellow of the China Academy

SAMUEL WEISER, INC.
York Beach, Maine

First published in 1976
by Routledge & Kegan Paul Ltd
London

Published in the U.S.A.
by Samuel Weiser, Inc.
Box 612
York Beach, Maine 03910

First paperback edition 1979
Revised edition 1980
Reprinted 1983, 1987

ISBN 0-87728-492-X

Printed in Great Britain

Contents

Contents

Figures

Tables

Preface

The Astrology of I Ching is based on a manuscript written in ancient classical Chinese, the title of which, translated literally, is 'Ho Map Lo Map Rational Number'.

The Astrology of I Ching is the product of translations and interpretations made by W. K. Chu, Ph.D., edited and amplified by myself. Dr Chu is among the rare Chinese scholars who are qualified to translate and interpret classical Chinese. Classical Chinese is written in ancient characters and without any punctuation. Many interpretations can be made, but few are the scholars who can truly provide the meaning and intent of what is written. I myself am a Sinophile and have lived in China several times in my life, as well as having studied *I Ching* at Fu Jen University in Taipei, Taiwan. The resultant book in English is such that it retains much of its ancient flavor, yet is modernized sufficiently to be understandable to and usable by Westerners.

W. A. SHERRILL

Introduction

The greater the understanding one has of *I Ching*, The Book of Changes, the more accurate will one's interpretations be of *The Astrology of I Ching*. Both are based on the same concepts and derivations. Both share in ageless Chinese knowledge and philosophy. This is only natural, since *I Ching* is reputedly the embodiment of all things, and its applications are universal. There is only one development of Yang and Yin and their evolution into trigrams and hexagrams. What is different between the two books, though, is the application here of the Celestial Stems and Horary Branches, as a basis for determining the appropriate natal hexagram with its controlling line, and the subsequent evolvement into yearly and daily predictions.

The systems for using *I Ching* for astrological purposes were first set forth by scholars of the Ming Dynasty. As frequently happens with Chinese works, when this astrology was first presented it was attributed to a famous scholar in order to get it accepted rather than who actually developed the ideas being revealed. The Ming scholars said they were merely presenting what Shao Yung (1011–77) had taught. Others claim that its origin goes back many centuries earlier. What the Ming scholars are reputed to have done in developing *The Astrology of I Ching* is to have synthesized and molded ancient concepts into something plausible and usable, and they began with the concept of time.

Time, as understood by the ancient Chinese, is quite different from the literal definition we give it today. Observations, studies and analyses of the cosmos and its influences, coupled with those of the earth and its manifestations, resulted in a sexagenary system of time. From the greatest division to the least division, the same system is applicable. From their studies, the scholars came to believe that there are two systems of forces acting on the earth, namely, those from out in space, called cosmic or celestial, and those generated within and by the earth itself. Five dominant cosmic influences were found, and these were given the names: wood, fire, earth, metal and water. Each of these has its positive and negative aspects. These five influences are also known as elements. The sequence in which they are given above comes from the way they react and interact with one another, and is the order in which they should always be considered. For ease of calculation, the five celestial influences, in their positive and negative aspects, are here designated by capital letters, A through J. They have repeated themselves in this sequence from the time when the sun, earth, moon, and all the planets of our solar system, were in a straight line at the time of the winter solstice. These same studies showed the earth's manifestations and radiations to repeat in cycles of twelve. Today they are called the twelve Horary Branches, the word 'horary' having been adopted from the West. The literal translation of the classical Chinese character would be 'Earthly Branch.' For ease of calculation, they are designated by the lower case alphabetical letters, a through l.

The matching of the ten Celestial Stems, A through J, with the twelve Horary Branches, a through l, produces sexagenary cycles, which are basic to the astrology set forth herein. The commencement of the cycle, naturally, is A and a, or Aa, then Bb, Cc, . . . Jj, Ak, Bl, etc. Carrying this forward, one finds sixty steps between each succeeding Aa.

The foregoing concept of time became the basis for Chinese culture. What we consider literally as time, i.e. hours, minutes and seconds, are but an advancement and refinement of the basic concept for practical purposes. In their striving to make practical use of their knowledge and their concept of time, the Chinese scholars developed, among other things, systems of astrology based on the sexagenary cycle. Using *I Ching* as one of the foundations for their astrology was but a natural and logical development.

The Astrology of I Ching is the most complete of the three astrologies associated with *I Ching*. The Nine House Astrology adopts the Lo Map and the meanings of the trigrams only. It does not consider the hexagrams as a whole, nor the meanings of the individual lines, so it is not truly worthy of being called *I Ching* astrology. The other system is the 'Iron Plate Divine Number' concept, but this is secret and not available.

Perhaps the reader has already observed that the Chinese had a concept of time being both positive and negative. This is not negative in the normal sense, any more than Yin and K'un are destructively negative. Rather, the positive and negative are parts of the eternal cycles, and should be considered as complements rather than opposites. Thus, everything that occurs has its right place and proper usefulness. This idea is, and has been, reflected in Chinese culture throughout its history, and has profoundly affected Chinese thought as well. The use of the positive and negative forces at any given moment plays a vital role in *I Ching* astrology.

The combination of the cosmic and earthly forces in play at any given moment are peculiar to the year, month, day, hour and minute in question. All of these cycles can be represented by the appropriate combinations of Celestial and Horary symbols. As will be seen in the text, by adding up all the odd numbers, one will obtain a total which will determine the heavenly trigram, while the sum of all the even numbers will determine the earthly trigram. The system as devised, regrettably, is only applicable for Northern hemisphere calculations.

Two dichotomies exist which need to be considered jointly. In *I Ching*, man is designated as positive (Ch'ien, Male, Yang) and woman, his counterpart, as negative (K'un, Female, Yin). Years in *I Ching* astrology are alternately positive and negative. A man's or woman's Celestial Stem influence is greatest in the years that match their respective nature, i.e. is uppermost in those years in which the polarities are the same. The year and the person then tend to harmonize with each other. Consequently, if born in a positive year, a man's heavenly trigram is at the top of his natal hexagram, while a woman's is below; conversely for negative years.

As stated above, the earth's influence follows the Horary pattern. As a result, in ancient times, the day was divided into twelve two-hour periods. The day begins at midnight; however, the Yang forces begin returning at 11 p.m., so for calculation purposes the first of the twelve two-hour segments was designated as from 11 p.m. to 1 a.m., and given the symbol 'a.' The additional two-hour segments up to 11 a.m. were designated 'b,' 'c,' 'd,' 'e,' and 'f,' with the Yin hours, 11 a.m. to 11 p.m., indicated by 'g,' 'h,' 'i,' 'j,' 'k,' and 'l,' respectively. The Yang force entering before the midnight of a new day harmonizes with the Yang force entering before the beginning of the new year, in accordance with its position in the Later Heaven Sequence of trigrams. Days and years parallel each other in the cycle of events.

Years also were divided by twelve, into months. The astrological year begins with the winter solstice, which is the mid-point of the eleventh month. The winter solstice is the basis for all yearly and subsequent calculations.

Out of the sum of the numbers representing the place, date, hour and minute of birth, one develops a natal or 'Pre-Heaven' hexagram, with a controlling line. This forms the basis for natal predictions, and governs the ascending phase of one's life. By reversing the trigrams one develops the Later Heaven hexagram, which controls the descending phase of one's life. Both, however, can be modified by karma and the exercise of one's free will. The lines in the two hexagrams each govern in turn a shorter cycle of one's life, and the numerical value of each is considered as if it were a moving line in the basic *I Ching*, i.e. a Yin line as six and a Yang line as nine. Therefore, a Yin line controls for a period of six years and a Yang line for nine years. Appropriate subcycles are thus formed for the different phases of life.

The predictions given are based on the interaction of the two trigrams making up each hexagram, with consideration of the position of the controlling line. When elements work in harmony or forces cooperate, then favorableness and success are predicted. The degree is determined by the known interaction of such elements or forces.

It will be noted that there are predictions for the 'Most Auspicious' and for the 'Least Auspicious.' This is based on the concept of reincarnation, whereby each soul returns at a certain level and under circumstances determined by his or her karma. Thus, two boys (or two girls) born in the same hospital at the same moment would have the same natal hexagram and controlling line, but one would be more auspicious than the other (except in extremely rare cases). Those born at the same time and in the same place on the whole have parallel influences in their lives, and are known as 'time twins.'

Fortunately, man has a certain degree of control over his destiny. By improving himself inwardly, a man can raise his level of auspiciousness. This can be done by observing the lessons to be learned during the course of the cycles of the hexagrams which repeat themselves frequently in his life. These hexagrams are of especial importance to him. Whether he increases his auspiciousness during his life will be determined by how well he learns the lessons set before him, coupled, of course, with his karma.

The forces acting on an individual's life are never static. Furthermore, there are no clear-cut starting or stopping points. Therefore, in addition to one's natal hexagram, one should look at two other hexagrams to obtain a more complete picture of oneself. These are (1) the 'inner' hexagram, which is composed of lines 2, 3, and 4 of the natal hexagram for the lower trigram, and lines 3, 4, and 5 for the upper trigram; and (2) the hexagram which would be formed by using the preceding or succeeding time group closest to the minute of birth; e.g. if born at 12.30 a.m., which is in the Yang 'a' period, one should develop a hexagram for the 'b' period and note the dominant characteristics, which are likely to have an influence on one. If, on the other hand, one was born shortly before midnight, one should develop a hexagram for the previous 'l' period and note the dominant aspects of it. The inner hexagram mainly shows what the individual is or should be like inwardly, while the natal hexagram itself covers the principal external considerations.

The daily predictions, in some cases, may be hard to understand. At first glance, what is said may not seem too appropriate. One must look at both the external and inner influences to discern the value and usefulness of the prediction. In some cases, too, it should be taken literally and in others figuratively. No two persons will extract exactly the same meaning from what is said. Furthermore, at different times in one's life, when a daily prediction is repeated, it will require a different interpretation as well. It is only by hindsight that the true meanings become fully manifest, hence it behoves one to analyze what is said in the light of occurrences. With considerable experience, interpretations will gradually become more lucid. Also, by following the advice given, one will slowly improve oneself inwardly, and have a better life externally. At some point in life one will

5

recognize that one's life has improved as a result of following the advice given, and from observing the cautions contained therein. At that point, one may also recognize that 'inanimate' objects have life and spirit as well as 'animate' beings, and thereby obtain an increased insight into the oneness of the universe.

Thus one can readily see that *The Astrology of I Ching* is far more than just a book of portents. It is a complete philosophy and way of life as well. Repeatedly, it points out the attributes and the value of 'the superior man.' It shows which courses are superior and which are inferior. At the same time, it shows how to handle any situation, and the improvements man can make by following the laws of heaven and earth.

The basic point to remember is that all life on earth is affected by the interaction of the earthly forces with the celestial forces at any given moment. The interaction of these forces is the basis of total time as far as our planet is concerned. The time expressed in the sexagenary cycles, both large and small, is a reflection of these influences and provides an expression for the particular influences at a particular instant. That, fundamentally, is why the vast majority of Chinese people believe in astrology and look for the best possible ways to interpret the celestial and earthly influences. Many feel the *I Ching*, with its universal application, is the best medium for such interpretation.

The value and benefits which can be found in *The Astrology of I Ching* are available to everyone. Find them, use them, and a rich and rewarding life can be yours.

W. A. Sherrill
Los Angeles, California

1 / Background and Computations

Foundations

What a truly superb document of ancient wisdom we have in the book *I Ching*! Properly understood, it is a guide for daily affairs and actions in all circumstances. According to the Chinese, it is the basis of all there is in the universe, and reflects the inter-relationship of all elements and aspects, spiritual and material. Any situation or condition man may find himself in, or can imagine, is included within the scope and meanings of *I Ching*. It is based on heaven and its laws as manifested on this earth, and thus is applicable to any science, discipline, or even the most remote mundane consideration. It embraces all that there is. Perhaps its greatest value, for those who can understand it, lies in showing man the right path for spiritual development. And now, in conjunction with the foregoing, it can be used for astrological predictions, based on the influences existing at the time of birth conjoined with the dimension of time. These follow the pattern of known laws, and hence matters are predictable. These predictions are for the material realm, but need not be inevitable, since man has free will, and the realm of spirit, in which free will operates, can override the material realm in which these natural laws operate.

The question naturally arises as to why a 'Book of Changes,' based on hexagrams, should lend itself to reliable astrological predictions. The answer, strange as it may seem, lies within the question itself. The Book is based on the manifestations of the universe converted into natural laws. Furthermore, the seeds of the past determine the present, and the seeds of the present determine the future. As an example, we can observe an oak sapling. We immediately know two things, namely, that it came from an acorn, and its approximate age, from its size and height. We can envisage that under normal circumstances it will become a full-grown oak tree, of a size befitting the climate and circumstances in which it finds itself. Another reliability factor is the fact that the hexagrams are the result of the evolutionary process of Yin and Yang, the two primal forces, and therefore reflect the various fundamental situations in the universe. Yin and Yang are the positive and negative forces through which the Universal Creative manifests itself. Thus the hexagrams symbolically represent any situation man can encounter. So, with the hexagrams representing the multifarious situations in which a man can find himself, and with the changes in these situations following natural and observable laws, the astrology of *I Ching*, properly understood and interpreted, can be used reliably by those who care to use it.

I Ching goes back as far as Fu Hsi who ruled before the Flood (c. 3000 B.C.),* and the basis of the astrology of *I Ching* may go back that far too. Evidence of the recording of sexagenary cycles goes back as far as Huang Ti (the Yellow Emperor). At that time, *I Ching* was being transmitted as easily memorizable verse. It may be assumed that knowledge of the cycles could have been transmitted likewise. It was not until around 1123 B.C. that King Wên and his son, the Duke of Chou, set *I Ching* down in writing, and provided explanations for the judgments and lines. Confucius (551–479 B.C.) wrote commentaries on *I Ching*, and later scholars were also interested in these matters. Some sources say that our present expanded system of astrology comes from Chen Tuan, a famous immortal during the Sung Dynasty, with the work subsequently being completed by Shao Yung during the same dynastic period. Others say that it was the work of Ming scholars, and attributed to Shao Yung.

As most scholars know, the shell and bone language and usage were developed to record oracular communications for kings. Evidence of astrological predictions has been found on shell and bone relics, but these are not as yet identifiable to any specific system. They have, however, been used to help trace the origin of the sexagenary cycles, on which this astrology is based.

* * *

* There are many dates given for the rule of Fu Hsi. Some even go back a million years.

Basically, there are three systems of *I Ching* astrology:

1. *T'ieh Pan Shen Shu,* which, translated literally, means 'Iron Plate Divine Number.' This is a secret system, reputedly developed by the same Shao Yung mentioned above. It is known only to a few chosen people, and is passed on verbally to a select few. It is a numerological system whereby one can compute a set of numbers for a specific purpose, e.g. if the computation came up with the numbers 1, 6, 7, 8, 9, 3, 2, the meaning could be 'You are going to bear a son as your first child.' This system is still secret today.

2. *Ho Lo Li Shu,* which translated literally means 'Ho Map Lo Map Rational Number,' the Ho Map being Figure 1, and the Lo Map referring to the Later Heaven Sequence of trigrams and the Magic Square of three (Figures 2 and 3).

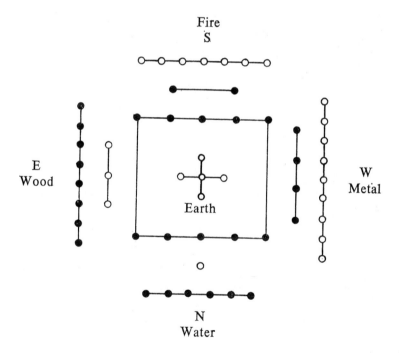

Figure 1. Ho Map

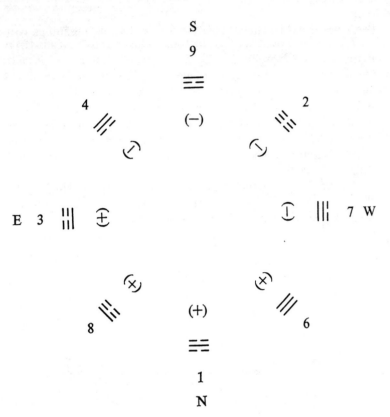

Figure 2. Later Heaven Sequence

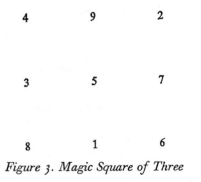

Figure 3. Magic Square of Three

The trigrams with their evolution and additional meanings will be discussed in detail subsequently (see chapter 2 pp. 61–4). This much will suffice here:

1 K'an Winter   6 Ch'ien
2 K'un   7 Tui, Autumn
3 Chên, Spring   8 Kên
4 Sun   9 Li, Summer
5 (to be discussed later)

There are two basic sequences of the trigrams, one is called the 'Later Heaven Sequence' and the other the 'Earlier' or 'Pre-Heaven Sequence.' The Earlier Heaven represents everything as it is in heaven, as well as all thoughts prior to their manifestation on earth. The Later Heaven is the earthly fulfilment and consummation of the Earlier Heaven, and represents conditions as they are on earth, as brought about by heaven.

Figures 1 and 2 can be turned into a numerological system, and this is what will be described in this book. As stated above, it was probably revealed by Chen Tuan and completed by Shao Yung.

3. *Chiu Kung Ming Li*, the third system, is the 'Nine House Astrology' or 'Nine Star Astrology,' but these words do not have the same meanings as 'house' and 'star' in Western astrology, and should not be confused with the latter. This system is developed from the Lo Map (Figure 2 above) but has nothing to do with the Ho Map (Figure 1). Rather, the nine numbers involved are associated with colors, which are equally symbolic and have many meanings. The color associations are:

1. white   4. green   7. red
2. black   5. yellow   8. white
3. jade green   6. white   9. purple

The Nine Star Astrology is the basis of the science of Chinese geomancy, which has developed as an important branch of this astrology. The Chinese use geomancy primarily for the determination of favorable sites for establishing businesses, for buying or renting houses, for ascertaining the most propitious rooms for specific purposes, and for selecting burial sites, etc. *I Ching* is also used for this.

Another branch of this astrology is known as 'directionology,' whereby one can determine the yearly, monthly, and daily directions to follow, for favorable, neutral or unfavorable results. It is used mainly for such matters as business, vacations, finding the right partner or party, tactics in battle, etc.

Systems 1 and 3 above are mentioned solely for the reader's general information, so that he is aware that such systems exist.

Some Chinese systems use the beginning of spring as their time base, but the system described herein uses the winter solstice as its starting point.

Referring back to Figure 1, it is to be noted that five elements are shown, namely, wood, fire, earth, metal and water. These, according to the Chinese, are the basic elements of the universe, and as they each act in both a positive and a negative aspect, the five, thus doubled in effect, become the ten Celestial Stems. It should be noted that these elements agree basically with those of the early Western philosophers, the Greeks in particular.

The names of the elements are extreme simplifications. While they represent many different things, among the more important we find:

Wood — vitality, east (when the sun rises in the east a sense of vitality and vigor comes over the earth), the spring, the liver, green (or the color of young shoots);

Fire — the sun, fighting, brilliance, summer, the heart, south, red;

Earth — yellow, middle, the spleen, the abdomen, the four seasons (the seasons are brought about by the interaction of the earth and the sun, but they belong, as a complete cycle, to the earth);

Metal — autumn, west (symbolizing decline), white, the lungs;

Water — winter, the kidneys, black, north, hidden things (from winter, when all things tend to hide or become inactive).

The progressive sequence of these elements in the material world (Later Heaven) is:

Wood gives birth to fire;
fire gives birth to earth;
earth gives birth to metal;
metal gives birth to water;
water gives birth to wood.

The above sequence is used in the astrology presented here.
Another sequence, used for different purposes, is:

Wood conquers (overcomes) earth;
earth conquers (overcomes) water;
water conquers (overcomes) fire;
fire conquers (overcomes) metal;
metal conquers (overcomes) wood.

From these sequences one observes that the five elements form
cycles, through creation or through subjugation. Furthermore, if
wood gives birth to fire, it means that the potentiality of fire is in
the wood itself; and, if fire gives birth to earth, the potentiality
of earth is in the fire, etc. Therefore, the five elements are not
five different and distinct things, but are one cosmic force,
differentiated into five appearances by time and space.

The five elements are very important in Chinese astrology and
in medical philosophy. For instance, all the parts of the body are
connected to form the whole. The parts should not be treated
individually, since a strong relationship with some other part
always exists, e.g. if the liver is not in good condition this will
have an effect on the heart, since wood (liver) gives birth to fire
(heart). The heart, in turn, will affect some other part of the body.
Strengthening medications will not only improve a particular
organ but others as well. Thus, if we strengthen the kidneys by
some means it will also vitalize the liver, because water (kidneys)
gives birth to wood (liver).

A similar sequential effect of the elements is considered as
taking place within the sequences of trigrams which generate
the computations for the astrological predictions. The relationship of the trigrams to the elements is shown in Fu Hsi's Earlier
Heaven (also called Pre-Heaven) Sequence. (Figure 4.)

The matching of the trigrams* (and their respective positive

---

* This varies from other pairings but is correct for *I Ching* astrology.

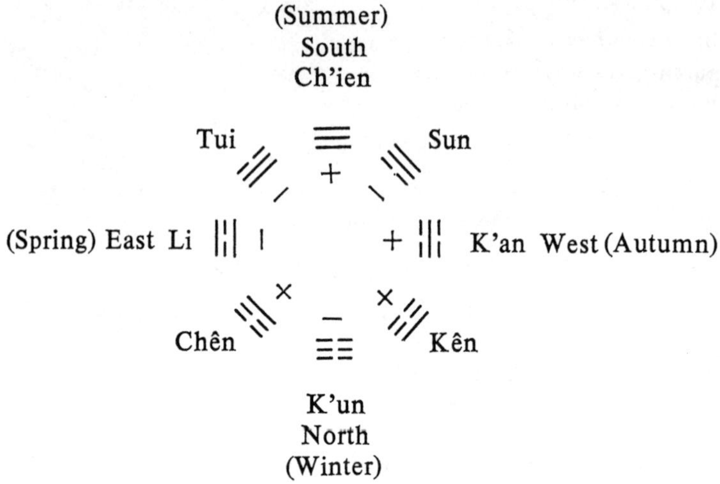

(Summer)
South
Ch'ien

Figure 4. *Fu Hsi's Earlier Heaven Sequence*

and negative natures) with the five elements, to produce the ten Celestial Stems, is as follows:

Name of Stem	Number			Element
Chia	6	Ch'ien (+)	☰	wood
I	2	K'un (−)	☷	
Ping	8	Kên (+)	☶	fire
Ting	7	Tui (−)	☱	
Wu	1	K'an (+)	☵	earth
Chi	9	Li (−)	☲	
Keng	3	Chên (+)	☳	metal
Hsin	4	Sun (−)	☴	
Jen	6	Ch'ien (+)	☰	water
Kuei	2	K'un (−)	☷	

Note that two of the elements share the same pair of trigrams and numbers, but the Celestial Stems are not identical, giving them different meanings and relationships. Also, there is no number five.

The astrological aspects of this book are based on the interrelationship and interaction of the foregoing ten Celestial Stems with the twelve Horary Branches. The effects produced are ascertainable from the system of rational numbers assigned to the Celestial Stems and the Horary Branches.

The twelve Horary Branches and their numbering are as follows:

Name of Branch	Numbers	Element
Tzu	1 and 6	water
Ch'ou	5 and 10	earth
Yin	3 and 8	wood
Mao	3 and 8	wood
Ch'en	5 and 10	earth
Szu	2 and 7	fire
Wu	2 and 7	fire
Wei	5 and 10	earth
Shen	4 and 9	metal
Yu	4 and 9	metal
Hsu	5 and 10	earth
Hai	1 and 6	water

Referring back to Figure 1 (page 9) it is to be noted that each element in the Ho Map has two numbers. These numbers are the same as those tabulated for each element above, the Ho Map having formed the basis for the values. Earth being represented four times is indicative of its interaction with each of the other four elements. The numbering, other than that of earth, which is given five and ten, goes from north to east to south to west. North (water) is also winter, the time when the new astrological year begins, and hence is logically given the number one.

The Sexagenary Cycles

A sexagenary (sixty-year) cycle is used in *I Ching* astrology. It is formed by the interrelationship and interaction of the ten Celestial Stems with the twelve Horary Branches. It would, at first glance, appear that the cycle should be 120 years, i.e. ten times twelve, or the product of the total number of Stems and Branches. As mentioned above, the Stems and the Branches each have their positive and negative aspects, but here only the positive are conjoined with the positive, and the negative with the negative, hence the number sixty. From the mathematical point of view, sixty is the lowest common denominator of ten and twelve.

The starting point of the sexagenary cycle is said to have been about a million years ago, at the time of the winter solstice when the sun, the moon, all the planets, and the earth were in a straight line at midnight. The sexagenary cycle has been computed from that time to the present and has had the calendar adjusted to it. It will be noted that there are three different sexagenary sub-cycles, called Upper, Middle and Lower. The use of three sexagenary cycles instead of just one began in the Ming Dynasty in order to match this astrology to the Nine Star astrology. The lowest common denominator for the two astrologies is 180 years, so since a sixty-year cycle is used here, three subcycles develop (three times sixty equals 180).

According to Chinese astrological calculations, the present sexagenary cycle is the Middle Cycle (extending from 1924 through 1983). The Lower Cycle will be 1984 through 2043. The previous Upper Cycle was 1864 through 1923. (See Tables 3a, 3b and 3c.)

For ease of calculation, capital alphabetical letters are assigned to the ten Celestial Stems, and small alphabetical letters to the Horary Branches. Their positive and negative characteristics are also shown in Table 1.

Table 1   *Alphabetical symbols and characteristics of the Celestial Stems and Horary Branches*

The ten Celestial Stems:

wood	fire	earth	metal
A (+) B (−)	C (+) D (−)	E (+) F (−)	G (+) H (−)
6 2	8 7	1 9	3 4

water			
I (+) J (−)			
6 2			

The twelve Horary Branches:

water	earth	wood	earth	fire

a (+)   b (−)   c (+) and d (−)   e (+)   f (−) and g (+)
1 and 6 5 and 10   3 and 8   5 and 10   2 and 7

earth	metal	earth	water

h (−)   i (+) and j (−)   k (+)   l (−)
5 and 10   4 and 9   5 and 10   1 and 6

Note: In the twelve Branches, each major element appears twice, once positive and once negative, while earth appears positive twice and negative twice.

The sexagenary cycle is thus formed of the following combinations, and the positive or negative character of each is also given (Table 2).

Table 2   *The sexagenary cycle*

1 Aa+	11 Ak+	21 Ai+	31 Ag+	41 Ae+	51 Ac+
2 Bb−	12 Bl−	22 Bj−	32 Bh−	42 Bf−	52 Bd−
3 Cc+	13 Ca+	23 Ck+	33 Ci+	43 Cg+	53 Ce+
4 Dd−	14 Db−	24 Dl−	34 Dj−	44 Dh−	54 Df−
5 Ee+	15 Ec+	25 Ea+	35 Ek+	45 Ei+	55 Eg+
6 Ff−	16 Fd−	26 Fb−	36 Fl−	46 Fj−	56 Fh−
7 Gg+	17 Ge+	27 Gc+	37 Ga+	47 Gk+	57 Gi+
8 Hh−	18 Hf−	28 Hd−	38 Hb−	48 Hl−	58 Hj−
9 Ii+	19 Ig+	29 Ie+	39 Ic+	49 Ia+	59 Ik+
10 Jj−	20 Jh−	30 Jf−	40 Jd−	50 Jb−	60 Jl−

The sexagenary subcycles

Table 3a   *Middle cycle* (1924–1983)

year	yearly cycle	daily cycle	year	yearly cycle	daily cycle	year	yearly cycle	daily cycle
1924	1	16	1925	2	22	1926	3	27
1927	4	32	1928	5	37	1929	6	43
1930	7	48	1931	8	53	1932	9	58
1933	10	4	1934	11	9	1935	12	14
1936	13	19	1937	14	25	1938	15	30
1939	16	35	1940	17	40	1941	18	46
1942	19	51	1943	20	56	1944	21	1
1945	22	7	1946	23	12	1947	24	17
1948	25	22	1949	26	28	1950	27	33
1951	28	38	1952	29	43	1953	30	49
1954	31	54	1955	32	59	1956	33	4
1957	34	10	1958	35	15	1959	36	20
1960	37	25	1961	38	31	1962	39	36
1963	40	41	1964	41	46	1965	42	52
1966	43	57	1967	44	2	1968	45	7
1969	46	13	1970	47	18	1971	48	23
1972	49	28	1973	50	34	1974	51	39
1975	52	44	1976	53	49	1977	54	55
1978	55	60	1979	56	5	1980	57	10
1981	58	16	1982	59	21	1983	60	26

Table 3b *Upper cycle* (1864–1923)

year	yearly cycle	daily cycle	year	yearly cycle	daily cycle	year	yearly cycle	daily cycle
1864	1	2	1865	2	8	1866	3	13
1867	4	18	1868	5	23	1869	6	29
1870	7	34	1871	8	39	1872	9	44
1873	10	50	1874	11	55	1875	12	60
1876	13	5	1877	14	11	1878	15	16
1879	16	21	1880	17	26	1881	18	32
1882	19	37	1883	20	42	1884	21	47
1885	22	53	1886	23	58	1887	24	3
1888	25	8	1889	26	14	1890	27	19
1891	28	24	1892	29	29	1893	30	35
1894	31	40	1895	32	45	1896	33	50
1897	34	56	1898	35	1	1899	36	6
1900	37	11	1901	38	16	1902	39	21
1903	40	26	1904	41	31	1905	42	37
1906	43	42	1907	44	47	1908	45	52
1909	46	58	1910	47	3	1911	48	8
1912	49	13	1913	50	19	1914	51	24
1915	52	29	1916	53	34	1917	54	40
1918	55	45	1919	56	50	1920	57	55
1921	58	1	1922	59	6	1923	60	11

Note: Daily cycle numbers are not interchangeable between the subcycles.

Table 3c   *Lower cycle* (1984–2043)

year	yearly cycle	daily cycle	year	yearly cycle	daily cycle	year	yearly cycle	daily cycle
1984	1	31	1985	2	37	1986	3	42
1987	4	47	1988	5	52	1989	6	58
1990	7	3	1991	8	8	1992	9	13
1993	10	19	1994	11	24	1995	12	29
1996	13	34	1997	14	40	1998	15	45
1999	16	50	2000	17	55	2001	18	1
2002	19	6	2003	20	11	2004	21	16
2005	22	22	2006	23	27	2007	24	32
2008	25	37	2009	26	43	2010	27	48
2011	28	53	2012	29	58	2013	30	4
2014	31	9	2015	32	14	2016	33	19
2017	34	25	2018	35	30	2019	36	35
2020	37	40	2021	38	46	2022	39	51
2023	40	56	2024	41	1	2025	42	7
2026	43	12	2027	44	17	2028	45	22
2029	46	28	2030	47	33	2031	48	38
2032	49	43	2033	50	49	2034	51	54
2035	52	59	2036	53	4	2037	54	10
2038	55	15	2039	56	20	2040	57	25
2041	58	31	2042	59	36	2043	60	41

Table 4   *The twenty-four seasons*

Name	Month	Hexagram	Date (1975)	Time (GMT)*	C.L.S.†
Little Cold			1–05–75	23:18	285
	(−)12th	䷒			
Severe Cold			1–20–75	16:37	300
Spring Begins			2–04–75	10:59	315
	(+)1st	䷊			
Rain Water			2–19–75	6:50	330
Excited Insects			3–06–75	5:06	345
	(−)2nd	䷡			
Vernal Equinox			3–21–75	5:57	360
Clear and Bright			4–05–75	10:02	15
	(+)3rd	䷪			
Grain Rains			4–20–75	17:07	30
Summer Begins			5–06–75	3:27	45
	(−)4th	䷀			
Grain Fills			5–21–75	16:24	60
Grain in Ear			6-06–75	7:42	75
	(+)5th	䷫			
Summer Solstice			6–22–75	0:26	90
Slight Heat			7–07–75	17:59	105
	(−)6th	䷠			
Great Heat			7–23–75	11:20	120
Autumn Begins			8–08–75	3:45	135
	(+)7th	䷋			
Limit of Heat			8–23–75	18:24	150
White Dew			9–08–75	6:33	165
	(−)8th	䷓			
Autumnal Equinox			9–23–75	15:55	180

Table 4 contd.

Name	Month	Hexagram	Date (1975)	Time (GMT)*	C.L.S.†
Cold Dew		䷖	10–08–75	22:02	195
	(+)9th				
Hoar Frost Descends			10–24–75	1:06	210
Winter Begins		䷁	11–08–75	1:03	225
	(−)10th				
Little Snow			11–22–75	22:31	240
Heavy Snow		䷗	‡12–07–75	17:47	255
	(+)11th				
Winter Solstice			12–22–75	11:46	270

* GMT: Greenwich Mean Time.   † C.L.S.: Celestial longitude of the sun.
‡ Note that the astrological year begins in the same month that the Yang line, i.e. the creative force, re-enters the hexagram at the bottom.

Table 5   *Monthly Celestial Stems and Horary Branches**

Month	Season		Applicable years				
			A and F	B and G	C and H	D and I	E and J
December (last half)	+	Winter Solstice	Aa	Ca	Ea	Ga	Ia
January	−	Little Cold / Severe Cold	Bb	Db	Fb	Hb	Jb
February	+	Spring Begins / Rain Water	Cc	Ec	Gc	Ic	Ac
March	−	Excited Insects / Vernal Equinox	Dd	Fd	Hd	Jd	Bd

April	+	{	Clear and Bright Grain Rains	Ee	Ge	Ie	Ae	Ce
May	−	{	Summer Begins Grain Fills	Ff	Hf	Jf	Bf	Df
June	+	{	Grain in Ear Summer Solstice	Gg	Ig	Ag	Cg	Eg
July	−	{	Slight Heat Great Heat	Hh	Jh	Bh	Dh	Fh
August	+	{	Autumn Begins Limit of Heat	Ii	Ai	Ci	Ei	Gi
September	−	{	White Dew Autumnal Equinox	Jj	Bj	Dj	Fj	Hj
October	+	{	Cold Dew Hoar Frost Descends	Ak	Ck	Ek	Gk	Ik
November	−	{	Winter Begins Little Snow	Bl	Dl	Fl	Hl	Jl
December (first half)	+		Heavy Snow	Ca	Ea	Ga	Ia	Aa

---

* The astrological year begins at the time of the winter solstice immediately preceding the calendar year. This system is not applicable to the Southern hemisphere.

23

Table 6 *Daily cycle values*

Month	Day														
	1	2	3	4	5	6	7	8	9	10	11	12	13	14	15
Jan.	0	1	2	3	4	5	6	7	8	9	10	11	12	13	14
Feb.	31	32	33	34	35	36	37	38	39	40	41	42	43	44	45
Mar.*	59	60	1	2	3	4	5	6	7	8	9	10	11	12	13
Apr.*	30	31	32	33	34	35	36	37	38	39	40	41	42	43	44
May*	60	1	2	3	4	5	6	7	8	9	10	11	12	13	14
Jun.*	31	32	33	34	35	36	37	38	39	40	41	42	43	44	45
Jul.*	1	2	3	4	5	6	7	8	9	10	11	12	13	14	15
Aug.*	32	33	34	35	36	37	38	39	40	41	42	43	44	45	46
Sep.*	3	4	5	6	7	8	9	10	11	12	13	14	15	16	17
Oct.*	33	34	35	36	37	38	39	40	41	42	43	44	45	46	47
Nov.*	4	5	6	7	8	9	10	11	12	13	14	15	16	17	18
Dec.*	34	35	36	37	38	39	40	41	42	43	44	45	46	47	48

Month	Day (contd)															
	16	17	18	19	20	21	22	23	24	25	26	27	28	29	30	31
Jan.	15	16	17	18	19	20	21	22	23	24	25	26	27	28	29	30
Feb.	46	47	48	49	50	51	52	53	54	55	56	57	58			
Mar.*	14	15	16	17	18	19	20	21	22	23	24	25	26	27	28	29
Apr.*	45	46	47	48	49	50	51	52	53	54	55	56	57	58	59	

24

May*   15 16 17 18 19 20 21 22 23 24 25 26 27 28 29 30

Jun.* 46 47 48 49 50 51 52 53 54 55 56 57 58 59 60

Jul.* 16 17 18 19 20 21 22 23 24 25 26 27 28 29 30 31

Aug.* 47 48 49 50 51 52 53 54 55 56 57 58 59 60 1 2

Sep.* 18 19 20 21 22 23 24 25 26 27 28 29 30 31 32

Oct.* 48 49 50 51 52 53 54 55 56 57 58 59 60 1 2 3

Nov.* 19 20 21 22 23 24 25 26 27 28 29 30 31 32 33

Dec.* 49 50 51 52 53 54 55 56 57 58 59 60 1 2 3 4

* Add one day during leap years.

The symbols for the hour of birth are obtained from Table 7. Enter the table with the exact time of birth and the capital letter designation for the correct day.

Table 7   *Hourly Celestial Stems and Horary Branches*

Exact time	Stem for correct day				
	A and F	B and G	C and H	D and I	E and J
Midnight to 1 a.m.	Aa	Ca	Ea	Ga	Ia
1 a.m. to 3 a.m.	Bb	Db	Fb	Hb	Jb
3 a.m. to 5 a.m.	Cc	Ec	Gc	Ic	Ac
5 a.m. to 7 a.m.	Dd	Fd	Hd	Jd	Bd
7 a.m. to 9 a.m.	Ee	Ge	Ie	Ae	Ce
9 a.m. to 11 a.m.	Ff	Hf	Jf	Bf	Df
11 a.m. to 1 p.m.	Gg	Ig	Ag	Cg	Eg
1 p.m. to 3 p.m.	Hh	Jh	Bh	Dh	Fh
3 p.m. to 5 p.m.	Ii	Ai	Ci	Ei	Gi
5 p.m. to 7 p.m.	Jj	Bj	Dj	Fj	Hj
7 p.m. to 9 p.m.	Ak	Ck	Ek	Gk	Ik
9 p.m. to 11 p.m.	Bl	Dl	Fl	Hl	Jl
11 p.m. to Midnight	Ca	Ea	Ga	Ia	Aa

TRUE LOCAL TIME

True local time must be used in determing the hour and minute of birth, before entering the appropriate tables. Since the calculations in this book are based on longitude 120 degrees East, it will be necessary to correct time: (a) for longitude; (b) for daylight-saving time, or other local time adjustments. (Hawaii, for example, for many years used time zone 10½.)

Longitude corrections should be made by adding one minute of time for each fifteen minutes of longitude the location is east of the standard time meridian, or subtracting one minute of time for each fifteen minutes of longitude the location is west of the standard time meridian (see Table 8a). An additional correction must be also made, using Table 8b.

Table 8a *Time corrections (standard meridian)*

Time Meridians East or West	Longitude variations from time zone							
	15′ of	30′ of	45′ of	1°	2°	3°	4°	
	Minutes of time							
o degrees	1	2	3	4	8	12	16	*
15 ,,	1	2	3	4	8	12	16	*
30 ,,	1	2	3	4	8	12	16	*
45 ,,	1	2	3	4	8	12	16	*
60 ,,	1	2	3	4	8	12	16	*
75 ,,	1	2	3	4	8	12	16	*
90 ,,	1	2	3	4	8	12	16	*
105 ,,	1	2	3	4	8	12	16	*
120 ,,	1	2	3	4	8	12	16	*
135 ,,	1	2	3	4	8	12	16	*
150 ,,	1	2	3	4	8	12	16	*
165 ,,	1	2	3	4	8	12	16	*
180 ,,	1	2	3	4	8	12	16	*

* For 5, 6, and 7 degrees from the standard time meridian the addition or subtraction would be:

    5 degrees 20 minutes of time
    6 degrees 24 ,, ,, ,,
    7 degrees 28 ,, ,, ,,

Beyond 7½ degrees, work to the next time meridian.
Note that all answers are given in minutes of time.

I Ching is based on observations of heaven and earth. The astrology of *I Ching* is, additionally, based on observations of the sun. Hence the sun's position with respect to the earth must be considered. The sun progresses roughly four minutes daily. Since 120 degrees East is the reference longitude, one must add one minute of time for each ninety degrees (to the nearest forty-five degrees) the location involved is west of 120°E., or as shown in Table 8b.

Table 8b   *Time corrections (longitude)*

1 minute for 30°E. ($\pm 45°$)
2 minutes for 60°W. ($\pm 45°$)
3 minutes for 150°W. ($\pm 45°$)

Examples   a. *Kialua, Hawaii.* December 17, 1935. Clock reading 10.58 a.m. Longitude 157° 43′ W. Time zone 10½, with the standard time meridian being 157° 30′ W. 157° 43′ W. is 13′ west of the standard meridian. Enter Table 8a, and nearest to 13′ one finds that a correction of one minute of time is necessary. Since the location (Kialua) is west of the time meridian, subtract the correction, i.e. 10.58 minus one minute is 10.57 a.m. From Table 8b, it is apparent that one needs to add three minutes as a longitude correction. However, as Hawaii was time zone 10½ at the date given, so one needs to correct to the nearest standard time zone, which in this case is 165° W. (Table 8a.) This correction is thirty minutes of time for 7½°, and since the location is east of this meridian, the thirty minutes are added. The true astrological time is, therefore: 10.57 a.m. + 3 + 30 minutes = 11.30 a.m.

b. *Charleston, South Carolina.* Longitude 80° W. 12.08 a.m. November 3, 1970. The standard meridian is 75° W., hence Charleston is eighty minus seventy-five, or five degrees west of the standard meridian. From Table 8a one finds that the correction is twenty minutes of time and in this case it is to be subtracted. For 80° W. the longitude correction is two minutes (Table 8b). So the true astrological time is 12.08 a.m. − 20 + 2 minutes = 11.50 p.m. November 2.

c. *Las Vegas, Nevada.* July 15, 1972. 1.15 a.m. reported time. Longitude 115° 30′ W. The standard time meridian is 120° W.

Therefore, Las Vegas is 4° 30' east of the standard time meridian. From Table 8a, this necessitates a correction of sixteen minutes for 4° and two minutes for the 30', or a total of eighteen minutes. July 15 is during daylight saving time, so an hour must be subtracted. Also, for 115° W., three minutes must be added for the longitude correction (Table 8b). Therefore, the true astrological time is 1.15 a.m. + (18 + 3 minutes) − 1 hour = 12.36 a.m. July 15.

The basic computation

The objective now is to find a numerical value for the date, time and place under consideration, in order to determine the heavenly and earthly trigrams, with which to construct the controlling natal hexagram from which the predictions are obtained. The year, month, day, and hour will each have three numbers. When these have been determined, all the odd numbers will be added together to provide the numerical basis for the heavenly trigram, while the sum of all the even numbers will provide the earthly trigram.

STEPS

1. Find the true astrological local time and date of birth, using Tables 8a and 8b, along with the instructions for their use.

2. Enter Table 3 and find the yearly cycle number.

3. Using this number, enter Table 2 to find the symbols for the year involved.

4. Enter Table 1 with these symbols, and find the numbers involved for the year. *Make a note of these numbers.*

5. Using the correct date and true astrological time (step 1), enter Table 4 to determine the month to be used in the calculations. The astrological forces overlap so that there is never a clear-cut beginning or ending. Consequently, if the date and time of birth are close to the end of one month or the beginning of another, develop natal hexagrams for both months and interpolate the predictions. The times given in Table 4 are good enough for most calculations, whatever the year, but for best results the double calculation should be performed. (For greater accuracy, see Appendix A, p. 438. Especially note leap year dates.)

6. Enter Table 5 with the Celestial Stem letter designation for the year (step 3) along with the astrological month determined in step 5, and find the symbols for the month.

7. Go to Table 1, and find the numerical designations for these symbols. *Make a note of these numbers.*

8. Enter Table 6 with the day and month, and find the cycle number. Note this. Remember to check whether a leap year is involved.

9. Enter Table 3, and find the daily cycle number for the year involved.

10. Add the numbers obtained from steps 8 and 9.

11. Enter Table 2, and find the alphabetical designation for the number obtained from step 10 (if necessary subtract sixty from the total to get a number between one and sixty).

12. Go to Table 1, and find the numerical designations for these, the daily symbols. *Make a note of these numbers.*

13. Enter Table 7 with the alphabetical designation for the daily Celestial Stem (step 11), and find the alphabetical symbols for the correct local time.

14. Enter Table 1 with the symbols from step 13, and ascertain their numerical value. *Note down these numbers.*

15. Add all the *odd* numbers from the four symbols (year, month, day and hour), the numbers obtained from steps 4, 7, 12 and 14. The total will be the heavenly number.*

16. Add all the *even* numbers from the four symbols (year, month, day and hour). The total will be the earthly number.*

Examples

1. Step 1. January 17, 1970. 3.50 p.m.†
        2. For 1970 the yearly cycle is 47
        3. From Table 2, 47 = Gk
        4. G = 3   k = 5 and 10   3   5 10
        5. Twelfth month
        6. Db +
        7. D = 7   b = 5 and 10   7   5 10

This system, using the odd and even numbers from the four symbols, was recorded and explained by Confucius in his commentaries on *I Ching*.
† This is true local time. Always determine true local time before proceeding with the computations (see pp. 26–8).

    8. 16

    9. 18

    10. 16 + 18 = 34

    11. Dj

    12. D = 7 j = 4 and 9   7 4 9

    13. Under column D of Table 7

      3.50 p.m. = Ei

    14. E = 1 i = 4 and 9   1 4 9

    15. Odd numbers 3 + 5 + 7 + 5 + 7 + 9 + 1 +

      9 = 46

    16. Even numbers 10 + 10 + 4 + 4 = 28

2. Step 1. September 18, 1934. 12.36 a.m.

    2. Yearly cycle = 11

    3. 11 = Ak

    4. A = 6 k = 5 and 10   6 5 10

    5. Eighth month

    6. Jj

    7. J = 2 j = 4 and 9   2 4 9

    8. 20

    9. 9

    10. 9 + 20 = 29

    11. 29 = Ie

    12. I = 6 e = 5 and 10   6 5 10

    13. Under column I, 12.36 a.m. = Ga

    14. G = 3 a = 1 and 6   3 1 6

    15. Odds: 5 + 9 + 5 + 3 + 1 = 23

    16. Evens: 6 + 10 + 2 + 4 + 6 + 10 + 6 = 44

Therefore the heavenly number is 23
and the earthly number is 44

Table 9   *The houses of the hexagrams* *

House of Ch'ien (metal)

| month | 4 | 5 | 6 | 7 | 8 | 9 | 2 | 1 |

* Developed by Ching Fan, a Han Dynasty scholar.

House of K'an (water)

month 10   11   6   1   2   9   8   7

House of Kên (earth)

month 4   11   12   7   2   3   8   1

House of Chên (wood)

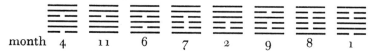

month 10   5   12   1   8   3   2   7

House of Sun (wood)

month 4   11   6   7   2   9   8   1

House of Li (fire)

month 4   5   12   7   8   3   2   1

House of K'un (earth)

month 10   11   12   1   2   3   8   7

House of Tui (metal)

month 10   5   6   1   8   9   2   7

Table 10   *Identification of the hexagrams*

Trigrams

Upper	Ch'ien	Chên	K'an	Kên	K'un	Sun	Li	Tui
Lower								
Ch'ien	1	34	5	26	11	9	14	43
Chên	25	51	3	27	24	42	21	17
K'an	6	40	29	4	7	59	64	47
Kên	33	62	39	52	15	53	56	31
K'un	12	16	8	23	2	20	35	45
Sun	44	32	48	18	46	57	50	28
Li	13	55	63	22	36	37	30	49
Tui	10	54	60	41	19	61	38	58

Table 11 *Auspicious pairings of hexagrams and months*

Hexagram number	Month	Hexagram number	Month	Hexagram number	Month
1	4	23	9	45	6
2	10	24	11	46	8
3	6	25	2	47	5
4	8	26	12	48	3
5	8	27	8	49	2
6	2	28	2	50	12
7	7	29	10	51	10
8	7	30	4	52	4
9	11	31	1	53	1
10	3	32	1	54	7
11	1	33	6	55	9
12	7	34	2	56	5
13	1	35	2	57	4
14	1	36	8	58	10
15	9	37	6	59	3
16	5	38	2	60	11
17	7	39	8	61	8
18	1	40	12	62	2
19	12	41	7	63	1
20	8	42	7	64	7
21	9	43	3		
22	11	44	5		

Enter Table 12 with the heavenly number, obtained from step 15 of the calculations. (The heavenly number will never exceed fifty.)

Table 12   *The heavenly numbers and trigrams*

1 ☲	2 ☵	3 ☷	4 ☴	5 see notes
6 ☰	7 ☱	8 ☷	9 ☳	10 ☶
11 ☲	12 ☵	13 ☷	14 ☴	15 see notes
16 ☰	17 ☱	18 ☷	19 ☳	20 ☶
21 ☲	22 ☵	23 ☷	24 ☴	25 see notes
26 ☵	27 ☷	28 ☷	29 ☴	30 see notes
31 ☰	32 ☱	33 ☷	34 ☳	35 ☶
36 ☵	37 ☷	38 ☷	39 ☴	40 see notes
41 ☰	42 ☱	43 ☷	44 ☳	45 ☶
46 ☵	47 ☷	48 ☷	49 ☴	50 see notes

Notes:
For Upper sexagenary cycle years use ☶ for a man.
For Upper   „   „   „   „   „   ☶ for a woman.
For Middle   „   „   „   „   „   ☰ for a man in even-numbered
years, and for a woman in odd-
numbered years.
For Middle   „   „   „   „   „   ☶ for a man in odd-numbered
years, and for a woman in even-
numbered years.
For Lower   „   „   „   „   „   ☴ for a man.
For Lower   „   „   „   „   „   ☴ for a woman.

Enter Table 13 with the earthly number, obtained from step
16 of the calculations.

Table 13   *The earthly numbers and trigrams*

2 ☷	12 ☷	22 ☷	32 ☷	42 ☷	52 ☷
4 ☵	14 ☵	24 ☵	34 ☵	44 ☵	54 ☵
6 ☰	16 ☰	26 ☰	36 ☰	46 ☰	56 ☰
8 ☷	18 ☷	28 ☷	38 ☷	48 ☷	58 ☷
10 ☵	20 ☷	30 ☷	40 ☷	50 ☷	60 ☷

The combination of the heavenly and earthly trigrams obtained from Tables 12 and 13 will give the Pre-Heaven hexagram. To determine which trigram will be the upper, and which the lower, consult Table 14.

Table 14   *The order of the trigrams*

For a man—   For 'positive' year of birth (even-numbered), the heavenly trigram is on the top (upper).
For 'negative' year of birth (odd-numbered), the heavenly trigram is on the bottom (lower).

For a woman—For 'positive' year of birth (even-numbered), the heavenly trigram is on the bottom (lower).
For 'negative' year of birth (odd-numbered), the heavenly trigram is on the top (upper).

The development of the basic Pre-Heaven hexagram

The astrology of *I Ching* is both a science and an art. It is a science in the computations that have to be performed, and in the basis on which these calculations are founded. It is an art in the making of the best possible interpretations from the scientific data obtained. As in all sciences, there is much that is not easy. The average person may have some difficulty at first in following the procedure, but with experience it will be found that it can be done with ease, and even by rote. As has been stated elsewhere, there is only the one book available giving details of this system, and it is written in the classical Chinese language. This is an ancient style, wherein the characters have several meanings and are different from their modern usage. Also, no punctuation is employed. Very few people are truly qualified to render acceptable translations. Another handicap is that it is very terse, with limited explanations or none at all.

The computations for the basic Pre-Heaven hexagram and for the controlling line, and the methods for determining the hexagrams for the yearly, monthly and daily cycles, are seemingly complicated. Whether difficult or not, they must be followed with care, and it is advisable always to double-check the work done and the interpretations made, since a minor error made along the way can completely alter the final presentation.

With the work being carefully done, and interpreted with understanding, one has a scientific and artistic system.

Perhaps one should consider the scientific aspects herein in somewhat the same light as one does the scientific aspects of an airplane. Most of us do not know why it was designed as it is, nor what makes it fly. But it gets us from here to there. So it is with the material which follows. We will use the data we have, and they will serve our purpose.

Up to this point the computations were all designed to produce a heavenly number and an earthly number, from which to develop the Pre-Heaven hexagram. In the study of *I Ching*, one learns that heaven, earth and man are coequal partners in the development of man, and in his experiences. Man, of course, has the option of exercising his free will. The influences of heaven and earth at any given time are fixed and predictable. At the moment of birth, one is *not* exercising free will, but heaven and earth *are* exercising their influence on one. Their influence is what we are about to determine. The situation can be likened to the planting of a seed. When influenced by nature alone, it will grow in a certain way. But when also influenced by man, the conditions of growth change. The hexagrams are considered as reflecting the influences of heaven, earth, and man, with the influence of heaven being primarily in the top two lines, that of man in the middle two lines, and that of earth in the bottom two lines. This pattern comes into play as life progresses, but the heavenly and earthly trigrams form the basis of all the lifetime influences.

For astrological purposes, one needs this basic hexagram representing the time and location of birth in order to derive the subsequent hexagrams that influence the phases of life. The basic hexagram is the seed from which the pattern of life unfolds. In this blossoming, good or unfavorable auguries can be determined. However, as stated above, man, with his free will operating in the realm of spirit, can override the realm of fate and either improve or impair the natural conditions prevailing (whether this astrology is used, or any other astrology).

Having carried out the basic computations described on pages 28–30, and having determined the heavenly and earthly numbers, one must enter Tables 12 and 13 to obtain the heavenly and earthly trigrams.

Using example 1 from page 30, one finds:

Heavenly number: 46   The trigram is ☱

Earthly number: 28   The trigram is ☵

Three things need to be done. The first is to ascertain whether the year of birth is positive or negative; the second, to note whether the subject is male or female; and third, in the event of the heavenly number being 5, 15, 25, 30, 40 or 50, one must note whether the year of birth is in the Upper, the Middle, or the Lower Cycle, i.e. 1864 to 1923, 1924 to 1983, or 1984 to 2043. (See Table 12, p. 34.)

Even-numbered years are 'positive' and odd-numbered years are 'negative.' (The first year of an Upper, Middle or Lower Cycle is always a positive year, e.g. 1864, 1924, 1984, etc.)

The time of birth in our example was 3.50 a.m. January 17, 1970. This is a positive year.

We shall work the example for a man and for a woman. The next step is to enter Table 14 on page 35. Since 1970 is a positive year, the heavenly trigram will be on top for a man, and in the lower position for a woman. The Pre-Heaven hexagrams are therefore:

	Man		Woman
Hexagram 39	䷦	Hexagram 4	䷃

It is clear at once that the life patterns for a baby boy and for a baby girl are likely to be entirely different, even if they were born at the same moment, in the same hospital.

Example 2 (from page 30) September 18, 1934 (positive year). 12.36 a.m.

Heavenly number: 23   Trigram ☳

Earthly number: 44   Trigram ☶

	Man		Woman
Hexagram 32	䷟	Hexagram 42	䷩

Example 3 October 5, 1941 (negative year). 7.26 a.m.

Heavenly number: 39   Trigram ☵

Earthly number: 26   Trigram ☰

	Man		Woman
Hexagram 44	䷫	Hexagram 9	䷈

Example 4 For a positive year in a Middle cycle, e.g. 1970.

		Man	Woman
Heavenly number: 25	Trigram	☲	☷
Earthly number: 30	Trigram	☲	☷

	Man		Woman
Hexagram 27	䷚	Hexagram 16	䷏

Example 5 For a negative year in an Upper Cycle, e.g. 1909.

		Man	Woman
Heavenly number: 15	Trigram	☲	☷
Earthly number: 42	Trigram	☳	☷

	Man		Woman
Hexagram 15	䷇	Hexagram 2	䷁

The development of the controlling line

While the Pre-Heaven hexagram gives the broad picture, it is the controlling line of the hexagram that is especially important. It is from this that all the subsequent patterns of hexagrams, for the yearly and daily cycles, develop. And, as one would imagine, it is the time of birth that is used as the basis for determining the controlling line.

The importance of the controlling line is that it is the foundation for the pattern of the subsequent age subcycles, and at the end of these becomes the foundation for the Later Heaven hexagram, which holds the seeds of the senior years of one's life. Since it influences all that follows from the moment of birth, it is rightfully called the controlling line.

The lines of the Pre-Heaven hexagram are given an alphabetical designation in a manner which will be described, and by this means the controlling line can be found. It is that line which carries the appropriate alphabetical designation obtained from Table 15.

Table 15   *Alphabetical symbols for the time of birth*

	Time of Birth Symbols					
	a	b	c	d	e	f
Hours Yang (+)	11 p.m.– 1 a.m.	1 a.m.– 3 a.m.	3 a.m.– 5 a.m.	5 a.m.– 7 a.m.	7 a.m.– 9 a.m.	9 a.m.– 11 a.m.
	g	h	i	j	k	l
Hours Yin (−)	11 a.m.– 1 p.m.	1 p.m.– 3 p.m.	3 p.m.– 5 p.m.	5 p.m.– 7 p.m.	7 p.m.– 9 p.m.	9 p.m.– 11 p.m.

Every hexagram has, of course, nought to six Yang and nought to six Yin lines in a specific combination. The system of designating these lines is shown for the seven possible combinations, each of the first five having one set of rules for the Yin hours and another for the Yang hours (see Table 15 for the Yin and Yang hours).

Case 1 For a hexagram that has only one Yang line:

a. Yang Hours

```
        — —
      — f —
      — e —
   a ——————— b
      — d —
      — c —
```

The Yang line is always a and b, the lowest Yin line c, and the other lines designated d, e and f, in sequence from bottom to top.

b. Yin Hours

Here the lowest Yin line is g and the other Yin lines above it are designated h, i, j and k. The Yang line is always l, no matter where it is.

Case 2 For a hexagram with two Yang lines:

a. Yang Hours

```
      — —
      — —
   b ——————— d
   a ——————— c
      — f —
      — e —
```

The lower Yang line is a and c, and the upper Yang line is b and d, with the two lowest Yin lines being designated e and f respectively.

b. Yin Hours

The Yin lines are designated g, h, i and j, starting with the lowest, with the lower Yang line being k and the upper Yang line being l.

Case 3 For a hexagram which has three Yang lines and three Ying lines:

a. Yang Hours

```
   c ——————— f
   b ——————— e
      — —
      — —
   a ——————— d
      — —
```

The lowest Yang line is a and d, the middle one is b and e, and the top one is c and f. The Yin lines are not designated.

b. Yin Hours

Only the Yin lines are designated, the lowest being g and j, the middle one being h and k, and the top one, i and l.

Case 4   For a hexagram which has four Yang lines:

a. Yang Hours	b. Yin Hours

```
   a. Yang Hours              b. Yin Hours

 d ——————                    ——————
 c ——————                    ——————
    — — f                 l ——————
 b ——————               h —   — j
 a ——————               g —   — i
    — — e                 k ——————
```

| The designations are in natural sequence, beginning with the lowest Yang, and lettering the Yang lines first, then the Yin lines. | Here the two Yin lines receive double lettering, the lower being g and i, and the upper, h and j. The lowest Yang line is k, and the next above it is l. |

Case 5   For a hexagram having five Yang lines:

```
   a. Yang Hours              b. Yin Hours

 e ——————                 g —   — h
 d ——————                    ——————
   — f —                     —————— l
 c ——————                    —————— k
 b ——————                    —————— j
 a ——————                    —————— i
```

| The Yang lines are lettered from the bottom upwards, and the Yin line is always f. | The single Yin line receives the double designation, g and h, and the Yang lines are lettered from the lowest upwards, with the uppermost remaining unlettered. |

Case 6   For the hexagram Ch'ien, The Creative. The rules for the sexes are different, thus:

Man

```
 i ——————— l
 h ——————— k
 g ——————— j
 c ——————— f
 b ——————— e
 a ——————— d
```

Woman

a. If born after the winter solstice and before the summer solstice	b. If born after the summer solstice and before the winter solstice

```
 a ——————— d           i ——————— l
 b ——————— e           h ——————— k
 c ——————— f           g ——————— j
 g ——————— j           c ——————— f
 h ——————— k           b ——————— e
 i ——————— l           a ——————— d
```

Case 7   For the hexagram K'un, The Receptive. The rules for
the sexes are different, thus:

Man		Woman

Man		Woman
a. If born after the	b. If born after the	i — — l
winter solstice and	summer solstice and	h — — k
before the summer	before the winter	g — — j
solstice	solstice	c — — f
		b — — e
		a — — d

i — — l	a — — d
h — — k	b — — e
g — — j	c — — f
c — — f	g — — j
b — — e	h — — k
a — — d	i — — l

It should be remembered in the development of the cycles of
life that the controlling line is more important than the basic
hexagram, since the interpretation of the lines is always more
specific than that of the hexagram as a whole. In a sense, the
hexagram can be considered as the 'cause' and the controlling
line the resultant 'effect.' It is the manifested 'effect' which is of
prime interest in astrological prediction.

Referring back to pages 37–8, and Examples 1 and 2, the
controlling lines for the hexagrams can now be determined.

Example 1   Time: 3.50 p.m. From Table 15, the controlling
letter is 'i,' and the time in the Yin hours. Consulting Case 2
above, it can be seen that the Yin lines are numbered in sequence
from the bottom upwards, followed by the Yang lines. Hence:

	Man		Woman
	— — j		———— l
	———— l		— — j
Hexagram	— x — i	Hexagram	— x — i
39	———— k	4	— — h
	— — h		———— k
	— — g		— — g

The controlling line is the 'i' line, line 4 in both instances. Since
it is a Yin line, the fact that it controls is shown by placing a cross
between the broken lines. In the event of the controlling line
being a Yang, a circle is added to show that it controls; i.e.

—⊙—

Example 2   The time is 12.36 a.m. This is case 3. The time is
within the Yang hours. Therefore all the Yang lines receive

double lettering. (Had the time been within the Yin hours, all the Yin lines would have received double lettering.) The controlling letter, from Table 15, is 'a.'

	Man			Woman	
	— —			——— c,f	
	— —			——— b,e	
Hexagram	——— c,f		Hexagram	— —	
32	——— b,e		42	— —	
	—ө— a,d			— —	
	— —ᵧ			—ө— a,d	

Note that the controlling line in both instances is the bottom Yang line. In one case it is line 1, and in the other, line 2. IMPORTANT: *Be sure to use the right time group (Yin hours or Yang), and check that you have lettered the hexagram according to the rules for the case involved.*

Computations for the subcycles of life

Basically, what is to be considered here is the pulse of cosmic influences on the life of the individual. These forces act on everyone, but individuals vary in their receptivity and reactions, depending mainly on their natal pattern. The subcycles are the major divisions of a man's life, and are determined from the lines of his natal hexagram. The length of the subcycle for a Yang line is nine years, while that for a Yin line is six years. This difference originates in the values placed on the lines in the fundamental theory of *I Ching*.

To determine the cycles, one begins with the Pre-Heaven, or natal, hexagram and its controlling line. If the controlling line is a Yin, then the first subcycle lasts for six years, if a Yang, then nine years. The other lines are considered in turn, moving upwards from the controlling line and assigning the years line by line, until the top of the hexagram is reached. Then one continues from the bottom, until the controlling line is arrived at once more. In our Example 1, this simple calculation would be:

	Man			Woman	
16 —	— 21		13 —	—— 21	
7 ——	— 15		7 —	— 12	
1 —	x — 6		1 —	x — 6	
34 —	—— 42		39 —	— 42	
28 —	— 33		28 —	—— 36	
22 —	— 27		22 —	— 27	

Note that the length of time involved is the same, but that different cyclic periods are applicable.

The numbers indicate the individual's age for the subcycle. When using these in subsequent calculations, the year of birth should be noted alongside, to ascertain whether positive or negative year rules apply. In this astrology the age of an individual is measured from winter solstice to winter solstice, the period from the date of birth to the first winter solstice after birth being year one.

The Later Heaven hexagram

The Later Heaven hexagram is the foundation for the individual's life subsequent to the years dominated by the Earlier (Pre-) Heaven hexagram. The Pre-Heaven hexagram determines the development of the individual, and the Later Heaven hexagram determines the second half of life, the reaping of the harvest. As such, the original influences have a tendency to be reversed, and, the Later Heaven hexagram is made up of the heavenly and earthly trigrams (with a slight modification), but with their positions reversed.

It is a simple matter of putting the inner trigram (the lower three lines) above the outer trigram (the upper three lines). One additional action, however, must be taken. The controlling line remains the controlling line in its new position, but if it was originally a Yang line it changes to a Yin, and vice versa. In our Example 1 this would give:

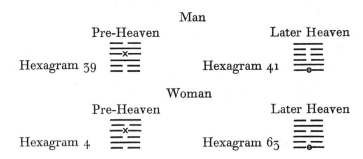

Man

Pre-Heaven   Later Heaven

Hexagram 39   Hexagram 41

Woman

Pre-Heaven   Later Heaven

Hexagram 4   Hexagram 63

The subcycle divisions for the Later Heaven hexagram are made in the same way as those for the Pre-Heaven hexagram (see previous section on subcycles of life, pages 43-4). These cycles then are:*

Man		Woman	
	79 ——— 87		82 — — 87
	73 — — 78		73 ——— 81
Hexagram	67 — — 72	Hexagram	67 — — 72
41	61 — — 66	63	58 ——— 66
	52 ——— 60		52 — — 57
	43 —●— 51		43 —●— 51

As is so often the case, there is an exception to the rule. In this astrology, special consideration must be given to three hexagrams, when the controlling line is in the fifth position and the individual born in a negative month (see Table 5 p. 22), or when the controlling line is in the sixth position and the individual born in a positive month.

These hexagrams are hexagram 29, hexagram 3, and hexagram 39.

Case 1 When the fifth line is the controlling line, and the individual born in a negative month:
Change the controlling line from Yang to Yin. Make no other change; i.e.:

Pre-Heaven		Later Heaven	
Hexagram 29	☵	Hexagram 7	
Hexagram 3		Hexagram 24	
Hexagram 39		Hexagram 15	

If the individual's birth month is positive, proceed according to the normal rule.

Case 2 When the sixth line is the controlling line, and the individual born in a positive month:
Change the controlling line from Yin to Yang. Make no other change; i.e.:

* The counting begins from the age at which the Pre-Heaven hexagram left off.

	Pre-Heaven		Later Heaven
Hexagram 29		Hexagram 59	
Hexagram 3		Hexagram 42	
Hexagram 39		Hexagram 53	

If the individual's birth month is negative, proceed according to the normal rule.

The development of the yearly cycles

The hexagrams for the six-year period for Yin lines and the nine-year period for Yang lines are developed from the appropriate subcycle line of the natal Pre-Heaven and Later Heaven hexagrams. The subcycle lines form the base from which the applicable yearly hexagrams are computed. Yin lines and Yang lines are treated differently.

The period covered by a yearly hexagram is from one winter solstice (w.s.) to the next. In the Chinese lunar system this was from the winter solstice about a month before the Lunar New Year's Day to the next winter solstice. The lunar year involved was the one wherein the vast majority of days were included. Converting this to the Western system means that 1978, for example, covers from winter solstice (December) 1977 to winter solstice (December) 1978. The character of the year would be positive since 1978 is a positive year even though the time began in 1977. For clarity's sake a few other examples are given:

    1931 — from w.s. 1930 to w.s. 1931 = negative year
    1954 — from w.s. 1953 to w.s. 1954 = positive year
    1967 — from w.s. 1966 to w.s. 1967 = negative year

It should be remembered that the age in question at any time is the year being lived up to the time of the ensuing winter solstice. Year 1 is from birth to the next winter solstice. Year 2 is from the preceding winter solstice to the next winter solstice, even though the child, at the start of the year had not reached its first birthday. Each ensuing year, of course, is of opposite polarity.

An example of how the foregoing applies can be shown by using Nelson Rockefeller, born July 8, 1908:

Year 1 = 7–8–08   to w.s. 1908 + year
     2 = w.s. 1908 to w.s. 1909 − year
     3 = w.s. 1909 to w.s. 1910 + year
     4 = w.s. 1910 to w.s. 1911 − year
     5 = w.s. 1911 to w.s. 1912 + year
     6 = w.s. 1912 to w.s. 1913 − year
     7 = w.s. 1913 to w.s. 1914 + year
     8 = w.s. 1914 to w.s. 1915 − year
     9 = w.s. 1915 to w.s. 1916 + year
   10 = w.s. 1916 to w.s. 1917 − year
   11 = w.s. 1917 to w.s. 1918 + year
   12 is the same as year 2 only 10 years later, i.e.,
       = w.s. 1918 to w.s. 1919 − year.

And so on.

Rockefeller's prediction for astrological year 70 would be from winter solstice 1976 to winter solstice 1977. 1977 is a negative year.

The best way to demonstrate the development of the yearly hexagrams is to apply the rules to an actual case.

a. For a Yin line Take the appropriate hexagram and change the line for the subcycle in question to a Yang. Use this new hexagram for the first year of the subcycle, and then change the lines above it for the ensuing years, changing one line for each year, e.g.:

Ex-president Nixon's subcycle for age fifty-four to sixty:

Later Heaven
  Hexagram

	55th year	56th year	57th year
55 [≡ ≡] 60	Hexagram 51	Hexagram 54	Hexagram 34

58th year	59th year	60th year
Hexagram 11	Hexagram 5	Hexagram 9

47

For the next year it is necessary to go back to the Later Heaven hexagram and develop the subcycle for age sixty to sixty-six.

Later Heaven
Hexagram

	61st	62nd	
61 ⚏ 66	year	year	etc.
	Hexagram 40	Hexagram 32	

b. For a Yang Line As stated before, the character of the *calendar* year for the beginning of the subcycle, i.e. whether it is positive or negative, determines the rules and methods that apply.

1. For positive (even-numbered) years, e.g. 1920, 1956, 1972, etc., the Yang subcycle line does not change for the first year of the subcycle, but becomes the controlling line for that year. For the second year, its counterpart in the other trigram changes from Yin to Yang or vice versa (line 4 is the counterpart of line 1, line 5 that of line 2, and line 6 that of line 3) and becomes the controlling line for that year. For the third year, the Yang subcycle line changes to a Yin, and becomes once again the controlling line. For the ensuing years, the controlling position moves up in sequence (returning to the bottom after reaching the top) with the line changing character each time.

It must be kept well in mind that for the most part the astrological year will vary from the normal calendar year by one year. This is because the first astrological year is from time of birth to the first winter solstice thereafter. Thus when checking ex-president Nixon's astrological age 34 to see whether it is a positive or negative year one must compute the calendar year for astrological age 34. Richard Nixon was born on January 9, 1913. Therefore his year 1 is from January 9, 1913 to winter solstice 1913. Consequently at winter solstice 1946 he is astrologically age 34 and this covers from winter solstice 1945 to winter solstice 1946. The calendar year 1946 is an even or positive year. The computations, according to the formula given above would be:

Pre-Heaven
Hexagram

34 ⚎ 42	34	35	36	37	38
Inclusive					

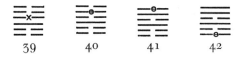

39   40   41   42

2. For negative (odd-numbered) years when the cycle begins, the controlling Yang line changes to Yin for the first year and remains the controlling line. For the second year the controlling line changes to its counter position (1 to 4; 2 to 5; 3 to 6; 4 to 1; 5 to 2; and 6 to 3) and also changes the nature of the line. For the third year the controlling line moves back to its original position and changes the line back to a Yang. For the ensuing six years of the cycle the controlling line moves up and the lines change their character in sequence.

For ex-president Nixon's astrological age 73 to 81 where he has a Yang line in the Later Heaven hexagram one finds that at the winter solstice of 1985 he reached the astrological age of 73 and that the calculations for age 73 will cover from the winter solstice 1984 to the winter solstice 1985. Since 1985 is an odd or negative year the yearly cycle computations for astrological ages 73 to 81 would be:

Later Heaven
  Hexagram

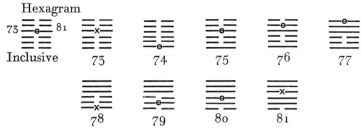

73   81
Inclusive   73   74   75   76   77

                    78   79   80   81

Checklist

1. Name.
2. Date of birth.
3. Hour of birth.
4. Sex.
5. Geographical location: Longitude.
6. Correction to standard time (if applicable).

49

7. Correction to standard meridian (Table 8a).
8. Correction for longitude west of 120° East (Table 8b).
9. True astrological time (steps 3, 6, 7 and 8).
10. Yearly cycle number for year of birth from Table 3.
11. Alphabetical designation for yearly cycle (Table 2).
12. Numerical designations for yearly cycle (Table 1).
13. Alphabetical designation for monthly cycle (Table 5).
14. Numerical designations for monthly cycle (Table 1).
15. Numerical designation for daily cycle (Table 3).
16. Numerical designation for day of month (Table 6).
17. Add values from steps 15 and 16. If greater than sixty, subtract sixty.
18. Determine alphabetical designation for step 17 (Table 2).
19. Determine numerical designations for step 18 (Table 1).
20. Determine alphabetical designation for hour of birth (Table 7).
21. Determine numerical designations for hour of birth (Table 1).
22. Add all the odd numbers from steps 12, 14, 19 and 21.
23. Add all the even numbers from steps 12, 14, 19 and 21.
24. Heavenly number (from 22).
25. Earthly number (from 23).
26. Is the year of birth positive or negative (even or odd)?
27. Develop the Pre-Heaven hexagram:
    (a) Heavenly trigram (use step 24 and enter Table 12).
    (b) Earthly trigram (use step 25 and enter Table 13).
    (c) Male or female? (Step 4.)
    (d) Check Table 14 for the order of the trigrams.
28. Enter Table 15, determine whether Yin or Yang hours apply, and note the alphabetical designation for the time of birth.
29. Count the Yang lines in the Pre-Heaven hexagram and determine which case is applicable.
30. Give the lines of the Pre-Heaven hexagram appropriate alphabetical designations for the case involved, and note the controlling line (from steps 28 and 29).
31. Begin with the controlling line, and determine the age sub-cycles. (See section on subcycles of life, p. 43.) Nine years for Yang, and six for Yin.
32. Develop the Later Heaven hexagram. (See section on the

Later Heaven hexagram, pp. 44–6.) (Be sure to change the nature of the controlling line.)

33. Begin with the next age subcycle beyond the Pre-Heaven, and determine the subcycles in the same manner as for the Pre-Heaven hexagram. (See section on the Later Heaven hexagram, pp. 44–6.) Note if one of the exceptions.

34. Determine yearly subcycles:
    (a) for Yin lines, and/or
    (b) for Yang lines when cycle begins in a positive year, and/or
    (c) for Yang lines when cycle begins in a negative year.

WORK SLOWLY AND CAREFULLY, AND ALWAYS DOUBLE CHECK.

Daily cycle calculations

The several aspects of the yearly hexagram control the daily cycles for the entire year. These are closely associated with the five elements: water, wood, fire, metal, and earth. (See Ho Map, Figure 1, p. 9, and pp. 12–15.) Each of these elements is considered dominant for about seventy-two days each year, with the exception of earth, which is given as the principal influence for seventy-seven days a year. The system described here is new, and is an integration of several ancient versions.

Earth is believed to interact with the other elements at all times, and to come into dominance over its associated element during the last stages before each of the solstices and equinoxes. In calculating the length of time between seasons it is found that between the autumnal and the vernal equinox the number of days is more or less exactly 180 days, whereas between the vernal and the autumnal equinox are 185 days plus. With this astrology being largely based on the influences of the sun and the earth, the extra days beyond 360 (5 elements multiplied by 72 days) are considered to be under the dominance of the element earth. Hence, as will be seen subsequently, the hexagrams representing the element earth will influence these extra days. Compensation is thereby made for the fact that the winter solstice varies in its time of commencement during the appropriate days.

In connection with the foregoing, when one is analyzing any

particular day one should also examine the preceding and succeeding days, as the cycles are not precisely defined as to where one begins and another ends, but rather represent a continuum of change.

An astrological year (beginning with the winter solstice) is dominated by the five elements approximately as follows:

(a) Water — 72 days
(b) Earth — 18 days
(c) Wood — 72 days
(d) Earth — 20 days
(e) Fire — 72 days
(f) Earth — 21 days
(g) Metal — 72 days
(h) Earth — 18 days

Seventy-two days is the length of time it takes for a hexagram to change to its opposite and then return to its original state, allowing each line to be the controlling line for a day. The days start at the bottom line and move upwards. Thus each hexagram controls a six-day period, before changing into the next hexagram (the changes entering at the bottom and continuing to the top) when another six-day cycle takes place. As may be seen below, a hexagram goes through its complete cycle of evolution in seventy-two stages, during which the controlling element (water, wood, fire or metal) goes through its seventy-two-day cycle and exerts its controlling influence for that period of time according to its stage of evolution on any given day. Example:

6 ———	12 ———	18 ———	24 ———
5 ———	11 ———	17 ———	23 ———
4 ———	10 ———	16 ———	22 ———
3 ———	9 ———	15 ———	21 — —
2 ———	8 ———	14 — —	20 — —
1 ———	7 — —	13 — —	19 — —
Hexagram 1	Hexagram 44	Hexagram 33	Hexagram 12

30 ———	36 ———	42 — —	48 — —
29 ———	35 — —	41 — —	47 — —
28 — —	34 — —	40 — —	46 — —
27 — —	33 — —	39 — —	45 — —
26 — —	32 — —	38 — —	44 — —
25 — —	31 — —	37 — —	43 ———
Hexagram 20	Hexagram 23	Hexagram 2	Hexagram 24

```
54 — —      60 — —      66 — —      72 — —
53 — —      59 — —      65 — —      71 ———
52 — —      58 — —      64 ———      70 ———
51 — —      57 ———      63 ———      69 ———
50 ———      56 ———      62 ———      68 ———
49 ———      55 ———      61 ———      67 ———
Hexagram 19  Hexagram 11  Hexagram 34  Hexagram 43
```

```
                    =====
                    =====
                    =====
                    =====
                    =====
                 73 —————
                 Hexagram 1
```

Returning now to the consideration of what takes place during a year, one must begin with the yearly hexagram. As is well known, each hexagram presents six different aspects, i.e. (1) itself; (2) its opposite; (3) its reverse; (4) its opposite reverse; (5) its inner hexagram; and (6) its inner opposite. Placed in proper perspective, these provide a three-dimensional picture. Take any hexagram as an example (here hexagram 37 was chosen):

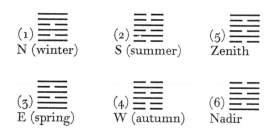

(1) N (winter)   (2) S (summer)   (5) Zenith

(3) E (spring)   (4) W (autumn)   (6) Nadir

As the yearly hexagram begins with the winter solstice, we therefore assign the hexagram to the position of North. The opposite of winter is summer, so the opposite of the yearly hexagram is placed in the South. The reverse hexagram is still consistent with original yearly hexagram, and is assigned to spring, with *its* opposite being assigned to autumn. Since earth interacts with all elements, the inner hexagram is considered as representing earth, with its influence tending toward the zenith in the first half of the year, and towards the nadir during the second half. (Figure 5.)

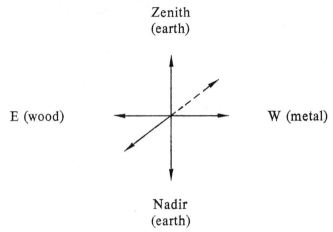

Figure 5. *Three-dimensional view*

Table 16   *Computation for the daily cycles*

	Days, beginning with the winter solstice
1. The yearly hexagram for	72
2. The inner hexagram for	18
3. The reverse yearly hexagram for	72
4. The inner hexagram (contd) for	20
5. The opposite yearly hexagram for	72
6. The opposite inner hexagram for	21
7. The reverse opposite hexagram for	72
8. The opposite inner hexagram (contd) for	18
Total	365 days

The daily cycles (Table 16) begin with the yearly hexagram and its controlling line. The change to the next hexagram after the yearly hexagram always takes place by changing the controlling line. Subsequent hexagrams are determined by moving onward (upward) from the controlling line. When the reverse and reverse opposite hexagrams come into play, the controlling line is inverted along with the rest of the hexagram, as shown in the following example. With the inner, opposite, and opposite inner hexagrams, the controlling line remains in the same position as in the basic yearly hexagram, i.e. if line 3 in the yearly, then it is line 3 in the inner, etc. In the example shown below, the yearly hexagram is hexagram 37, with line 3 as the controlling line. The computation for the daily cycles then becomes:

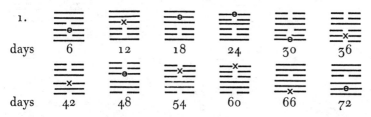

1.

| days | 6 | 12 | 18 | 24 | 30 | 36 |

| days | 42 | 48 | 54 | 60 | 66 | 72 |

The first hexagram governs the first six days, the second hexagram the next six days, etc. (To determine the line for an individual day, always start counting with the bottom line, and work upwards.)

2.

| days | 6 | 12 | 18 |

3.

| days | 6 | 12 | 18 | 24 | 30 | 36 |

| days | 42 | 48 | 54 | 60 | 66 | 72 |

4.

| days | 6 | 12 | 18 | (20) |

5.

| days | 6 | 12 | 18 | 24 | 30 | 36 |

| days | 42 | 48 | 54 | 60 | 66 | 72 |

55

6.

days	6	12	18	(21)

7.

days	6	12	18	24	30	36

days	42	48	54	60	66	72

8.

```
— x — 3          ——— 9          ——— 15         ———
—  — 2           —  — 8          —  — 14        —  —
——— 1            ——— 7          ——— 13
—  —             —  — 6          —  — 12        — x — 18
—  —             —  — 5          — x — 11       ——— 17
———             —e— 4          —  — 10        —  — 16
```

days	(1–3)	(4–9)	(10–15)	(16–18)

Note: Stage 4 is a continuation of stage 2, seventy-two days later.

Stage 8 is a continuation of stage 6, seventy-two days later.

Observe that line 4 is shown as day 1 and that only the top three lines of the hexagram apply here.

Starting the daily cycles

This system of astrology is based on the commencement of the year at the winter solstice. If one wishes to be exact, one should take the length of time between one winter solstice and the next, divide it by 365, and apply these divisions. The result would be 365 periods of 24 hours and 1 minute (approx.) in length. In rare cases this may be useful.

For practical purposes, however, we will use the 365-day calculations shown on page 54, and apply them as follows:

When the solstice falls between midnight and noon (00.00–11.59 hrs)

Man born in a positive year or woman in a negative year } Use calendar date

Man born in a negative year or woman in a positive year } Use next succeeding calendar date

When the solstice falls between noon and midnight (12.00–23.59 hrs)

Man born in a negative year or ⎱ Use calendar date
woman in a positive year   ⎰

Man born in a positive year or ⎱ Use next succeeding
woman in a negative year   ⎰ calendar date

Sometimes there will be a gap of a day between one 365-day cycle and the next. The solstice, however, will fall on this day, so part of the day will belong to the old year, and part to the new year. In these cases it is necessary to synthesize a prediction, taking that for the last day of the old year along with that for the first day of the new year. Example:

Man (positive year) Winter solstice—December 22; 7.00 hrs.
                                                    Year A.

Computation:

First calendar day for daily cycles = December 22. Year A.
One year   = 365 days.
Therefore last day of cycle   = December 21. Year B.
Winter solstice for year B   = December 22; 13.00 hrs.
First calendar day for daily cycles = December 23 (for a man
                                        born in a positive year).

The 'missing' day is December 22 (year B) and the prediction must be synthesized from the prediction for December 21 and that for December 23, the first day of the new astrological year. This is logical, anyway, since thirteen hours belong to the old year and eleven hours to the new. In fact, in nearly all cases, the preceding and succeeding days have an influence on any day in question, and should be given consideration if the greatest accuracy is desired or required. As will have been noted, this synthesizing procedure applies sometimes when the person concerned was born in a positive year, and sometimes when he or she was born in a negative year. This procedure should be considered independent from calendar leap years, even though sometimes the same years may be involved.

2 | *Auspiciousness*

The basic and primary concepts of I Ching

The fundamental philosophy of *I Ching* is truly deep. It covers all that there is, and there are a number of primary and basic concepts contained therein which provide the foundation for the astrology of *I Ching*. Many commentaries and explanations have been written about *I Ching* over the centuries, among them being those by Confucius. These may be examined by the scholar who is interested. Here, however, it is sufficient just to say what the basic concepts are, without going into details. Many the reader will already know, and most of them are self-explanatory.

1. The hexagrams are the evolution of the primal forces of Yin and Yang, as derived from the Universal Creative manifesting itself.

2. The hexagrams symbolically represent all possible situations and conditions relating to the human, animal, vegetable and mineral kingdoms.

3. Basic laws and patterns of the Universal Creative are in, or are generated by, the Pre-Heaven cycle of trigrams.

4. The basic laws and patterns are made manifest in the universe in accordance with the Later Heaven cycle of trigrams.

5. Man is an equal partner in the laws governing heaven and the laws governing earth, while operating in the material realm.

6. The laws of heaven and the laws of earth are fixed (from man's point of view). In actuality they are evolving very, very slowly, but not in a manner perceptible to the vast majority of human beings.

7. Man has free will: freedom of choice in what he thinks, does or says.

8. Man has good fortune and success when he works (consciously or unconsciously) in keeping with the laws of heaven and the laws of earth.

9. A man does best for himself when he acts selflessly, and in harmony with the laws of heaven and earth.

10. Karma returns to the originator in Universal Time. It can and often does override free will in the material realm.

11. Karma is not inevitable. Man can develop himself mentally and enter the realm of spirit (even if only for brief periods of time) through refinement and purification. The realm of spirit supersedes and overrides the material realm in which karma operates.

12. Man manifests divine will when he works in harmony with the laws of heaven and the laws of earth.

13. Man progresses spiritually as he further discerns the laws of heaven and earth, and consciously uses them.

14. *I Ching* is fundamentally a guide for spiritual development.

15. Since the hexagrams represent all conditions and circumstances (see 2 above), the hexagrams can, with proper understanding and interpretation, be used for any matter a man can think of.

16. There are no measurable changes in the laws of heaven or the laws of earth during the lifetime of any individual. Therefore, the laws affecting an individual at birth are the laws governing his life.

17. Man is an equal partner with heaven and earth in the action of the hexagrams. The influences of heaven and earth on the life of an individual are those forces and laws operating at the moment of that person's birth. The moment of one's birth is thought of as part of one's exercise of one's free will. (This can be understood by the theory of reincarnation, or as the influence of a superior guiding purpose, whichever belief one may care to hold.)

18. The influences existing at the time of birth are those of Time, Space and the relative positions of everything in the universe at that moment. In this astrology the influence of the sun is given major consideration, with the moon a poor second, and the rest of the stars and planets a long way behind.

19. In the light of the above, the hexagrams can justly be used for astrological purposes.

20. The value of using the hexagrams in this way emerges only if proper rules are established for their astrological determination, and applied with a sensitive understanding of their meanings.

21. The system described here has been used for many centuries and has withstood the tests of time, demand and experience, and it remains foremost, in spite of parallel systems having been devised.

22. The degree of reliability of this astrology will depend on the qualifications, spiritual development and experience of the interpreter.

23. The full import of the horoscope, with all its ramifications, will only be perceivable by hindsight. The study of past forecasts, however, will be very useful for improving future forecasts.

24. Only the individual himself can ever know the real truth about himself and his life. This is a part of his individual freedom.

The elements of the hexagram

The elementary evolution of the universe proceeded, according to *I Ching*, from a quiescent Universal Creative desiring to manifest itself. This desire generated two forces, one positive, called Yang, and the other negative, called Yin. From these, by a process of further evolution, all the various dichotomies were produced, and by the interrelationship and interaction of Yin and Yang in their limitless combinations, all else in the universe came, or is still to come, into being. Figure 6 is a simple diagram showing the evolution of Yin and Yang and then the trigrams.

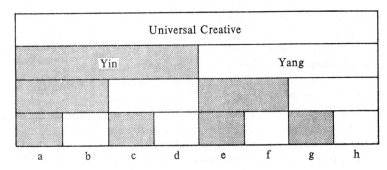

Figure 6. The evolution of Yin and Yang and the trigrams

Looking vertically above each of the alphabetical letters, one can see that the evolution consists of various combinations of Yin and Yang. These combinations are the basic eight trigrams.

a.	3 Yin	☷ K'un	Mother
b.	1 Yang below 2 Yin	☳ Chên	Eldest son
c.	1 Yang between 2 Yin	☵ K'an	Middle son
d.	1 Yin above 2 Yang	☱ Tui	Youngest daughter
e.	1 Yang above 2 Yin	☶ Kên	Youngest son
f.	1 Yin between 2 Yang	☲ Li	Middle daughter
g.	1 Yin below 2 Yang	☴ Sun	Eldest daughter
h.	3 Yang	☰ Ch'ien	Father

Continuing the evolution for three more stages, one obtains Figure 7, showing the sixty-four hexagrams. These are found in the same way that the trigrams were found in Figure 6.

In any hexagram there are certain favorable and unfavorable aspects, and some are more so than others:
a. The action of a hexagram is from the bottom to the top.
b. In the hexagram, lines 1 and 2 represent earth; lines 3 and 4, man; and lines 5 and 6, heaven. Thus, man is an equal partner with heaven and earth (in the material realm).
c. Lines 2 and 5 are generally the most favorable, and usually line 5 is more favorable than line 2.
d. Lines 2, 3, 4 and 5 represent the principal action of the hexagram, in most cases.
e. The ruler of a hexagram is usually line 5, or else a single Yang or Yin amongst five of the opposite polarity (because of the basic principle that one rules many). There are, however, a few exceptions.
f. Lines 1 and 6 are often outside the main action of the hexagram, line 1 reflecting considerations before the activity can commence, and line 6 representing a decline after the peak of activity. Also, they are often unfavorable.
g. In general, the order of favorability is: 5 more than 2, more than 4, more than 1, more than 3, more than 6.
h. There is a correspondence between lines 1 and 4; lines 2 and

61

1 43 14 34 9 5 26 11 10 58 38 54 61 60 41 19 13 49 30 55 37 63 22 36 25 17 21 51 42 3 27

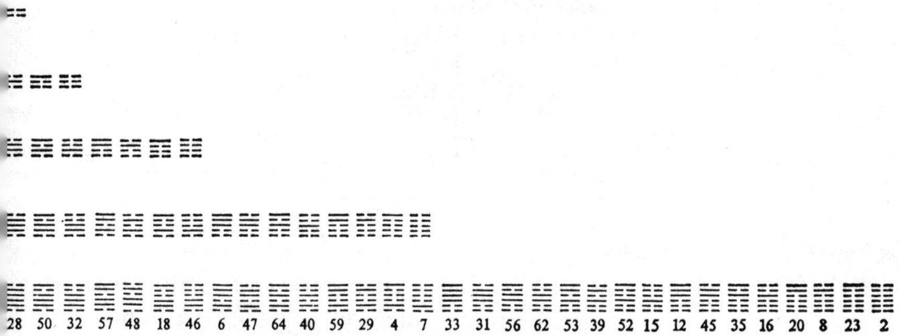

Figure 7. *Shao Yung's Sequence*

5; and lines 3 and 6. The correspondence is favorable if the upper of the two lines is a Yang and the lower a Yin, i.e. symbolizing a man leading a woman; it is usually neutral if both lines are of the same nature. A Yang leading a Yin is more favorable than if a Yin is uppermost and a Yang below because a woman leading a man is supposedly an indication of weakness. i. Even though the hexagrams are formed in the sixth stage of the evolution of Yin and Yang, they are most frequently considered as being made up of two trigrams. Both of these points of view are correct. During any analysis one should bear in mind throughout whether one is considering the hexagram as a whole, or the effects of the separate trigrams. j. In a trigram, the top line represents heaven, the middle line, man, and the bottom line, earth. Therefore, when analyzing a hexagram according to its trigrams, one should approach it thus:

$$
\begin{array}{lll}
\text{Line 6} & \text{heaven} \\
5 & \text{man} & \left.\right\} \text{Upper trigram} \\
4 & \text{earth} \\
3 & \text{heaven} \\
2 & \text{man} & \left.\right\} \text{Lower trigram} \\
1 & \text{earth}
\end{array}
$$

The value of doubles

One Chinese concept that is particularly germane to the interpretation of the hexagrams for astrological purposes is the belief that doubling anything, or the manifestation of doubling, is especially propitious. Opposites, on the other hand, are viewed adversely, unless they are obvious counterparts and complement each other. As examples of propitious doubling one finds that October 10, 1911 was the date of the birth of the Republic (the tenth day of the tenth month), and that Lovers' Day is August 8, the eighth day of the eighth month. ('Eight' is pronounced 'ba.' 'Baba' in Chinese means 'father,' so eight doubled is likewise 'father.') This value attributed to doubling is said to date from Fu Hsi and his development of the hexagrams, wherein the eight trigrams are doubled with propitious effects. King Wên (c. 1123 B.C.) was the first to set down the value of doubles in his expositions regarding *I Ching*. Therefore it is only logical that one finds doubling considered of value in *I Ching* astrology.

The finding of a trigram in an individual's Pre-Heaven or Later Heaven hexagram that matches the favorable Primeval (Celestial Stem) Trigram for the year of birth, is believed to mean that riches, fame, honor, good fortune and love will be forthcoming in his life. As previously stated, the Pre-Heaven hexagram governs one's rise in life and the Later Heaven hexagram reflects the reaping of one's harvest. The Primeval influence is exerted favorably through the trigrams as shown in Table 17.

Table 17　*Favorable Primeval trigrams*

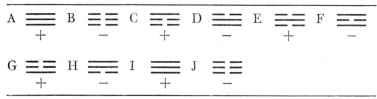

To find out whether one is favored or not, one must refer back to the Celestial Stem, the capital alphabetical letter obtained from Tables 2 and 3, pp. 17–20, e.g. if one was born in an 'A' year, and one has the trigram ☰ in either the upper or lower position in either one's Pre-Heaven or one's Later Heaven hexagram, then one is likely to enjoy fame, riches, good fortune, etc. For instance:

Pre-Heaven　　　　　　Later Heaven

In this example there are three ☰ trigrams, and this state of affairs would be considered exceptionally favorable.

Similarly, with the Horary Branches (given by the lower case alphabetical letters), one's life will be highly favorable if one's Pre-Heaven or Later Heaven hexagram contains the trigram corresponding to one's Horary Branch letter in Table 18.

Table 18　*Favorable Horary Branch trigrams*

a	b and c	d	e and f
g	h and i	j	k and l

For example, if from Tables 2 and 3 one discovered that one's year of birth was 'Ag,' and if one had a Pre-Heaven or Later Heaven hexagram containing ☳, as in ䷗ or ䷚, it would be favorable. It would be even more favorable, since the year is Ag and the favorable trigram for A is ☰, if the hexagram were ䷪ or ䷉.

Among the most favorable Pre-Heaven and Later Heaven hexagrams are those in which the trigrams are doubled. (Note that Hexagrams 30 and 58 do not exist as Pre-Heaven hexagrams), i.e.

Ch'ien	K'un	Li	Chên
Kên	Tui	Sun	K'an

A dichotomy exists in the effects of the Celestial Stems and Horary Branches, just as with other matters in our dualistic world. Consequently, there are circumstances in which a negative influence is exerted through the Celestial Stem and Horary Branch Trigrams. The unfavorable trigram is in each case the opposite of its counterpart in Table 17 or 18.

Table 19   *Unfavorable Primeval trigrams*

A and I	B and J	C	D
E	F	G	H

Table 20   *Unfavorable Horary Branch trigrams*

a	b and c	d	e and f
g	h and i	j	k and l

Examples (taking into account positive and negative influences):

A year	䷀	䷀	Adverse fortune
a year	䷀	䷀	Adverse fortune
Cj year	䷀		Very unfortunate
Ea year	䷀		Very unfortunate
Aa year	䷀		Good fortune and bad

The correspondence of months

Check Table 4, pp. 21–2, to determine your month of birth. Check Table 9, pp. 30–1, or Table 11 p. 33 and see if your natal hexagram matches any of the hexagrams applicable to your month of birth. If so, it will increase your auspiciousness. For example, born July 8 (sixth month), natal hexagram is 33 with favaurable correspondence.

Additional favorable and unfavorable aspects

1. HELP FROM OTHERS

When the controlling line has a counterpart of the opposite polarity (in the Pre-Heaven hexagram only) one will receive much help from others, from one's leader, one's superiors, and even from unknown sources. Achievements will only come to others (whose Pre-Heaven hexagram does not show this correspondence) as a result of their own efforts.

Examples:

Help forthcoming ䷀   No outside help ䷀

In the first example, the controlling line is line 5 and a Yang, with its counterpart, line 2, being a Yin. In the second example, both the controlling line and its counterpart are Yang lines.

2. LEADERSHIP OF OTHERS

When the Pre-Heaven hexagram has a single Yang or Yin line as ruler, and this line is the natal controlling line as well, the person involved will be a leader of others, both professionally and socially, and, for the most part, will be surrounded by a large number of people. This is because 'one controls many,' i.e. one Yang (Yin) controls five Yin (Yang).

Example:

3. EFFECTS OF THE MAGNITUDES OF THE HEAVENLY AND EARTHLY NUMBERS

For favorable conditions there should be a degree of rapport between the heavenly number and the earthly number, already obtained, when compared with the basic hexagram representation for the month of birth of the individual under consideration. The existence or nonexistence of this rapport, and its relative strength, depend on the ratio of Yang to Yin lines in the hexagram depicting the month, as compared with the heavenly number, representing the odd (Yang) aspect, and the earthly number, representing the even (Yin) aspect. To determine the favorability or unfavorability, one must compare one's heavenly and earthly number values with the relevant monthly situation elaborated below.

a. December ☰☰ Heavy Snow—Winter Solstice—Eleventh Month

Here the Yang force is reentering the hexagram from below, and consequently its influence should not be too weak or it will not make favorable progress; hence a heavenly number of less than five is considered unfavorable. On the other hand, if the Yin value (earthly number) is greater than thirty it is too strong, overpowering the Yang, and consequently unfavorable.

Optimum values: Heavenly number: eight to twelve.
Earthly number: less than thirty.

b.   January ☰☰ Little Cold—Severe Cold—Twelfth Month

Here the Yang force is considerably stronger; hence to be favorable the Yang value should be greater.

Optimum values: Heavenly number: greater than twelve but not more than twenty-five.
Earthly number: not greater than thirty.

c.   February ䷒ Spring Begins—Rain Water—First Month

The optimum conditions are when the heavenly number is about twenty-five and the earthly number about thirty. Conditions are unfavorable to the degree in which the numbers vary from the foregoing.

d.   March ䷊ Excited Insects—Vernal Equinox—Second Month

The heavenly number should be greater than twenty-five but less than thirty, and the earthly number less than thirty, for the most favorable conditions. If the heavenly number is greater than thirty it is like having summer weather in the springtime, and therefore not favorable.

e.   April ䷡ Clear and Bright—Grain Rains—Third Month

Note that there is only one Yin line. The Yang lines are trying to drive it out, therefore the heavenly number should be greater than twenty-five, and as large as possible, with the Yin number being very low, for the most favorable conditions.

f.   May ䷀ Summer Begins—Grain Fills—Fourth Month

With the absence of Yin lines, the heavenly number should be as large as possible, preferably over thirty, whereas the earthly number should be very low, for favorable conditions to prevail.

g.   June ䷫ Grain in Ear—Summer Solstice—Fifth Month

The Yin force is beginning to return but is still minimal, so the earthly number should be low. The heavenly number is most favorable between twenty-five and thirty-five.

h.　　July ☰☷ Slight Heat—Great Heat—Sixth Month

For the most favorable conditions the heavenly number should be between twenty-five and twenty-nine, and the earthly number close to thirty.

i.　　August ☰☷ Autumn Begins—Limit of Heat—Seventh Month

With the balance of Yin and Yang in the hexagram, the heavenly and earthly numbers should be more or less equal for the most favorable conditions, i.e. heavenly number: twenty-five to thirty, and earthly number: thirty to thirty-five.

j. September ☰☷ White Dew—Autumnal Equinox—Eighth Month

Since the Yin lines now predominate over the Yang in the hexagram, so the heavenly and earthly numbers should be further apart, with the heavenly number around twenty-five, and the earthly number between thirty and forty, for the optimum conditions.

k.　　October ☷☷ Cold Dew—Hoar Frost Descends—Ninth Month

The heavenly number should be around twenty-two to twenty-five, and the earthly number around forty, for the most favorable conditions.

l. November ☷☷ Winter Begins—Little Snow—Tenth Month

With the absence of Yang lines in the hexagram, the most favorable conditions are when the heavenly number is minimal, and the earthly number between forty and sixty.

As a general guide, it is better for a man to have a large heavenly number, and for a woman to have a large earthly number. This factor must, of course, be considered in relation to the other determining aspects.

If a man was born in a positive year and his heavenly number is insufficient (with regard to the month of birth), then his father will die before his mother. If a woman was born in a negative year and her *earthly* number is insufficient, then her mother will die before her father.

4. UNFAVORABLE YEARS
In the event of a yearly hexagram being the 'opposite' or the 'reverse' of either one's Pre-Heaven or one's Later Heaven hexagram, that year will be unfavorable.
The 'opposite' is that hexagram in which every Yang line has been replaced by a Yin, and every Yin by a Yang, e.g.

Basic hexagram	Its opposite

The 'reverse' hexagram is that obtained by turning the basic hexagram upside-down, e.g.

Basic hexagram	Its reverse

Example of unfavorable yearly hexagrams:

Pre-Heaven or Later Heaven hexagram	Unfavorable yearly hexagrams	
33	19	34

5. MARRIAGE. See Chapter 4 (p. 432).

6. OMENS RELATING TO THE FIVE ELEMENTS (see pp. 9–15).
The action and interaction of the five basic elements of wood, fire, earth, metal and water (they should always be considered in that order) have a continuing influence on natal conditions. Referring back to Figures 1 and 2 (pp. 9, 10) one will note that they are assigned symbolic trigrams and are found in certain directional positions, e.g. Fire, Li, ☲, South, Summer. While each element is dominant in its directional and seasonal positions, its influence begins to be felt eighteen days before its season begins.

Fame, fortune, honor, leadership, wealth and love will accrue to those whose Pre-Heaven hexagram contains the trigram for their season of birth, as shown below. For a woman, this correspondence indicates that she will make a good wife and mother.

Date of birth	Favorable trigram	Its opposite (unfavorable)
between winter solstice and vernal equinox	☵	☲
between vernal equinox and summer solstice	☳	☴
between summer solstice and autumn equinox	☲	☵
between autumn equinox and winter solstice	☱	☶

3 | The Predictions

BASIC FACTORS

Certain basic factors enter into the development and use of the sixty-four hexagrams for making predictions on an astrological basis. The background and history of *I Ching* play a vital role in the manner in which this book is to be understood. The elements which come into play in the use of *I Ching* itself are equally applicable in this branch of its philosophy. This combination of attitudes and elements is here distilled into usable, comprehensible predictions.

One of the principal factors is that *I Ching* has been used throughout its existence as a guide for the conduct of good government. In its early days (c.3000–c.1000 B.C.) it was used by kings and nobles, the only literate people. In 1123 B.C., King Wên and the Duke of Chou set *I Ching* down in writing, with some amplifications. Confucius (551–479 B.C.) added to its usefulness by writing explanatory comments. In 136 B.C., examinations for the filling of government positions at all levels were initiated in China. The 'Five Confucian Classics' and *I Ching* were the books from which the examination questions were drawn. Many of the interpretations of *I Ching* consequently relate to rules and officials, and one finds this carried over into the astrology of *I Ching* as well. Keeping this in mind, one can interpret the statements to fit one's own situation, for, after all, governing a country, a family, or oneself have much in common. Actions taken in one situation can be paralleled in the others. In some instances one must examine the portents closely for their applicability to the individual concerned.

The fundamental basis for interpretation, however, rests on the fact that *I Ching* symbolizes all conditions and circumstances in life. This is because the trigrams, each with its wide variety of

73

meanings, between them embrace all things. Consequently, detailed consideration of the trigrams composing any hexagram is vital to the astrology, i.e. what the trigrams represent, which one is above, whether they are cooperating, whether their tendency is to rise, fall or separate, what their basic natures are, what support the lines give each other, etc. From a deep study and an understanding of these elements, predictions have been set forth for each line of each hexagram.

Sometimes, what is written about one of the lines may be somewhat at variance with the commentary on the hexagram as a whole, owing to the line's position, the support received, and/or its strength, etc., demonstrating the fact that nothing, according to *I Ching*, is ever all black or all white. There is a little of the Yin in every Yang, and a little of the Yang in every Yin. Some favorableness can therefore be expected in every hexagram, and for every line, however difficult. Similarly, there will be reason for the exercise of caution, even with the most favorable of predictions.

The predictions and commentaries are quite succinct. What is written is primarily addressed to the superior man, as with the basic *I Ching*. The more the commentaries and predictions are used, the better will be one's understanding of them, and the nearer one is to becoming a superior man, the more accurate will be one's interpretations.

HEXAGRAMS 1–64, WITH NATAL, YEARLY AND DAILY PREDICTIONS

Hexagram 1   Ch'ien ☰ *Creative (Innovatory) Action*

The universe has been revolving continuously, and changing continually, since its inception. Fu Hsi started *I Ching* with the hexagram Ch'ien so as to teach mankind to emulate the way of heaven, to be creative, active and diligent throughout each day, and to persevere with ceaseless constancy.

SIMPLE TRANSLATION OF TEXT
Creative Action. Sublime success. Persistence in the firm and correct is advantageous.

74

COMMENTARY

The Universal Creative, in manifesting itself, first produced the Yin and the Yang. In three subsequent evolutionary stages it produced the Yang and seven other trigrams. In six stages it produced the Yang or Ch'ien hexagram and sixty-three other hexagrams. The Ch'ien hexagram is composed of two Yang trigrams or a total of six Yang lines. Yang lines in the first, third and fifth positions are in their right places. Here we have Yang lines in the second, fourth and sixth positions as well. Strong lines in places where weakness should normally prevail can often be damaging. Creative strength must be properly and wisely directed for it to be truly propitious. Since this creativity is throughout the hexagram, it is considered as stemming from the Primal Source, and a person born under this hexagram will receive outside help and support, as well as being exceptionally strong inwardly. He will be a man of action and creativity. Hence the predictions for success, fame and riches for those carrying out their intentions with wisdom.

It is well known that some paths are smoother than others, and so it is here. The position of the controlling line sets forth the favorable and unfavorable conditions. Whether one's path will be smooth, rough, or somewhere in between, depends on the position of the controlling line and how one uses the blessings available to one through the exercise of one's free will (see also Chapter 2).

In the lines, mention is made of 'dragons.' The meaning is not literal but, rather, symbolic of forces, powers and spirits which do not only exist here on the surface of the earth, but also in its very core, and in the skies, anywhere and everywhere. Related to man, this signifies the inner force which can transcend time and space.

Those born in the fourth month will be more auspicious.

CONTROLLING LINES (FROM BOTTOM TO TOP)
Line 1 Hidden dragon. Work quietly.

The hidden dragon means that the primeval forces are not operating out in the open here, implying that one should remain withdrawn, hiding one's talents and abilities; however one should be mentally active. These are persons who quietly direct matters from behind the scenes.

Most auspicious: He will be a learned scholar with wide knowledge, who knows how to direct and control others to get the best out of them. He may have a tendency to be lackadaisical, and will not be a seeker of fame or fortune. Even so, some may reach him. Least auspicious: His level of activity will be quite low and his living standards poor. Since this is the Ch'ien hexagram, he will have the wherewithal successfully to overcome and rise above these conditions.

In yearly hexagram:

Officer or official	No promotion or demotion.
Business and professional	Conditions dormant.
Ordinary people	Excellent for those leading a quiet life. Do not start any major new activity. Inferior persons will experience troubles.

Line 2　The dragon appears in the field. It is beneficial to meet the superior man.

The primal forces are now operating on the surface of the earth, symbolizing that this man not only has great talent and ability but should demonstrate his talent and worth to the world. Doing so will result in successes for him. He is resourceful, and capable of working at all levels. Working in cooperation with superiors will be especially beneficial for him.

Most auspicious: He will become noble and rich in character, wealth and position. He will rise to a high position and his services will be sought after by many. He will also have a highly favorable personal life.

Least auspicious: He will attain limited fame, honor and wealth, coupled with a modest family life, adequate in all respects.

In yearly hexagram:

Officer or official	He will meet and work with a good manager or superior who will help promote him.
Business and professional	He will gain profits and be successful.
Ordinary people	A good year. Profits and acquisitions can be expected.

Line 3　Superior persons should be careful all day to avoid mistakes.

I Ching is designed for superior persons, and offers no advice to inferiors. It does, however, make predictions regarding them.

By being cautious yet diligent, a man can avoid mistakes. Many important matters will confront an individual throughout his life. The persons indicated here will have a tendency to procrastinate and be indecisive. They should beware of this. These persons have ample ability, and their strong traits, if used, will play an important part, not only in their success but in that of others dependent on them.

Most auspicious: He will be a noble, honest and learned man, achieving gains and fame by always being cautious, and by converting the difficult into the easy, both in his personal and professional life.

Least auspicious: He will be indecisive, unstable and changeable, sometimes diligent, sometimes lazy, and often not respecting others. The potential to improve is there, and, if brought to the fore, such a person will be able to enhance his circumstances.

In yearly hexagram:

Officer or official	He will have many assignments and will always be required to be busy. With exceptional care he can avoid mistakes. Chances for promotion are remote.
Business and professional	Much activity but little profit. Check and double-check financial position, for safety. Any impetuousness will be dangerous.
Ordinary people	A generally unstable year, without much cooperation.

Line 4 The dragon is wavering. No blame.

Each individual must determine for himself what his course will be. Whatever course this individual elects to follow will be right for him. He will have the requisite judgment and experience to make proper progress or retreat as circumstances dictate. No blame will occur, no matter what courses he follows.

Most auspicious: He will know when to move and when to stop. He will also tend to cultivate a highly moral and religious character. He will be willing to share his knowledge and abilities with others and be of service to them. This will result in many benefits to him.

Least auspicious: While admiring riches and fame, his indecisiveness will probably keep him from gaining them, except to a minor degree. Unless he exercises care in all he does, such a person may become a failure both in his personal and professional life.

In yearly hexagram:

Officer or official	He will have to wait for a position to become vacant, or for promotion. Nevertheless he should be constantly active.
Business and professional	The potential for success is available. Rendering service and following the right courses will be advantageous and fruitful.
Ordinary people	A propitious year for all activity. Obstacles encountered, generally, will be easily overcome.

Line 5 The dragon flies in the heavens. One should see the great man.

The achievements of this man will be greater than those of many others. The primal forces are operating in the sky, and favor all activity in which such a person may engage, whether it be mental or physical, spiritual or material. Such an individual will be progressively successful, and, depending on how much he exerts himself, his successes can be limitless. He will be continually blessed by heaven. It is especially of such a person that the saying 'God helps those who help themselves' truly applies, even though others, seeing the individual's affluence and achievements, might be inclined to say that he did not need God's help. Some scholars say that this controlling line is the most auspicious of all those in *I Ching*.

Most auspicious: He will achieve fame and fortune and attain high positions throughout his life. He will be sought-after and highly respected, and his services can, and probably will, be used for the benefit of the nation and the world. His personal life will be highly favorable.

Least auspicious: He will have a strong desire for fame and glory, but the results he attains will not be as high as he would like, in that his influence will be primarily at a local level rather than at a national or international level. He will be successful, and will have a good family life as well.

In yearly hexagram:

Officer or official	Rapid advancements and new positions, favoring the attainment of fame and wealth.
Business and professional	Much activity and profit.
Ordinary people	He will obtain help from superiors, and will make favorable progress.

Line 6 The highest dragon has regrets.

Since line 6 is the topmost position, the symbolism is that the dragon has travelled so high that it has become isolated. No person or thing is independent of all else, so if one strives too high the results are unsatisfactory and there is cause for regret. These persons will have such tendencies, but the superior man heeds this warning, and guides himself accordingly.

Most auspicious: He will be learned and quite influential. Fortunately, he will have the know-how to remain humble and to employ caution. This will enable him to attain modest fame and fortune, and to retain it.

Least auspicious: He will be arrogant and ostentatious, and will have a generally troublesome and unfavorable life. He may die young.

In yearly hexagram:

Officer or official	Demotion or retirement is likely.
Business and professional	If he is too hard in his dealings and is obstinate, he will run into many difficulties.
Ordinary people	He can expect moderate difficulty throughout the entire year.

KEYNOTES

1. Quietude is sometimes a virtue. Use it judiciously.
2. Resourceful creativity brings success.
3. Be cautious whenever it is indicated.
4. Select activities suited to your disposition.
5. Progressive activity leads to success.
6. Always beware of excesses.

CONDENSATIONS FOR DAILY CYCLES

1. Do not make important decisions today. Further thought should be given. Also, new information may be forthcoming. Do not disclose matters of importance if this can be avoided.
2. A favorable day for every aspect of life.
3. Doubt exists as to the best course to pursue. Use extreme care in thought and deed in order to avoid mistakes.
4. You know intuitively how far to proceed in any enterprise. Be guided accordingly, and you will achieve favorable results.
5. Your actions today will be those of a superior person, and whatever you do will produce favorable results.
6. Even though your present conditions may be favorable, beware of arrogance and ostentation. Remain humble, and with extra care possible stumbling-blocks can be avoided.

Hexagram 2   K'un ☷ *Receptiveness (Responsiveness)*

SIMPLE TRANSLATION OF TEXT

Receptiveness. Sublime success. The firmness of a mare advantageous. If the superior man takes the initiative he goes astray, but if he follows he finds guidance. Favorable friends will be found in the south and west, but those in the north and east will be lost. Gentle persistence leads to good fortune.

COMMENTARY

One immediately notes a similarity to the text of the Ch'ien hexagram. This is because the Yin and the Yang, the Receptive and the Creative, are equal, and complement each other rather than oppose. It is true that their basic characteristics are very different, but there is no such thing as only one path to a particular goal, whether it be spiritual development, fame, fortune, riches, a long life, happiness, or whatever. The symbol for Yin is the earth. Therefore, this person should be like the earth, i.e. strong, receptive, responsive, and, above all, inwardly correct. Whenever the earth is correct inwardly it is productive externally, useful, beneficial, and a thing of beauty, It is responsive to the laws of heaven, and works to consummate what is required of it, without external display or complaint. Those born here should try to emulate the earth. It is of such a person that it can be said, 'He never seems to do anything yet he always gets results.' Another attribute of these persons is that, generally, they never let you know what they are thinking.

Since the predominant quality here is receptiveness, like the nature of a mare, these persons will fare best if they let others do the leading. The south and west are the directions in which there are many people, and the places where things are brought to fruition. The north and east are the directions from which orders emanate. Here, the north and east are to be avoided, but following established paths will lead to good fortune. This hexagram is expecially favorable for women. One born under this hexagram will be kind, gentle, virtuous, and will marry a good man, with whom she can rear a fine family and have a good life.

Those born in the tenth month will be more auspicious.

CONTROLLING LINES (FROM BOTTOM TO TOP)
Line 1   With the coming of frost, winter is not far behind.

This is the lowest position in the earth, and indicates the beginning of growth. This person will face many quandaries in life, and will have trouble learning how to make proper decisions. He also will have to learn many lessons regarding patience and the length of time it takes for seeds (ideas or actions) to mature, just as there is a natural interval between the first frost and winter. Care, caution, and the making of detailed observations will then become routine.

Most auspicious: This person will be active and studious in childhood and through his school years. He will probably stand high in his class, which will help him in his subsequent work or position in life, and he will gain fame and fortune relatively early. This line is especially auspicious for a child born in a positive month.

Least auspicious: He will have a tendency not to follow an accepted or proper way of life. He will take advantage of people, especially through confidences, and will be easily angered and highly susceptible to flattery. He is likely to be artful or villainous, and more likely to be notorious than famous.

In yearly hexagram:

Officer or official	Much malicious and damaging gossip is likely. Be very careful.
Business and professional	Government policies, competition, and professional jealousies will make this a difficult year.
Ordinary people	Be careful of the troubles stemming from the jealousies of others.

Line 2 Strong, broad and straight in capacity and ability. Affairs prosper, even though no action may be taken.

The second line is the ruler of this hexagram and hence holds within it all the most favorable portents. This person will be highly developed spiritually, and will carry out the will of heaven rather than his own will. Working thus, his every thought and action will be furthered and blessed by heaven, as long as he does not try to override heaven's will.

Most auspicious: He will be a noble, broadminded and capable person, attaining a high position in whatever work he chooses. He may serve some time in the government, and will be very influential. His personal and professional life will be worthy of emulation by others

Least auspicious: He will be an honest man, respected by his peers, and will be well known locally. He will have a reasonably good life, however he will be frequently restless.

In yearly hexagram:

Officer or official	He will achieve advancement and promotion.
Business and professional	He will become well known, and will make gains.
Ordinary people	He will gain considerable profit from his investments.

Line 3 Hide or play down your talents. Let others seek the glory and recognition. Immediate successes are not to be expected, but ultimate success will be achieved.

Humility, perseverance and patience are the qualities which will achieve the greatest success, under this controlling line, when these are coupled with wisdom. Those especially favored will have these qualities. Others born under this hexagram will learn to acquire them to a greater or lesser degree.

Most auspicious: He will become learned and well known, and perhaps even, by dint of especial effort, become famous and achieve wealth at various times in his life.

Least auspicious: He is likely to be cautious and somewhat dull, yet upright and helpful in dealings with others. He will only have mediocre achievements.

In yearly hexagram:

Officer or official	A promotion may be imminent.
Business and professional	Advancement and a broadening of responsibilities is to be expected.
Ordinary people	He will attain that upon which he concentrates.

Line 4 Calmness. No blame. No praise.

Troublesome conditions seem imminent. By handling them quietly and with reserve, they can be overcome or avoided. The judicious exercise of wisdom and reserve produces neither blame nor praise for the results achieved. These persons will be diligent and responsible, and will be capable of becoming outstanding executives. Since many difficulties will be encountered, great achievements are not presaged.

Most auspicious: He will attain a high and influential position, but will not attain renown. His successes will be positive but limited in scope. He will have a generally favorable life.

Least auspicious: This person will be a loyal, honest, sincere and reliable individual. He will probably have a moderate or low income. His life also will be quite favorable.

In yearly hexagram:

Officer or official	Exercise judicious caution. No promotions are to be expected.
Business and professional	It will be difficult to make any progress. He will have small gains only.
Ordinary people	A stagnant year. Stay where you are, and avoid new ideas and activities.

Line 5 A yellow-lined coat. Supreme good fortune.

Yellow is the color of the golden mean, the earth, and of purity. It is also a symbol of humility. These persons will be innately pure, inwardly strong, and will express humility, even when richly endowed mentally, physically and spiritually. They will possess an inner beauty, nurtured by an inherently noble spirit. That which they are inwardly will come into being and reach fruition outwardly, hence supreme good fortune can be expected. Most auspicious: He will be noble, virtuous, helpful and beneficial to others, both professionally and personally, and all possible good will be his for the taking.

Least auspicious: He will be revered yet modest, achieving better than average results, and wealth as well, along with a favorable reputation and a good life.

In yearly hexagram:

Officer or official	He will advance to a more important position.
Business and professional	A favorable year for profit and expansion.
Ordinary people	A stable year, good for attaining anything upon which he concentrates.

Line 6 Contending with a true dragon results in black and yellow blood.

In this sixth position, the Yin force has run to an extreme, and if it tries to lead and take the place of a creative dragon (see the explanation of 'dragon' under hexagram 1), the result will be bloodshed and injury. Yin activity should remain receptive and responsive, no matter how high it rises. A person born with this controlling line will be inclined to lead, but if he notes the warnings given and guides himself appropriately, even though it is likely to be difficult, he can be successful and avoid serious injury. Such a person may never have peaceful enterprises or great happiness, yet by virtue of possessing qualities inherent in the hexagram he will be able to attain a full and rewarding life. Most auspicious: He will achieve a high position, but unless he exercises humility constantly he will become arrogant, always blaming others for mishaps or mistakes, and eventually losing all he has gained.

Least auspicious: He will become a man of bad character, boastful, ostentatious, unreliable, and changeable in thought and action; he will have many hardships.

In yearly hexagram:

Officer or official	Demotion is likely, or a reduction in salary.
Business and professional	He can expect worries and conflicts.
Ordinary people	A generally troublesome and difficult year.

KEYNOTES

1. Slow growth is never wrong.
2. With rectitude, unrestricted progress can be made.
3. Express humility and fortitude in relations with others.
4. When perplexed, exercise exceptional care and forethought.
5. Intuitive receptivity makes for successful productivity.
6. Attempts to lead are dangerous when one is destined to follow.

CONDENSATIONS FOR DAILY CYCLES

1. Whatever one has in mind, good or bad, will take a natural, steady course of development.
2. Through inner correctness, all situations can be dealt with successfully today.
3. Seek no glory for yourself. Make no display of talents or abilities.
4. Troublesome conditions may be close, but with forethought difficulties can be circumvented.
5. Receptiveness coupled with intuitiveness, followed by quiet activity, can produce favorable results.
6. Trying to lead today, unless directed to so do, could result in the failure of your efforts, and endanger your enterprise.

Hexagram 3   Chun ☷ *Difficulty in Infancy*

SIMPLE TRANSLATION OF TEXT
The superior man advances, despite difficulties at the beginning, through cooperation and perseverance in what is right.

COMMENTARY
Whenever heaven, Ch'ien, and earth, K'un, unite, offspring are produced in the mental, physical and spiritual realms. These, like all progeny, need to be nurtured and cared for in infancy, with righteous persistence, in order for them to become independent.

85

The kind of person depicted here is a superior man who knows what to do and how to do it with persistence and constancy. These individuals will bring new ideas into being, help whatever is small to grow big, and do so using proper methods and principles. This type of leadership, which is difficult to exercise, is productive of success, and will result in benefits, riches and fame. As a general guide, action will initiate inspiration.

Those born in the sixth month will be more auspicious.

CONTROLLING LINES (FROM BOTTOM TO TOP)
Line 1 The way of righteousness must be pursued, despite uncertainties and difficulties at the beginning.

The actions and character demanded of this person are of the highest quality and strength. Very few will be able to meet these arduous demands. The beginning of anything holds the seed of all that is to follow. What happens at the beginning will largely determine the degree of success or failure later. Life will not be easy for those with this controlling line. Fortunately, these persons are innately endowed with the qualities necessary for coping with whatever faces them.
Most auspicious: He will achieve greatness in his position or enterprise, but this will be precarious. While results will be attained, nothing will be easy, either in his personal or his professional life.
Least auspicious: Basically, he will be an honorable man, but likely to be quite suspicious of others and frequently indecisive, resulting in few or no achievements.
In yearly hexagram:

Officer or official	His abilities will probably be recognized this year.
Business and professional	Many difficulties will be overcome if handled properly.
Ordinary people	Follow set standards and patterns to avoid difficulties. A below average year.

Line 2 Back and forth, hither and thither. No progress. The maiden has lost her veil but remains modest. The man will woo at the right time without obstacle.

This man has advanced a step, but there are still many difficulties and uncertainties. The man neither knows nor recognizes the right course to pursue, at the beginning of the line, and wanders this way and that in his efforts to find the correct path. He seems to make no progress. The situation appears quite adverse, like that of a man wooing a maiden only to find she has lost her veil, the symbol of purity and correctness. The truth is, however, that she has merely been robbed of something which was beyond her control. Thus the situation looks dire, but is not in reality what it seems on the surface. In due course the man will see things for what they are, and he will then be able to proceed without encountering obstacles. These individuals will have many trials and tribulations in early life, but through diligent and persistent effort they will eventually find the right and successful way.

Most auspicious: He will experience much solitude and will receive no help in the early part of his life. Later, the situation will reverse itself. He will achieve fame on a local basis, and modest riches. The latter part of his life will be happy.

Least auspicious: He will be too ambitious, and will not wait for the right time to act. This impatience and rashness will be resented, so he will run into much opposition and achieve but little. This man's morals may also be questionable.

In yearly hexagram:

Officer or official	He will carry out duties in a good and wise manner, and will advance to a better position.
Business and professional	A troublesome year, with growth stagnating.
Ordinary people	For the most auspicious: He is likely to marry this year or increase the size of his family. For the least auspicious: Many hardships, and possible litigation.

Line 3 When pursuing a deer in the forest, without a guide, a hunter is likely to find himself lost. The superior man discerns the situation and desists from going forward, since so doing would lead to needless troubles.

This line shows that by not acting properly one can get into difficulties. Great care and caution are suggested.

In a general way, there are four types of individuals, namely, (1) the wise and energetic, (2) the wise and lazy, (3) the foolish and lazy, and (4) the foolish and energetic. It is of these last that one must be wary, and they, for themselves, must exercise great care in order to be successful. It is this fourth type that is symbolized here, with the warning that they should take their time and become wise before (wrongly) releasing the energy they possess, i.e. through diligence and care to advance from category (4) to category (1). The potential is there. It can be worked on, and some of these persons will do so.

Most auspicious: He will be a superior **person,** knowing when and how to act at all times, thereby achieving successes. Also, acting thus he will avert troubles.

Least auspicious: He will move from place to place searching for the right work and associates, but never truly finding them.

In yearly hexagram:

Officer or official	He is likely to be accused of corruption. A troublesome year.
Business and professional	He is likely to suffer from insults and the erroneous thinking of others.
Ordinary people	Any deviations from the norm could result in the individual being arrested and jailed.

Line 4 Indecisive, trotting to and fro, he waits for marriage. Subsequently, every action will prosper and good fortune will prevail.

One should seek to associate with a wise and clever man, or to join an enterprise in a propitious situation. Through thus uniting, one will be able to overcome one's difficulties and have one's wishes fulfilled.

The fourth line of a hexagram is the higher position of man, and one born under this line should normally be firm, positive, persevering and correct. The Yin line here is weak and not in the proper place, hence at the start this man is indecisive, and hesitates. In this situation it is right that he do so, until he finds the right person or situation to unite with (symbolized by the marriage). Once this is done he will be working in harmony with the will of heaven, because of the Yang line immediately above, and good fortune and success will then be attained.

Most auspicious: This man's early life will be spent in the search for an association with one of superior talents. Eventually he will meet a person in an authoritative position who will recognize his merits and appreciate him. He will then rise to a high position and achieve success.

Least auspicious: He may remain indecisive through timidity and lack of courage, never becoming independent. He will have a tendency to wander, in both his private and his public life, even though superior persons may try to help him.

In yearly hexagram:

Officer or official	Promotion and fame is likely.
Business and professional	Advancement and profits are to be expected.
Ordinary people	A generally favorable year, provided he receives help from friends.

Line 5 Nourishing is difficult. Doing small things brings good fortune, but great enterprises should be avoided.

This man's character is not sufficiently expansive to bring great results from his actions. This is the ruling line of the hexagram, which is normally an indication of auspiciousness. Unfortunately, the individual symbolized here is still relatively weak in overall growth, especially in intelligence and character. He will have good potential for growth, but for the most part will lack the experience to be able to cope with, and successfully overcome, major difficulties. Consequently, if he stays within proper limits for himself he can be successful to a modest degree. On the other hand, if he becomes pushful and tries to force results in other than small matters, he will experience misfortune.

Most auspicious: He will know how to cooperate with others, as well as how to act independently. He will achieve some small successes, local fame, and some wealth.

Least auspicious: He may be over ambitious without possessing adequate experience or making necessary preparations, and as a result meet with misfortune, unless through diligence he becomes wise enough to change his ways and character.

In yearly hexagram:

Officer or official	Small gains can be expected.
Business and professional	Take small steps only, and with care.

Ordinary people	Avoid expansiveness of any sort, and matters will go well.

Line 6   Horse and chariot part. Blood and tears flow.

This line holds little opportunity for further advancement; hence there is considerable consternation and concern.

Symbolically, this man has advanced too far, without being adequately prepared; it is like going into battle with poor equipment so that one's horses become separated from the chariot. Naturally, blood and tears will flow. These conditions are paralleled in this man's life. He should never go so far in any one direction that there are no alternative possibilities, or blood and tears will ensue. A person born with this controlling line will probably have a very unfavorable life, unless taught the right path, and unless, through his personal efforts and will, he manages to overcome the power of fate.

Most auspicious: Even the most auspicious omens are not good. It will be a life of hardships and difficulties, with constant dilemmas as to when and how best to act. No fame, and little fortune, is indicated.

Least auspicious: He will have a poor marriage and family life, and may suffer a disabling injury and/or imprisonment.

In yearly hexagram:

Officer or official	The probability of malicious gossip, investigations, and false reports, demands that extreme care be exercised.
Business and professional	Slanderous competition will be damaging.
Ordinary people	Beware of possible disaster. Make sure that you are well insured. You, or one of your parents, may die this year.

KEYNOTES

1. When starting something new, seek cooperation.
2. *Laissez-faire* can often be employed to advantage.
3. Inexperience can be dangerous.
4. Act only when you feel intuitively that the time is right.
5. As far as possible be impartial.
6. Overstepping limits will prove disastrous.

CONDENSATIONS FOR DAILY CYCLES

1. A precarious situation may be developing. Secure the co-operation of others.
2. If difficulties are being encountered, wait for conditions to return to normal before taking further action.
3. Beware of inexperience or a tendency towards rashness. It would be easy to lose your way today.
4. Further hesitation will get you nowhere. Diligently pursue that which you know intuitively to be right.
5. Stay within your limits, as discovered from previous experience. Favorable results can be had if care is used.
6. Take heed, and make no moves. One should never go so far that one becomes isolated. This may be a very difficult day.

Hexagram 4   Mêng ☶ *Immaturity*

SIMPLE TRANSLATION OF TEXT

Youthfulness, despite its lack of wisdom, can still achieve success. The teacher does not seek the tyro, but when sought and questioned, answers fully. If the student importunes, no further information is given. Correctness promotes success.

COMMENTARY

This hexagram depicts a spring at the foot of the mountain, and symbolizes uncultured youth. The spring shows the potential of ever increasing nourishment, and the mountain signifies the heights that can be attained. The superior man develops his worth with every step he takes in life.

To understand *I Ching* and its guidance, one must remember that it is based on the theory of reincarnation or a divine plan whereby all people do not come into this world equal in mental and physical endowments. Each is different, each is at a particular level, each has his own experiences to encounter and each has certain lessons to learn. Those born with Mêng as their ruling hexagram are not stupid, but merely lacking in certain areas of experience and wisdom, which they must seek out. Their immaturity will be overcome through proper learning and learning methods. Continuing effort will secure success. Such persons' lives will be far from dull, and more than likely very interesting. Those born in the eighth month will be more auspicious.

CONTROLLING LINES (FROM BOTTOM TO TOP)
Line 1   To cultivate maturity in a youth it is advisable to apply discipline, but never more than is necessary, while removing the fetters of his mind.

A teacher conducting the training of a youth is depicted here. Thus two interpretations are possible, i.e. one for the teacher and another for the student. Since the hexagram as a whole is concerned with immaturity, this line will generally relate to the inexperienced person. An individual born with this hexagram and controlling line will find himself surrounded by limitations, visible and invisible. His progress will be determined by how quickly he learns his lessons. Since the line is a Yin, led by a Yang in the second position, his chances for success are quite good.
Most auspicious: He will be close to people in high positions. He will cultivate a just and moral character and be blessed. He also has the potential to become rich or famous, or both.
Least auspicious: He will be a good, useful and loyal citizen, with a better than average life.
In yearly hexagram:

Officer or official	He will probably be assigned to a position involving education or law enforcement.
Business and professional	Something new and beneficial will come to pass.
Ordinary people	A year of disputes with relatives and friends. Imprisonment is a possibility.

Line 2   Tolerating initial weaknesses brings good fortune. Sons will be capable of taking charge of the household.

Whatever one's position in life may be, it will involve the leading of others to a greater or lesser degree. This person will be kindly and considerate, as symbolized by 'tolerating weaknesses.' He will also know how to treat women, and will find himself a good wife, since he is qualified to take charge of the household. All in all, this reflects inner strength and outer reserve. Whatever such a person undertakes will be productive and beneficial. His life should be favorable, whatever activities he pursues.

Most auspicious: He will be a wise, broadminded person, kind and considerate, putting others before himself. He will be loyal to his family, and patriotic, and will have a highly satisfactory life.

Least auspicious: He will have an average life, with a good wife and family, and good partners and/or friends.

In yearly hexagram:

Officer or official	His position will be stable, and he will have fruitful achievements.
Business and professional	He will be successful, and an example to others.
Ordinary people	Whatever he concentrates on will be accomplished. Also, he may get married or increase the size of his family.

Line 3 Do not marry a maiden who, on seeing a wealthy man, loses control of herself. Nothing advantageous.

Just as many women will give up their honor in the hope of catching a wealthy man, so, likewise, immature men may sell their souls in the hope of acquiring quick gains. One is warned against such surreptitious conduct, since what is not rightfully and dutifully earned will not remain in one's possession. Persons with this controlling line will have a tendency towards recklessness, while still lacking in wisdom, experience and learning. Unless corrective measures are taken, such actions will bring no favorable advantage to such a person.

Most auspicious: He will be learned, but inclined to use his knowledge for selfish purposes only. There will be periods of gain and loss throughout his life, in both the personal and professional realms. A woman will quite likely become an accomplished mistress.

Least auspicious: He will be a person of bad character, inclined to hurt people behind their backs. He will have many hardships in life and no worthy accomplishments.

In yearly hexagram:

Officer or official	It is likely that he will be insulted, demoted, or punished for greed.
Business and professional	Something unexpected will occur which will keep him from attaining his goals this year.
Ordinary people	He should maintain calm and quietude. He may become involved in a serious dispute, or have troubles through an excessive use of alcohol.

Line 4 Opinionatedness, stubbornness, and immaturity bring humiliation.

This line shows the student enmeshed in erroneous thinking, and the teacher having no recourse but to leave him alone to suffer humiliation, in order to bring him to his senses.

Many people are born, or become, impractical in thought and action, and, through obstinacy, immaturity, opinionatedness or deluded imagination, demand to follow their own course despite the propitious guidance of others. Often, friends, teachers and superiors have no recourse but to leave such an individual alone to suffer from his self-generated folly, until remorse sets in and he once again desires to follow the right path. There are apparently several important lessons that these persons are destined to have to learn in their lives, lessons which others have already learned. What befalls these individuals is right for them at this particular stage of their evolution, for each is serving a divine purpose, despite the difficulties in which they find themselves.

Most auspicious: He will be a man of talent and ability, but these qualities will not be recognized, so he will either tend to withdraw within himself, or go and live in seclusion. His attainments will only be small.

Least auspicious: He will have but few friends, being of a difficult nature, and having a tendency to show off. He will be a wastrel, and will probably not marry or have children.

In yearly hexagram:

Officer or official	He can expect no cooperation from others this year, and no promotion either.

Business and professional	No one will recommend him. He will not be highly respected, and so will have difficulty making progress.
Ordinary people	A stagnant year, with many hardships. He may lose some friends. It would be best to keep quiet and be patient.

Line 5 Childlike innocence brings good fortune.

Knowing how to trust one's teacher, and accepting what he says, brings success.

When, having selected a qualified teacher, a man subordinates himself to his instructor, accepting his teachings and guidance in good faith, he will certainly be helped further, and will achieve success by utilizing what he has learned. In life. an ardent seeker of knowledge will usually be able to find that which he needs to know for the next step in his progress. He will obtain it from another person, or from written material, or it will come to him intuitively. Those born under this line will also know what to accept, and how to put it to practical use. Many of these people will be researchers in their chosen field, scientists, inventors or innovators.

Most auspicious: He will be clever and intelligent from childhood, and will be helped by parents, relations, teachers and friends. He will become quite successful in his profession, and will have a good personal life.

Least auspicious: He will be able to go through life, in all its aspects, calmly and without hardships.

In yearly hexagram:

For everyone	A good and fortunate year.

Line 6 Strict and just discipline can prevent further wrong doings on the part of the tyro. Advantageous.

Improperly applied discipline may lead the young to hate those whom they are expected to love. Yet, sometimes strict discipline is the only answer to incorrigibility.

Different people act and react in different ways. There is no one best way to teach others, no one punishment to fit every crime, etc. Here we are primarily concerned with correction. A light punishment may tempt some persons to try and get away with the same thing again, whereas it may be all that is needed to correct others. A person capable of administrating corrective punishment will be a good teacher and leader. Some of these persons will possess such qualities innately; the others will be able to acquire them.

Most auspicious: He may achieve renown in a military career, or in a law enforcement agency. He will set an example to others.

Least auspicious: He will be ambitious, but since not greatly endowed, he will only be well known locally.

In yearly hexagram:

Officer or official	If in the military, or in law enforcement, advancement can be expected.
Business and professional	He will have well disciplined organization, and few troubles.
Ordinary people	He may be subjected to robbery, have to go to court because of a dispute, or have difficulties with servants or subordinates.

KEYNOTES

1. Thoughtlessness or playfulness always needs correction in education.
2. Express consideration of others; understand their points of view.
3. Calmness is always propitious.
4. Obstinacy or immaturity makes for impracticality.
5. A humble search for knowledge will attain results.
6. Skilful correction is propitious.

CONDENSATIONS FOR DAILY CYCLES

1. Punishment is sometimes necessary to correct thoughtlessness and playfulness.
2. If you try and put yourself in the place of others and see their points of view it will be helpful in your endeavors.
3. The time is not propitious for taking action to consummate whatever one has in mind.
4. Try not to be obstinate or unrealistic today. If you are, results could be unfavorable.

5. Your search for knowledge, guidance or assistance will be answered appropriately.
6. Deliberate violation of rules may result in severe punishment. If meting out punishment, do not debase yourself to the level of the culprit. Use corrective measures only.

Hexagram 5 Hsü ☰☰ *Waiting*

SIMPLE TRANSLATION OF TEXT
Confident, joyous, deliberate waiting. Perseverance in righteous action brings success.

COMMENTARY
In life, there are right times to advance, right times to retreat, and right times to wait. Here, the proper time and way to wait are shown, along with the results which can be expected from the various phases of such a course. Proper waiting is a sign of strength and not of weakness. It reflects confidence and patience, with an inner knowledge that one's goal will be attained. Rare is the person who is not faced with doubts while waiting in times of difficulty. The persons symbolized here will be at ease in any circumstances, knowing that they are in control through their inner correctness, and that sooner or later they will achieve success. They will have ordered and generally happy lives.

Those born in the eighth month will be more auspicious.

CONTROLLING LINES (FROM BOTTOM TO TOP)
Line 1 Remain firm, following that which you know to be right, and wait on the outskirts.

There are many different types of individual in this world, each of which can do some things better than any other type. This man should be in a supporting role, letting others lead. He should let someone else be the salesman, while he quietly waits on the sidelines, lending guidance and support. Each member is an equally valuable part of the team. This is the kind of activity that persons with this controlling line should pursue, no matter what career they elect to follow. In general, more success will be achieved by working as part of a group than by operating independently.

Most auspicious: He will be an honest and incorruptible official in local government or business. He will exert influence, mainly from behind the scenes, and will achieve modest success.

Least auspicious: He will be a mild-mannered, mediocre person, living a rather uneventful life.

In yearly hexagram:

Officer or official	He will keep his present position, with no promotion this year.
Business and professional	Nothing spectacularly good or bad will occur this year.
Ordinary people	There will be few or no difficulties of note, except for those persons who are accident-prone.

Line 2 Waiting on the sand by a stream. There is some injurious gossip, but in the end good fortune.

In ancient times, when *I Ching* came into being, there were no bridges, so to cross a stream one waited on the bank, either for a boat, or for the water to subside. Water symbolizes danger. One standing on the sand by a stream is very near the water (danger), and may be overcome by it if it suddenly rises and surges in his direction. Crossing the water symbolizes the carrying out of some great enterprise. Therefore, those depicted here are desirous of achieving progress, and are willing to face the dangers that their prospective enterprise will entail. Others, less visionary and daring, will talk adversely about the projects, which may do them some temporary harm, but this will not stall the activity and in the end good fortune will ensue. Persons with this controlling line are quiet individuals who make careful plans with vision, and execute them with daring. Their lives will be centered around these dominant characteristics.

Most auspicious: Good omens will prevail throughout his life and he will become honored and well known.

Least auspicious: He will be a happy-go-lucky wanderer, and a persuasive talker, possibly a confidence trickster. His later years will be more stable and personally beneficial.

In yearly hexagram:

Officer or official	He will act as a leader, speaking

	for a group of people (but hampered by some gossip).
Business and professional	He will be daring, and successful in overcoming difficulties, which will be numerous.
Ordinary people	Those who are generous and have forgiving natures will have no troubles. Forceful individuals will face disputes and lawsuits, but can win if the right courses are followed.

Line 3 Waiting in the mud (next to a stream) invites the approach of injury and evil.

The persons symbolized here are similar to those born under line 2, but not so wise or clever. They want to be daring and accomplish major enterprises (crossing the water), but while waiting they are standing in the mud. Anyone so doing will be limited in the speed with which he can take action and the directions in which he can move. An enemy can easily catch and harm one so mired. This is most evident in the animal kingdom, where predators stalk their prey at watering-places. Hence these persons are not wise and knowledgeable, as they ought to be for the things they are trying to accomplish. Since *I Ching* is a guide not a book of facts, such persons can circumvent this portent by learning wisdom and gathering wise persons about them, or by setting their sights on less difficult goals than those originally selected. (Read also what is written under line 2.)

Most auspicious: He will attain some wealth and fame, but will be worried and melancholy much of the time.

Least auspicious: He will be obstinate, headstrong and hardhearted. He will not listen to good advice, but will find recklessness, and vain and foolish talk pleasing. He will have no real achievements in life.

In yearly hexagram:

Officer or official	Demotion or grief is likely.
Business and professional	He will suffer insults and economic injury.
Ordinary people	He may be burgled, or suffer injury on a journey.

Line 4 Waiting in a pit amidst blood.

Remembering that *I Ching* was developed in ancient times, one can see the image here is of one who has fallen into a pit or trap along his course. No action is possible. He can neither advance nor retreat. The person is either injured himself, or in the midst of blood from an injury to someone, or something, else. The persons born under this line are unfortunate individuals, who, no matter what they try and do, never manage to achieve much success. Here again though, the adversity of fate can be overcome through proper self-development. If the path of self-improvement is not attempted, then such persons should stand firm in what is right and let fate take its course. In the end, all will be released from the pit.

Most auspicious: He will be a talented and upright person, who will learn how to avoid trouble, but will face severe difficulties in both his personal and professional life.

Least auspicious: He will leave home early in life, and there is a possibility that his parents may die during his childhood. He will have only a poor education, and will be a wanderer, performing menial tasks.

In yearly hexagram:

Officer or official	Wise persons, noting the situation, will avoid demotion.
Business and professional	Those having the backing and support of others will have some of their wishes fulfilled.
Ordinary people	This year will be unfavorable, to a greater or lesser degree. He should seek cooperation and assistance from friends to achieve success.

Line 5 Waiting at the banquet. Perseverance brings good fortune.

The feast has been prepared, and there is an abundance of all things available for the taking. One can relax and enjoy the bounty available to one. Perseverance, as used here, means knowing when and how to act propitiously. There is a right time at a banquet to eat certain foods, and these persons will know all that they need to know, and will do everything that needs to be done, wherever they find themselves. The result will be that they will have an abundance available to them, as at a banquet.

These persons are blessed by heaven.

Most auspicious: He will be a man of noble character, occupying a high position. He will carry out his duties and responsibilities well, and will be highly respected. He will exercise good judgment at all times. There will be no hardships in his life.

Least auspicious: He will attain only a modest position professionally, but will have a good family life and no major problems.

In yearly hexagram:

Officer or official	He will gain promotion and an increase in salary.
Business and professional	He will be noticed, and will make profits.
Ordinary people	He will make profits and life will be good. He may marry, or increase the size of his family.

Line 6 Waiting in a cavern. Three unexpected guests arrive. Honor them. There will be good fortune in the end.

Here at the top of the trigram K'an, meaning danger, the man represented seems to have tried every possible way to overcome the danger, without success, and has withdrawn within himself. Everything seems to have been in vain, and no way out is in sight. Suddenly, three unexpected guests arrive; (these may represent persons or ideas). He asks himself if they are friends or enemies. The advice is to honor them, and they will reciprocate by either showing, or helping him to find, a way out of his difficulties and the path to success. Often, thoughts or people strange to us, regarding which we have doubts, later prove to be our salvation. Those persons born under this line are daring and enterprising individuals, who are willing to try almost any means of achieving success. By their continued activity, new inspirations arise. Sometimes, however, they must temporarily relax in order to let new thoughts enter. When these do, if they are respected and explored, regardless of how strange they may seem at the time, then difficulties will be overcome.

Most auspicious: He will become an eminent scholar or civic leader. He will be very ambitious early in life, but will quieten down appreciably later. He may become a recluse in his senior years.

Least auspicious: He will be humble and modest, giving and receiving help, and in general will avoid troubles. He will have a modest, uneventful life.

In yearly hexagram:

Officer or official	He is likely to be transferred to a position of importance. Beware of misrepresentation.
Business and professional	New ideas will increase his reputation and profits. Scholars may attain national prominence.
Ordinary people	This can be a very good year, if care and caution are exercised. Imprudent persons may suffer degradation, or death.

KEYNOTES

1. Waiting for or avoiding action is better than impulsiveness.
2. Take note of signs, and know when you are impeded.
3. Whenever action is bogged down, beware of encroaching dangers.
4. When progress is halted, retreat and regroup.
5. Determination and persistence bring success.
6. Employ wisdom constantly, since nothing ever has a final ending.

CONDENSATIONS FOR DAILY CYCLES

1. Some danger may be near. Keep outside its imminent sphere. Do not do anything out of the ordinary.
2. Watch what is taking place without participating in it. Then strike at the right time.
3. It is as if one were stuck in mud, with danger near. Exercise extreme care.
4. There is still danger near. Let matters take their own course.
5. Success is certain, so you can relax and wait. Retain the determination to act when the time is ripe.
6. Your creative strength and wisdom come to the fore from within yourself. Put your trust in your intuition.

Hexagram 6   Sung ☰☵ *Conflict*

SIMPLE TRANSLATION OF TEXT
In conflict, righteousness and sincerity are not sufficient by themselves. Plans should be made carefully before any enterprise is begun. If conflict develops later, use caution, and do not force matters to their ultimate conclusion, nor force the advancement of any enterprise.

COMMENTARY
In this hexagram, Ch'ien, strength, is in the outer or external position, over K'an, cunning, within. External strength leading internal cunning is certain to result in conflict, unless channelled and guided correctly. The strength without tends to make individuals with this natal hexagram persons of great external drive and forcefulness, to which most people react unfavorably. In the vast majority of cases it would be better for them to halt half way, rather than try and take matters forcibly to an ultimate conclusion, whereby misfortune would be likely as a result of the antagonisms generated. The wisdom needed by such persons should be sought from those of kingly character. By following their advice, good results can be expected. If such help is not available, it would be best for these persons to forgo any major enterprises. Fundamentally, persons born under this hexagram have some strong inner conflict to overcome before their external actions will be productive of major success.

Those born in the second month will be more auspicious.

CONTROLLING LINES (FROM BOTTOM TO TOP)
Line 1   Do not press disputes through to the end. If left alone they will end propitiously.

Pressing a conflict through to the end makes enemies, which will quite likely result in further difficulties. Ways should be found to solve problems quickly, without either side losing face. The advice for individuals with this controlling line is to become aware of their basic traits, and use them to become negotiators rather than domineering tyrants, into which they could easily degenerate. Remember too that problems often solve themselves when left alone. Keep striving for ever greater wisdom.
Most auspicious: He will be intelligent, wise, quick thinking, open-minded and considerate. He will be aware of changes in

affairs in advance, and for the most part will avoid trouble and difficulties. He is likely to be an orator, historian, counsellor or writer, and his life, in general, will be beneficial and interesting. Least auspicious: He will be unable to envisage changes and situations correctly, and hence will have but few achievements. In general, he will not be sufficiently knowledgeable or persistent, in either his personal or professional life.

In yearly hexagram:

Officer or official	He will be injured by defamation or misrepresentation. In the end, the situation will clear up by itself.
Business and professional	As above.
Ordinary people	He will be bothered by lawsuits and misrepresentations, but these will finally be settled in his favor. A chronic illness may be miraculously cured, or, for the least auspicious, death may occur.

Line 2 Unequal conflict cannot be resolved. Retreat. Numerous family members and friends will benefit from such a course.

A man of good common sense and practicality is depicted here. It is a wise course, when faced by a superior enemy or circumstance, to retreat and reformulate plans, adopting reasonable ways rather than dogmatically pressing forward without hope of victory. The lower trigram is representative of water, which does not force its way when impeded but quietly builds up until it overcomes its obstacle. Retreat is not surrender. It is taking advantage of time and space in order to renew the struggle subsequently with better hope of success.

Most auspicious: He may become a respected official, able to withstand defamation and denunciation, or he may be sufficiently rich to be able to withdraw into seclusion, thereby avoiding troubles.

Least auspicious: He will not like others getting ahead of him and leaving him in second place. He will be pushful, and will encounter difficulties in striving for advancement, but inwardly he will know the value of retreat, and will occasionally use it, reluctantly, in order to maintain a stable life.

In yearly hexagram:

Officer or official	He will probably have an increase in salary.
Business and professional	Conservatism is the keynote. Competitiveness on a large scale is to be avoided.
Ordinary people	A stable and quiet year for most. Some may face lawsuits, or have to escape from a difficult situation.

Line 3 Nourishing oneself on tried and true methods. Danger at first, but in the end good fortune. Keep in the background, even though elements try to force one deeper into the situation.

The third line is the lower position of man, and in this hexagram the symbolism is predominantly indicative of character building. This man has found something of great value to him personally, and he tries to make a complete conversion at once. He is not successful because the old weeds have not been fully eradicated, but through persistence he will achieve his goal in the end. In such circumstances, while undergoing change, it is best to keep in the background, even though there may be external pressure for advancement. In life, such a person will probably branch out into a new field or career foreign to his rearing or his parents' endeavors, and will experience difficulties in the early years but will achieve his goals later in life.

Most auspicious: For the first half of his life he is likely to be under the protection and guidance of his parents, grandparents or close friends of the family. His success in nearly everything will come with the aid of outside support.

Least auspicious: He will receive little or no outside support, but through diligent study and constancy he will be able to overcome the numerous difficulties he will encounter. Regrettably, he will not rise very high in life.

In yearly hexagram:

Officer or official	He will stay on in his position, without difficulty.
Business and professional	An ordinary year, with little fluctuation.
Ordinary people	A dull, routine year.

Line 4 The conflict cannot be carried out successfully, so one

retreats and carries out divine will. This change in attitude brings good fortune.

This man is inclined to carry on a conflict and to try and improve his situation. This is contrary to divine will, so he has to retreat, attain inner peace, and then follow the course he intuitively knows to be right for him. The striving comes from being ambitious and trying to get as far ahead as possible, possibly beyond where he has earned a right to be. This person should remember that nothing is useless in the hands of the Creator, and that each human being serves a purpose, wherever he is and whatever he is doing. Riches, fame and fortune are not ends in themselves but are only valuable for the uses to which they are put. Man is but a custodian. Usefulness is demanded here. When a career of usefulness is selected and followed, this man will find even greater inner peace, and will have good fortune.

Most auspicious: He will be a consistent, persevering, merciful person, following and promoting peaceful paths for himself and his country, with good results.

Least auspicious: He will be too ambitious, and will offend people easily. He will not know how to control himself inwardly, and so will not have good fortune or a peaceful life.

In yearly hexagram:

Officer or official	If cooperative, he will achieve progress.
Business and professional	Considerateness and helpfulness will result in success.
Ordinary people	If he reforms from error and resorts to doing good deeds, he will be free from troubles and will have a peaceful and satisfying year, otherwise he will have difficulties.

Line 5 Bringing conflicts before a qualified arbiter results in supreme good fortune.

This line is very favorable in all aspects, and reflects a wise person endowed with good judgment, who knows the right course to·take in all situations and circumstances. Consequently, he will have many highly favorable achievements. He will also be energetic, persistent and consistent in all that he undertakes.

His actions will be worthy of emulation by others.

Most auspicious: He will be learned and practical. He will have many advancements in life, and will attain a high position from which he will exert great influence.

Least auspicious: With the occasional help of a qualified arbiter he will follow the right courses, and will achieve a very favorable local position and influence.

In yearly hexagram:

Officer or official	He will achieve a major advancement or promotion.
Business and professional	He will win unusual honors and success.
Ordinary people	Strong desires will materialize.

Line 6 Contentions without end. Even rewards earned three times will be taken away.

This is the topmost position in the cycle of contention and conflict, symbolizing that conflict has been carried on to victory and rewards have been received. This peace, however, does not last, because the right way in which to terminate the conflict was not found. The top men in the professions, industry and business are symbolized here, those who have attained their goals through persistence and ruthlessness. Such people are dynamic, but they do not realize that what is won by force can be taken away by force, and so they are involved in endless difficulties and never find true peace or happiness. They should not feel sad about this, since such people are needed, and serve useful purposes for others, even though they suffer appreciably themselves.

Most auspicious: He will be very ambitious, and will dare to try when others dare not. He will disregard personal safety in favor of a high goal, and he may gain considerable wealth and status, but he will have a struggle to keep it.

Least auspicious: He may attain more than the average person does, but will lose it later. His household and business affairs will generally be in a state of disorder.

In yearly hexagram:

Officer or official	He will have successes and failures, advances and retreats.
Business and professional	As above.

Ordinary people   He will also have successes and failures, and may possibly have a major dispute.

KEYNOTES
1. Avoid disputes, or else terminate them quickly.
2. When necessary, retreat, reorganize, and revise plans.
3. Sometimes it is right to keep in the background.
4. If difficulties arise, see whether a change of attitude might be required.
5. Only make use of qualified persons or ideas, for success.
6. Avoid force or obstinacy.

CONDENSATIONS FOR DAILY CYCLES
1. Terminate any dispute quickly, and good fortune will be yours.
2. You will perhaps encounter a superior force today. Retreat, regather your strength, and take a new approach even though you might be inclined to continue the original argument.
3. Keep in the background. The use of force here could get you into deeper trouble. Follow tried and true methods and you can achieve success.
4. Your conflict cannot be carried on successfully today. Change your attitude and accept divine will, and the troubles in your situation will be resolved.
5. Take any major argument before a qualified arbiter. If right is on your side you will have much good fortune.
6. What is won by force can be taken away by force. Do not recklessly take arguments to their ultimate conclusion through force.

Hexagram 7 Shih ☷☵ *Military Expedition (The Army)*

SIMPLE TRANSLATION OF TEXT
Water in the earth. The Army. Perseverance, along with correct and strong leadership, brings good fortune.

COMMENTARY
Man is a microcosm of the macrocosm. Water in the earth indicates a reservoir of strength and power available for use when

needed. Similarly, the people of a nation are a reservoir of strength and power, hence the symbol of an army. Man, as the microcosm, has within himself a vast reservoir of strength and power which is his own army, and which he can call upon as his expeditionary force as he ventures through and contends with the vicissitudes and obstacles of life. There is no question about it; perseverance, along with correct and strong leadership, will bring good fortune. Persons born with this hexagram as their base are destined to be self-willed and generally independent individuals. They will be wise with regard to their own resources, and will use them judiciously, as a general would when conducting a military expedition. Naturally, some will be more wise than others, as is reflected in the various controlling lines. Sages use all their resources, mental, physical and spiritual, in the most propitious combination, to the best advantage.

Those born in the seventh month will be more auspicious.

CONTROLLING LINES (FROM BOTTOM TO TOP)
Line 1   Discipline is a fundamental requirement for a successful army. Without it, misfortune is imminent.

The persons symbolized here are learning how to marshal together all their varying resources, for whatever enterprises face them. Some learn more quickly than others and hence are more successful. Out of the ordinary persons are depicted here, since ordinary people tend to act without deep thought, using visible factors only. These persons understand that there is more to life than just what is observed, and are beginning to use all the other factors. With continued use and experience they will progress and make improvements. Those who do not think, plan and act in this manner will find their lives ruled solely by chance, and will consequently be subject to much misfortune.
Most auspicious: He will be a good, unselfish leader with a love for people, and will accomplish much for the benefit of others. He will make good fortune for himself and will probably become rich and noble.
Least auspicious: He will be fascinated continually by new things and new styles, with a disregard for ancient culture and lore. He will be unstable. If he becomes rich early in life, he will lose his riches.

In yearly hexagram:

Officer or official	If loyal to the government, he will receive honors.
Business and professional	An increase in reputation and profits can be expected.
Ordinary people	An increase in wealth and goods can be expected. Any rashness may lead to failures.

Line 2   The general in the midst of his army. Good fortune. No errors. The king decorates him three times.

In the interpretation of *I Ching*, the fifth line is usually the ruler, or the 'king.' In this hexagram, line 2 is the ruler, so a general is depicted.

Applied to man, this shows a strong leader operating his forces in a skilful and successful manner. He is equal to the demands made of him, and so capable, that, on the whole, he will make no major errors. The receiving of triple decorations signifies that he is blessed by heaven. Such a person must at all times be aware of the responsibility he shoulders and the fact that he cannot separate himself from it without evil creeping in. Here he carries out what is required of him, and is appropriately honored or rewarded.

Most auspicious: He will be courageous, firm, upright, non-tyrannical and considerate. He will exercise good leadership, and give nourishment and benevolence to the masses.

Least auspicious: He will be a local leader of note, receiving much respect and honor. His life will be free from major errors.

In yearly hexagram:

Officer or official	He will be honored by the government, and may be offered a position in the capital or abroad.
Business and professional	He will be a consultant to the government, and may win national acclaim for his individual effort.
Ordinary people	A very prosperous year.

Line 3   Improper leadership. Many corpses.

The leadership and organization are incorrect. Neither the principal leadership nor the subordinate or delegated authority are being exercised properly, as might be the result of a weak man being in an important position without being qualified for it. Such a person has found the means of rising in status or position, but as a result of poor judgment and improper values, leaves a trail of corpses in his wake. Basically, this is a warning for one with this controlling line as his base to note these characteristics, and to take steps to overcome and eliminate them in order to achieve success in life. The correct qualities and traits are available. He should find them and use them.

Most auspicious: He will be a weak leader, neither trusted nor respected unless he takes firm steps to improve himself.

Least auspicious: He may make some attempts at leadership, but with poor results. He will have a hard and short life.

In yearly hexagram:

Officer or official	Demotion is probable. Some matter with a long-term adverse influence is likely to occur.
Business and professional	Possible failure of business or enterprise (or partial failure) is indicated.
Ordinary people	There will be grief, sorrow and sadness. One parent may die.

Line 4 The army retreats. No censure.

Cautious leadership is depicted here. This is a valuable trait in many walks of life. Even the most daring leader must retreat occasionally and alter his tactics. Here, deliberateness in all activities is presaged. Often such people will not make moves, even when haste is apparently indicated. This can be annoying to others, but in the end it is seen that the leadership was correct and that no error was made. This type of deliberate leadership stems from wisdom and not in any way from weakness or cowardice. The situations that such a person will face in life will be those in which this type of leadership is appropriate.

Most auspicious: In good times he will have a position of leadership in a business or profession, or with the government. In adverse times he will take steps to help avoid disasters and troubles. His leadership will be worthy of emulation by others.

Least auspicious: He will find stability if he remains humble and calm, rather than trying to force his methods and ideas on others.

In yearly hexagram:

Officer or official	He will find himself in a position or on an assignment without many inducements.
Business and professional	Motivation for professional progress is lacking. Cultural studies would be propitious.
Ordinary people	His actions should be deliberate, and he will live peacefully and be content with his occupation. He may build a house or travel.

Line 5 There is game in the field. Catch it. The eldest son leads the hosts. If the younger does not transport the corpses, calamity.

Correct organization and leadership are depicted here. Game is available, and this signifies opportunities. The eldest son, in other words the most experienced, must take the lead, just as in any successful business enterprise the best qualified are the leaders in all departments. The youngest, the least experienced, must not be left idle but should be assigned a specific task or responsibility in support of the major effort. Persons here must do the same in the conduct of their lives. Opportunities are available to them. Their duty to society demands that they go after the 'game.' Each of their inner resources must be organized properly and propitiously, and none should be left idle. All must cooperate and work in harmony for the accomplishment of major goals, with each doing that for which he is most capable. Unless this responsibility to self and to others is carried out, there will be misfortune.

Most auspicious: He will advance readily in a proper way, and will perform acts of merit and achieve great respect. He will be famous and popular, and will have a good family.

Least auspicious: He will be learned, and may become a 'country gentleman.' His household will be in good order, with the eldest son capable of handling all affairs. If he acts rashly he will encounter difficulties.

In yearly hexagram:

Officer or official	He will either be in, or be assigned to, an important position.
Business and professional	He will gain advancement in his enterprise or profession.
Ordinary people	Gains in goods and position are likely. Favorable results can be expected from all cooperative efforts. Watch out for troubles stemming from an inept leader or peer.

Line 6 The mission is accomplished. The ruler issues his mandates for the new order to his prince, and rewards the faithful with land. Inferior persons should not be employed.

Proper assignments need to be made. Some persons are great leaders of men (in the field of battle) while others are great administrators. Results have been achieved by the expeditionary forces, and the military leaders are rewarded. The troops are paid off and sent home. Peacetime rule is implemented in both the new and old territories. Rare are the men who are great leaders in the field and capable administrators as well. All effort must be duly rewarded, but for continued progress the right people must be employed, in every circumstance and condition one encounters. In a man this should be reflected in flexibility at all times, mental, physical and spiritual, and the utilization of those attributes which best suit any given set of circumstances. Those persons with this controlling line will have the innate ability to accomplish these things.

Most auspicious: He will be a person who knows and follows the right way, and who will be honored by superiors. He will have worthy achievements and a long life, and he may inherit wealth from his ancestors.

Least auspicious: He may be a wolf in a lamb's skin, presuming upon people and cheating them by false pretenses. His life will probably be unfortunate.

In yearly hexagram:

Officer or official	He will be in a position of authority, and administer it well.
Business and professional	New administrative methods will produce favorable results.

| Ordinary people | Family affairs will be put in order, and he will have a good year. He may receive an inheritance. Beware of confidence tricksters. |

KEYNOTES
1. Establish proper order at the beginning.
2. Ideal leadership brings blessings.
3. Inept leadership is damaging.
4. In difficult situations, exercise deliberate leadership.
5. Good leadership always consummates whatever is begun.
6. Delegate responsibilities appropriately.

CONDENSATIONS FOR DAILY CYCLES
1. The right measure of discipline must be introduced at the beginning of any enterprise for it to be successful.
2. If in an authoritative position one has complete freedom of action. Exercise leadership today and good fortune will result.
3. The assignment of inept or inefficient personnel or ideas could lead to bad results. Exercise care.
4. Halt or retreat on the course you are pursuing. The time is not propitious for action.
5. Whenever opportunities present themselves, take action with appropriately experienced persons.
6. Your goal has been achieved. Now employ only highly suited personnel or ideas to administer it.

Hexagram 8   Pi ☵☷ Uniting

SIMPLE TRANSLATION OF TEXT
Water over the earth. Uniting. Consult further as to whether you possess the qualities and sublimity necessary for leadership. Those of like mind assemble. Laggards meet misfortune.

COMMENTARY
The hexagram is composed of the trigram K'an, water, over K'un, earth. Waters on the earth all flow towards the sea, joining one another and uniting. The inner hexagram, the hidden

influences, i.e. lines 2, 3 and 4, and 3, 4 and 5, form the hexagram Po, Splitting Apart. Hence the advice to discover whether one is a true leader before assuming that office. It is also the reason for stating that laggards meet with disaster. Persons born under this hexagram will have a natural bent towards leadership, in whatever activities they choose to engage in. A humbleness within is dictated for success, and this includes full analyses and firm decisions before accepting and assuming any leadership. One's natural talents and abilities must be suited to the circumstances. If they are, there will be a natural gravitation that will be productive of success. Those not appropriately attuned will meet with difficulties, either through being late, or through attempting to make progress individually.

Those born in the seventh month will be more auspicious.

CONTROLLING LINES (FROM BOTTOM TO TOP)
Line 1 Seeking unity with sincerity is without blame. Confidence, like a full earthen bowl. Unexpected good fortune.

Sincerity is the keynote of any successful union. With confidence as an added factor, the union should be propitious, even though no gains are sought in the beginning. These persons will be of strong character, and will have firm goals which they will pursue with persistence and resolution. Their inner being will act like a magnet, attracting others favorably. Their sincerity has the power to attract benefits from without. The results will be plentiful, 'like a full earthen bowl.'
Most auspicious: He will be a sincere, truthful, plain-spoken and substantial person, in a good position, attracting others readily and leading them beneficially.
Least auspicious: He will be helpful to others. He will have virtually no hardships in life, and everything will seem to flow freely and easily.
In yearly hexagram:

Officer or official	He will receive an unexpected promotion.
Business and professional	He will gain unanticipated profits and benefits.
Ordinary people	He will associate with a friend who will help him make gains.

Line 2 Unification and attachment proceeds from one's own circle (mind). Favorable results through perseverance.

The person depicted here will be a strong and natural leader. Since this line is in the center position of the trigram K'un, earth, his success will be primarily in the material and physical spheres rather than the spiritual and mental. Also, as this is the first stage of the inner hexagram, things are not as auspicious as they would be if another inner hexagram were involved. While this person will have moderate leadership qualities, the implication is that he should devote some of his time to developing himself mentally and spiritually, for a balanced life as well as a more productive one.

Most auspicious: He will be a sincere, honest, honorable and distinguished leader, held in high esteem, and possessing much good fortune, especially in a material sense.

Least auspicious: He will also be honest, upright and sincere, and will attain modest success. He may receive some help from his wife's family.

In yearly hexagram:

Officer or official	He is likely to be transferred to a position close to those principally in authority.
Business and professional	Local success and some good fortune will be forthcoming.
Ordinary people	He will receive outside support from superiors, and plans will materialize. Women marrying this year will be fortunate in their choice of a husband.

Line 3   Seeking unity with the wrong people.

These persons are poor judges of human nature and have difficulty in selecting proper goals. This controlling line is at the top of the trigram K'un, earth, and in the middle position in the lower inner trigram. It is this latter inner tendency which yearns for leadership and unity, but since it is at the height of earthly matters, the unities sought are of the wrong kind. Such persons will have a tendency to try and do things the easy way, which in the end will prove more difficult. Those with this

controlling line as their base are advised to seek and follow the counsel of wise persons, rather than relying on their own judgments and inclinations, even though this may seem difficult. Most auspicious: He will have inferior relatives and friends, and will have bad relations with them. He will not attain his goals, and though he may acquire wealth temporarily, he will not keep it. He will probably have a short life and no heirs.
Least auspicious: He will be a poor scholar, enjoying the company of mean and disreputable persons. He may become afflicted with a serious illness, or incarcerated.
In yearly hexagram:

Officer or official	He will quarrel frequently with colleagues, and will not win.
Business and professional	The year is likely to be troublesome, and he may be dismissed.
Ordinary people	He will be suspicious, unfriendly and provocative. He may suffer injury, and will probably also lose some friends.

Line 4 Seeking cooperation outside your own circle, you should work through leaders. Perseverance brings good fortune.

While every human being is a salesman to a greater or lesser degree, those depicted here will be salesmen in a superior capacity, e.g. entrepreneurs, diplomats, statesmen, and negotiators. Such persons will have a special gift for dealing with leaders in many fields, and, to go with it, the necessary fortitude and persistence for success. Since the fourth line is the upper line for man in the equal partnership between heaven, man and earth, he will constantly strive to improve himself, and will keep abreast of the times.
Most auspicious: He will be a modest man, rendering superior service to his organization and its leaders. He will attain prominence and riches, which he will be able to retain. He will have a good family life, and will render much service to others.
Least auspicious: A life similar to that for the most auspicious is indicated, generally favorable but to a lesser degree.
In yearly hexagram:

Officer or official	He can expect promotion, and an increase in personal possessions.

| Business and professional | He will have increased prominence and work, with substantial profits. |
| Ordinary people | He may be helped by an intimate friend or a stranger. All things will go very well. |

Line 5   Illustration of seeking union and attachments. The king used beaters on three sides but lost the quarry on the other side. The people understood this. Good fortune.

Kingliness and benevolence characterize these persons. In ancient times, when *I Ching* was developed, the kings used beaters on three sides when hunting game, allowing an access for escape on the fourth side. It was considered that destiny was active here, and that only such game as was fated to be caught did not escape. Persons with this controlling line as their base will develop their inner characteristics to the point of kingliness, and will have a natural attraction. Their purposes and aims will be high, but they will not force anyone to join in their enterprises against their wishes. Hence, those who come will do so voluntarily, and will be those who are meant to join. This will result in blessings and benefits for all concerned.

Most auspicious: He will be a just and impartial person, helping others and rendering service to mankind. He will most likely have a government position at some time, at the executive seat of such activity (local, state, national, etc.).

Least auspicious: He also will be a just and upright person, and an open-minded man, willing to help others. He may have hardships early in life, with things improving considerably later. In yearly hexagram:

Officer or official	Promotion is likely. A good year.
Business and professional	He will be honored in his own sphere. Profits will increase.
Ordinary people	Favorable conditions will prevail.

Line 6   Striving for unity without a head. Misfortune imminent.

The person depicted here is somewhat deficient in virtue, and others will not readily obey him. Trying to lead without proper qualifications results in disaster. Similarly, if unity is sought without a suitable leader, misfortune is probable. People cannot be brought together for the common good in such cases. Man, the microcosm, cannot unite the resources within himself without providing the proper leadership for himself. This is advice for those born under this line to constantly re-assess themselves, since what they externally reflect and achieve stems from, and is dependent on, what is within.

Most auspicious: If he does not improve, although he is a man of good personality, he will lack in substance, and so will lose chances for advancement. He may well regret his ways, and repent, too late.

Least auspicious: He will probably have a short life with many hardships; he may withdraw into solitude.

In yearly hexagram:

Officer or official	He will be isolated, and will not be helped by friends or associates.
Business and professional	Achievements will be difficult.
Ordinary people	A difficult year. He may be faced with lawsuits, disaster, or serious quarrels.

KEYNOTES

1. Attraction is attained through sincerity.
2. External unity begins inwardly.
3. Look to yourself if you are attracting the wrong people.
4. For successful accomplishments, work with leaders.
5. Kingly qualities produce supreme results.
6. Ineptitude destroys unity.

CONDENSATIONS FOR DAILY CYCLES

1. Work with one who is an innate leader, and good fortune will result.
2. One's inner disposition and aspirations parallel those of the leader or ruler. Show loyalty openly.
3. Beware of associating with, or seeking to associate with, the wrong people.
4. When seeking unity outside your own circle, cooperate and work with the leaders first.
5. Natural confidence prevails. You should exercise firm and just leadership. Good results can then be expected.
6. Striving to achieve unity without proper leadership results in failure. Heed this warning.

Hexagram 9   Hsiao Ch'u ☰☰ *Small Power*

SIMPLE TRANSLATION OF TEXT
Restrained Small Power. Dense clouds in the west. No rain yet.

COMMENTARY
This hexagram symbolizes the wind (trigram Sun) blowing across the sky (trigram Ch'ien), producing dense clouds but no rain. Rain falling symbolizes the completion of an enterprise. The wind blowing across the sky advises one to display one's mental, physical and material accomplishments in preparations for the achieving of results. The persons depicted here are likely to be liaison personnel, salesmen, or in advertising, the graphic arts or electronics. Progress relates primarily to the development of new ideas, or goods, with success for the individuals themselves as well as for the matters they work on.

Those born in the eleventh month will be more auspicious.

CONTROLLING LINES (FROM BOTTOM TO TOP)
Line 1   Returning to the way. How can this be blameworthy?
Good fortune.

This person knows intuitively the right path, and the proper courses to follow. The first line indicates beginnings, so if he returns to the beginning and follows the path that he knew was right all along, what error can there be? Naturally, such action is in keeping with divine will, so he will have good fortune. Persons of common sense and good judgment are symbolized, who are also enthusiastic and ambitious.
Most auspicious: He will follow the right way through life, aware of deviations, and knowing when to stop and when to proceed. His life will be good, and no one will be able to harm him. He will be loyal to the ruler of his country and to his leaders. He will also be helpful to his family and to others.
Least auspicious: He will also be a resolute, straightforward and upright man, not vain and not admiring hollow fame or titles. He will also have a good life. The least auspicious of all will be lonely, or recluses.

In yearly hexagram:

Officer or official	He will return to a very active position and attain good results.
Business and professional	The advancement of new models, materials and methods will be propitious.
Ordinary people	A quiet year. Beware of being suspicious; it could lead to trouble.

Line 2 Drawn into returning. Good fortune.

A still more intelligent person is represented here. This man has begun to progress, and is wise enough to see impediments and restraints occurring when improper courses are followed, and hence returns to the way which he knows will achieve success. He will know also how to cooperate with others, and will be a very successful communicator of ideas.

Most auspicious: He will be a self-disciplined and self-willed person. He will choose good friends, and will communicate well with his family, superiors and associates. He is likely to have a high position, and at some time work for the government. He will attain his aims and purposes.

Least auspicious: He will be communicative and cooperative, but sometimes with the wrong people, which will injure his chances for achievement and success. However, he will have no great hardships.

In yearly hexagram:

Officer or official	He will be at the head of his organization or unit.
Business and professional	He will be a leader in national or world affairs. Gains are predicted.
Ordinary people	He will have the cooperation of others, and will be successful. The least auspicious may experience failures.

Line 3 Carriage and spoked wheel part. Husband's and wife's eyes glare.

These individuals are the type who readily say, 'Why isn't it done this way?' or 'Do it that way,' etc., without reference to the realities and the facts of the situation, and believing their opposition to be slight. In general, they will be mistaken in their evaluations, and, as often happens in a marital situation, annoying arguments will occur, with each person trying to blame the other. Little hope is offered to such persons, as it is their innate judgment which is deficient. It would be best for them not to try to rise high in status or position. By remaining at a low level, they will be able to find reasonable contentment.

Auspiciousness: Not auspicious for anyone. A few may establish some merit. All will tend to be stubborn and greedy, and quarrelsome with their wives, families and others. They will readily blame others for their own faults and deficiencies.

In yearly hexagram:

For everyone	A troublesome year, with illnesses, partings, separation from family or friends, as well as difficulties professionally.

Line 4   Sincerity and confidence cause bloodshed to be averted. Apprehensions give way. No error.

Persons acting with sincerity and confidence induce trust in others, and consequently apprehensions disappear. These persons should be upright and reliable, and their leadership will generate emulation by others, and no errors will be made. Those who are both intelligent and wise will exercise great influence. Those who are immodest and stupid are likely to cause bloodshed.

Most auspicious: He will be open-minded, modest, sincere, and confident, following the right paths. He will be a noble person with no great sorrows or hardships. He will be helped by his seniors, and will have a good family life.

Least auspicious: He is likely to be jealous and suspicious, with no firm goals, ideas or opinions. He may be ill frequently and subject to many hardships and sorrows, with few or no friends.

In yearly hexagram:

Officer or official	He will be transferred, or promoted to a better position, on the recommendation of his colleagues.
Business and professional	His life will be enhanced and advanced by his peers and associates, and by his seniors.

Ordinary people	His desires will mostly be accomplished, with modest success. The least auspicious may receive a serious injury.

Line 5 Trustworthiness binds like a cord. Enrichment between neighbors.

These persons are strong in virtue, even more so than those described by line 4, and are leaders primarily by example. Trustworthiness and sincerity induce confidence in others, both at higher and lower levels. Their inner strength is so great that it will automatically influence the hearts of others in beneficial ways. This will be true whether their work is at a purely local level, or in a business or governmental enterprise, but especially true in matters where protection against adverse or evil influences is involved.

Most auspicious: He will be rich, and will share his opulence with others. He will be noble in mind and character, and humble in dealings with others. He will be admired and respected by many people.

Least auspicious: Though not able to be independent, he will receive help from persons possessing both material and mental riches, and will thus be able to enjoy a good life, even though his achievements will be indifferent.

In yearly hexagram:

Officer or official	He will receive trust from his seniors and respect from his juniors, and he will be promoted.
Business and professional	He will be respected by the public, and will find that others share his views. He may attain fame.
Ordinary people	He will receive outside help, and will thus attain his aims.

Line 6 The rains come. It is now the time for rest. Persistence brings troubles to the woman. The moon is nearly full. If the superior man ventures further, calamity is probable.

The gathering of the clouds mentioned at the beginning of the hexagram has now produced rain. The enterprise has been consummated as a result of the extensive application of small power. To try to proceed further, before the time is ripe, either with the persistence of a woman or with the strength of a superior man, would be wrong, and would produce calamity since the moon is nearly full, signifying that negative influences are close to their maximum. It is these negative influences which govern here. Persons born under this line are advised that the energetic development of a positive force is the only way to counter and overcome the negative. They must work on their inner selves so that the positive force can later be manifested externally. Any major external activity at first could result in calamity.

Most auspicious: He will be rich and powerful enough to be of benefit to others, and will enjoy a life free from great losses or serious troubles.

Least auspicious: He will have many ups and downs. After acquiring profits he will lose them quickly. Women will tend to be cruel and shrewish, and will probably have a short, unhappy life.

In yearly hexagram:

Officer or official	One following an evil path will be dismissed. Lesser offences will be reprimanded.
Business and professional	Improper practices will result in litigation, and loss of reputation and profits.
Ordinary people	Upright and calm persons may have a fair year by virtue of their good character. Others, if not deceitful or crafty themselves, may be besieged by such persons, with bad results.

KEYNOTES

1. Returning to the right path cannot be wrong.
2. Cooperating with others is beneficial.
3. Heedless actions will result in disaster.
4. Use sincerity and confidence at all times.
5. Trustworthy leadership brings success.
6. Convert negativity to something positive whenever possible.

CONDENSATIONS FOR DAILY CYCLES

1. If you have overstepped your bounds, return to what is right.

This will lead to good fortune.

2. Instead of forging ahead independently, good results can be obtained by going back and cooperating with others.

3. The opposition seems slight. Beware of over-confidence. It is possible that you may have misjudged the situation.

4. Be sincere and confident, with flexibility; then no errors will occur.

5. You are equal to whatever task is at hand. Your mental attitude and resources will win the support and cooperation of others.

6. Results have been achieved. Now is the time to relax and curtail further activity. Beware of negative influences.

Hexagram 10   Lü ☰ *Treading (Conduct)*

SIMPLE TRANSLATION OF TEXT
Treading on the tail of the tiger. It does not bite him. Progress and success. Heaven above, lake below. The superior man consults the high and the low and fortifies the people's thinking.

COMMENTARY
This hexagram basically relates to the development and use of correct conduct at all times and in all circumstances, resulting in progress and success along one's chosen path. The words 'treading on the tail of the tiger' are an ancient Chinese way of signifying hazardous conditions. The reason why the tiger does not bite the man comes from the lower trigram, Tui (joy, lake), being below and reflecting the upper trigram Ch'ien (heaven). How could there be a mirroring of heaven and joy if one were in the fangs of a tiger? The persons depicted here are, however, faced with many hazardous conditions. Fortunately, they have the innate capacity to discriminate between good and bad, right and wrong, using elements of both the high and the low as the foundation for their decisions. Persons born under this hexagram can be found in any walk of life where analytical activity is involved and discriminatory powers are a necessary attribute.

Those born in the third month will be more auspicious.

CONTROLLING LINES (FROM BOTTOM TO TOP)
Line 1   Simple conduct. Going forward produces no errors.

At the beginning, i.e., the bottom line of any hexagram, a man has, unless otherwise stated, an obligation to take the initial steps by himself and of his own free will. At this point he is not yet bound by contracts. By conducting his life simply, this man will be able to make progress without blame or error. He will do this on his own, without the assistance of others. He will have much activity in his life, and will act with firmness and correctness. Hence he will be following the right paths, and will benefit both himself and others.
Most auspicious: He will be vigorous and courageous, but somewhat conservative, simple in desires and without external show. His leadership will be strong and dignified, and his influence will extend to many persons, both nationally and internationally. Least auspicious: He will attend to improving his own conduct and virtue in privacy; he may even become a recluse or a monk. His development will be continual, and his life modestly good.
In yearly hexagram:

Officer or official	He will foster and encourage right methods and the progress of other people. Promotion is likely.
Business and professional	A year of hard work, using known methods. He will increase his reputation and profits.
Ordinary people	Hard workers will make gains. For the least auspicious: a member of the family may die.

Line 2   The solitary man treads his path peacefully. He brings good fortune to himself.

The path trodden here is higher and more noble than that trodden in line 1. This man is more introspective, desirous of accomplishing major goals, and inclined to keep his deepest thoughts to himself. He will know the golden mean, and for the most part will follow it. His goals are firm, and he will not let himself become confused. These persons are somewhat unusual in that they are quite self-sufficient, men of peace doing whatever is set before them, for the benefit of others.

Most auspicious: He will be deeply interested in mental and spiritual matters, and will follow the way of Tao, i.e. action through inaction. He will only be ambitious to a limited degree, but persistent in completing whatever he begins. He will not seek unattainable fame or honors, and will find much happiness in contemplating, and being surrounded by nature. He will achieve peace of mind.

Least auspicious: Principally, he will be a man of leisure, following the right paths. He will make no demands on others, and will not seek fame or fortune, nor will he be defamed. He will have a reasonably good life.

In yearly hexagram:

Officer or official	He may be assigned to an easy position, or retire with honor.
Business and professional	Destiny will seemingly be inactive.
Ordinary people	He will be content, and will enjoy peace and harmony. Communicating and cooperating with the right people may bring him gains. The least auspicious may die.

Line 3 The one-eyed man (thinks he) can see. The lame man (thinks he) can walk. He treads on the tail of the tiger and is bitten. Disaster. The warrior (thinks he) battles on behalf of his lord.

Here is a weak person using strength beyond his capacity, with dangerous results. A one-eyed man can see, but his perceptions are imperfect. A lame man can walk, but not fast enough to make progress with others. This line is in a position of strength, so bravado and brashness are implied. When meeting hazardous conditions, one does not overcome them properly through such behavior, and disaster results. One should act in such a manner only when fighting for one's lord. Persons born under this line are likely to have little knowledge or experience, but use great strength and drive. By the exercise of caution, and through self-development, they may be able to overcome their weaknesses.

Most auspicious: He will pride himself on being out of the ordinary, but without justification. He will despise and look down on other people. His plans are unlikely to be achieved, and his hard, tough attitude will result in continual troubles.

Least auspicious: He will be a person of low station in life, possibly even crippled or deformed. He is likely to be a stupid person, and will probably have a short life.

In yearly hexagram:

Officer or official	Demotion in rank, position or salary is likely.
Business and professional	He may suffer loss of reputation, accompanied by a decrease in profit.
Ordinary people	There will be disputes and lawsuits. He may be incarcerated, ruin his family, or die.

Line 4 He treads on the tail of the tiger. Prudence is required. Good fortune in the end.

Self-reliance, self-confidence and good judgment are indicated here. These are founded on knowledge, common sense and experience. This man will know where he is going, and is sure in himself that he will get there. With this controlling line, in this position, he should not forge ahead rashly or act impetuously, but rather proceed steadily and with caution. He will meet many difficult situations which he will overcome, and in the end he will have good fortune.

Most auspicious: He will serve his family, his work and his nation with diligence, respect and care. He will be able to overcome dangerous situations through calm speech and a gentle attitude, and will convert likely disasters into good fortune.

Least auspicious: He will experience many hardships early in life, but will have a fairly good, routine life later.

In yearly hexagram:

Officer or official	He will probably be assigned to the charge of an important activity.
Business and professional	He will achieve new recognition and increased profits.
Ordinary people	Difficult situations are probable. Advance with caution.

Line 5 Resolute advancement. Despite firmness and correctness, peril.

This man is constantly striving to improve his conduct through resolute advancement, in consonance with the meaning of the hexagram, and this would normally have good portents. In keeping with the law of physics which states that to every action there is an equal and opposite reaction, resolute advancement, despite firmness and correctness, will meet with opposition and perils. Primarily, this is the result of his striving too hard for rapid advancement. He should be aware that the higher he rises, the greater may be his fall.

Most auspicious: He will be courageous in cultivating his virtue. He will strive to follow the right way at all times, and will drive out evil whenever and wherever possible. He will encourage and promote good, and will carry out his purposes regardless of the consequences. His life will be beneficial to others. Least auspicious: He will face many hardships, have few friends, and will possibly encounter a major disaster. He will tend to be a wanderer, seeking to find himself.

In yearly hexagram:

Officer or official	He will have great achievements, without any reward.
Business and professional	He will be honest and virtuous, without gaining any fame or profit.
Ordinary people	If he is honest and upright, he will have good results. The least auspicious may be reckless, easily provoked, and cause trouble, or may even die.

Line 6 Analyze your conduct. Note the omens. If all is complete and favorable, supreme good fortune.

This line is at the top of the cycle of Conduct, and the advice is virtually self-explanatory. If progress has been favorable, favorable results can be expected. If not, changes have to be made. The persons represented here will be analytical, and, since they already have made considerable progress, will be individuals with above average capabilities. How they use their attributes, and how well they heed the results of their analyses, will determine the nature and effectiveness of their lives.

Most auspicious: He will be a man of wisdom and virtue, rich, fortunate and famous, and he will be of great benefit to others.

Least auspicious: He will use his analytical and other abilities for evil purposes. He may make gains, but however hard he tries to hold on to them, his efforts will be in vain.

In yearly hexagram:

Officer or official	Those in high positions will retreat, and withdraw to a peaceful life.
Business and professional	He will gain in reputation, position, and profits.
Ordinary people	He will increase his possessions. The least auspicious may die.

KEYNOTES

1. Simple conduct is without criticism.
2. There is no blame in treading paths peacefully.
3. The lowly should not try to be greater than they are.
4. Exercise prudence when danger is imminent.
5. When the time is ripe, advance resolutely.
6. Through analyses, you can learn what results you may expect.

CONDENSATIONS FOR DAILY CYCLES

1. If one acts in accordance with accepted rules of conduct, at the beginning, no mistakes will be made.
2. Conduct yourself as does a hermit, i.e. be quiet and unassuming, and make no demands. By so doing, you will achieve results and not become confused.
3. If one acts heedlessly with respect to superiors, adversity is sure to be forthcoming. The exercising of a strong will here can be dangerous.
4. Provided caution and tact are exercised, one can deal successfully with dangerous situations and people.
5. Be gentle in conduct and show humility, otherwise you will stumble.
6. Review your situation. If the steps taken so far have been favorable, good fortune can be anticipated. This is the only way you can know what to expect in the future.

Hexagram 11   T'ai ☰☷ *Peace*

SIMPLE TRANSLATION OF TEXT
Peace. The small is gone. The great approaches. Progress. Success. Good fortune.

COMMENTARY
The communion of the Creative and the Receptive, in a state of balance, brings peace. Ch'ien, heaven, is below and moving upward into K'un, earth, above and moving downward. They are blending equally in perfect harmony and complementing each other. Working together in this manner brings peace. Hence, this man should make progress in life, which will bring success and good fortune. The high will help the low and the low cooperate with the high. It is a time of service and benefit, bringing blessings to all. Wise, magnanimous, and productive leadership is depicted here. These persons are peacemakers, bringers of prosperity, and successful innovators. Generally speaking, they are superior persons who will set an example worthy of emulation by others.
   Those born in the first month will be more auspicious.

CONTROLLING LINES (FROM BOTTOM TO TOP)
Line 1 When grass is pulled up, sod and roots come too. It is auspicious to advance now as planned.

Progressive leadership is indicated, whereby the leader draws others, well grounded and of like mind, along with him in public matters. Such persons will all have the instinct to advance, and will find themselves naturally drawn to the leader. This co-operative effort of minds and bodies is bound to be productive, and, since the time is right, the results will be successful. The leaders are very capable, but they must recognize that they shoulder grave responsibilities which cannot be shed.
Most auspicious: He will be intelligent, lofty of purpose, upright, and pure in mind. He will associate and be intimate with superior men, and will not become involved with evil-minded persons. He will be just and impartial to all. He will attain honors, have worthwhile achievements, and may even become famous and rich.
Least auspicious: He will be a leader on a small scale or in a

local way. He will communicate well with his family, friends and associates, and will have a good life.

In yearly hexagram:

Officer or official	He will be helped and respected by associates and peers. He can expect promotion and other gains.
Business and professional	He will be honored, and will advance mentally and materially.
Ordinary people	Planning and cooperating with friends and associates will result in gains.

Line 2 Bearing with the uncultured. Fording the stream. Aware of what is distant. Remembering his associates left behind. He follows the golden mean.

Men of great ability, using their potential effectively, are depicted here. They recognize that no person or material is useless in the hands of the Creator, and they adhere to this principle in their lives. Fording the stream means engaging in enterprises. This such men will do independently. They are true leaders, pioneers in government, business and industry, and the many arts and sciences. Their greatness is further illustrated by their possessing the common sense to know what lies ahead of them and being able, therefore, to act correctly at all times. In addition, they will always remember their friends and associates from the past, never discarding them as is done by so many who rise to high position.

Most auspicious: He will be wise and broad-minded, sensible, upright, impartial and just. He will possess the ability to help bring peace to the world, and will enjoy a long, rich, noble and rewarding life.

Least auspicious: He also will possess noble traits, but he will use them only at a local level. He may become rich, and his life will be good.

In yearly hexagram:

Officer or official	He will be assigned to an important and influential position, and will be successful.
Business and professional	He will have advancements, gains and fame.

| Ordinary people | He will meet, and make, influential friends, and will have material gains. A good year. |

Line 3 Every plain is followed by a slope; every going by a return. Consistency and persistence amid danger. No error. Knowing this, he maintains faith and joy.

Here the law of change is exemplified, namely, that all things and all situations are subject to inevitable rise and fall, coming and going, growth and decay, etc., with the passage of time. Even the states of peace depicted in this hexagram are not left undisturbed. This man recognizes the law of the universe for what it is, maintains his goals, and acts with consistency and persistence, while being flexible with regard to changing conditions. He will certainly have faith in the world, and will experience much joy. Negotiators and arbiters are depicted here. Their principal mission will be to restore peace under hard and trying conditions.

Most auspicious: He will be steadfast in purpose, and will maintain his uprightness even in difficult situations and circumstances. He will do his utmost to carry out divine will. He will enjoy the fruits of his labors, and will have an easy and restful later life.

Least auspicious: He will have some successes and some failures, and his good fortune will be self-made. He will also render beneficial service to others.

In yearly hexagram:

Officer or official	His job will be difficult. He should beware of deceitful and dishonest persons, and of jealousies.
Business and professional	He should hold on to what he has, and should not take chances but seek only attainable goals.
Ordinary people	By restricting himself to his own household and immediate affairs, he will have a good year. The least auspicious may be cheated by deceitful or dishonest persons.

Line 4 Vacillations and fluctuations. Supported by the wealth of neighbors. Trusting and sincere.

Many situations are fraught with difficulties. In keeping with the symbolism, here, of the lines for man, i.e. the third and fourth lines, line 4 is a Yin line leading a Yang, and in addition line 4 has two more Yang lines behind it, pushing upward. This makes the situation difficult, and the Yin, being weak, makes for vacillation here in goals, intentions and actions. These will be aimed in the right direction, but are unlikely to produce great consistent successes. The wealth which comes from neighbors is given by the three Yang lines, the neighbors of the Yin line 4, tending to rise and come to the support of those having difficulties. The persons depicted here are ever sincere, and will never lose their trust and faith in people, especially their close friends. This reflects the inner sentiments of all concerned. These persons will not, however, be as wise as they ought to be for the work that they seek to accomplish, or the positions they wish to fill. Their vacillation will come mainly from a lack of knowledge and confidence.

Most auspicious: He will face many hazardous conditions in life. He will have many doubts and will be unable to keep his mind concentrated on his goals and aims, lacking singleness of purpose. He will make some gains and some losses, and his life will not be easy.

Least auspicious: Basically, he will not have a strong character, and he will have to depend on friends and relations for support. He will not be qualified to act independently.

In yearly hexagram:

Officer or official	He should hold fast or perhaps even retreat. Extreme caution must be exercised to avoid serious trouble.
Business and professional	As above.
Ordinary people	Stick to tried and proven methods to avoid difficulties.

Line 5 The emperor gives his daughter in marriage. Felicity and good fortune.

A fundamental message of *I Ching* is expressed here, namely, that to rule truly is to serve. (This is also shown in Hexagram 42, I, Increase.) The emperor referred to is Ti Yi, the last emperor of the Yin dynasty, who decreed that daughters of the emperor, after marriage, should take precedence only as befitted the wife of their espoused. This avoided many difficulties and embarrassing situations, and resulted in understandings and good relations which were a blessing to the realm. Those born under this line will likewise fare well and be a blessing to others, if they subordinate some of their abilities, and delegate their authority and responsibilities.

Most auspicious: He will be a great and good leader and find it easy to obtain honors, riches and fame, if he desires them. He will always remain humble, and will be reverential in nature. He (or she) will have a good wife (husband) and a noble heir. He rules primarily through the proper choice of subordinates to whom he delegates appropriate authority and responsibility.

Least auspicious: He also will be of benefit to others, and prosperous. He will enjoy a good life, and will be honored and respected.

In yearly hexagram:

Officer or official	He will either be promoted or have occasion for much joy.
Business and professional	He will make progress and gains.
Ordinary people	He will be respected by others, and will have much good fortune. He may get married or increase the size of his family.

Line 6 The wall falls into the moat. Refrain from fighting. Maintain order in your city. Even with correctness and firmness, some blame cannot be avoided.

Disuse results in disintegration. This is a universal truth. Once the decay has set in it is difficult to maintain order and discipline. Even efforts at firmness and correctness prove somewhat ineffective, since they were not instituted in time. The persons depicted here have gained some knowledge and experience, but have failed to use these further. They have not remained flexible, nor have they kept up to date so that their abilities would continue to be of use. Everyone knows that if you do not practise a foreign language you lose your ability to use it, no matter how well you once knew it. So it is with other matters. Heed this warning.

Most auspicious: If humble, modest and mentally active, he may be able to establish some gains and benefits. He will have a life full of hazards and difficulties.

Least auspicious: He will be conceited and boastful, impudent, intimidating, and perhaps sometimes violent. He will make difficulties for others, and perhaps even ruin his own family.

In yearly hexagram:

Officer or official	Degradation is indicated.
Business and professional	He will experience shame and defamation.
Ordinary people	Enterprises will collapse, and he will have illnesses and other troubles. By remaining modest and humble, some of the difficulties can be averted.

KEYNOTES

1. Cooperation brings progress.
2. If you have talents, use them.
3. The law of change is never inactive.
4. Vacillation and fluctuating get one nowhere.
5. To rule is to serve.
6. Unintelligent neglect brings about disintegration.

CONDENSATIONS FOR DAILY CYCLES

1. You will associate with persons of like mind, who also desire progress and are willing to participate actively. Going forward will result in good fortune.
2. A man of clarity and vision is in control, who sees everything clearly and in its proper perspective. Follow the golden mean in all thoughts and actions.
3. Even in peaceful situations the law of change is operative, and your situation will become adverse unless new elements are injected to replace the old.
4. You are anxious to achieve results, and run to and fro in your thoughts and efforts. Your peers are in accord with you, and are willing to help. Make use of them.
5. Be impartial in your leadership. By carrying out what is right, in a humble manner, you will achieve good fortune.
6. Neglecting to keep up to date, being inflexible, and not mending your deficiencies in a timely manner, can result in troubles and losses.

Hexagram 12   **P'i** ☰☷ *Standstill (Stagnation)*

SIMPLE TRANSLATION OF TEXT
Standstill. Lack of understanding between the high and the low.
The great departs. The small approaches.

COMMENTARY
Heaven and earth are not in communion, hence stagnation and
standstill. Ch'ien, heaven, is above and moving upward. K'un,
earth, is below and moving downward. When heaven and earth
do not cooperate and work together, nothing productive is
accomplished. This is where the symbolism of the high and the
low not being in accord comes from. Weakness is within and
strength without, e.g. weakness at the seat of a government,
with strength in its armies throughout the country. In a man, it
is weakness of intellect, purpose, and mental activity, while
being externally and physically strong. Mistrust prevails in the
government, and gainful activity is not possible in private life.
The superior man does not allow himself to be tempted by
honors and fame, and withdraws from public life. Others are
advised to study and prepare themselves within for subsequent
activity. Those born under this hexagram would do well to keep
themselves up to date.
   Those born in the seventh month will be more auspicious.

CONTROLLING LINES (FROM BOTTOM TO TOP)
Line 1   When grass is pulled up, sod and roots come too.
Righteous persistence brings good fortune and success.

At the onset of evil, removing oneself from it through active
persistence in righteous courses leads to good fortune and success.
This man is a leader who draws others along with him into
seclusion. He will possess common sense, intelligence and good
judgment. He will know when and how to act correctly, and
will follow such courses as will be good for him and others.
Most auspicious: He will be a man born to a family of honor and
fame. He will further his lineage and cultural heritage in a
proper and beneficial manner. He will engage in enterprises

designed to help protect the nation and those who render service to the people. His life will be a blessing to others.

Least auspicious: He will know when to advance and when to retreat. He will meet with hardships occasionally throughout his life, and will have difficulty in following the right path. He will not be ruined, and will be able to maintain himself and his family.

In yearly hexagram:

Officer or official	Beware of injury and misrepresentations.
Business and professional	It will be hard to find good opportunities for successful activity.
Ordinary people	A routine year, but be on the lookout for trouble from mean people.

Line 2 Authorities favor the obsequious now. This means good fortune for the inferior. The superior man adjusts himself to the standstill and has success.

The inferior are very weak, but the superior man remains steadfast. Even though the weak are favored they are so weak that they cannot accomplish their purposes. The strong follow the right path, regardless of external circumstances and conditions. Since *I Ching* is designed for the superior man it is right to assume that a person with this controlling line will have superior qualities. He will be a leader, and will see through the motives and actions of others, avoiding any association with their meanness. He will take actions accordingly, bearing in mind the serving of others.

Most auspicious: He will be noble, broad-minded and intelligent, following the golden mean and right paths. He will quietly await the right moments for action, and then strike effectively. He will have the potential to turn deviations into righteousness, to break down obstructions in the way of peace, and to turn misfortune into good fortune. He will not be disturbed or destroyed by the difficulties he meets along the way.

Least auspicious: He will be an ordinary person, with some good and some bad. He should be cautious throughout his life to avert injury and disaster.

In yearly hexagram:

Officer or official	He should be conservative, and retreat if necessary until the right time for action.
Business and professional	As above.
Ordinary people	He should be tolerant, cautious, and well-intentioned, otherwise he will be involved in troubles.

Line 3   He endures his shame.

Mean people would like to harm the good, but are held back. Line 3 is at the top of the trigram K'un, and therefore indicates meanness, but the trigram Ch'ien is immediately above, so these people are restrained from taking the actions they would like to take. Persons having this controlling line will be more unfortunate than most, to a greater or lesser degree. Their destiny is such that they cannot do much more than make a living. They have several important lessons they must learn in this life, in order to overcome and rise above fate.

Most auspicious: He will meet a noble or superior man who will trust him and help him mentally and materially, and may also help him more than once to obtain professional employment. His best course, however, would be to become a monk, a priest or a recluse.

Least auspicious: He will be unable to follow the right paths. Furthermore, he will be so poor in mental and material wealth that he is likely to pursue evil paths.

In yearly hexagram:

Officer or official	He will retire, or be demoted in salary or position.
Business and professional	Defamations and insults are likely and will possibly be damaging.
Ordinary people	Disputes and lawsuits are likely.

Line 4   Whoever follows the will and ordinations of heaven will remain free from censure. Associates of like mind share in his blessings.

A strong and wise leader is depicted here. How many people can discern the will and ordinations of heaven? Such a person has found the true *tao* (or 'way'). His inner strength is such that he will automatically draw others to him. They will think and act in accord with him, and will therefore be blessed too.

Most auspicious: He will be a noble man of many achievements, from which he will derive fame and good fortune. His life will be one of service to others, and it will be long, satisfying, and filled with many friendships.

Least auspicious: He also will have a long life of beneficial service from which he will attain good fortune. He will acquire appreciable property and wealth, and will be constantly active until his death.

In yearly hexagram:

Officer or official	He will receive help from colleagues, and will also be promoted.
Business and professional	He will be recommended by authorities, and will probably achieve fame.
Ordinary people	He will have an increase in property and money, and several minor good fortunes.

Line 5 The standstill is coming to an end. Fortune favors the superior man to restore conditions. Dangers still prevail. He strengthens himself like a bound cluster of mulberry trees.

A leader capable of restoring peaceful conditions is now at hand. Time has nearly fulfilled itself in the cycle of stagnation and standstill. However, some dangers are still present, and therefore, in order to be certain of overcoming them, the superior man holds himself together, as one might bind together a number of mulberry trees for added strength. This means that such a leader should marshal all his abilities for the greatest possible strength in order to overcome the dangers and restore conditions of peace. Another point of view is that such a person instructs and unites others, so likewise obtaining added strength for overcoming whatever difficulties they mutually face, as well as providing a method for maintaining the new conditions. This person will be a wise, knowledgeable, experienced and fearless leader.

Most auspicious: He will be a wise and virtuous man, impartial and cautious, knowing how to restore order and how to avoid troubles in advance. He will be able to withstand mental, physical or spiritual stagnation, and will enjoy long friendships, riches and honors.

Least auspicious: He will be a virtuous man of modest talents, who cannot achieve all he would like to accomplish. He will have an easy life with adequate wealth and possessions, but no fame.

In yearly hexagram:

Officer or official	He will be assigned to a high and influential position.
Business and professional	Old troubles depart. New fortune is on its way, with gains and profits.
Ordinary people	Sorrows will turn to joy. Losses will be recovered. There will be new gains as well.

Line 6 The standstill has been overcome. First there was standstill; now great joy.

The cycle of stagnation and obstruction has run its course and is now over. The topmost line is a Yang, signifying a strong leader who works in keeping with the law of change, and helps bring about an end to adverse conditions. This leadership will be founded on deep and intimate knowledge of ancient wisdom and lore. This person will work with the will of heaven, and will be the focal point for bringing about peaceful conditions, either consciously or unconsciously. These persons will usually be found in key positions in their chosen field.

Most auspicious: He will be a man of great ambitions, and clever enough to carry them out successfully. He will have some hardships early in life, with all matters smoothing out later, to make life very enjoyable in his senior years. He will be noble in character, and a blessing to all his associates.

Least auspicious: He will find it difficult to attain a favorable reputation and make profits. He may be subjected to serious injury. Becoming a monk or a recluse would make for a simpler life.

In yearly hexagram:

Officer or official	If unemployed at present, he will obtain a good position.
Business and professional	Things are slowly picking up, with the prospect of advancements.

Ordinary people The situation is improving, and those who have troubles with drawnout lawsuits will soon have them settled in their favor.

KEYNOTES
1. When retreat is inevitable, withdraw cooperatively.
2. Take independent action when this is deemed necessary.
3. Being expansive without proper qualifications is wrong.
4. Always try to act in accordance with the will of heaven.
5. When matters are discordant, unite the divergent elements.
6. Strong leadership is required to bring any stagnation to an end.

CONDENSATIONS FOR DAILY CYCLES
1. Like attracts like. Quietly proceed, with firmness and righteousness. The results should be good.
2. Today you must work alone. Take superior actions, and restore peace.
3. If one attempts to achieve something beyond one's authority and ability, one must bear the shame which will ensue.
4. Whoever acts in accordance with the will of heaven will commit no errors. Be correct and obedient with respect to authority.
5. Bring stagnation or standstill to an end by uniting the divergent elements.
6. The law of change is active. Take firm steps to inject new life into the situation.

Hexagram 13 *T'ung Jên* ☰ *Fellowship, Brotherhood*

SIMPLE TRANSLATION OF TEXT
Fellowship in the open. Success. It is advantageous to cross the great stream. The superior man benefits from maintaining firm correctness.

COMMENTARY
Unions between men are based on having a common goal, coupled with clarity and strength within the individuals. This

hexagram fulfills these requirements by having clarity within, i.e. the lower trigram, Li, and strength without, trigram, Ch'ien. When the goals are such that they can be known and agreed on by everyone, meetings can be held in the open. This augurs success. Enterprises can be begun. Regrettably, in any union there is a danger of selfish or separatist attitudes creeping in. Therefore the superior man benefits by maintaining firm correctness. A systematic arrangement, with everything having its proper place, is presaged. Persons who are destined to be leaders in uniting people are depicted here. How well they fare in accomplishing their aims is determined by their controlling line.

Those born in the first month will be more auspicious.

CONTROLLING LINES (FROM BOTTOM TO TOP)
Line 1 Union at the gate. No blame.

Organizers forming unions 'at the gate,' i.e. in the open for everyone to see, will engender no blame. The true leaders among these persons will fully investigate matters before engaging in any enterprise. They will separate and arrange elements in their appropriate order, and will cope capably with divergent views. They will have the inherent qualities to be able to accomplish their purposes.
Most auspicious: He will be highly respected, broad-minded and impartial, and will have a natural attraction, drawing many persons to him. He may be appointed to an important post, such as a cabinet position, the president of a college, the head of a religious or fraternal organization, or something similar.
Least auspicious: He will be an itinerant organizer with no firm roots. He will probably leave his family circle and associate mainly with his wife's family. He will travel extensively in his profession. He may become a priest or a monk.
In yearly hexagram:

Officer or official	Will be transferred to an inner circle position, and/or promoted.
Business and professional	He will receive recommendation for a position of leadership.
Ordinary people	Through united effort and co-operation with others he will have

gains and profit. He may take a
long journey, or buy or build a
house.

Line 2 Intimate relationship with members of the clan.
Humiliation.

The persons depicted here are much sought after, but they are
weak in character. This is the single Yin line in the hexagram,
with which the five Yang lines all seek to unite. The second line
is a position of leadership in a hexagram. So these persons will
tend to be leaders, but having weak natures they will be adversely
affected by all the attention they receive. Many may be inclined
to use their natural ability for selfish purposes or in factions. Low
motives will naturally lead to humiliation. Furthermore, one
should always beware of the danger of being too intimate with
members of one's own clan. The tendency here to be too intimate
is a sign of weakness. Remember that members of the clan are
often more difficult to deal with than strangers. With care, the
possibility of humiliations can be avoided.

Most auspicious: He will be talented and will have wide
knowledge, but he will also have a tendency to be mean and
prejudicial. He may have a high and influential position in an
organization of limited scope.

Least auspicious: He will be influential to a minor degree, with a
life full of worry and sorrows. He may have an intimate association with someone of his own ancestry. Later he may retire
to a secluded life.

In yearly hexagram:

Officer or official	His influence will be circum-scribed.
Business and professional	Small gains are conceivable, but not likely.
Ordinary people	Much suspicion and discord, and an unstable year, are indicated.

Line 3 He conceals his weapons in the thicket. He mounts a
high hill. For three years matters are adverse.

These persons are seeking unity without sincerity. They have only
hidden their weapons, and will retrieve them when they want to.
They climb a hill to look around for the most likely group to join.

The truly superior man does not seek others, rather he waits and lets others seek him. Therefore, those depicted here are likely to be inferior, with perhaps a trace of cowardice and instability. Also, mistrust may have replaced true fellowship. 'Three years' relates to a cycle of events. These persons must endure and progress through this cycle, learning to develop superior qualities. Most auspicious: He will be a lover of eminence, no matter how great or how small. He will mistrust others, which in turn will cause them to mistrust him. He will vacillate in his goals, and will be an inveterate worrier. He will not rise to a high position, and his most likely employment will be in work of a hard nature. Least auspicious: He will seek fellowship for the wrong reasons, and will be an evil doer. He will not obey the law, but he will run into disaster and be punished.

In yearly hexagram:

Officer or official	He is likely to make big mistakes, and demotion is probable.
Business and professional	He will seek or obtain wrong contracts or associations.
Ordinary people	A difficult year. He may face law-suits, and one of his parents may die.

Line 4 He climbs up on his protective wall. He cannot attack. Good fortune.

Courage, common sense and strength are the dominant characteristics here. The superior man reviews his situation and examines himself to see if he has the adequate qualities for establishing fellowship, and whether he should advance, or wait before launching his plans. This man will have an intuitive sense of what is right, and will maintain his goals and intentions even under difficult situations. He will continue to develop himself inwardly, so that his innate strength acts like a magnet and draws the fellowship to him which he desires. This will result in benefits and good fortune.

Most auspicious: He will know when to advance, when to wait, and when to retreat. He will know what is right and the best courses to pursue to attain his aims, and he will be satisfied with what is attainable and not be greedy. He will be noble and may become rich. He is likely at some time to be assigned to a high position away from the seat of his career.

Least auspicious: He will be able to advance, but will find it difficult. He will be trusted and respected by his juniors and seniors alike, but he will have much to learn. He will have a generally good life.

In yearly hexagram:

Officer or official	He will receive promotion, or be awarded a title for merit.
Business and professional	A stable year, but with little chance of any major gains.
Ordinary people	With care and caution, this year could be auspicious. Some suspicions and disputes are likely.

Line 5   Men destined for fellowship first weep and cry; afterwards they laugh. After great struggles they join together.

The key to establishing fellowship is depicted here. It is beautifully expressed thus by Confucius. *

> Life leads the thoughtful man on a path of many windings.
> Now the course is checked, now it runs straight again.
> Here winged thoughts may pour freely forth in words,
> There the heavy burden of knowledge must be shut away in
> silence.
> But when two people are at one in their inmost hearts,
> They shatter even the strength of iron or of bronze.
> And when two people understand each other in their inmost
> hearts,
> Their words are sweet and strong, like the fragrance of
> orchids.

These persons will be strong, purposeful, idealistic, persistent, intelligent, knowledgeable, warm-hearted, considerate, and willing to render service and nourishment to others.

Most auspicious: He will be a true gentleman and leader, following the right way, talented, full of virtue and honor. He will experience hardships at first, then later attain his goals, for which he will achieve fame and profit. He will attain a high position, and will execute his office successfully, as he will all his enterprises.

* Richard Wilhelm/Cary F. Baynes (trans), *The I Ching, or Book of Changes,* Routledge & Kegan Paul, 1968, p. 59.

Least auspicious: He will have hardships and sorrows which he should eventually largely overcome, although he may be plagued with troubles all his life. At some point he will be honored in his profession, and thereafter will amass modest wealth.

In yearly hexagram:

Officer or official	Demotion in rank or salary is probable, with an attractive increase later.
Business and professional	There will be some initial barriers to his enterprises, but these will be broken through later by the actions of leaders or authorities.
Ordinary people	A generally better than average year, with some early hardship easing off later. He can expect some sorrows and some joys.

Line 6 Fellowship in the countryside. No error or regret.

Fellowship in the country is not as wide as that in towns. This indicates that the time for the greatest fellowship is past, but that efforts towards fellowship, by those possessing qualities for organization and leadership, should continue. The results will be limited but the effort will be worth while, engendering no error or regrets. These persons will have above average leadership abilities, capable of persisting towards a desirable goal, and will be able to act independently. They will be ambitious but not with a compelling ambition, and will be content with whatever gains they manage to make.

Most auspicious: He will be an intelligent, broad-minded leader or organizer, of a noble and rich nature.

Least auspicious: He will become a monk, or person of similar activity in which fellowship is circumscribed.

In yearly hexagram:

Officer or official	He will be assigned to a position away from the executive seat.
Business and professional	His clientele will be smaller, with a consequent limitation of achievements.
Ordinary people	A generally dull year, without much fellowship.

147

KEYNOTES
1. Be devoid of secret designs.
2. Keep all relations on a moral basis.
3. When there is mistrust, reclarify your aims.
4. If you are not amid fellowship, pause and reassess your situation.
5. Persevere in successful courses.
6. Always work towards universal fellowship.

CONDENSATIONS FOR DAILY CYCLES
1. This is the beginning of a fellowship. Meet openly. Be sure that the seeds are the ones you would like to see mature.
2. Relations not in keeping with accepted mores will lead to trouble. Keep all relations on an ethical and moral basis.
3. Mistrust has entered. Reclarify your goals and purposes, and persevere in what is good.
4. Review the situation. Reassess your abilities. Determine whether you are ready to exercise the leadership requirements facing you.
5. The zenith of fellowship has been achieved through overcoming many difficulties and handicaps. The attainment is blissful and gratifying. Continue on your successful course.
6. Join and work with some group having a universal goal, no matter how large or small, or establish one for yourself.

Hexagram 14   Ta Yu ☲☰ *Great Possessing (Amassing)*

SIMPLE TRANSLATION OF TEXT
Great Possessing. Supreme success.

COMMENTARY
These auspicious persons are endowed with great perspicacity. Light and clarity are above, with creative strength below. While the previous hexagram represented fellowship and brotherhood on earth, those born under this hexagram, through proper development, can achieve much fellowship in spiritual matters. Thus the creative power within these individuals expresses itself in a graceful and cultured way. Possessing and amassing naturally

follow the acquisition of great inner spiritual power. The degree will vary, depending on the degree of spiritual development. The path is not smooth or easy, and some set-backs may occur. In general, those with this hexagram as their base will be blessed and will have a better than average life. This will come from being in accord with heaven, and gladly carrying out divine will, which is affirmed by love and goodness, and by the curbing of evil.

Those born in the first month will be more auspicious.

CONTROLLING LINES (FROM BOTTOM TO TOP)
Line 1 No contact with evil. No blame. Realization of difficulties ahead. He remains without fault.

The tyro is beginning to make progress. He is a man of culture, learning now to seek a greater understanding of life, and the universe. He has resolved not to associate with evil, which is commendable, but he is only just beginning, and he will have to face and overcome many practical difficulties. If he has a true realization of the difficulties, he can remain without fault. Being a tyro, his successes and failures will be determined by the firmness of his resolve. He should recognize that in metaphysics there is action and reaction, just as in physics.
Most auspicious: He will be a man of virtue, and very talented. He should keep his spiritual strivings in the background, and help others by generating profits which he then puts to altruistic use. It is best for him not to seek fame.
Least auspicious: He may strive too high too soon and face difficulties. He is likely to receive serious slanders. If conservative and cautious, he can avoid troubles, or cope with them successfully even in times of hardship.
In yearly hexagram:

Officer or official	He should wait or retreat until the right moment for action.
Business and professional	He should not do anything out of the ordinary this year.
Ordinary people	Care and caution can avert difficulties, otherwise trouble and worries are likely.

Line 2 Large supply wagons. Set forth on a goal. No error.

A favorable time and favored persons are indicated. Spiritual wealth is available in great quantities. Persons knowing how to draw on it can set forth on any enterprise in any direction and be confident of success. It is most propitious if the goals chosen are universal in nature, no matter how humble. While the spiritual wealth is available it must be used as a blessing, and the more it is used the less chance there is of error. Individuals with this hexagram as their base will be found in various walks of life and at many levels, but all will have the common purpose of striving for good and for the improvement of the world.

Most auspicious: He will have great virtue and be very talented, and he will establish great merit. He will be able to calm anarchy and quell disorders, and he will have a good and beneficial life.

Least auspicious: He also will have a long life and great good fortune, with no major worries or troubles. He may attain wealth.

In yearly hexagram:

Officer or official	He will gain promotion or a new position. If in a position of leadership, he will win a victory (not necessarily in war).
Business and professional	He can expect advancement in the size of his organization, or in status and reputation.
Ordinary people	He will also gain in status and possessions.

Line 3 The prince presents his offering to the emperor. An ordinary man cannot do this.

'The Prince' symbolizes a man of superior talents, experience and ability. Furthermore, this person is presented as being in the right position to render service to his lord. An ordinary man is insufficiently qualified to do this. These individuals will fare best when their service includes service to mankind in addition to the personal fealty depicted. Any attempts at taking over leadership could be disastrous.

Most auspicious: He will act impartially, and he will be virtuous and talented, possessing wide experience. He will not be egotistic. This person's advice will be sought and followed, even in matters affecting the nation.

Least auspicious: He may falter, and begin to work with selfish motives. This could be disastrous. He will find it hard to establish anything of lasting benefit.

In yearly hexagram:

Officer or official	He will have important duties, perhaps of national scope.
Business and professional	He will make gains and win distinction.
Ordinary people	He will have a dull year, with possibly some trouble.

Line 4 Very discriminating. No error.

This person has an intuitive insight into nearly every situation. The fourth line is the topmost position for man; here it is strong, the lowest line of the trigram Li, clarity, and next to the ruler of the hexagram, line 5. Lines 4 and 5 are of such a nature that they work together favorably, hence this person knows his work well, yet is cautious and guards against mistakes. Such a person can, and should be, in a position of leadership, both in spiritual and material matters. Regrettably, as a strong line is in a weak place, these persons will have a tendency towards ideal solutions which are not always practical in this material world, or a tendency to use their unusual capabilities for selfish purposes.

Most auspicious: He should be exceedingly careful at the beginning of any enterprise to be sure that the seeds are rightly sown and properly nurtured. He will exercise capable supervision, so that the results are always propitious.

Least auspicious: He may be greedy regarding small things, expressing some jealousy, and thereby cause trouble. He will have difficulty in achieving his goals and in managing his household successfully.

In yearly hexagram:

Officer or official	A stable year, with troubles gradually eliminated.
Business and professional	A year of waiting and making preparations for advancement.
Ordinary people	A routine year. He may contract an eye disease.

Line 5 Exemplification of clarity and truth. Good fortune.

Leaders and rulers possessing sincerity, clarity and truth, who rule majestically and set a good example to others, will experience good fortune. These persons have found the right way, or *tao*, in both the spiritual and material realms. They will be cultured, well-mannered, intelligent, wise and discerning rulers, whom others respect and try to emulate. This will result in much good for all. Since this is a weak line in a strong position, not all these persons will be successful, even though they will attempt to do that which is right.

Most auspicious: He will be kind, magnanimous and just in leadership, rewarding others graciously and freely. He will lead with dignity and virtue, and will attain fame. He will be respected and honored, and will communicate well with others.

Least auspicious: He will be disastrously unsuccessful, owing to his inner self being inadequately developed, and not as clear as it ought to be. He will reward graciously, but will be defamed and insulted in return. He will do good for others, but will receive complaints in return.

In yearly hexagram:

Officer or official	He should lead in a dignified manner but be ready to retreat if necessary.
Business and professional	He will take steps towards progress, and make timely advances.
Ordinary people	He should act at the right moments. If he is flippant, proud or insincere, troubles will occur.

Line 6   Blessed and protected by heaven. Advantages and good fortune.

The height of clarity, supported by heaven, is depicted here. These persons will have the same fine attributes as those described by line 5, but they will be even more highly favored, supported and blessed by heaven. These persons will sincerely walk in truth, and will be the devoted stewards of both material and spiritual possessions; they will be a blessing to others.

Most auspicious: He will be valiant, devoted, reliable and modest. His virtue and talents will be in accordance with the will of heaven, which he will intuitively carry out throughout a long, beneficial and rewarding life.

Least auspicious: He also will be a man of virtue, and blessed, but not to such a high degree as the most auspicious.

In yearly hexagram:

Officer or official	Promotion and fame can be expected.
Business and professional	He will have advancement and gains.
Ordinary people	A good year. He will receive help from leaders and authorities. If a farmer, he will make good profits.

KEYNOTES

1. The diligent tyro progresses satisfactorily.
2. When spiritual wealth is available, use it.
3. Superior persons know intuitively how to be successful.
4. Analyze and discriminate constantly.
5. Kingly leadership is productive.
6. Great clarity is blessed by heaven.

CONDENSATIONS FOR DAILY CYCLES

1. In any amassing, be wary of dangers creeping in.
2. It is a propitious time for acting on those goals which are universal.
3. Do not indulge in pretence or in airs. Superior persons may proceed, if they are careful.
4. Great discriminative powers are evident. Use them realistically.
5. You are highly trusted and respected. Continue this quality of leadership.
6. You are blessed by heaven. Be a worthy steward of matters put in your care.

Hexagram 15 Ch'ien ☶☷ *Modesty*

SIMPLE TRANSLATION OF TEXT
Modesty brings success. The superior man successfully carries matters through to completion.

COMMENTARY
Humility, modesty, and impartial justice are the dominant

characteristics of individuals born under this hexagram. The hexagram is made up of the youngest son, Kên, mountain, the representative of heaven on earth, under (within) K'un, the receptive, earth. The wealth of the mountain is hidden, yet it is there to be taken and used at the right time. Also, soil from the mountain is used to fill up the low places on the earth. Persons with these qualities are found in all walks of life. They not only strive to reduce fullness and to develop the modest, but they carry out the will of heaven, which likewise favors modesty. That is why the Chinese regard this characteristic so highly. It is also why people everywhere love the modest, hating pride and boastfulness. With modesty as a handle, a man can face any difficulty with confidence.

Those born in the ninth month will be more auspicious.

CONTROLLING LINES (FROM BOTTOM TO TOP)
Line 1   Adding humility to modesty. One may cross the great stream. Good fortune.

Self-disciplined persons readily exemplify modesty as a dominant characteristic. Line 1 represents the beginnings of modesty. Therefore, these persons would do well to add humility to modesty in their early progress. If they do so, they will be able to commence any enterprise, no matter how dangerous, and be certain of good fortune. They should remember, however, that good fortune frequently comes in a manner which at first seems strange. Regrettably, line 1 is a weak line in a strong place. This indicates that not all will be successful in the matter of appropriate self-discipline.

Most auspicious: He will be modest and moral in behaviour. He will be gentle in relations with others, and reverent to the divine will. He will be trusted by his juniors and seniors alike. He is able to change dangerous situations into safe circumstances, and is likely to be in government or another high position of authority. Least auspicious: He could be lazy. If so, his attempts to advance will end in retreat. He may also be dull and stupid, and content to remain in a low position.

In yearly hexagram:

Officer or official   He will be in a position to lead and
                             guide many people.

Business and professional	He should be honest and reliable, following right courses and awaiting an opportunity for expansion.
Ordinary people	A routine year. It will be auspicious for making a long journey.

Line 2 Expressed modesty is recognized. Righteous persistence brings good fortune.

Modesty is such an innate part of these individuals that others readily perceive it. This then is their inner influence, the strength of which is such that lasting benefits will be derived therefrom. Those born with this controlling line may be found in nearly any walk of life. It is more than likely that they will engage in a full or part-time activity of service to others.
Most auspicious: He will win fame and honors through his talents, virtue, and his unselfish and honest thoughts and efforts. He is likely to be in a position where the guidance of others is involved.
Least auspicious: He will also be recognized for his ability, and will give assistance to others. He will have a good life.
In yearly hexagram:

Officer or official	Promotion in position and/or salary is possible.
Business and professional	He will make advancements, and will be honored.
Ordinary people	He should hold back this year, and not try to push forward.

Line 3 The superior man, by his merit, carries everything through to conclusion. Good fortune.

These persons will be superior, full of virtue, and richly endowed with noble traits. They will make good leaders, excellent examples for others to follow, and will carry matters through to conclusion. This will be easy for them since their character is of a high and noble order, as well as being of a nature which automatically attracts others, and is reflected in all that they do. They will never begin anything they do not intend to finish, and they will finish everything they begin. They will be intuitive and beneficial leaders of others, and will be sought after by many.
Most auspicious: He will be able to assume great responsibility

and able to establish or control a successful organization. He will have a deep sense of honor and justice, which he will exemplify at all times. He may be very good at writing, especially in dealing with worthy subjects in article or book form.

Least auspicious: He will also be a noble person, but only known and respected locally. He will be of help to others, without seeking anything in return.

In yearly hexagram:

For everyone   A very favorable year.

Line 4 Advantageous to cultivate and express modesty.

Modesty, like everything else, should be cultivated and expressed in accordance with the golden mean, i.e. nothing should be done to excess. This implies a strong nature, and one who knows both what is right and the right time to act. These persons will have the patience to wait, and the strength to retreat if necessary, to act without impulsiveness, and to bring matters to the fore, often in the face of possible adverse opinions or reactions. These persons will be wise, practical, full of common sense, confident and courageous.

Most auspicious: He will have great talent and virtue, and will be respected by the high and the low alike. He will be honest and sincere, and will promote matters of benefit to the community. He may become highly respected and rich.

Least auspicious: He will be an upright person, and will associate with, and be close to, good, intelligent and capable people. He will exert considerable influence in his circle.

In yearly hexagram:

For everyone   A good year, passing smoothly, if one remembers to be modest and yielding; otherwise there may be some trouble.

Line 5 Modest dealings with neighbors. Everything contributes to success, even attacking with force (if necessary).

Noble, kingly rulers and leaders are symbolized. These persons are wise and intelligent, and have great understanding of the psychology of human nature. They respect their neighbors and treat them as equals. They use modesty as their tool, rather than rules, regulations and precepts, which control through punishment and fear. They are strong, and know when to use their strength advantageously for the assertion and (re)establishment of justice, with the use of force only when necessary.

Most auspicious: He will be a leader who naturally attracts other leaders and men of quality and ability. He will automatically move people favorably, and his wishes will be carried out readily. He will be a man of virtue and nobility, achieving much honor and merit.

Least auspicious: He also will establish fame as a pioneer, perhaps in a military career or in the field of literature. He will help to overcome evil wherever he is, in many ways.

In yearly hexagram:

Officer or official	He will hold, or be assigned to, an influential position.
Business and professional	He will make gains in status, reputation, and material possessions.
Ordinary people	He will succeed with the help of some noble person, and will gain considerable profit. If he falters in virtue he may have disputes.

Line 6 Modesty disseminated. It is propitious to send one's army forth to subdue one's own country and cities.

As in hexagram 15, where universal brotherhood has not yet been attained by line 6, here universal modesty has not yet been attained. The injunction given is to begin with oneself, and discipline every part of one's inner being, in order to establish modesty as a virtue of one's wholeness. When this has been achieved, it will be reflected externally and will be emulated by others, and be a blessing to all who one comes in contact with. These persons will have much modesty innately, but will need to be diligent and cautious in their careers, to be sure that quality is improved and quantity is used judiciously.

Most auspicious: He will be courageous and will carry out *tao* (divine will). He will be ever diligent to improve his modesty, and will express it in his leadership. He may have a career in the Corps diplomatique, the military, or some peace-keeping agency.

Least auspicious: He will be able to maintain his household in good order and condition on a modest scale, and at the same time exercise modest influence.

In yearly hexagram:

Officer or official	He will be in a position of command, and able to subdue enemies and competition.
Business and professional	He will make minor advancements honorably.
Ordinary people	Disputes will resolve themselves. He will avoid or avert losses.

KEYNOTES

1. Self-discipline is always necessary.
2. Exercise righteous persistence in whatever you do.
3. Modesty must be carried through to the end.
4. The cultivation of modesty is endless.
5. Kingly modesty attracts.
6. Complete your self-development.

CONDENSATIONS FOR DAILY CYCLES

1. Greater modesty can be achieved through self-discipline. If this is done, one can commence any enterprise or journey.
2. Great responsibilities can be laid on those who are modest and humble. Carry matters through correctly, and good fortune will ensue.
3. Carry everything you begin through to completion. You will be honored and respected.
4. You will be supported by your leader in your activities, and you will be successful.
5. Remain quiet, or take such actions as may be appropriate, but make clear decisions with the right motives.
6. You must exercise self-discipline for the fulfilment of the modesty required today.

Hexagram 16   Yü ☷ *Broadcasting**

SIMPLE TRANSLATION OF TEXT

Broadcasting. The people are set in motion advantageously.

* This hexagram is the opposite of hexagram 15, which was translated as 'Modesty.' Hexagram 15 shows the proper characteristics to display from an earthly point of view. Here in hexagram 16 we are dealing more with the

COMMENTARY

This hexagram principally represents thunder over the earth, and movement over people. Thunder emanates from heaven and is heard on earth. Chên, movement, the upper trigram, and symbolic of heaven's actions, is above K'un, earth, representing the people. The ancient kings used this situation to develop special music to express reverence for the will and blessings of heaven, and also to stir up and generate feeling in the people, thereby controlling them either for peaceful or for warlike purposes. The single Yang line, the ruler of the hexagram, is a strong leader to whom the others are devoted. This produces enthusiasm, tranquillity and repose. The upper trigram, Thunder, sugge ts making sounds known to others. Hence individuals with this hexagram as their base will make themselves known to others, in varying ways according to their specific controlling lines. These individuals will be found in nearly every walk of life, with many being successful through understanding and use of the principles of this hexagram, while others will be failures through personal neglect.

Those born in the fifth month will be more auspicious.

CONTROLLING LINES (FROM BOTTOM TO TOP)
Line 1   Boastfulness brings misfortune.

The modern expression for the kind of person depicted here is 'name dropper.' These persons brag about whom they know, and use the knowledge and the fame of others egotistically, as if it were their own. There is a definite lack of personal will power for self-development and self-improvement. These people would like to progress by riding on the coat-tails of others.
Most auspicious: He will receive some strength and help from people in a higher position than himself, and will make some gains. He can only make very small gains on his own.
Least auspicious: He will be very narrow-minded, a braggadocio,

spiritual realm, signified by heaven's creation and the manifestation of thunder. This hexagram is the foundation for the use of music and words to influence others. To us today, broadcasting most aptly describes the influencing of others on a large scale through words and music. In other translations, Legge did not assign a descriptive name to this hexagram. Wilhelm called it 'Enthusiasm,' and Blofeld called it 'Repose.' It is, in fact, a combination of both.

with self-destructive tendencies reflected in all his thoughts and actions. He will have a poor family life.

In yearly hexagram:

Officer or official	He will presume on being the favorite of the leader or ruler.
Business and professional	He will make some astonishing temporary gains.
Ordinary people	He will have much worry and some unpleasant surprises. Not a very good year.

Line 2 Stable as a rock; not for a whole day. Righteous perseverence brings good fortune.

Persons with this controlling line are wise and discriminating, following the golden mean, stable and steadfast in their goals and purposes. These persons will express their nobility through lasting creativity, by writing influential books or music, painting memorable works of art, creating poetry, etc. The words 'not for a whole day' are symbolic of these persons never reaching the end of their capacity. Their working in this manner for the right reasons will result in good fortune.

Most auspicious: He will be active, quickwitted and communicative. He will be diligent in all matters, especially in pursuit of virtue, and will live by the golden mean. He will have a stable character and disposition, unmoved by riches or poverty or temptations. He will become noble, and will achieve fame.

Least auspicious: He will also be a person of good character, and attain good fortune through modest accomplishments.

In yearly hexagram:

Officer or official	Remain steadfast. Wait for the right time. If action is propitiously taken he will gain fame.
Business and professional	An increase in profits can be expected.
Ordinary people	There will be gains in family, status and possessions.

Line 3 To gaze enviously brings regret. Delayed action brings remorse.

Line 3, a weak line in the wrong place, looks to its strong

neighbor, line 4, for care and support. He is weak and envious, and would like to be provided for as if he were still a child. These characteristics are predominant in persons having this controlling line. They like possessions, status and respect, but are unwilling to exert the necessary energy to attain them. They would like to have these things presented to them. Additionally, they make efforts to avoid responsibility while seeking love, pity and care from others. They do not understand the principle that to give is to receive. Procrastination and failure to take action in a timely manner brings remorse. Fortunately, many of these persons recognize these traits in themselves, and consequently repent and reform, thereby overcoming their deficiencies.

Most auspicious: He will be faced with many obstacles as a result of his own attitude and can accomplish but little. If he reforms himself he will achieve a reasonably satisfactory life in his later years.

Least auspicious: He will vacillate continually in his ambitions and work habits. He will have no worthy achievements, but many worries and troubles.

In yearly hexagram:

For everyone   On the whole, plans will fail. There will be many fluctuations. It is best not to try and advance, but hold as firm and as stable as possible.

Line 4   From the fountain great results accumulate. Be confident. Friends readily gather round.

The advice, guidance, example, and control of a true, dynamic and communicative leader are a fountain from which great results can be achieved and blessings derived. Every age in history develops such persons when they are needed. It should be remembered here that *I Ching* is designed for superior persons as a guide to self-development. It can, however, reflect and symbolize others who are not striving for the good of humanity. Among those are leaders who are egotistical, factional and selfish. These are equally discernible. All leaders have difficulties at one time or another, and conditions are never smooth for a great leader. In fact, it is the manner in which they overcome impediments that makes for their greatness. Every leader probably wavers on occasion, when difficulties are truly immense. But by being confident he is able to carry out his will, and gather others spontaneously to him. Everybody likes a winner, and those depicted here are winners.

Most auspicious: He will be in a powerful and influential position, and will exercise his responsibilities judiciously and dynamically. He will carry out great enterprises, and will establish virtue and achieve merit. He will have great good fortune.

Least auspicious: He will also be a reputable man, of virtue and good fortune. He will be respected and sought after, both personally and professionally. He will have an exceptionally harmonious domestic life.

In yearly hexagram:

Officer or official	He will advance to fame, and will be recommended for a higher position.
Business and professional	He will establish a favorable reputation, and become a leader in his field.
Ordinary people	He will make substantial profits.

Line 5 Chronic illness. No death.

Line 4 is so strong that in its efforts to advance it puts much pressure on the weak line above it. This incessant pressure is like an illness. There is no let-up, so that these persons have little time for anything other than work and solving problems. Since the position of the line is central there is a possibility of some successes. There will be many periods of fluctuation, but never complete failure or disaster. Chronic illness also suggests a lack of adequate preparations. These persons will be involved in much hustle and bustle, with much talk and many attempts to exert influence on others. They will have few firm and lasting accomplishments.

Most auspicious: He will be pressured by himself and others, and will be involved in much activity. Many times he will find his efforts hampered and delayed for no apparent reason. If truly auspicious, he may become known through the support and efforts of others. He may have a long life, but will probably be ill much of the time.

Least auspicious: He will be too weak and too timid to be independent, and will be plagued by illnesses or injuries.

In yearly hexagram:

Officer or official	He will presume himself to be a favorite of the upper classes and act accordingly.
Business and professional	He will be hampered in efforts at advancement.
Ordinary people	He will not be able to accomplish his goals. He may have a serious illness.

Line 6   Confused. Wasted efforts. Change can take place. No blame.

Line 6 is the height of the thunder in the heavens, and consequently striving upward produces no effect on earth. Efforts in this direction are confused and wasted. If the thunder finds some way to change its direction, such as being reflected by a sound barrier, it still can be heard on earth. This symbolizes persons who strive too high without the proper background, who are not clear in their goals or are too idealistic in trying to influence others. They cannot achieve sound results. If they become aware of their deficiencies they can reform, with an expectancy of greater subsequent effectiveness. Such a sober awakening frees them from blame.

Most auspicious: He will make mistakes, but will listen to sound advice and reform without bearing grudges. If the new courses are continued for long enough he will make some gains and profits. Least auspicious: He will have no lasting achievements. Even if he gains prosperity by a lucky chance, he will probably lose it later, and end his life in sorrow.

In yearly hexagram:

Officer or official	He will be blamed for decay or corruption, and is likely to be demoted.
Business and professional	He will suffer defamations and insults.
Ordinary people	He may suffer from disputes and lawsuits, but if he reforms and follows a virtuous path, mistakes can be avoided.

KEYNOTES
1. Avoid boastfulness.
2. Be dependable and firm.
3. Wishful thinking alone is harmful.
4. Be a source from which others can draw.
5. Beware of incessant pressures.
6. Overcome emptiness.

CONDENSATIONS FOR DAILY CYCLES
1. Be taciturn. Bragging about your preparations demonstrates a lack of will power.
2. Be stable, firm and consistent and others will place confidence in you.
3. Looking for help and wanting things to be done by others when you should be taking action yourself can lead to regrets.
4. Be full of confidence and optimism, and friends will automatically gather around.
5. If one gives way to lust and pleasure instead of remaining firm in one's duty, the result may be an illness.
6. The preparations are of the wrong kind. Re-evaluate, reform and begin again.

Hexagram 17   Sui ☰☱ *Following*

SIMPLE TRANSLATION OF TEXT
Following. Supreme success. Persistence in the correct and the firm. No error.

COMMENTARY
In this hexagram we have Chên, movement, led by Tui, joy, a condition which automatically produces a following. Chên is the beginning of spring, so it is a time of joyous progress. In addition, this hexagram shows the completion of a cycle, in that Chên, thunder (as well as movement), is below Tui, lake. The fall is therefore indicated by the thunder returning within the earth. Consequently, we have a cycle of service beginning with a joyous movement and ending with a time of rest. If one

considers this hexagram as symbolic of the course of a day, then the superior man is active during the hours of light and at nightfall rests and recuperates. These persons will primarily have daytime careers wherein they render service to others. The more service they render, the greater will be their following. Persistence in being firm and correct in their actions will produce supreme success without error. The keynote here is rendering service.

Those born in the seventh month will be more auspicious.

CONTROLLING LINES (FROM BOTTOM TO TOP)
Line 1 Authorities subject to change. Persistence in right ways. Go out in public and mingle freely. Substantial results.

Flexibility, persistence in virtue, open-mindedness, a rising above selfish motives, and an absence of preconceived opinions are the dominant characteristics of these persons. Such individuals keep abreast of the changing times and are eclectic in their studies and ideas. They know that merely having knowledge is not sufficient in itself. Others must be nourished as well as additional personal illumination being sought. Hence, these persons go out among the public in their careers of service. As a result of their joyous and energetic actions they naturally acquire a following. Knowledge and service makes for influence and power.

Most auspicious: He will be a noble person of great virtue, wisdom, energy and talent. He will be able to lead, and to quell even major calamities in his nation. He will be highly respected.
Least auspicious: He will be a similar person to the most auspicious, but to a lesser degree. He will establish some merit and achievements, but may need the support of powerful and influential persons to attain his aims.
In yearly hexagram:

Officer or official	A change to a more influential position is indicated.
Business and professional	There will be many good opportunities for mental and material gains.
Ordinary people	He will gain considerable profit.

Line 2 He who follows a boy loses a superior man.

Individuals who have inferior goals and put forth only minimal effort will never become superior. Such persons have a tendency to be lazy, and to procrastinate, and accomplish only that which is forced upon them. Such persons might go to college or a technical school, and, after leaving, never again pick up a text containing new material relating to their field. They will come in contact with virtue and ambition, but will not possess the courage to pursue these qualities very far on their own. They will, on the whole, be followers all their lives.

Most auspicious: He will be a man of little talent, prone to vacillation. He may be close to persons following the primrose path. Least auspicious: He will be a laborer or servant. Women may become concubines.

In yearly hexagram:

Officer or official	He should hold firm or retreat.
Business and professional	He should analyze his own actions carefully, and know when to advance and when to retreat.
Ordinary people	Not a peaceful year. There will be many troubles, and he may even face being jailed.

Line 3   He who follows the superior man loses the boy. He gains what he desires through following firm and correct courses and goals.

In general, the conditions and situation are the opposite of those set forth in line 2. Those depicted here are constantly seeking new knowledge and new ways to be of service to others. Their degree of success is largely determined by the intelligence with which they are endowed. They will be independent persons to whom additional duties and responsibilities can be assigned, with reliance on their appropriate fulfilment.

Most auspicious: He will complete everything he begins, with some degree of success in all matters. He will be assisted by those of higher status or position, but will receive negligible help from subordinates. He should beware of impatience, be cautious and thorough, and avoid mean people.

Least auspicious: He will achieve some substantial results, from which local fame and profit may arise. His children, regrettably, will not be dependable.

In yearly hexagram:

Officer or official	He will be recommended for a better position, and possibly promoted.
Business and professional	He will be assisted by seniors in a generally favorable year. He may attain some fame.
Ordinary people	If he follows the right path his wishes and desires will materialize. He should be cautious, and firm in what is right.

Line 4 A following develops. Continuation brings misfortune. Sincere in his loyalty. What harm can develop?

The strong and natural leader acquires a following, and many adherents. The fourth line is the position of the minister or second in command. To generate and develop a following for its own sake, or for ulterior motives, would be a grievous mistake. If such persons recognize what is taking place they can, primarily through their sincerity, convert their personal following into a loyal following for their leader, ruler or cause. Acting in this manner is a true rendering of service both to his leader, whom he thus serves correctly, and to the subordinates, since then everything is in proper order. What error or harm can develop if such a course is followed? The greater the wisdom and the greater the loyalty of the minister, the greater the overall success.

Most auspicious: He is sincere, upright and virtuous, following the true *tao*. His seniors and juniors alike repose confidence and trust in him. He will be kind, considerate and non-dictatorial. He will be highly successful in all that he undertakes.

Least auspicious: He will do well as long as he remains impersonal. Personal involvement, and the seeking of gain for selfish reasons can lead to serious trouble. He may be reprimanded frequently by his seniors, and his juniors may become suspicious of him. He is likely to be an inveterate wanderer in his field of work.

In yearly hexagram:

Officer or official	He will be in a prominent position, exercising much power.

Business and professional   He will gain in status and reputation.

Ordinary people   A very good year. He will be supported by an influential person.

Line 5 Sincere towards universal good. Good fortune.

Genuine, unaffected sincerity should be exercised in the rendering of service to others, by fostering and promoting matters for universal good. These persons exemplify the meaning of the hexagram as a whole. To fulfil this they must be dedicated to the service of mankind, in keeping with divine will. They will be wise, intuitive, judicious, communicative and intelligent, blessed with common sense, practicality and inexhaustible energy. They will be men of vision.

Most auspicious: He will be a wise person of great virtue, who likes to communicate and associate with superior men. He will know inwardly that he has a great mission to accomplish, and will persistently and consistently strive to achieve it. He may earn a large salary and be in a high position.

Least auspicious: He will also be a good man, but to a lesser degree. The golden mean will be the rule in his life.

In yearly hexagram:

Officer or official   He will enjoy promotion.

Business and professional   He will receive accolades and make gains.

Ordinary people   A year free from major troubles with everything going nearly as wished.

Line 6 Firm allegiance. Adherents cling to him. He accompanies the king in sacrifice on the Western Mountain.

Symbolized in this line are leaders, teachers and sages, who desire to withdraw from worldly affairs. They are good people who have achieved much in life, and their followers wish to remain with them. The king's sacrifice at the Western Mountain was a ceremony in which the king worshipped God, and paid reverence to his ancestors in the highest degree. It was the highest form of worship of the ancient kings. To be invited to participate was an honor symbolizing the granting of equal status to the individual concerned. These persons will be innately noble and good, but will not have a strong desire to participate in the affairs of the world. Their natural inclination is more towards spiritual matters, and they devote a great portion of their time to developing and improving themselves inwardly. Status, position and wealth mean very little to such persons. Most auspicious: He will be honest, sincere, gentle, merciful, following righteous ways. His personality will automatically move people. His aims can be attained, but, in general, these are simple and non-demanding. In his cultivation he can communicate with heaven, and invite good fortune. Least auspicious: If he lives in seclusion, in the mountains or in the forest, he will have a good and auspicious life. If he tries to enter worldly affairs he will encounter difficulties.

In yearly hexagram:

Officer or official	Hold back, and hold firm. Beware of misrepresentations.
Business and professional	As above. He may also face insulting conditions.
Ordinary people	Exercise care that no losses occur.

KEYNOTES (render service)
1. Always maintain flexibility.
2. Low goals and purposes are destructive.
3. High goals and purposes are constructive.
4. Work for universal, unselfish purposes.
5. Sincerity is productive.
6. Seek spiritual wisdom.

CONDENSATIONS FOR DAILY CYCLES
1. A change is taking place. Keep flexible and strong. Mix freely with others, giving and gaining opinions.
2. No man can serve two masters. He who follows someone weak will lose the beneficence of a strong leader.
3. Use caution and discrimination. Turn away from the weak to follow the strong, and you will find what you seek.
4. One is not yet in a true, ruling position and able to act independently.
5. He who leads with sincerity, confidence, and trust in his subordinates, is certain to accomplish great deeds. Good fortune.
6. Cultivate yourself inwardly and seek greater spiritual wisdom.

Hexagram 18 Ku ☶ *Decay (Correcting)*

SIMPLE TRANSLATION OF TEXT

Correcting decay augurs sublime success. Advantageous to cross the great stream. Three days before beginning. Three days after beginning.

COMMENTARY

This hexagram has the trigram Sun, wind, at the foot of Kên, the mountain. The foot of the mountain is where things collect and stagnate. Therefore this hexagram is symbolic of stirring up decay and making corrections. Since *I Ching* is a guide for individual development, the statements in the controlling lines relating to correction of the mistakes of the father and mother have reference partly to the characteristics inherited from one's ancestors. This is representative of but another step in man's never-ending growth. The symbolism applies to other situations, such as family life, government and business, and wherever the old must be cast out before the new can enter. It is advantageous to set forth and work on such matters, but important steps should not be taken lightly nor hastily. 'Three days before beginning' and 'Three days after beginning' enjoin this man to thoroughly study changes in advance and to follow through after their initiation with proper care and nourishment, so that the changes develop in a propitious manner and the seeds sprout into productive growth. Individuals with this hexagram as their base will be constantly involved in matters of correction, both great and small, i.e. in the household, in the community, in business, in states and in nations. For many this will include spiritual as well as material matters.

Most of those born under this hexagram will build their life out of meager or hard beginnings. Some may inherit a household, but they will find it difficult to maintain. Many will not get on with their parents. Those born in the last two months of the year will be less auspicious, while those born in the first month will be more auspicious.

CONTROLLING LINES (FROM BOTTOM TO TOP)

Line 1 Children correct the mistakes of the father. If done ably there is no residue of blame on the father. Perilous conditions end in good fortune.

Great corrections are not required here, so even though they may be considered perilous they can be readily accomplished, and result in good fortune. No one and nothing is perfect here on earth. There are always possibilities for improvement, even when the conditions are good, when corruption exists. Persons with this controlling line will gravitate to positions requiring their special qualities and talent to bring about reforms in a propitious manner.

Most auspicious: He will cultivate virtue and know how to rectify mistakes. He will have the courage to advance with deliberate and determined action. He will be loyal to his parents and country. He is able to work through danger, and his character and conduct will be a model for future generations.

Least auspicious: He will be independent of his family and relations. He will fight through hardships, for accomplishment rather than for glory or personal gain, and he will be modestly successful.

In yearly hexagram:

Officer or official	He will be assigned to a position by the government or other authority to make good bad conditions.
Business and professional	He will make gains, which will include recognition for written efforts.
Ordinary people	A modest year for most. Older persons may die.

Line 2 Making corrections for the mistakes of the mother. One should not go to extremes.

Persons in such positions as vice-president, special assistants, head of departments, etc., are symbolized here. They will render full support to their superior, or organization, through diligence, talent, loyalty and obedience. They are well-qualified persons, who merit the positions they occupy. They are endowed with sound judgment and common sense, and they act wisely, avoiding extremes.

Most auspicious: He is greatly talented, and exemplifies the golden mean, with sincerity. He employs correct measures, well thought out in advance. He will improve his home situation, his enterprises, and his country. Opulence is not predicted but he may become moderately wealthy.

Least auspicious: He will also be a good man working hard for the improvement of his household, his undertakings, and his country. He will attain modest results.

In yearly hexagram:

Officer or official	His position will be stable. He will clear away old business and useless matters.
Business and professional	He will render loyal support, as well as instituting modest changes and corrections.
Ordinary people	He will do something special for his parents. He may correct himself, or start something new.

Line 3 Handling mistakes of the father. There may be some regret. No great blame.

Whenever one tries to make corrections too hastily and with too much intensity, unfavorable reactions set in; but some corrections need to be made quickly and acting in such a manner is not subject to great blame. Persons acting thus will tend to be impatient, and intolerant towards those who act in ignorance or from stupidity, and especially with those who make errors when they should know better. These persons are clever enough to see what needs to be done, and courageous enough to carry it out, even when occasionally there is opposition, or when it involves stepping on the toes of others. When they act for themselves they believe that being right is sufficient in itself.

Most auspicious: He is courageous and determined to do what he knows should be done, with a disregard for consequences, either for himself or for others involved along the way. He readily rectifies his own mistakes, and those of others. He will have strong friends and strong enemies, and will have a good and auspicious life, without losses.

Least auspicious: He will also be courageous and effective, but will face many hardships early in life. Conditions will improve slowly later.

In yearly hexagram:

Officer or official	Beware of rash actions which could cause regret later.
Business and professional	Study and caution are presaged.
Ordinary people	Keep clear of evil thoughts and deeds, and the year will be satisfactory.

Line 4 Tolerating troubles caused by the father. Weakness in going forward. Humiliation.

The controlling line here is a weak line in a weak position, indicating that these persons have neither the strength nor the ability to correct the decay and corruption they see. Such persons are wise enough to discern difficulties and errors, and may bring them to the attention of others. They will talk about them freely, but cannot shoulder their own responsibility in connection with them. They are mentally, morally, and physically weak and lazy. They let things run their own course if others do not take action.

Most auspicious: Although talented, he is easily dispirited and lacking in fortitude. He will not have any major achievements.

Least auspicious: He is lackadaisical, jealous and suspicious, with many vacillations and worries. He may be successful in small matters, but cannot handle big enterprises.

In yearly hexagram:

Officer or official	He will be blamed for inactivity.
Business and professional	It would be a mistake not to keep up to date.
Ordinary people	He will be lackadaisical and indulge in pleasure, with later regrets. He may become seriously ill.

Line 5 Correcting and restoring conditions which are inherited wins praise.

Wise, energetic, courageous, patriotic and loyal persons who carry out the will of their leader, and who govern enterprises, government agencies, or political parties, judiciously and effectively, are depicted here. To such persons the successful accomplishment of their mission, especially in those matters which benefit a great number of people, is far more important than any gain or personal reward that might be attainable. They are truly altruistic and unselfish.

Most auspicious: He will be far superior to the average person, possessing great virtue, talent and personality. He will establish great merit in the world, and have a beneficial and richly rewarding life.

Least auspicious: He will be a superior man, and effective, but only in a local way.

In yearly hexagram:

Officer or official	He will gain promotion to an honorable position, and will attain some fame.
Business and professional	He will achieve success in his ventures, and a favorable reputation.
Ordinary people	He will start a new enterprise or business. He will experience many joys, including an increase in the size of his family.

Line 6 He does not serve kings and nobles. He serves loftier purposes.

Self-correction and self-improvement at the highest levels are indicated. The results are not used selfishly, nor in public affairs, but rather for universal matters and goals. Such persons have progressed beyond participation in the mundane, and will live in relative seclusion while working for the benefit of mankind.

Most auspicious: Although he is noble, talented and dynamic, with great virtue, he will live and work creatively in seclusion, rather than engage in public affairs. His efforts will benefit mankind as a whole.

Least auspicious: He is also a man of high virtue and noble character who prefers to follow his own way, apart from the customs and practices of ordinary life. He will derive much satisfaction from his work.

In yearly hexagram:

Officer or official	He will probably retire, or withdraw almost entirely from public activity.

| Business and professional | He will improve himself while waiting for new opportunities for service. |
| Ordinary people | The auspicious will receive help from their superiors. Others will experience nothing new |

KEYNOTES
1. Correct the mistakes inherited from the father.
2. Correct the mistakes inherited from the mother.
3. Analyze and correct one's own mistakes.
4. Weakness in correcting mistakes is disastrous.
5. Restoring decayed conditions is beneficial.
6. Work for universal goals.

CONDENSATIONS FOR DAILY CYCLES
1. Correct the traits inherited from the father. Even though this may be perilous the results will be good.
2. Exercise strict observance of what is correct and proper. Eliminate weaknesses inherited from the mother.
3. Do not correct mistakes too hastily nor with too much intensity, or an unfavorable reaction will set in.
4. Being lackadaisical and weak about the making of corrections will lead to difficulties. Study matters thoroughly.
5. Taking the initiative to bring about reforms, including organizing the help of others for this purpose, wins praise.
6. Develop and improve yourself spiritually, and take actions for the benefit of mankind.

Hexagram 19   Lin ☷☱ *Approach*

SIMPLE TRANSLATION OF TEXT
Approach. Supreme success. Persistence in righteousness advantageous. In the eighth month misfortune.

COMMENTARY
This hexagram, which depicts a huge reservoir of water under the earth, is linked with the twelfth month, when a new year and conditions of renewal are approaching. The lower trigram,

Tui, also indicates joy, and its movement is upward toward K'un, or the people, which trigram tends to move downward. A third symbol of approach is in the depiction of the time of the year when the Yang is trying to enter from the bottom and push upward. This is augmented by the lower inner trigram, Chên, movement, pushing upward into, and blending with, K'un, people, the upper inner trigram. Thus the persons symbolized here have great strength and depth, and are willing to teach, care for, and support others. The persons described by the three lower lines are rising to power and influencing those above them, while those described by the upper three lines use their strength primarily in support of those below them. Since the reservoir is huge, this indicates inexhaustible nourishment for the earth and the people, from those who dispense it. Nothing hinders these persons in the caring for and protection of the people. Such a time is truly great. 'In the eighth month' cautions one to remember that the law of change is always operative.

Those born in the twelfth month will be more auspicious.

CONTROLLING LINES (FROM BOTTOM TO TOP)
Line 1 Mutual Approach. Righteous persistence brings good fortune.

Lines 1 and 2 work together, cooperating in their movement upwards. They are thus far stronger and more effective in their total effort than if working on their own. It is the work of the positive and the creative for the purpose of establishing good. These are the teachers in all walks of life who help, guide, support, protect and care for others at all levels. Some of them may be teachers by profession. There will be many levels of attainment among these people.
Most auspicious: He will be a widely talented man, of great virtue. He will exercise modesty, sagacity and respectfulness, and will show mercy and love to all. He will be a noble character, cultivating himself and others continuously. He will be a blessing to many, and will accomplish worthwhile projects.
Least auspicious: He will be a just and upright man, desirous of helping others, but effective only on a local basis.
In yearly hexagram:

Officer or official	He will coordinate and cooperate effectively with others, and will be promoted.
Business and professional	He will communicate effectively, and gain in position and fame.
Ordinary people	Enterprises will be effective and profitable.

Line 2 Joint Approach. Good fortune. Everything advantageous.

Line 2 is the leader of the united approach of lines 1 and 2, but is a strong line in a weak place and hence not as favorable as line 1, yet quite strong and active. As the leader and the more advanced this person has greater and more important matters to deal with than his partner, but some opposition is indicated. His principal characteristics are wisdom, courage and fortitude.

Most auspicious: He will be diligent and will cultivate intelligence and virtue, following the right path and the golden mean. He will be able to control violence and correct it with humaneness. He is easily able to cope with adverse situations and conditions. He desires to establish good, and to leave the world in a better state than that in which he finds it.

Least auspicious: He will also be a fine and worthy person with much courage and a strong personality. He will advance household and external enterprises propitiously and profitably.

In yearly hexagram:

Officer or official	He will expose and destroy some extensive corruption and be respected.
Business and professional	Advancements will be smooth and gainful.
Ordinary people	He will know when to grasp opportunities, and to make gains or profits.

Line 3 Volitional approach. Not advantageous to set forth. With reflection, no error.

The position of this line is such that the way seems clear ahead; one has the upward support of the Yang line underneath. These persons recognize that there are many ways to go and innumerable things to be done. This can easily produce over-confidence, along with careless and relaxed moods in dealing with others. It is not advantageous to set forth on matters relating to approach with such attitudes. Reflection permits one to select a firm goal and a straight course and to act in a manner which frees one from error. Regrettably, this is a weak line in a strong position, so great things are not accomplished. These persons will be knowledgeable in their fields, and will be able to communicate well with others, especially in imparting their knowledge.

Most auspicious: He will know how to correct and compensate for losses and mistakes. He will be a capable guide but not too strong in leadership. He will have a good position, such as being a director in the educational field, or some other major enterprise.

Least auspicious: He will use his knowledge and talents for evil purposes. He will use flattery, and become a confidence trickster, cheating people. In later life he will reap just reward for his efforts, by experiencing many setbacks and considerable sorrow.

In yearly hexagram:

Officer or official	He will be bothered by the mistakes of others, and by misrepresentations and wrong evaluations.
Business and professional	He may make mistakes by flattering when making solicitations.
Ordinary people	He can expect considerable sorrow and grief.

Line 4 Mature approach. No error.

The upper trigram, K'un, has the tendency to sink, thus symbolizing that the approach of these persons will be carried out by using their power and strength to influence those below them. Hence a mature approach is necessary if no error is to be occasioned. These persons will be calm, poised, knowledgeable, full of common sense, and possessing a strong liking for others.

Most auspicious: He will be a man of virtue and noble character, in a moderately high position, and respected by friends and associates. He will find it easy to establish merit in all he does, and he will be engaged constantly on some worthwhile goal. His life will be full of blessings and benefits.

Least auspicious: He will also be an auspicious person, with few hardships and an easy life. He has the skill to lead, guide, and associate with others successfully. He may also achieve fame.

In yearly hexagram:

Officer or official	He will be supported by his colleagues.
Business and professional	An advantageous year for helping others, with beneficial results.
Ordinary people	He will have good friendships, and enterprises will go well if forethought is used.

Line 5 The wise approach of a great king. Good fortune.

All the noble and virtuous qualities, of wisdom, justice and executive ability, thought to have been held and exercised by the three early Emperors, Fu Hsi, Shen Nung and Huang Ti, can be assigned to persons with this controlling line. One of their highest attributes is their ability to choose proper subordinates, and rule expertly and beneficially through the delegation of authority, while retaining full responsibility.

Most auspicious: He enjoys association with persons of virtue and distinction, as well as keeping abreast with the needs of the people. He is a modest, clever, philosophical, virtuous and honest man, respected by rulers, leaders and the people alike. He will have a high position of authority, probably in the government.

Least auspicious: He will have similar qualities to the most auspicious, but not in such a high degree.

In yearly hexagram:

Officer or official	He will become known for effective and efficient management.
Business and professional	He can expect an increase in responsibilities and gains.
Ordinary people	Strong desires will be fulfilled.

Line 6 High-minded approach. Good fortune. No error.

The persons depicted here are beyond striving for the physical nourishment, support and care of others, and are seeking to improve the moral and spiritual values of individuals and the nation. These persons are wise and use the best means for inculcating these principles, directly or indirectly. Furthermore, they may take part in public life or be withdrawn, whichever best suits their purposes. They are unselfish, great-hearted and, magnanimous in their efforts.

Most auspicious: He will be a sage person of great virtue, using his abilities wisely to improve public morality through artistic or professional endeavors, privately or in public.

Least auspicious: He will also be a sage man of virtue, who may leave his family for the purpose of accomplishing his mission. He will be reasonably well off financially.

In yearly hexagram:

Officer or official	He will be appointed to an inner position in his field, or in the government.
Business and professional	He will have the opportunity to obtain the best knowledge currently available in his field.
Ordinary people	A good year for gains in possessions.

KEYNOTES

1. Cooperate wherever you are.
2. Be progressive in your activities.
3. Observe warning signs and be cautious when caution is indicated.
4. Strive for ever greater maturity.
5. When in positions of authority, behave in a kingly manner.
6. Balance your activities in all departments.

CONDENSATIONS FOR DAILY CYCLES

1. Commencing activity in cooperation with others of like mind, and persevering to completion, brings good fortune.
2. Keep activities correct. Apply the law of change and fate can be overcome.
3. The situation is not right for advancing. Pause and reflect. The right way will make itself known intuitively.
4. One knows exactly what to do and should do it.
5. A wise ruler or leader is indicated. Take actions in a kingly manner, obeying the golden mean.
6. Be unselfish, magnanimous and great-hearted. Good fortune will result.

Hexagram 20   Kuan ☴☷ *Contemplation*

SIMPLE TRANSLATION OF TEXT
The ablution has been made but not the sacrifice. He is reverenced
with sincerity.

COMMENTARY
This hexagram shows Sun, the wind, blowing over K'un, the
earth. It also represents 'penetration' over 'people,' hence the
concept of contemplation, or looking down over the people to see
what effects have been produced. At the same time, the people
look up to observe the manifestations of those above them. The
symbol of all this is the ancient sacrifice. The persons depicted
here are found in many walks of life and at various levels of
understanding. All of them have found certain keys to success,
i.e. through contemplation of the effects they produce on those
below them and on those above them. It is by these effects that
they can judge their success or failure, and begin to know the
seeds of the future. From these observations they establish rules
and guidelines for their actions. They tend to be active, judicious,
courageous, analytical and ambitious, to varying degrees,
largely dependent on their experience and intelligence. They are
respected for the successes they attain. Among the more successful,
one will find diplomats, lawyers, doctors, researchers and
politicians.
   Those born in the eighth month will be more auspicious.

CONTROLLING LINES (FROM BOTTOM TO TOP)
Line 1   A youthful point of view is blameless in the ordinary
person, but blameworthy in the superior man.

Here, at the beginning of contemplation, are persons who have
insufficient talent, experience, character, intelligence or common
sense to make correct observations and formulate judicious
opinions. Thus their courses of action are not the best. This is not
their fault, but rather it is because their innate endowments are
limited. All types of individuals are required in this world, and
these, too, serve a useful purpose in their own way.
Most auspicious: He can learn but little academically, or from

experience. He is able, however, to support himself and his family.

Least auspicious: He has a mean and base character, and is short-sighted, niggardly and ineffective in nearly everything he does.

In yearly hexagram:

Officer or official	He will find himself in a difficult position, with his hands tied.
Business and professional	Wait or retreat this year. Do not commence any major enterprises.
Ordinary people	Judiciousness is lacking, and many things will tend to go wrong. Beware of evil people.

Line 2   Observing through a cracked door. Advantageous to women.

Looking out from behind a cracked, or partially open, door indicates that this person has a limited and narrow field of view and, consequently, a 'restricted viewpoint.' Also, he likes to operate secretly and unobserved. As noted under Hexagram 13 (and others), the most propitious way of operating is through fellowship in the open. There are some circumstances where secrecy and a limited outlook are advantageous when considered in the light of their ancient role. Men with this controlling line will tend to be opinionated, narrow-minded, limited in intelligence, and restricted in abilities.

Most auspicious: He will be a person of little virtue and meager talent. He will probably be stupid or ugly and in a low position. He will have a tendency to blame others for his mistakes, and because of jealousy will 'take it out on others,' to compensate for his own deficiencies. He may receive help from a noble or rich woman. Women can expect a much longer life than men.

Least auspicious: He will have similar traits to the most auspicious, but will be poor and live in miserable conditions.

In yearly hexagram:

Officer or official	He will be regretful of his inability to accomplish anything worth-while.
Business and professional	He will be limited by the scope and precision of his materials, and their value.

| Ordinary people | Women will experience more joy than men. There will be uncertainties over gains and losses. Avoid difficult business methods and transactions. |

Line 3 Analyzing own life determines advance or retreat.

Childishness and narrow points of view have been outgrown, and here one contemplates one's own life (and the biographies of others, to determine their value and application) for the establishment of the guide lines one wishes to use and the direction in which one elects to go. This is a continuous process. These persons never do anything without a reason. Spontaneity is lacking throughout their lives, often to the irritation of others. These persons would do well in business, industry and government, in assignments involving research and analysis.

Most auspicious: He will begin to cultivate all phases of his life, especially the mental and moral aspects. He will know when to act and when to hold back or retreat. He will exercise wisdom and have many accomplishments of merit, and his life will be smooth with virtually no hindrances.

Least auspicious: He will advance and retreat throughout his life. This will be due in part to external conditions, and in part to his own vacillations. He will face many hardships.

In yearly hexagram:

Officer or official	There will be much uncertainty, with both advances and set-backs.
Business and professional	He will suffer much competition, with others often having the advantage.
Ordinary people	There will be uncertainties over gains and losses. Avoid difficult business matters.

Line 4 Contemplating conditions of the kingdom. It is propitious to be the guest of the king.

Cultivated and knowledgeable persons are depicted here. In ancient times (in the Confucian era, c.500 B.C.) kings sought new wisdom and enlightenment from visiting scholars and dignitaries. They often changed the methods of governing their realms on the advice of such people. The persons depicted here are capable of giving sound advice to the leaders of realms and enterprises. Their vision is much broader than that of those in line 3. They contemplate and analyze kingdoms as well as individuals, to obtain their guide lines, and they are naturally communicative persons as well. Since the controlling position in this hexagram is line 4, these people are likely to be found in cabinet posts, on boards of governors, and in legislative positions rather than executive.

Most auspicious: He will be an important personage in government or big business, capable of shouldering great responsibilities with sagacity. He will be faithful and loyal to his God, his country and its leaders, his duties, and his family.

Least auspicious: He is also a talented man, achieving merited fame. He will be respected, and duly rewarded for his efforts.

In yearly hexagram:

Officer or official	He will find himself in, or be assigned to, a lofty position.
Business and professional	He will advance. He may participate in a renowned convention, seminar or workshop.
Ordinary people	An auspicious year for doing business. Profits are to be expected.

Line 5 The superior man contemplates his own life, and the lives of others.

The persons depicted here recognize that the greatest good comes from being a worthy example, and bringing benefits to, others. While being interested in the realm as a whole, he knows that real accomplishments and advancements come from and through people. A nation or business can temporarily achieve much by executive action alone, but for truly great achievements, what is done must be a part and parcel of the people's will.

Most auspicious: He will be a gracious, wise, considerate, beneficent ruler or leader, setting high standards through personal example and excellence. He will strive to eliminate injustices, and to raise the virtue of the people as a whole. He will work for and serve others, even though he is a ruler or leader.

Least auspicious: He will also be a good and just leader, with a long and fruitful life.

In yearly hexagram:

Officer or official	He will be in a respected position as a leader, or else help the leader or ruler promote benefits for the people.
Business and professional	He will create and promote material for the benefit of others. He may receive some accolades.
Ordinary people	It will be a good year. He will work with the cooperation of others. If subject to a long-term illness, he will recover.

Line 6 Contemplation of his inner self. No blame.

The highest contemplation (in consonance with the position of the line) is that of one's inner self, whereby one recognizes one's oneness with the Creator, and that therefore the inner self is that which controls external conditions. These persons are sages, who, for the most part, are beyond mundane matters and matters of the ego. They tend to disguise their personal virtue and abilities, and lead and guide indirectly, letting others receive the praise and the credit. There is no blame attached to them for choosing this type of behavior. They inspire others to take actions that they know will bring benefits to many. They also achieve their purposes through literature, art and music.

Most auspicious: He will be a sage person and will be venerated. He will be a model of virtue, and will do much for the benefit of mankind.

Least auspicious: He will also be a model of virtue, but in seclusion or within a religious or altruistic organization.

In yearly hexagram:

Officer or official	He should exercise introspection for the benefit of his mission.
Business and professional	He will not be satisfied with present conditions, but will find the advancement of new ideas difficult.
Ordinary people	It will be a dull year. However, long-term illnesses will be cured, and those who are pregnant will have an easy birth.

KEYNOTES
1. Immature considerations are harmful.
2. Incomplete contemplations are damaging.
3. Self-analysis is always beneficial.
4. A broadened outlook is very useful.
5. A wide outlook is valuable for leadership.
6. Wise contemplation is most beneficial.

CONDENSATIONS FOR DAILY CYCLES
1. It is bad if one contemplates superficially, like a boy. Obtain, and use, a broader point of view.
2. Trying to gain enlightenment, knowledge or information, secretly, is not a manly way to act. Beware.
3. Contemplate the past to know the seeds of the future, and thus find the way to proceed ahead.
4. Determine for yourself the general or universal cause you should endeavor to join or support.
5. By noting the effects you have on others, you can determine whether the future bodes good or evil.
6. Search within yourself and discover if you are working without ulterior motives or desire for personal gain. In this way one can overcome karma, if that is what one wishes.

Hexagram 21   Shih Ho ☲☳ *Gnawing Through*

SIMPLE TRANSLATION OF TEXT
Gnawing through. Success. The time is favorable for the enforcement of justice.

COMMENTARY
Lightning is above thunder; clarity is above movement. The air is clear, the life of nature renewed; tensions are released, and beauty is restored once more, after a thunderstorm. This hexagram symbolizes the gnawing through of obstacles and adverse conditions. To do this, rulers and leaders must initiate, disseminate and enforce proper laws, vigorously and firmly. The three lower lines refer, on the whole, to people who need to correct themselves or be corrected, while lines 4 and 5 symbolize

how correction should be made. Line 6 reflects the completion of the cycle, with conditions reverting to their opposite. Persons depicted by this hexagram may be in a legal career, or involved with legal matters, in any of the three fields, legislative, executive and judicial, as determined by their controlling line and degree of auspiciousness.

Those born in the ninth month will be more auspicious.

CONTROLLING LINES (FROM BOTTOM TO TOP)
Line 1   His feet are in the stocks. Toes now are useless. No error.

When a person first transgresses, making small mistakes, he should be corrected and punished mildly but appropriately so that he will stop making mistakes, big or small. In this way no blame or error will occur. Every hexagram, through the changing of lines can change into any other hexagram, and it is to be noted that a complete change here would bring about a condition of rapid progress (hexagram 35). This is the most auspicious possibility here, and implies that those born with this controlling line will tend to be audacious, to violate rules, and to enjoy skirting authority. Some may be in high positions, others in low, but by changing their traits and habits, and by using their talents for the purpose of furthering good, they can make excellent progress.

Most auspicious: He will know how to, and will, take precautions to avoid troubles and mistakes. He will correct his own faults through the energetic cultivation of virtue. He will probably start life in poor or humble circumstances, which will gradually improve to an average, and then well above average, standard. He will become a noble person.

Least auspicious: He will be a mean and cowardly person, who fails in nearly every endeavor to advance.

In yearly hexagram:

Officer or official	Demotion of some sort is likely.
Business and professional	Efforts at promotion fail. Hold back.
Ordinary people	He should beware of serious illness; and he may be punished or put in jail. Caution can prevent most difficulties.

Line 2   Gnaws through soft flesh. Nose disappears.

Whatever these people do is like biting through soft flesh, but it may be for right purposes or for wrong ones. The nose disappearing could mean, in ancient times, either that the meat was soft so that one's nose disappeared into it when eating a large piece, using one's hands to hold it, or, that this was the punishment an offender received, i.e. to have his nose cut off for some transgression. The lower trigram is 'movement,' and a change in this line would convert it into 'joy.' Here, too, one could be seeking the right kind of joy or the wrong kind, depending on one's character, intelligence and motives.

Most auspicious: He will be a man of good character, ambitious and talented. He may become an officer in the military, or some law enforcement agency, either in the apprehension or punishment of transgressions. He will carry out his responsibilities well.

Least auspicious: He may use his talents for wrong purposes, with bad results. He could become a cripple, and will face many troubles and hardships. It would be best for him to become a monk or a recluse.

In yearly hexagram:

Officer or official	He will be hurt, physically or in reputation, by tough persons who are hard to govern or manage.
Business and professional	New efforts at advancement and promotion will fail.
Ordinary people	It will be hard to advance or retreat. There are likely to be many illnesses in the family.

Line 3 Gnawing on dried meat. Strikes tainted portion. Some indisposition. No blame.

If one were strong and in the right position one would be eating fresh meat and not dried meat, so old that some of it is apparently spoiled. This is symbolic of not governing properly, and having difficulties with people through insubordination. This is primarily the result of insufficient clarity and foresight, which are the characteristics that this man must seek in order to achieve a more auspicious life. If this is done, then his efforts and accomplishments will be without blame.

Most auspicious: He will tend to be low in intelligence and talent, but very ambitious. He will probably fail to recognize his weaknesses, and consequently have but few achievements. Self-improvement is needed.

Least auspicious: He will be less adequately talented than the most auspicious. He will find it very hard to advance and develop professionally, and to support himself and his family.

In yearly hexagram:

Officer or official	He will be criticized severely for not being adequately qualified for the position he holds.
Business and professional	Lack of facilities and capabilities will prove damaging.
Ordinary people	There will be considerable troubles, and possible disaster.

Line 4 Gnawing on dried gristly meat. Receives metal arrows. Determination in spite of difficulties. Good fortune.

A strong person, in the position of an arbiter or executive who has to try to administer justice in difficult legal situations, is depicted. In olden days such persons received metal and arrows before they adjudicated matters. Therefore these persons have the innate ability to be great and noble in fulfilling such duties. Gristly meat signifies that very serious and entangled matters are under consideration, yet through talent, wisdom, courage and determination, these can all be decided correctly, and good fortune will result.

Most auspicious: He will be a highly competent and courageous individual, who can be assigned to even the highest judicial positions in the nation, and will carry out his duties and responsibilities in a firm and beneficial manner. His personal life will be on a high level too.

Least auspicious: He will have considerable wealth and perhaps a good position, but will be subject to graft and corruption.

In yearly hexagram:

Officer or official	He will be promoted.
Business and professional	His reputation and effectiveness will be enhanced.
Ordinary people	He will make a good profit in his business or work.

Line 5 Gnawing on choice dried meat. Meets piece of gold. Aware of dangerous position. No error.

This is the ruling position for this hexagram, and also the center of the trigram 'clarity.' Rulers and leaders must overcome difficulties and mistakes, as well as correcting others. Choice meat indicates a large and potentially favorable enterprise. The gold indicates that this man should be mild and pure like gold in his rulings. It further signifies that the people do not readily submit to him. He must carefully discern the requirements of his enterprise, and the needs and abilities of his personnel, and judiciously match the two. If he recognizes the nature of his situation and handles it properly, no errors will occur. The position is not easy, but those depicted here are well qualified to attain successful results.

Most auspicious: He will be a wise and clever man who can turn adverse situations into favorable conditions, who can change erroneous ideas into healthy and progressive ones, and who can turn deviations into *tao* (the right path), on a large scale. He will have many auspicious events in his life.

Least auspicious: He will also be a rich man, but may live a comfortable and self-satisfying life, rather than one of major public service or service to others.

In yearly hexagram:

Officer or official	He will establish a favorable reputation, and become widely known and acclaimed.
Business and professional	He will make substantial advancements.
Ordinary people	If ill, he will recover. If in jail, he will be released. If sued, he will win the suit. A generally favorable year.

Line 6 He wears a wooden cangue. His ears cannot hear. Misfortune!

Obstinate and impractical persons, who are not willing to listen to others, are depicted. Even if they do hear something, they do not pay attention to it. They are persons of low intelligence and wisdom, who do not and will not recognize their difficulties. With such characteristics they are virtually incorrigible. They must be made to suffer for the manner in which they live their life with respect to others. Hence, misfortune will be their lot during most of their existence.

Most auspicious: If riches are inherited they will be a constant source of worry and trouble. He will make a few gains on his own, but will not find much happiness in life.

Least auspicious: He will be ruthless, domineering and stubborn, and frequently involved in disputes and troubles. He may commit felonies and end up in jail, or suffer serious injury.

In yearly hexagram:

Officer or official	He will receive unmerited blame, and is likely to be demoted.
Business and professional	Personal and business defamations are likely.
Ordinary people	He will encounter many disputes. A poor year.

KEYNOTES

1. Correct evils while they are small.
2. Hardened criminals must be punished.
3. Punishments should be carried out only by those who are duly authorized and qualified.
4. One must be firm and just in meting out discipline.
5. Mitigation and leniency should be exercised by rulers.
6. Incorrigibility leads to misfortune.

CONDENSATIONS FOR DAILY CYCLES

1. Outside influences would deter you from taking action. Heed the warning.
2. Initiate broad reforms, or take ample corrective action.
3. One is involved in troubles brought on by others, and deprived of effective action. Hold back. Your aims can still be attained.
4. Take direct action now, and follow through with prudence.
5. Find a true, just course, and follow it.
6. Beware of the danger of being deaf to counsel.

Hexagram 22   Pi ☲☶ *Ornamentation*

SIMPLE TRANSLATION OF TEXT

Ornamentation has success. Favorable for small matters only.

COMMENTARY

Just as ornamentation and adorning have their advantages in nature, so likewise there are times in man's life when it is propitious. In nature one finds ornamentation a matter of attraction, or for disguise and protection. Man can always do well by emulating nature under the right circumstances. This man should recognize that this condition applies to small matters and is favorable for them. Important matters require other approaches and deeper considerations. These persons tend to be ostentatious on the surface, in both their personal and professional lives, and would do well in advertising, public relations, and related fields where attraction in its various aspects is a requirement. Some of these individuals will display external characteristics which will hide their inner merit. Most will have a clear insight into conditions facing them, since the trigram Li, clarity, is in the lower position. Externally, their actions should be quiet and firm, like Kên, mountain, the upper trigram.

Those born in the eleventh month will be more auspicious.

CONTROLLING LINES (FROM BOTTOM TO TOP)
Line 1   Ornamentation of his feet. He leaves the carriage and walks.

The symbolism is that of a person who knows the right way and wants to follow it through the application of his own efforts, rather than take advantage of any easy conditions made available to him by others. The person depicted, knowing that he would walk, paid special attention to being well shod. Individuals of this type are highly independent, self-reliant and proud. Their pride is in doing what is right, rather than the pride of egotism. They are willing to accept life as it is dealt to them, and advance step by step.

Most auspicious: He will be a man of talent and virtue, yet content to be in whatever situation he finds himself. He is not given to great emotion, and rarely desires to express either great joy or great sorrow. He will climb steadily in life, and will ceaselessly endeavor to improve himself.

Least auspicious: He will face many hardships and have a routine life, but will not complain.

In yearly hexagram:

Officer or official	He may be demoted or dismissed.
Business and professional	He may be defamed or derogated.
Ordinary people	A year of hardships. Actions bring hope; inaction leads to failure.

Line 2 He adorns his beard.

Often social and professional situations demand adapting oneself to certain customs and traditions, as well as to modes of respect. This is what is symbolized here, but, in keeping with the hexagram as a whole, such actions are external only and do not stem from one's inner self. Consequently, even though these persons conform they do not do so from desire or with ulterior motives. They remain true to themselves under all conditions. These persons have the strength of character, which, when coupled with ability, can produce great results.

Most auspicious: He will be professionally learned, and socially cultivated. He will be sought by those in high places, and will render valuable service to others.

Least auspicious: He will also be well educated and enjoy social status. His life may become quiet when he is older. In general, he will be fortunate.

In yearly hexagram:

Officer or official	He will be promoted through the help of others.
Business and professional	He will gain advancement through writing something creative and professionally valuable.
Ordinary people	He will profit through the help of others.

Line 3 His ornaments are sparkling. Righteous persistence brings good fortune.

These persons have much natural good luck, as opposed to auspiciousness brought about by their own personal development. They must be careful to follow right paths and recognize that advancements must be of their own making. Indolence would nullify the benefits that naturally accrue as long as they continue to progress. Basically, they are calm, peaceful and considerate persons, who are at ease with the world, their family and their circumstances.

Most auspicious: His efforts and abilities will help the growth of the people and the nation, especially economically. He will attain major results and become famous. He should be assigned to influential positions.

Least auspicious: He will be helped by others, as well as attain some achievements on his own. He will have a long and generally easy life.

In yearly hexagram:

Officer or official	He will be supported by influential persons and assigned to a better position.
Business and professional	He will have many adherents and supporters. Fame is likely.
Ordinary people	An auspicious year. He will be helped by many people.

Line 4 Complete ornamentation like a white Pegasus. Not a despoiler but desires betrothal.

A white horse with wings is symbolic of winged thoughts that transcend time and space. Thus this person adorns himself inwardly with modern and ancient wisdom; this gives him the external appearance of being superior. Some people therefore are afraid of him and imagine that he will use his knowledge and power for wrong purposes. They see him in an adverse light but he is not what they think. His objective is to cooperate to the maximum extent, using his broad knowledge to be of service and benefit to others.

Most auspicious: He will be learned in both ancient and modern writings, and will be a creative writer himself. He may have many hardships early in life, but as he progresses he will make concrete gains, and possibly even amass great wealth. He may achieve fame.

Least auspicious: He will also have hardships early in life, which will slowly change to good fortune later. He will have faithful friends, and his family life will be moderately good.

In yearly hexagram:

Officer or official	There will be many obstructions early in the year, with things smoothing themselves out later.

Business and professional He will have minor losses early in the year, with major gains later.

Ordinary people Quarrels followed by reconciliations. Sorrows followed by joys. Dangers followed by safety.

Line 5 Ornamented with a roll of silk of poor quality, he strolls through the hills and gardens. Some humiliation, but ultimately good fortune.

Here are depicted the Emperor's hills and gardens surrounding Peking. These serve as objects of admiration by the people, and help to satisfy inner yearnings as well as a desire to be associated with success. Some Emperors even like to display moderation in their dress, but people expect a greater show of superiority and nobility. This causes some temporary humiliation, but since the goals and motives are right good fortune ultimately prevails. Consequently, wise leaders will recognize the value of example, and will use external ornamentation befitting their station even though they may personally dislike doing so.

Most auspicious: He will be pure and honest, leading his country or his enterprise well. He may have a tendency to be parsimonious, but not to a dangerous degree. He will gain considerable wealth and possessions as a result of good leadership, and can expect a long life.

Least auspicious: He will be a man of small mind and limited vision, who will find it hard to support himself, let alone lead others beneficially.

In yearly hexagram:

Officer or official He will find himself in a position of leadership and will fare well.

Business and professional Expansions and developments are propitious.

Ordinary people If goals are proper it will be a good year.

Line 6 Simple ornamentation. No blame.

Those described here are beyond the necessity for ornamentation or adornment. They are the ones who are noticed wherever they go, no matter what they may be wearing. They present an external reflection of a highly developed inner self, which is similar to what a Zen master or guru can see when he looks at those students who are meditating truly and gaining in spirituality. Such persons have found the true, real values in life, and know that simplicity is among the highest attributes of the most good. These people are a blessing wherever they are, and whatever they are doing.

Most auspicious: He will lead a simple and natural life as a result of his great innate, and cultivated, wisdom, along with his ever increasing intelligence. Despite his simplicity he will render true service to others, have good fortune and become rich.

Least auspicious: He will have a good and quiet character, and will serve mankind, but to a lesser degree than the most auspicious. He will be quite able to take care of himself appropriately, as well as others who may be dependent on him.

In yearly hexagram:

Officer or official	He will advance in status and salary.
Business and professional	Some ambitions will be fulfilled, and he will make gains.
Ordinary people	Simple, straightforward methods will result in a good year.

KEYNOTES
1. Be willing to do whatever needs to be done.
2. Conform externally if necessary.
3. Be at peace with yourself.
4. Let your thoughts be cooperative.
5. Purity and honesty are highly valued in self-development.
6. Simplicity frees one from error.

CONDENSATIONS FOR DAILY CYCLES
1. Be ready and willing to engage in self-cultivation.
2. Conform externally without yielding your internal worth.
3. You will be aided by your friends and peers. Good fortune.
4. Answers to our questions often come in a manner which at first seems strange.
5. Beware of set-backs due to negligence over details. In the end good fortune prevails.
6. Abandon ornamentation when it has served its purpose. Return to simplicity. Your wishes will be achieved.

Hexagram 23   Po ☶☷ *Cleavage*

SIMPLE TRANSLATION OF TEXT
Cleavage. No movement in any direction advantageous.

COMMENTARY
The trigram Kên, mountain, is resting on the trigram K'un, earth. The law of change and the law of equalization are operative here. The action of the latter is to try and reduce the mountain and fill up the valleys, and by the former, the five Yin lines are trying to cast out the one remaining Yang. The action is symbolized by the pattern of the lines representing a bed, with, presumably, someone on it. Efforts are being made to separate this person from the situation. Basically, this hexagram presents inferior persons trying to climb, using surreptitious and nefarious methods, with a desire to replace the one at the top. Cleavage of interests and actions naturally results. Fortunately, the inner hexagram is K'un, the Receptive, hence there is considerable hope for those wise enough to discern the valuelessness of climbing methods, and to let themselves be led into correct ways and cooperative efforts. As for strong persons, they will become even stronger from their trials and experiences. 'Cleavage' is primarily symbolic of the separation of good from evil, of the Yang from the Yin, and hence actions taken are not advantageous. The Yang and the Yin ought to cooperate, and are most propitious when they are in balance, not opposition. When they are in opposition nothing productive is accomplished. Persons with this natal hexagram would do well to cultivate and increase their virtue to recapture this balance.

Those born in the ninth month will be more auspicious.

CONTROLLING LINES (FROM BOTTOM TO TOP)
Line 1 Cleavage of the leg of the bed. Lack of steadfast rectitude. Misfortune.

These individuals may be either good persons whom mean persons are trying to cast out, or the mean persons themselves. It is quite possible that they will neither be wholly good nor wholly mean, since everyone has some good and some bad in him. Their traits can range from those of a sour misanthrope to those of a virtuous scholar. They are not gifted in any particular field, and can be found in most careers. What distinguishes them from others is their motivation.

Most auspicious: Will be, or will become, a virtuous and upright person, but not in a very high degree. He will face many problems, but will be able to overcome them with rectitude.

Least auspicious: He will be an insincere and supercilious climber, or a self-righteous avenger. He will be a wanderer, and, on the whole, will have an unstable and difficult life.

In yearly hexagram:

Officer or official	He will face serious difficulty, and must grasp the right moment for retreat.
Business and professional	A quarrelsome year with one's peers, and associates at work. Try to follow the middle way.
Ordinary people	A good year for construction work. He may have quarrels with his brother, and other troubles.

Line 2 Cleavage of the edge of the bed. Lack of steadfast rectitude. Misfortune.

The cleavage of the good from the bad is even more pronounced here than in line 1. The good person finds it hard to avert the evil that is closing in about him. The evil persons are similar to those in line 1, but wiser and stronger in their ways. The good must take action to escape from evil, as often and as quickly as possible. However, it must be done with flexibility, or else errors will occur which could lead to misfortune.

Most auspicious: He will become a rich, upright and virtuous person, but subject to many slanders, lawsuits, intrigues, and attempts by others to obtain money.

Least auspicious: He is likely to be obsequious, and to have ulterior motives. Those somewhat more elevated in character will work hard, but will find it difficult to support their family and have good family relationships. No help from friends or relatives should be expected

In yearly hexagram:

Officer or official	He will be blamed for some serious problem, and perhaps demoted as well.
Business and professional	All matters will be harder than normal to accomplish this year.
Ordinary people	He will have troubles and arguments, with many suspicious and harsh words exchanged.

Line 3   He cleaves (it). No error.

The five Yin lines, pushing upward, are uniting and working together to cast out goodness, i.e. the Yang line at the top. Line 3 is central among the five Yin lines, and so is the one most concerned and involved in the effort. It is the only one, however, with a correct correspondence, and since this is with line 6 no error is made. This correspondence causes the more auspicious to try to dissociate themselves from evil and support the good. Since line 3 is a Yin in the wrong place, some of these persons will succumb and join in the majority effort, whatever its nature. The more auspicious work well in solitude, are studious, diligent and full of fortitude. The less auspicious have a herd instinct and need companionship for their efforts, especially if they are nefarious. When by themselves they are practically useless.

Most auspicious: He will be better than average in virtue and in his efforts to lead a good and purposeful life. He will be generally very persistent.

Least auspicious: He will have but little virtue, and scant good fortune. He will tend to be an iconoclast.

In yearly hexagram:

Officer or official	He will meet a superior who recognizes his ability.
Business and professional	He will face opposition at every turn. He may have a few successes, but they will only be small.
Ordinary people	He will have no profits, and much difficulty with his family.

Line 4   Cleavage of the mattress of the bed. Misfortune.

In ancient times, the 'mattress of the bed' was no more than a piece of cloth or skin stretched across the frame. When this is torn, the bed becomes useless and the occupant faces danger. This imminent danger keeps such persons from being as effective as they normally would be. This symbolism is carried over into their lives. They are prone to experience sudden handicaps, dangers and misfortunes instigated by others. Furthermore, there is no one close to them nor near them to help them in their efforts to progress and advance. Hence, these persons need to have exceptionally strong characters to survive such conditions and not be pulled under or overcome by the dangers and evils surrounding them. Lines 1, 2 and 3 also have adversities associated with them. Here the evil is even stronger than in the previous three lines. Fortunately line 4 is virtually independent of, rather than cooperating with, lines 1, 2 and 3. Therefore the evils, even though great, can be overcome by the individual himself. How well one does depends solely on the individual.

Most auspicious: The truly strong will put trepidation into the hearts and minds of evil persons approaching them. They will automatically draw away from evil by virtue of their innate goodness. Their lives will be difficult but successful.

Least auspicious: The evil is great, and hence these egregious persons will have a tendency to destroy themselves by their actions. They may make temporary gains occasionally. They will have no surviving heirs.

In yearly hexagram:

Officer or official	He will be in, or close to danger, all year.
Business and professional	Nothing favorable is indicated. Defamations are likely.
Ordinary people	There will be many troubles and disputes. Lawsuits are likely.

Line 5 School of fishes. Favored like court ladies. Everything favorable.

This line is the leader of the five Yin lines and leads them like a school of fishes. Being close to line 6, it is influenced by it, changing its nature to goodness. Leading a group to cherish goodness and virtue merits great reward, hence everything is favorable. Religious, political and military leaders, primarily, are depicted here, those who have a natural attraction for others, the gift of the gab, and a professional expertise that commands respect and a following.

Most auspicious: He will be a great and noble person, who fosters the welfare of the nation and the betterment of mankind. He will greatly aid the evolutionary process, and will be adept in both civil and military matters, even if in a religious order. He will leave a favorable impression wherever he goes.

Least auspicious: He will be above average in his personal and professional ability and management. He may however need, and receive, some help from his superiors (mentally and spiritually).

In yearly hexagram:

Officer or official	He will be promoted, and will assume increased responsibility.
Business and professional	He will be well rewarded for some of his personal efforts.
Ordinary people	A good year with many benefits. Harmony and love will exist between himself and his family.

Line 6 The large fruit remains uneaten. The superior man acquires a carriage, whereas the inferior loses his house.

Those who survive the difficulties to this stage find a truly great cleavage between the good and the evil. The good, the Yang line, has remained in the hexagram and become exalted. There is much nourishment available to others, as symbolized by the large, uneaten fruit. Regrettably, the inferior does not want it, consequently he suffers by separation from the good. The goodness here is compounded of innate wisdom, strength, virtue, fortitude, and leadership. The person having these qualities acquires whatever he seeks, and has the support of the people as well. 'The inferior loses his house' indicates that those who are not good will be unstable, have no firm roots to rely on, and will probably lose their most precious possessions.

Most auspicious: He will be a man of great virtue, assigned to a highly influential position, capable of dispelling calamities and of pacifying the nation. He will be impeccant.

Least auspicious: He will be of low intelligence, vicious, vituperative, virtueless and mean. He will probably lose his friends, family, and possessions, and be a constant source of trouble to others.

In yearly hexagram:

Officer or official	He will be assigned to an influential position.
Business and professional	He will be assisted and recommended by peers and associates. He will be very active, and will attain a highly favorable reputation.
Ordinary people	If cautious and diligent, he will have a good year, in particular for building and for major transactions.

KEYNOTES
1. Eliminate evil early on.
2. It is dangerous to lack a firm purpose.
3. Beware of isolation.
4. Great good counters great bad.
5. Cooperation leads to success.
6. Virtue generates its own rewards.

CONDENSATIONS FOR DAILY CYCLES
1. The situation seems to be deteriorating. Get rid of hindrances, and disloyal persons.
2. Beware of competition setting in. Take appropriate action.
3. Use extreme caution. You have temporarily lost contact with your juniors and your seniors alike.
4. You are in the midst of some danger which cannot be avoided. Be of renewed courage.
5. The overall situation is still dire, but you can pursue your goals with some assurance of success.
6. If you are a superior person you will receive much respect. If inferior, you will be castigated.

Hexagram 24   Fu ☷☳ *Return*

SIMPLE TRANSLATION OF TEXT
Return. Success. All going forth and coming in is free from error. Friends come and no error is involved. They return and repeat. Seven days are required. Advantageous to have a firm goal.

COMMENTARY

This hexagram illustrates concisely the law of change and its operation in this world. All physical changes take place in six stages or actions. Going further then leads to a return of former conditions, and the completion of the cycle. (Another view is that what is sent out will return in kind.) Hexagram 1, Ch'ien, is entirely Yang. Changes enter from the bottom. In six stages the hexagram becomes entirely Yin, or K'un, the Receptive. With the seventh stage the Yang starts to return, and the hexagram then formed is this one, Fu. The cycle can repeat itself endlessly. The 'seven days' mentioned in the text are the seven stages of change, and with this last change being the entering of a Yang at the bottom, with all the lines above being Yin, it is a time to advance and make much progress. Hence it is advantageous to have a firm goal. By profession, the kind of people symbolized here are inventors, innovators, founders of businesses, organizers, promoters and entrepreneurs; they are men of clarity, vision, sound judgment, and fortitude. In their private lives, these individuals will use the foregoing qualities to change themselves within.

Those born in the eleventh month will be more auspicious.

CONTROLLING LINES (FROM BOTTOM TO TOP)
Line 1 Returning a short distance. Need for contrition. Supreme good fortune.

This line is the ruler of this hexagram, and hence those depicted here are exceptionally strong and courageous, mentally, physically and spiritually. The trigram Chên, thunder and movement, is under (within) trigram K'un, the earth. This tremendous inner force is bound to create something great externally. As the ruler, this man leads and guides sincerely, with self-discipline, docility, humility and loving kindness. This endears him to others, and they support his efforts and progress.

Most auspicious: He will be a man of great talent and noble character, and one who enjoys accomplishments. He will cherish goodness and personal development. He will be an expert organizer, and capable of founding a new government, a new business, or a new society. He will become rich and famous.

Least auspicious: He will be a person primarily cultivating himself in *tao* (the right way), and not seeking fame or fortune. However, he will render beneficial support to others when it is vital.

In yearly hexagram:

Officer or official	He will find himself in a high position, close to the ruler or leader, and a staunch adviser.
Business and professional	Creative efforts will be highly successful.
Ordinary people	A good year with substantial profit.

Line 2 Praiseworthy return. Good fortune.

The law of karma is symbolized here in that persons treating others with consideration, tolerance, guidance, and loving kindness reap good fortune in return. This, naturally, is praiseworthy. This meaning is also revealed if one considers the lower trigram. A change in line 2 from Yin to Yang produces the trigram Tui, joy. These persons are individuals who exercise a very high quality of leadership, whether in public or private life. They know that they personally are accountable for their every thought and action, and consistently strive to make these the best possible.

Most auspicious: He will be a just and richly endowed man, who follows the golden mean. He will not be boastful or egotistical, but will be sincere and loyal to all his personnel, and to his professional obligations. He will be highly trusted and reliable, and will obtain riches and some fame.

Least auspicious: He will also be a man of good character, but one content to live a private life, no matter what kind of life it may be. He will serve others quietly and unobtrusively.

In yearly hexagram:

Officer or official	He will regain his reputation and grow in favor with his superiors.
Business and professional	His position and activities will expand or be rejuvenated.
Ordinary people	Substantial profits can be expected. Past troubles will be favorably resolved.

Line 3 Repeated returns. Precarious position. No error.

Line 3 is a weak, Yin line in a strong place. It is not strong enough to take the action that is necessary. Were it so, it could change to its opposite, which would produce the trigram Li, clarity. Many abortive attempts towards goodness, half-heartedly carried through, result in repeated returns. Such unstable and vacillating action makes one's position precarious. Since these individuals are striving to do what is right, no damage will be done to their inner selves. These persons are individualists who have some idea of what is right and what produces the best results, and who make many experiments. They are to be commended for their efforts, even though their accomplishments in their chosen field are not great.

Most auspicious: He will strive to cultivate his virtue and character, as well as improve himself professionally. He will readily reform whenever he notes an error. He will frequently advance and frequently retreat; at times he will be lucky, and at others unlucky. He will not attain greatness.

Least auspicious: He will have many hardships in life, along with, regrettably, considerable sorrow.

In yearly hexagram:

Officer or official	He will be in an unstable position.
Business and professional	He will achieve fame for literary efforts.
Ordinary people	A slow year, with frequent doubts and indecisions.

Line 4   Walking in the company of others. Returning alone.

The symbolism here comes from this line being the middle line of the five Yin lines, and hence walking among them. Fortunately, line 4 is a correlate of line 1, and this aids it favorably, but it is the only line which has a proper correlation. Line 1 is very strong and this influences line 4 to return to what is right without any promises of favoritism or reward. These persons do not let themselves be swept along blindly with the crowd, or over influenced by their associates. They evaluate matters for themselves, and then try to do what they think is right. Basically, they lack sufficient strength to accomplish great results, and would do well to constantly cultivate themselves mentally and spiritually, and try especially to keep themselves up to date. Such actions will promote auspiciousness.

Most auspicious: With diligence and persistence he will become a man of virtue and wealth. He will be calm in times of anarchy, rebellion or danger. He will not be stirred by demagogues, whatever their allegiance. He will follow *tao* (the right path).
Least auspicious: He may work in a large organization, and strive for independence of thought and action. He is likely to be in a position demanding considerable travel. He may find restful conditions later in life.
In yearly hexagram:

Officer or official	He will regain an influential and important position.
Business and professional	He will achieve a favorable reputation.
Ordinary people	He will make a good profit.

Line 5 Magnanimous return. No regret.

The fifth line is normally the ruling line in a hexagram, so these persons have a tendency to dominate a situation with their own thoughts and efforts. Inwardly they know that this is not for the best, so they nobly and unselfishly return to fundamentals to discover guide lines for their actions, development and achievements, irrespective of the nature of their goal, whether mental, physical or spiritual. Their motive is to build on firm foundations, only using suitable methods and materials, in great and small matters alike, both personally and professionally. Doing thus leads to success, not regrets.
Most auspicious: He is likely to be in a high and influential position and well qualified to meet his situation, both personally and professionally. He will be noble in character, rich in friends, and respected by adversaries. He will attain wealth, property and possessions.
Least auspicious: He will strive to become a more auspicious person, and will make some worthy achievement on a modest scale.
In yearly hexagram:

Officer or official	He will move to a better position.
Business and professional	His services will be sought by others.
Ordinary people	He will be able to put aside some savings. His father may become seriously ill or die.

Line 6 Confused. Uncertain return. Misfortune. Calamities and disasters. If armies are set in motion by the ruler, defeat. For ten years it will not be possible to attack again.

One's external world reflects that which is within oneself. This man is confused within, and muddled in his thinking. He has considerable innate wisdom, but his position (line 6) places him in circumstances with which he is inadequately qualified to cope. This results in disasters. The situation becomes so dire that 'ten years' are required to put things right. 'Ten years' as used here means a cycle of experience. Therefore a whole new cycle must be undergone to attain success. If *this* 'return' is missed he will suffer many misfortunes. He must place his faith and trust in the Creator and divine law. These persons will have extremely active lives, with many successes and failures, both great and small, until they learn the lesson of converting themselves inwardly into men of *tao* and the golden mean.

Most auspicious: He will know how to effect reforms nationally, locally and within himself. He readily learns the lessons of life, and after some trial and error, will gain and retain wealth, along with a favorable reputation. His personal life will also be favored.

Least auspicious: He will be a stupid, dull person, learning slowly. He may be crippled or ill for long periods of time. He will cause troubles for himself, his family and his country.

In yearly hexagram:

Officer or official	He will be held in contempt for sticking to his position and accomplishing nothing worthwhile.
Business and professional	He will suffer indignity if his actions are not outstanding.
Ordinary people	If confused, hold firm and wait for difficulties to clear up.

KEYNOTES
1. A quick return from minor transgressions is favorable.
2. Self-mastery is highly beneficial.
3. Inner instability is dangerous.
4. Be prepared to tread a lonely path, if necessary.
5. Magnanimity in character and actions is advantageous.
6. Act when you know reform is required.

CONDENSATIONS FOR DAILY CYCLES

1. A strong reform meets with little opposition and achieves good fortune. Exercise self-discipline.
2. Consummate reforms in company with others of like mind whenever possible.
3. Stop wavering. Strengthen your will power and you will become free from blame.
4. Remain firm, even if others try strongly to lead you astray.
5. Reforms brought about by self-discipline and self-mastery bring advantages.
6. Beware of the consequences of stubbornness, or failure to reform at the right time.

Hexagram 25   Wu Wang ☰ *Circumspection (The Unexpected)*

SIMPLE TRANSLATION OF TEXT

Circumspection. Supreme success. Righteous persistence furthers. If some one does not pursue rectitude, misfortune, and it is not advantageous for him to undertake anything.

COMMENTARY

Primal movement, Chên, the lower trigram, is surrounded by heaven, the upper trigram, symbolizing circumspection and innocence. These persons have great inner strength and capacity, which, if properly trained and developed, can be of true benefit to mankind. They will be blessed with common sense, innate intelligence and communicativeness. This last quality is apparent when one considers the hexagram from an external point of view, i.e. thunder below heaven, making itself known and heard everywhere. In this respect these persons are capable of giving abundant and timely nourishment to those willing to receive it. This nourishment is in the form of knowledge of the laws of heaven, the reflection of innocence, and the taking of actions free from guile. Heaven, however, does not follow the laws of man and often injects what it deems most fitting. Hence there is an element of the unexpected here too.

Those born from the second to the eighth month, the months of thunder, will be more auspicious, with those born in the second month being the most auspicious of all.

CONTROLLING LINES (FROM BOTTOM TO TOP)
Line 1   Circumspect advancement brings good fortune.

By the sequence of changes entering at the bottom and moving upwards, this hexagram becomes the next step in the evolution of Hexagram 12, Standstill. When things first begin to move again, under the primal guidance of heaven, they are bound to be circumspect, with much good resulting therefrom. These persons will have dynamic personalities and forceful minds. They will make forthright progress with intrepidity. Their degree of success will be measured largely by the wisdom of their actions. In general, what they will is done.

Most auspicious: He will keep his mind active by a progressive attitude, and will keep abreast of changes in his profession, his community, and his country. He will have great ambitions relating to national goals and purposes; he will become an important personage, and lead a highly favored life.

Least auspicious: He will also have a good and beneficial life, filled with modest success and good fortune.

In yearly hexagram:

Officer or official	He will be supported and trusted by his ruler or superior, and by the people.
Business and professional	He will gain fame and a reputation through creative efforts.
Ordinary people	A good year with considerable profit.

Line 2   Do not count the harvest while ploughing, or anticipate the results of your efforts. It is propitious (however) to have a firm goal.

A universal law is stated here. Man never has full control over any situation. Heaven exercises control, and this is symbolized here by the trigram Ch'ien, heaven, being above, i.e. the upper trigram, which controls the lower trigram. It is probable that from this comes the saying 'Heaven helps the man who helps himself.' If one has firm goals and devotes oneself constantly and persistently towards them one is bound to obtain results at a time that is in keeping with universal time (i.e. the time decreed by heaven). What is accomplished is sufficiently abundant that the individual need have no concern over when results will occur. Can a farmer count his harvest when he ploughs? Can a business definitely know its prospective sales? Many things can happen between the ploughing and the harvest. Diversification, of course, increases the chance of success, but each activity must have a firm goal. This man, likewise, should do many different things, and do all that is necessary in pursuit of his goals. Success and good fortune then will be his. Broadminded and perspicacious individuals of noble character will know what to do at all times, and will do it propitiously.

Most auspicious: He will be a foreseeing and lucky individual, following the golden mean. He will not be concerned about fame or profit, but will achieve them anyway. He will have an easy and adventitious life.

Least auspicious: He may be lazy and indulgent, gratifying selfish desires, or a wanderer with no fixed destination or strength of character. He will find it hard to support himself and his family.

In yearly hexagram:

Officer or official	He will gain promotion in status, position or salary.
Business and professional	He will achieve his dominant aims.
Ordinary people	It is propitious to buy land or make investments. He will make a profit in an enterprise. A good year.

Line 3   Unexpected adversity. The tethered ox was taken by a passer-by. The owner's loss.

Having gains made by others at our expense is unexpected adversity and a true loss. This indicates that the law of karma is operative, reminding us that sometimes unexpected things happen to us which are not our (apparent) fault. On the other hand one should not put temptation in another's path, as symbolized by the unguarded ox. Nor should one consider goodness by itself to be sufficient. One must guard and protect one's endowments, both material and spiritual. It behooves these persons to strive for a balanced life, and many will be successful.

Most auspicious: He will be a man of driving energy and strength, who knows how to make and keep gains, whose virtue is adequate to dispel calamities, whose fortitude overcomes adversity, and who establishes and maintains excellent family and community relations.

Least auspicious: He will lead a wandering life, restless in goals and aims, and exercise a cunning personality. He will have much uncertainty, with many gains and losses, and will find family life difficult.

In yearly hexagram:

Officer or official	A good year for the high official, but a poor year for the small administrator.
Business and professional	He will have several fluctuations in his endeavors, and will find it difficult to advance.
Ordinary people	He will have both profits and losses, and, on the whole, these will offset each other.

Line 4   Persevering in rectitude. No error.

Here in line 4, the position of the minister, one is enjoined to devote thought, time and effort to carrying out the meaning of the hexagram as a whole. If this is done with rectitude there will be no error. The implication is that if these persons are not circumspect, troubles will develop. To remain circumspect at all times is difficult. (This is also suggested by this being a strong line in a weak place.) Consequently, greatness is not predicted. These persons will be in above average positions, and will carry out their duties and responsibilities diligently and with honor.

Most auspicious: He will be a gentleman of considerable honor, talent and morality, who readily helps others while privately cultivating his own virtue. He will have a favorable life, with many worthwhile accomplishments.

Least auspicious: He will receive ample remuneration for his services to be able to live a life without financial difficulties.

In yearly hexagram:

Officer or official	His position will be unchanged.
Business and professional	Everything will proceed according to routine this year.
Ordinary people	A routine year. Move slowly in any attempts at progress, or else failure will result.

Line 5 Unanticipated illness. Use not untried medicine, and it will be joyful.

This line is the ruler of the hexagram and depicts the leader and minister working together, laying plans in case of unanticipated changes or difficulties. Their actions are right and proper (a strong line in a strong place) and thus they keep things under control. These persons should study nature, and follow the laws of heaven and earth rather than try to be innovators. Their far-sighted plans and actions will achieve favorable results. Individuals with this controlling line will be leaders and high officials in their chosen field, who have the potential to avert possible disasters for the group with which they are associated. They will do their best if they follow proven methods.

Most auspicious: As a leader, he will be a man of virtue, vigor, vitality and vision, who is audacious yet follows the golden mean. He will know how to keep or restore peace in all his associations. He will have an excellent family, coupled with wealth and much joy.

Least auspicious: He will also be an auspicious person with few difficulties, and the recipient of a long life and much happiness.

In yearly hexagram:

Officer or official	Even if troubles develop they will disperse of their own accord. Do not worry.
Business and professional	There is the possibility of a setback. Hold firm, and it will correct itself.
Ordinary people	He may have an illness that cures itself. Business should be successful.

Line 6 Uncircumspect actions bring misfortune.

Here at the top of the hexagram, one has passed the time for propitious action. Therefore, to push forward would be contrary to this stage of progress, and would be reprehensible. Action could lead to much opposition and exhaustion. Those depicted here should be calm, thoughtful, far-sighted, up to date, and modest individuals if they are to achieve success. Patience is a great virtue. They should not try to oppose fate, but should keep their motives pure and innocent.

Most auspicious: He will be able to attain a good position, and will know how to hold it. He will know also how to guard against troubles, both professional and personal.

Least auspicious: He will be very ambitious, but a dullard, unable to consummate his goals. He will wander for most of his life, and work in solitude. He will frequently feel the need of assistance from others, but will not receive it. If sufficiently wise, he will seek out seclusion to the maximum extent practicable.

In yearly hexagram:

Officer or official	He will be demoted, dismissed, or sent to a remote position.
Business and professional	He will be disgraced for obvious deficiencies.
Ordinary people	He will have disputes, largely due to inadequate knowledge or preparations.

KEYNOTES

1. Progress circumspectly.
2. Do not count the harvest while ploughing.
3. Unanticipated events do occur.
4. Rectitude is always beneficial.
5. Be far-sighted and broadminded.
6. Exercise proper patience.

CONDENSATIONS FOR DAILY CYCLES

1. Applying knowledge of what is right, and advancing, brings good fortune.
2. Take actions for their own sake. Do not expect long term results too quickly.
3. Adversities due to your fate (karma) may occur. Remain inwardly firm.
4. Your innocence and sincerity are being tested. Do only that which is right and just.
5. An unexpected adversity may occur. Do not use untried methods to overcome it. The right solution will present itself.
6. The time for action has passed. Do not attempt anything new at this time.

Hexagram 26   Ta Ch'u ☰☶ *The Great Restraining*

SIMPLE TRANSLATION OF TEXT

The Restraining Power of the Great. Good fortune from not eating at home. Advantageous to cross the great water.

COMMENTARY

Several important aspects of this situation are symbolized. Heaven, below, is rising up into the mountain. This implies a daily renewal of strength. It is also a time for accumulation, but along with this amassing, superior persons should be nourishing others as well as paying reverence to the ancients and their knowledge. The mountain further signifies that these persons pursue their courses with judgment and proper restraint, retreating or holding firm when necessary. 'Good fortune from not eating at home' indicates that this is a time for initiating further external actions. These may be material, physical or spiritual, and they will be in accord with the will of heaven as long as they curb and correct evil. These persons will be perspicacious, judicious, consistent, reliable, courageous and wise.

Those born in the twelfth month will be more auspicious.

CONTROLLING LINES (FROM BOTTOM TO TOP)

Line 1   Danger is at hand. Wise to desist from efforts towards progress.

Persons with this controlling line are very observant and analytical. They are constantly aware of a great many things that need to be done. Regrettably, their natal position is such that they are held back by circumstances and powers beyond their control. Even though there are many things they would like to do, they will find that they can get the most satisfaction out of life by improving themselves, rather than by endeavoring to improve external circumstances in their profession.

Most auspicious: He will be a wise person, who knows how to survive within the limits by which he is circumscribed. He will take good care of himself mentally, physically and spiritually, while limiting his external aspirations. He will lead a personally satisfactory life.

Least auspicious: He will be weak-willed, and will occasionally succumb to the dangers surrounding him. He will have a generally troublesome life.

In yearly hexagram:

Officer or official	He should retreat, or withdraw from conflicting matters.
Business and professional	He should be passive and wait for conditions to change.
Ordinary people	He should not try anything new, or troubles will ensue.

Line 2   The carriage axle is broken.

Self-restraint is being exercised here. The fifth line is the normal correlate of the second. Since both here are in wrong positions, the result is judicious restraint rather than fortuitous advancement. The Chinese text implies that the axle is the person to whom this line relates. These individuals are of the type who work quietly behind the scenes, developing master plans which others execute. They themselves are always in the background.

Most auspicious: He will be a talented, judicious, upright, quick-witted and intelligent individual, possessing much knowledge. He will master-mind matters of lasting benefit. He may assume important positions for short periods of time, but will be readily willing to give them up. He will lead a personally satisfying life.

Least auspicious: He will have an unfortunate childhood. His professional efforts later will not be of great or lasting benefit. He will have frequent ailments or injuries, some, perhaps, to the feet, and will have a short life.

In yearly hexagram:

Officer or official	Watch out for disputes or other troubles.
Business and professional	Take steps to protect your investments.
Ordinary people	An unfavorable and unlucky year.

Line 3   Steeds galloping in companionship. Realization of danger. Persistence advantageous. Beneficial to practice charioteering and defensive methods daily. Favorable to have a goal.

The 'steeds' are lines 5 and 6, working together in freedom.

The exercise of too much freedom can be dangerous, therefore they are enjoined to exert righteous persistence. Doing so will be advantageous. With two Yin lines ahead of line 5, the way is open for these persons to advance. By keeping their professional standards high, and at the peak of proficiency, they will achieve many benefits. Their rise can be rapid if they choose the right goals, and pursue them single-mindedly.

Most auspicious: He will be learned, clever, and judicious, and endowed with innate common sense and practicality. He may be assigned to a high industrial, business or governmental position (more than likely involving a considerable amount of travelling). Least auspicious: He will have aspirations similar to those of the most auspicious, but acts without due consideration and mature deliberation. He is impractical and does not take care of himself, professionally or personally, and will therefore experience unavoidable losses. He will have many hardships.

In yearly hexagram:

Officer or official	Promotion can be expected.
Business and professional	His scope for action and his responsibilities will be enlarged in a favorable manner.
Ordinary people	He will get help from his superiors and friends. If he works hard he will make some gains.

Line 4 Headboard on the young bull. Great good fortune.

A headboard on a young bull restrains the horns from doing damage. Line 4 has the trigram Ch'ien immediately below it, with the latter's creative strength driving upward. This has the effect of making these individuals exercise special care and attention on restraining and guiding the strength and aspirations of those below them, and on curbing evil or erroneous propensities at the start. Such persons are great natural teachers, in all walks of life. Their unselfish and devoted efforts are very effective, and great good fortune arises from them.

Most auspicious: He will be well qualified both personally and professionally, and possess a deep, innate knowledge of psychology which he will use instinctively as occasion demands. He will achieve considerable wealth, and a high status.

Least auspicious: He will either be in a small, independent

position, or an assistant to some auspicious person. His knowledge, mentality and experience are insufficient to handle great responsibilities.

In yearly hexagram:

Officer or official	He will be promoted, and be very pleased about it.
Business and professional	His reputation will be enhanced, and his responsibilities broadened.
Ordinary people	A generally favorable year, with something especially joyful occurring.

Line 5   A gelded boar's tusks. Good fortune.

As one of the rulers of this hexagram, in a ruling position, this line symbolizes leaders among men, who need to repress and restrain evil. 'A gelded boar's tusks' represents that which needs to be restrained and shows the method by which it can be done. A wild boar is very dangerous and uses its tusks to harm others, Once a boar is gelded, it no longer cares to use its tusks. Therefore 'gelding' evil is a good way to restrain and eradicate it, rather than trying to combat it directly. Good, wise, steadfast, and strong men, with courage and vitality, are required to carry out such matters. Most auspicious: He will be highly talented, both personally and professionally, with innate qualities of leadership. He will be assigned to positions involving the establishing of policies, and controlling or influencing large numbers of people. He will make positive contributions within his sphere of influence, and will have a good and rewarding life.
Least auspicious: He will not be a man of great vision, and so his life will be on a small scale, self-circumscribed to within narrow limits. He will have a better than average, modest life, with some joyful events.

In yearly hexagram:

Officer or official	He will be promoted, in salary, status or position.
Business and professional	Creative efforts will generate professional gains.
Ordinary people	A good year, with some desires achieved.

Line 6   Applying heaven's way. Success.

These are sage individuals, who have studied the manifestations of heaven and the laws of earth, and know how to apply them in a manner similar to that in which heaven does. These persons are perspicacious, helpful, judicious, profound, erudite, sagacious, far-sighted and dynamically courageous. Regrettably, a few have an inner negativity which prevents them from being highly successful. If you are not achieving your desired results, correct yourself inwardly.

Most auspicious: He will be one of the great and noble persons of his time, highly respected and greatly sought after. He will achieve results that will benefit mankind as a whole, or, at least, a great many people. He will become renowned for his efforts towards peace and the improvement of mankind. He will have a very rewarding life, rich in friends, health, joy and material pleasures.

Least auspicious: He will be very ambitious, but will be set back by an inner negativity that will keep him from being successful, both personally and professionally.

In yearly hexagram:

Officer or official	He will be promoted, through the acclaim and desires of others.
Business and professional	He will achieve a highly favorable reputation, and will be supported by others.
Ordinary people	A good year, with influential and cooperative friends.

KEYNOTES

1. When the time is not propitious, desist from advancing.
2. Always exercise self-control.
3. Persevere in your goals.
4. When extraordinary caution is required, use it.
5. It is best to restrain evil indirectly.
6. Try to follow the way of heaven.

CONDENSATIONS FOR DAILY CYCLES

1. You feel yourself repressed. Do not try to press forward yet.
2. You are held back by forces beyond your control. There is no blame attached to this. Continue to exercise self-control.

3. Progress seems rapid, but one should continue to act cautiously, keeping one's goal firmly in mind at all times.
4. Extraordinary caution, in one's enterprises and in the distribution of nourishment, will bring good fortune.
5. The use of indirect restraints is better than combating evil directly. Use them now and blessings will accrue.
6. Act in accordance with the will of heaven, and success will be yours.

Hexagram 27   I ☶☳ *Jaws (Nourishment)*

SIMPLE TRANSLATION OF TEXT
Jaws. Righteous persistence brings good fortune. Observe the nourishing of others, and what they provide for themselves.

COMMENTARY
The principal trait of individuals with this natal hexagram is that they are diagnosticians. This hexagram is made up of the trigram Kên, mountain, over Chên, thunder, or movement. The hexagram looks rather like an open mouth, with two strong lines at each end and all Yin lines in the middle. The upper Yang line is stable, like the upper bone of the mouth. The lower Yang line is unstable, like the moveable jaw-bone. The four Yin lines represent the cavity of the mouth. Consequently the hexagram is named 'Jaws,' and in such a manner in the Chinese text that it relates to nourishment. The three lower lines have reference to material nourishment and the three upper lines to the spiritual. Being persistent in righteousness naturally leads to good fortune. Being observant of what people seek, and how they desire to be nourished, helps the superior person to help others. The superior man is deliberate in his speech, and modest in his own eating and drinking. Confucius enjoins students to note what parts of their bodies other people are concerned about, and how those persons nourish themselves; they can then know what types of individual these persons are. This advice is still valid, with the up to date adjunct that behind every man's desire are needs he is trying to fill. Broadly speaking, the persons depicted here will be leaders, with greater or lesser responsibilities for nourishing others. They can be found in nearly every walk of life, depending on their

personal desires and choice. They will diagnose the needs of people, and try to find ways and means to satisfy them.

Those born in the eighth month will be more auspicious.

CONTROLLING LINES (FROM BOTTOM TO TOP)
Line 1 You release your magic tortoise and stare at me with jaws open. Misfortune.

Basically, these persons are not exercising proper control over their own destiny. The magic tortoise is the animal the shell of which was used for divination in early times. To lose one's magic tortoise means that one lets one's life become subject to chance rather than positive control. 'With jaws open' is symbolic of wanting to be fed like a baby. Either such persons do not want to bite (work hard) for their nourishment, or else they are so lackadaisical that they do not care. These persons would gladly be parasites if circumstances permitted. In any event, they are unable to persist in following true goals, but tend to follow mirages on the horizon.

Most auspicious: He will seek his fortune in a foreign country where he imagines life will be easier. He will be poor in worldly wealth, and mean in disposition. He will be greedy but lazy. Although he may make some slight gains, he will mainly have large losses.

Least auspicious: He will be anomalous, disloyal and corrupt. He will have a difficult life, which will end in disaster.

In yearly hexagram:

Officer or official	He will be blamed for some serious corruption.
Business and professional	He will be blamed for corruption and immorality.
Ordinary people	He will have troubles and disputes over money. A quiet year with some good fortune.

Line 2 Nourishment at the mountain top. Digressing from the normal way of nourishment from the hills. Misfortune.

The best nourishment in this hexagram comes from the top of the mountain, line 6. Normally, the second line should correlate with, and seek nourishment from, the fifth line, i.e. in this case, half-way up the mountain, equivalent to 'the hills.' Seeking nourishment in the wrong place or in the wrong way naturally leads to misfortune. This line depicts persons who separate from their own kind, and seek nourishment for which they are not duly prepared.

Most auspicious: He will lead a quiet and unhurried life, keeping out of troubles, and sustaining himself and his family modestly. He will have a safe and relatively uneventful life, and will seek to improve himself inwardly.

Least auspicious: He will have unstable characteristics and a vacillating personality, with others never knowing what to expect from him. He will not concentrate or persevere, and he will have a propensity for cheating or getting things the easy way. He will have many hardships, and some serious troubles.

In yearly hexagram:

Officer or official	Demotion of some sort is likely.
Business and professional	Defamations and derogations are probable.
Ordinary people	It will be difficult to either advance or retreat. He will have disputes over money matters, and he may become seriously ill, or die.

Line 3 Deliberate forgoing of nourishment. Misfortune. Ten years are wasted. Advancement not advantageous.

Line 3, as the lower center of the mouth, looks to the jaw-bone, line 1, for its nourishment rather than to line 6, its normal correlate. The lesson here, as elsewhere, in *I Ching* is that man must develop his inner self, from which an auspicious external life will follow. A change of this line to its opposite produces hexagram 22, Pi, which is concerned with external embellishments. A whole cycle of life (ten years) is wasted in pursuing such a course. Any advancement in this direction will only make matters worse. Heed the warning.

Most auspicious: He will be reasonably talented, and sufficiently wise to be able to restrain and repress damaging desires, as well as to reform if he makes mistakes. His life will be on a humble scale, but good.

Least auspicious: He will be a violent, base and dishonest

person given to pursuing evil goals. He will have a difficult life, which will end in disaster.

In yearly hexagram:

Officer or official	He will be defamed, and tempted by, or subject to corruption.
Business and professional	Moral values will be at a low ebb, resulting in difficulties.
Ordinary people	He will over-indulge in sensuality and dissipation. Many troubles.

Line 4 Nourishment at the mountain top. Good fortune. Staring around like a starving tiger. No error.

The heavenly and true nourishment is at the mountain top, line 6. Those depicted here know something about it, but as they are at the foot of the mountain, line 4, they are looking everywhere with keen eyes, trying to discern how they can become genuinely nourished themselves, as well as how to provide nourishment for others. Since the fourth line is the position of a minister, these persons are looking for the right people to help and support them in this effort, in addition to seeking the proper nourishment for themselves. These individuals will be executives, or others involved with the assignment and supervision of personnel, or matters relating to their welfare.

Most auspicious: He will be a man of many capabilities, knowledgeable, broadminded, visionary and magnanimous, who will accomplish worthwhile results for the people, and perhaps even help bring peace to the nation.

Least auspicious: He will use his talents and efforts for selfish purposes, and especially in striving for money, glory and power. He will experience many difficulties in all phases of his life.

In yearly hexagram:

Officer or official	He will be the favorite of his ruler or master.
Business and professional	He will make substantial gains and achieve some fame.
Ordinary people	He will get help from good people, and attain some of his desires.

Line 5 Forsaking established ways. Abide in and follow what is right. Good fortune. Do not cross the great water.

Normally, the fifth line is the controlling line, the ruler or leader who nourishes, guides and supports others. Here, however, this function belongs to line 6. Therefore line 5 has to forsake established ways and gains its strength and support from line 6. If he abides in and follows what is right, good fortune ensues. Unfortunately, the persons depicted here have inadequate strength, knowledge or experience to engage in great enterprises on their own. They will fare best when they let someone superior to themselves do the leading.

Most auspicious: He is likely to inherit independent means, or receive considerable help from others, such that he has a good life. He will render some service to others, but his accomplishments will not be great.

Least auspicious: He will probably have little or no inheritance; otherwise he will have a similar life to the most auspicious.

In yearly hexagram:

Officer or official	He can keep his position, but should avoid taking on additional responsibilities.
Business and professional	Little advancement for himself or his enterprises is to be expected.
Ordinary people	He will receive beneficial help from others. He should not make a sea voyage this year.

Line 6 The source of nourishment. Recognition of the grave responsibilities brings good fortune. It is favorable to cross the great water.

Line 6 in this hexagram (see also the commentaries on the other lines) is the source of nourishment. The persons depicted here have great wisdom, and recognize their grave responsibility for the nourishment being correct and proper, so that no harm is done to those being nourished. When one is so sagaciously endowed, it is also incumbent on one to pass one's knowledge, virtues and experience on to others, hence the admonition to cross the great water. These persons are truly great and noble.

Most auspicious: He will be a man of great virtue and exceptional talents, perspicacious and sagacious. He will attain a high position, either in civil or governmental activity where the welfare of the nation is one of the principal concerns. He will be trusted by superiors and respected by the people, and will accomplish much of great merit and lasting benefit. He will have a long and rewarding life.

Least auspicious: He will also have good fortune and a long and beneficial life, but on a lesser scale. He will be renowned locally.

In yearly hexagram:

Officer or official	He can expect a rise in position and salary.
Business and professional	Creative efforts will be highly successful and appropriately rewarded.
Ordinary people	An auspicious year with everything running smoothly.

KEYNOTES

1. Work to control your life.
2. Work among your peers.
3. Cooperate by giving and receiving.
4. Analyze how best to help others.
5. Help superiors nourish others.
6. Nourish others impartially.

CONDENSATIONS FOR DAILY CYCLES

1. It is man's duty to God to determine for himself what his duty is. If he forgoes this, misfortune will result.
2. Seek nourishment among your peers. Work in seclusion only if it is with deep sincerity.
3. He who believes himself to be self-sufficient, neither giving nor receiving nourishment, will experience a period of misfortune.
4. Be like a hungry tiger. Find the right nourishment. Be willing to share it with others.
5. One is not qualified to give nourishment independently. Continue working with superiors and good fortune will result.
6. Awareness of the need to give nourishment to others impartially brings good fortune. The task is great, but one can overcome all the difficulties involved.

Hexagram 28   Ta Kuo ☰ *Inner Preponderance*

SIMPLE TRANSLATION OF TEXT
Inner Preponderance. The ridgepole sags precariously. Pursuing a goal is advantageous. Success.

COMMENTARY
This hexagram is heavy in the middle with Yang lines, with a weak Yin line at each end. The inner hexagram is entirely Yang. The visual appearance of this hexagram reminded ancient sages of the ridgepole used to support the roofs of their early houses. The pole rose diagonally from the ground. Being heavy in the middle, here, it sags precariously. This hexagram consists of the trigrams Tui, lake, over Sun, wood, with the meaning of penetration. Externally, these persons have the wherewithal to nourish others. Inwardly, they are firm and stable, like wood. Hence, it is desirable for these persons to have a goal where the potential of nourishment can be used. If this is done they have success. They are always in danger of being too one-sided in their thoughts and deeds. This could be dangerous if they use their great, innate inner strength selfishly. They must be impartial, to the maximum extent possible. On the other hand their great inner strength permits them to be undaunted, even if they have to stand alone. So it can be a blessing or a drawback, depending on how it is used.

Those born in the second month will be more auspicious.

CONTROLLING LINES (FROM BOTTOM TO TOP)
Line 1   Place white reed mats underneath. No error.

Strong and courageous individuals are depicted, who use deep sincerity and exceptional care in all they do. They are very meticulous. They should be differentiated from those persons who are small-minded and who devote their time to details out of fear. Those with this controlling line are very considerate to everybody and everything, and give forth loving care as if all these were their own cherished possessions. These individuals can be found in nearly all walks of life.
Most auspicious: He will be a man of impeccable character and

behaviour, highly respected and widely known. He will treat everyone as a worthwhile person, and be exceptionally careful and considerate to his subordinates. He will have a favorable life, with many joys, good fortune and wealth.

Least auspicious: He will be content with his lot, neither envious nor greedy. He may choose to live in seclusion; and he will make no major errors.

In yearly hexagram:

Officer or official	His position will be firm and unassailable.
Business and professional	He should exercise great care and economy in his endeavors; he will advance slowly.
Ordinary people	He should be cautious and frugal and he will have adequate money for his basic needs. One of the parents of the less auspicious may die.

Line 2 New shoots grow from the withered willow. An older man has a young wife. Blessings accrue.

With the strong preponderance of Yang lines in the middle, line 2 cannot join its normal correlate, line 5, and hence chooses line 1. Line 5, for the same reason, chooses line 6 for its partner, hence here it is an older man choosing a young wife, while in the upper case it is an older woman taking a younger man for a husband. Exceptional strength and vigor are thus coupled here with the wisdom of age. Despite the unusualness of this it is a productive union. Many blessings accrue from the fortuitous combination of the characteristics of a wise old man and the dynamic vitality of a young girl.

Most auspicious: He will be a person who knows what he wants, and who goes after it correctly and diligently. He will fight for what is right and for his possessions, even if he must do so independently. He has a commendable and respectable character, and will gradually abandon waywardness for *tao*. He will have a fortuitous life, with meritable achievements.

Least auspicious: He will have many hardships early in life, but will be moderately prosperous, and somewhat influential locally, in his senior years.

In yearly hexagram:

Officer or official	He will hold his position, or, if unemployed, will return to a favorable position.
Business and professional	With unusual effort or ideas he will make considerable progress, personally and professionally.
Ordinary people	The size of his family will increase; otherwise it will be a routine year.

Line 3 The ridgepole sags dangerously. Misfortune.

Too much of anything is dangerous. One should follow the golden mean, i.e. not go to extremes. Those depicted here are not judicious, and do not know when to stop nor when to seek the support of others. Their actions in general are rash, wilful, self-centered and, above all, excessive. They are reluctant to delegate authority and responsibility to others. As a result of their traits their friends and their accomplishments are few.

Most auspicious: He will be a brave, ambitious and impetuous person, anxious to help people, and his country, but too tough and fierce to be truly effective. His results, in most cases, will be negative rather than positive.

Least auspicious: He has little or no judgment or common sense. He is very violent and fierce, and disasters follow in his wake.

In yearly hexagram:

Officer or official	He may be dismissed, demoted, or seriously reprimanded.
Business and professional	His position will be precarious, and his efforts not readily accepted.
Ordinary people	A generally troublesome year. He may have difficulty with his feet or eyes.

Line 4 The ridgepole is arched. Good fortune. If independence is not exercised, humiliation.

The arching of metal or glass structures makes them able to uphold more weight or withstand more pressure than they could otherwise. Therefore these are individuals who have found that little something extra which makes for true greatness. Their knowledge, wisdom, habits, actions, thoughts, and conversation are all superior. It is divine will that if one has gifts and talents one should use them to help nourish and sustain others. If this is not done, humiliations will result.

Most auspicious: He will be greatly talented, wise, valiant, far-sighted and energetic. He will be a pillar of the nation, accomplishing many things of great merit, and will be respected both nationally and internationally. He will have a good life.

Least auspicious: He will have a similar life to the most auspicious, but not to such a high degree. He will be quite valuable wherever he is assigned or finds himself, and his work and household will flourish.

In yearly hexagram:

Officer or official	He will be appointed to a high position.
Business and professional	He will advance, and achieve a highly favorable reputation.
Ordinary people	A good year. He may build or remodel his house.

Line 5 The withered willow produces blossoms. An older woman has a young husband. No blame. No praise.

This symbolism stems from the correlation with line 6 (see the commentary under line 2). Basically, it says that individuals who wait too long in life to try and accomplish something worthwhile, when they finally convince themselves that they are ready find that the persons then willing to join them are of the wrong kind, so that nothing fruitful results. Such people are not to be blamed for their late effort, but when nothing truly worthwhile is accomplished they cannot be praised either. Such persons demonstrate dual characteristics throughout their lives, until they eventually reach a firm decision. Subsequently, they are no longer flexible.

Most auspicious: Will be vacillating early in life, and later extremely unyielding. He will enjoy the association of strong but mean people, but with a good possibility of changing in this regard later in life. While he will have adequate food and shelter he will not accomplish anything worthwhile, and hence have no fame. His actions will not be subject to blame either.

Least auspicious: He is likely to have an older, shrewish, vigorous wife, or be subject to a domineering mother. What ability and talents he will have will be ordinary, and his life will be difficult. In yearly hexagram:

Officer or official	He should not stay in his present position long. Change is indicated.
Business and professional	It will be hard to advance or make gains.
Ordinary people	Adverse circumstances early on, becoming favorable later.

Line 6 Fording the stream. The water goes over his head. Misfortune. No personal blame.

In life there are circumstances that demand great effort, courage and self-sacrifice from a limited few. These persons are adventurers and explorers, scientists, engineers, astronauts, etc. They will have much in common with the early American pioneers. In combat, they are the leaders of advance units. They are the master-minds and executors of worthwhile movements, and their sacrifices pave the way for the less courageous.

Most auspicious: He will have great strength, talent, and courage. He will be in high positions and face serious dangers, and he will be righteous and selfless. He may die for his cause and have his name recorded in history.

Least auspicious: He will be ambitious and will strive with high intentions, but he will be limited in talent and tend to be reckless and to act without due consideration, which will result in troubles and disasters.

In yearly hexagram:

Officer or official	He may sacrifice himself professionally for some cause.
Business and professional	Only the exceptional will make gains.
Ordinary people	He will have troubles and illnesses, and may die.

KEYNOTES
1. At the start of anything use extraordinary care.
2. Join with persons of lesser status for greater cooperation.
3. Carelessness results in misfortune.
4. Talent plus inspiration makes for superiority.

5. Sometimes waiting too long can be disastrous.
6. Pursue only worthy goals.

CONDENSATIONS FOR DAILY CYCLES

1. Extraordinary care must be exercised at the beginning of any enterprise so that no errors are made.
2. Success will be achieved best if one joins with persons of lesser rank or status.
3. If the extraordinary situation is not handled correctly misfortune will result.
4. You now know the right way to deal with the situation and good fortune will result.
5. Using ancient or outmoded methods will not be productive, even though nothing wrong or unjust is done.
6. Striving for success when one is inadequately prepared to master the situation leads to failure, but one should not be condemned for the attempt. If adequately prepared, be adventurous and willing to take the consequences.

Hexagram 29   *K'an* ☵ *The Abyss*

SIMPLE TRANSLATION OF TEXT

Abyss upon Abyss. Maintaining a sanguine attitude and a stable mind induces respect, and results in success.

COMMENTARY

Water never stops from its source to the sea. When it meets obstacles it pauses, builds up until it can go over or around them, and then proceeds onward. Water is not strong, yet through continued application it can wear down rocks and metal. It succeeds in reaching its goal going forward step by step, yet ever true to itself and its purpose. The words 'abyss upon abyss' refer to the appearance of the two trigrams, each having a deep ravine between mounds of earth. Water flows through these ravines as well as overcoming impediments in its path. Those depicted here should emulate water and be ever true to themselves in heart and mind, and firm in their purposes. They should maintain sanguineness and keep their minds stable. By doing these things they can attain success upon success, both small and great. Emulating water is a matter of knowing how to use situations for protection as well as for advancement. Great wisdom and advantageous progress go with those well versed in the laws of nature applicable here.

Those born in the tenth month will be more auspicious.

CONTROLLING LINES (FROM BOTTOM TO TOP)
Line 1 Abyss upon abyss. In one he encounters a fissure. Misfortune.

Those depicted here have a similar character to that described in the commentary for the hexagram as a whole, but regrettably they have some great weakness of character which drains their potential or energy. 'A fissure' is indicative of such weakness, in that fissures let water flow off elsewhere or become absorbed within the ground. This weakness could be gambling, alcohol, sex, a sport or a pastime, etc., which may not be wrong in other circumstances but becomes too important to these persons, because of the extensive degree to which its effects are felt.

Most auspicious: He will recognize the deficiencies within himself, and will adjust to them or compensate for them, so that even though he will have many difficulties his principal goals will eventually be achieved.

Least auspicious: He will be timid, injudicious, non-analytical and shy. Fortune will not favor him, and he will find it difficult to make his own way.

In yearly hexagram:

Officer or official	He may be dismissed, demoted or reprimanded.
Business and professional	Some actions will result in damage to his reputation.
Ordinary people	Only monks or recluses can avoid troubles.

Line 2 Danger in the abyss. One can bring only small things to completion.

Here a great many divergent matters have to be taken care of along the way, so that forward progress is but slight. The situation resembles an obstacle in the path of the Colorado River in the Grand Canyon. As the water builds up it has to fill many side canyons before the level is high enough for the water to advance again. Such obstacles are circumstances beyond one's control, but in man's progress there are certain lessons he must learn, and perhaps even repeat, before he is duly qualified to proceed further. These persons are enjoined to be content with that which is available and attainable.

Most auspicious: He will be a person of strong character, persevering in his purposes, and doing everything that is necessary to achieve them. He will be a leader in times of grave necessity for the nation, and will have the wisdom with which to bring and keep peace among the people.

Least auspicious: He is unable to do anything on a large scale. He is annoyed by any multiple requirements placed on him, but can achieve some small gains on a limited basis.

In yearly hexagram:

Officer or official	He will have several small accomplishments, but no great ones.
Business and professional	As for officer or official.
Ordinary people	An average year with many activities.

Line 3 Forward and backward. Abyss upon abyss. He falls into a pit in the abyss. Do not act.

When there is heavy rain, or snow melts in areas where there are no regular streams, the water first tries to find its way out through one abyss after another, flowing back and forth, searching for the right way to advance. Here the rivulet reaches a pit and no advancement is possible. The best one can do in such a circumstance is to remain true to oneself and not try to accomplish great things. These persons are apart from the main stream of life, and have no fixed goals that they are capable of attaining.

Most auspicious: While not being able to assist, lead or guide others, he is able to sustain himself and his family without serious troubles.

Least auspicious: He will be very poor, with many hardships all his life. He will have little or no ambition, yet be critical of others.

In yearly hexagram:

Officer or official	A year for retreat or quiet preparations.

Business and professional	A year for renewing or improving professional knowledge.
Ordinary people	Many disputes and other troubles.

Line 4 A jug of spirits. A bamboo basket of rice, and earthenware bowls. Introduced to him through an opening. His actions are free from blame.

Remembering that this hexagram refers to an abyss, and that the fourth line is the position of the minister, this pictures the minister living next to the king, perhaps in caves in the side of the abyss, and the minister supplying emergency nourishment to the ruler through an opening between the two dwellings. These persons will be in high positions, aware of the needs of their families, their work, their rulers and their nation, and will give support freely, generously, sincerely and honestly. They will do this within due bounds and limits, such that no obligations accrue. They will not seek any gain from their support.

Most auspicious: He will be quite wise, with his advice sought and accepted. This advice can be used to advantage, nationally and internationally. He will be modest, honest and sincere, and will not seek luxury or fame, but he may obtain both.

Least auspicious: He will find everything easy to accomplish, but will have insufficient wisdom for great things, and his will will fluctuate. Hence he will have easy gains and easy losses, some good fortune and some bad luck, some good years and some bad. Throughout it all he will still have adequate means to support himself and his family.

In yearly hexagram:

Officer or official	He is likely to be appointed to a planning, or staff position.
Business and professional	He will make some gains and also sustain some losses.
Ordinary people	An average year. Someone in the family will marry.

Line 5 The abyss is not filled to the top. It will adjust itself. No error.

Here we have water seeking its own level and ready to overcome obstacles as necessary. Furthermore, it has the potential to produce energy or nourish. However, this potential must be used in the service of others. These persons are in a ruling position (line 5) and make great and wise administrators. They give their subordinates ample latitude and let them perform their duties, while themselves retaining responsibility for their actions. They exemplify the natural law that water has only to rise high enough to surmount the obstacle in order to advance. They especially avoid excesses.

Most auspicious: He will be a man of wide knowledge and great wisdom, full of human understanding and kindness, following the golden mean, and guiding and supporting others with sound judgment and common sense. He will be a man with a cosmic destiny to fulfil for the benefit of the world and the universe. He will enjoy rendering service, and will consider his life quite serene and joyful.

Least auspicious: He will have above average talents and character. He will be able to quell small disturbances and settle disputes readily. On the whole, he will have an easy and smooth life.

In yearly hexagram:

Officer or official	A good year.
Business and professional	He will make small gains. Large gains will come later.
Ordinary people	Plans will go smoothly. An enjoyable year.

Line 6 Bound with thongs and ropes. Restrained by a thorn hedge. Three years of failures in his quest for a course. Misfortune.

The individual depicted here, instead of following the flow of the water, has tried to get out of the abyss by using the sides. He has become entangled in a hedge of thorns, no doubt there for the protection of someone else's property or possessions. These individuals are prone to try quick remedies, quick escapes, and quick paths to their goals, instead of the longer but safer, proven methods. They will experience many entanglements and difficulties as a result of their short-sightedness, their fear of moving forward step by step, and the follies associated with their thinking. Eventually they can learn the right way to overcome their difficulties, and make normal progress again.

Most auspicious: It will be beneficial for these individuals to live in seclusion to the maximum extent practicable, disregarding

worldly matters, and developing themselves inwardly. Life will
not be easy, but something worthwhile may eventually result.
Least auspicious: He will be quite unfortunate. He will separate
from his family, and have many troubles and insults; he may
even be imprisoned. He will have a short life.
In yearly hexagram:

Officer or official	He may be arrested, or demoted.
Business and professional	He will have difficulties continuously in his enterprise.
Ordinary people	Disputes, lawsuits, and even incarceration are likely.

KEYNOTES

1. Always be on the lookout for incorrect ideas.
2. At most times it is best to proceed directly ahead.
3. When in a quandary, do not advance.
4. Maintain serenity to the best of your ability.
5. When moving ahead, advance in the manner of water.
6. Rashness leads to entanglements.

CONDENSATIONS FOR DAILY CYCLES

1. You are muddled regarding some important matter. Reevaluate the situation, and begin again later.
2. There is danger on both sides. Proceed slowly ahead.
3. Do not act. Any step taken, in any direction, will lead to difficulties.
4. You are mixed up in troubles which are not your fault, or of your own making. Maintaining clarity and serenity keeps one free from making errors.
5. Just as water only rises high enough to overcome its immediate obstacles, so you should do likewise in your forward progress in these circumstances.
6. In keeping with the law of change, a period of inevitable decline is taking place. Hold back.

Hexagram 30   Li ☲ Clinging Light (Fire)

SIMPLE TRANSLATION OF TEXT
Clinging Light. Persistent correctness advantageous. Success.
Care of the cow. Good fortune.

COMMENTARY

The trigram Li doubled symbolizes duration of the light. There are two bright flames, which by perpetuating their brilliance, can light up the four corners of the earth. For there to be light there must be something for it to cling to, a medium against which it is contrasted. 'Care of the cow' symbolizes nourishment and the protection of docility and usefulness. These persons are men of strong faith and firm principles to which they adhere in the conduct of life. They have the potential to be leaders but are inclined to be narrow-minded. They tend to become experts in specialized matters of interest to themselves, at the same time laying a path for others to follow. They have leanings towards extremes; e.g. in spiritual matters they may be devoted ascetics or possibly saints. They perform a very valuable service by being examples to others. Usually, their actions and lives will become well known, and with the exercise of care their lives can be of great benefit to others and bring good fortune to themselves.

Those born in the fourth, fifth and sixth months will be more auspicious.

CONTROLLING LINES (FROM BOTTOM TO TOP)

Line 1 Walking with confused steps. Reverence, care and sincerity evade errors.

Confused steps are invariably made at the beginning of any enterprise or state of affairs. So it is here at the beginning of clarity. In general, these persons will be energetic and ambitious, with a goal of sorts in their minds. They will be diligent in their efforts yet ever seeking something more, but uncertain as to what exactly this should be. They will make considerable progress throughout their lives, but cannot be expected to rise to great heights.

Most auspicious: He will be reverent and loyal to his obligations, and responsibilities, and meticulous in their execution. He will be wise in a limited way, and will seek opportunities to be useful and of service. He will make modest gains.

Least auspicious: He will also know how to perform his duties, and will carry them out reasonably well within narrow limits. He will make many mistakes early in life, but will reform and enjoy a good life later.

In yearly hexagram:

Officer or official	Haste can result in waste. Be slow and deliberate.
Business and professional	Haste or unthoroughness in carrying out activities will be damaging.
Ordinary people	Stay within established limits, or trouble will ensue. He may be injured by a slip or a fall.

Line 2 Yellow Light. Sublime good fortune.

When someone is working with great clarity for someone else, and doing so fairly and impartially, sublime good fortune can result. This line is the strong correlate of line 5, the ruler; hence this man is in a key supporting role, helping to provide good administration and government through exceptional clarity. These persons will have the innate ability to see things clearly and in their proper perspective, at whatever level they may be operating. Their life will be one of service and benefit to others, and they will set a good example.

Most auspicious: He will be an advisor to, or an administrator for, the leader of his country, the local government, or a commercial enterprise, and thereby help the nation to flourish culturally and economically. He will be a man of virtue, modesty, gentility and consideration, following the golden mean. Good fortune will be his in all phases of his life.

Least auspicious: He will also be a careful and forthright person, paying close attention to his every activity, whether personal or professional. He will have an easy and happy life.

In yearly hexagram:

Officer or official	He will be honored and rewarded.
Business and professional	He will excel over others when in competition with them.
Ordinary people	A good year with many gains.

Line 3 In the light of the setting sun the young do not beat their pots and sing; the old bemoan their age. Misfortune.

In the trigram Li, the bottom line represents sunrise, the middle line the main part of the day, and the upper line the period of the setting of the sun. The beauty of sunsets is fluctuating and transient, and the time bodes of darkness to follow. Hence these persons are inveterately pessimistic, and always think that where they have been is better than where they are going. They glory in the past and try to avoid the future, and their energies are spent in the wrong directions. In general, they are not very helpful to themselves, their families, or any activity or enterprise with which they are associated.

Most auspicious: He will be knowledgeable regarding the cycles in life of rise and decline, gain and failure, etc., and will act solely in keeping with the law of change, without striving to overcome it. He will be content with his lot, whether it is good or bad.

Least auspicious: His actions and endeavors will probably result in serious damage to himself. He may lose any wealth he possesses or accumulates. He will have an unfortunate family life as well.

In yearly hexagram:

Officer or official	He will probably retire.
Business and professional	He will experience a major setback.
Ordinary people	There will be all sorts of difficulties this year.

Line 4   Meteoric clarity. Its coming is sudden. It flares up and dies away.

These persons have great energy and dynamism when they first start a new job or any project. They show characteristics of being truly great but these usually fade away quite quickly. Their knowledge is limited in scope, their energies are rapidly expended, and their durability is questionable.

Most auspicious: He will be over ambitious, and unable to hold any position long, constantly chopping and changing, and hence never rising very high. Endurance will be lacking in almost everything he does, but despite this he will have an above average status in life.

Least auspicious: He will not follow the golden mean, and will be unjust, arrogant, unruly, and offensive. He will have many difficulties throughout a probably short life.

In yearly hexagram:

Officer or official	He may try to usurp authority, or at least be suspected of it.
Business and professional	Some quick gains will be made, but he will not be able to enjoy them, owing to mistakes.

| Ordinary people | He will offend superiors, and meet with troubles and possible disasters because of it. |

Line 5   Great tears of dismay and regret. Good fortune.

This is the position of the king or ruler. He sees everything with great clarity, and seeks the best for his country and his enterprises. He is very knowledgeable and wise, and understands the weaknesses and frailties of human nature. He observes the inept attempts by those who try their best to do right but as yet are not on the right path. He would like to help each and every person to improve himself inwardly and outwardly, and he does his best to set a proper example, and to promulgate such rules and regulations as will best help the maximum number of people.

Most auspicious: He will be a man of great vision and clarity working for the good of mankind, with his life and actions resulting in much harmony. He will be peaceful and gentle in nature, yet firm in his purposes and goals. He will enjoy a long, rich and noble life.

Least auspicious: He will have much clarity, but will lack the stamina and courage to carry out what he knows needs to be done. He is unable to assume the necessary authority to be great and successful. He will have many hardships, but his senior years will tend to be smoother through reaping the rewards of some of his earlier efforts.

In yearly hexagram:

Officer or official	Those 'in' will be very fortunate. Those 'out' will be quite unfortunate.
Business and professional	Only tried and proven methods will be successful.
Ordinary people	The more auspicious will make gains. Those less auspicious will probably experience sorrowful circumstances.

Line 6   The king goes forth and chastizes the rebels. He punishes the leaders but grants amnesty to the followers. No error.

These individuals are amongst those who are required to ferret out erroneous aims and procedures, in whatever profession and at whatever level they are operating. The gamut of possibilities is boundless since perfection does not exist on this earth. These persons are filling a definite need in eradicating the wrong rules or procedures and wrong leadership. This is a necessity, consequently they will experience no error in their so doing.

Most auspicious: He will be courageous, wise, valiant and effective, in either, or both, civil and military matters, with sufficient talents and abilities to be a blessing to the nation. He will have a rich and rewarding life.

Least auspicious: He will not have a high status or station in life, yet will assist in making corrections. He will not be destitute, but will not have much wealth either. He may suffer from head or eye troubles.

In yearly hexagram:

Officer or official	He will establish merit. If a military officer, he may be assigned to combat duty.
Business and professional	He will advance and profit through corrective activities.
Ordinary people	A joyful year, with gains.

KEYNOTES

1. Light needs contrast to be seen.
2. Follow the middle way.
3. The beauty of the sunset is transient.
4. Meteoric clarity is inadequate.
5. Overcome fears through clarity.
6. Make corrections with clarity.

CONDENSATIONS FOR DAILY CYCLES

1. In beginning anything one is not certain as to the best way to proceed. Maintain seriousness, and the right way will be found.
2. Follow the golden mean in thought, word and deed, and much success will result.
3. Your clarity is dimming. Act according to the dictates of the circumstances. Do not dwell on the past.
4. Meteoric clarity bodes no permanent good. Base clarity on sound foundations, and maintain it constantly.
5. Conquer fears. Inwardly adhere to what is right and proper, and good fortune will result.

6. Make whatever corrections are necessary, and pass on quickly to other matters.

Hexagram 31   Hsien ☱☶ *Stimulation (Compelling)*

SIMPLE TRANSLATION OF TEXT
Stimulation. Success. Persist in what is right and just. It is favorable to marry a young wife.

COMMENTARY
Here we have a lake on the top of a mountain, i.e. the trigram Tui above Kên, indicating the potentiality of great nourishment over a wide area and a variety of conditions, where the water, when used, will stimulate growth and development. Some lakes on mountains are large and of great value. Others are small and of but little intrinsic worth. All, however, serve useful purposes. Their value depends on where they are, and their availability for useful purposes. These persons will have potentialities in whatever fields or enterprises they elect to involve themselves. Their inherent usefulness is great wherever they may be, but it will depend largely on themselves as to how they want their gifts to be used. This, of course, will determine the quality and magnitude of their successes. Working with those full of dynamic energy will prove favorable.

Those born in the first month will be more auspicious.

CONTROLLING LINES (FROM BOTTOM TO TOP)
Line 1   Stimulation of the big toe.

The lake over the mountain, as it is used in the hexagram, is also symbolic of man. A man's progress in movement begins with the big toe. The lowest line in this hexagram is also the foot of the mountain, so we therefore have the beginning of stimulation, with its consequent influence. Since it is only the big toe it is not of great consequence, and as yet the 'stimulation' is neither good nor bad. Matters are more or less still in the planning stage, and these persons will, by and large, be planners on a modest scale. The number of actions that they initiate will be small.
Most auspicious: He is likely to be born into a family of low

status, and he will be ambitious to rise above his background. He has the power to make good plans, but his influence will not be great, and hence his achievements will be modest. He will enjoy a more substantial life in his later years.

Least auspicious: In general, his plans will exceed his capabilities, and he will not be successful. He will leave his home in middle age; however, he will not be a pauper.

In yearly hexagram:

Officer or official	Only slow progress will be made.
Business and professional	Modest expansions may be beneficial.
Ordinary people	Plans will tend to go awry. Stick to known methods and procedures.

Line 2 Stimulation in the calves of the legs. Misfortune. Waiting brings good fortune.

The calves achieve nothing by themselves, i.e. they represent followers. Their stimulation alone is of little purpose unless it serves higher aims and goals. In general, these persons have a specialized function which they must use to cooperate in a larger enterprise. They are vital cogs in the machinery as a whole.

Most auspicious: He will be well qualified to perform his assigned duties, and will have a keen sense of timing, especially relating to initiating actions and following them up. He will have a pleasant personality and an innate goodness of character. His life will be free from disasters, and will be quite favorable in many aspects.

Least auspicious: He will be selfish, egotistical, greedy and over ambitious. He will face many troubles in supporting himself and his family.

In yearly hexagram:

Officer or official	Those who remain at the center of activity will fare well. Those sent into the field will experience difficulties.
Business and professional	Hold back. The time is not propitious for advancement or expansions.
Ordinary people	Much effort will be expended, with but few concrete results.

Line 3 Stimulation of the thighs. He holds close to whom he follows. Continuing will lead to regret.

The divine Creator would like everyone to have independence within limits. Here the thighs are following on the torso so closely that there is no room for independence. Hence, this situation is like that of a man following the lead of his wife, or following rules and regulations too literally, without exercising judgment regarding intentions and thereby being inflexible in thought and opinions. Unless these persons amend their thoughts, words and deeds they will have cause for regret.

Most auspicious: He will not be very independent, but will know when to advance and when to stop. He will do well in a subordinate position of leadership, where the execution of the promulgated policies and procedures is vital. In general, he will be free from major mistakes.

Least auspicious: He will be good at planning, but his execution will leave much to be desired. He will do well working for someone else, but will fail if he proceeds independently.

In yearly hexagram:

Officer or official	Prepare for possible demotion through being blamed for failures.
Business and professional	In general, below average results are to be expected.
Ordinary people	He will fare well by adhering to normal leadership.

Line 4 Persistence in correctness results in good fortune. Remorse vanishes. Agitations and inconsistencies; vacillations. Only those on whom he concentrates follow.

This line is the ruler of this hexagram, and the place of the heart is indicated. The external results one attains are the product of the inner self, i.e. the influence and actions stemming from the heart. If these are correct they stimulate all, impartially. However, if one pursues narrow goals only those on whom one mentally concentrates will follow (by telepathic stimulation). These persons will, on the whole, exert much influence on their surroundings, their associates and their families. The quality of their endeavors will depend on their inner worth and the goals they set themselves.

Most auspicious: He will be a person with lofty aims and definite goals, which he will pursue with diligence and persistence. He will be flexible in mind yet firm in purpose, and will be just and sincere, having no evil intentions. He will be a leader in a high position, establishing progress and order to the satisfaction of a great many people. He will have a good and rewarding **life.**

Least auspicious: He will be muddle-headed, and will taste the toil and hardships of a normal struggle for existence. His influence will be local only, yet of value, since he is inwardly striving for what is right and just.

In yearly hexagram:

Officer or official	He will be assigned to a powerful position, with possible promotion.
Business and professional	The area and scope of his influence will increase.
Ordinary people	Small things are favored. Great enterprises should not be undertaken.

Line 5 Stimulation of the shoulder muscles. No regret.

These muscles exert little influence by themselves, but they protect the vital spinal column and the associated nerves. Hence these individuals may be found in such positions as treasurer, public accountant, quality controller, or in any other position which helps protect the vital elements and communication networks in government, business or industry.

Most auspicious: He will have lofty aims and will carry them out with the support and backing of his superiors. He will possess great fortitude and be quite imperturbable; he will consider that he has a good life.

Least auspicious: He will be narrow in vision and phlegmatic in action. He may use his position for selfish purposes, and will have very little good fortune.

In yearly hexagram:

Officer or official	He will maintain a stable position.
Business and professional	Progress will be difficult.
Ordinary people	Disputes are likely. He will have very few gains, if any.

Line 6 Stimulation through the tongue and jaws.

The possibilities of stimulation and influence through the tongue and the jaws range from the effect of idle chatter to the revelation of what lies deep within one's inner self. The latter is usually of great and lasting benefit, whereas the former may have no real worth, and may be seductive or erroneous. In general, these persons will be loquacious, as well as being fluent writers. Their natural propensities will be to try and influence others or stimulate them into actions through the use of words.

Most auspicious: He will be a deep thinker of dynamic personality, whose orations and or writings will greatly influence people, nationally and internationally. He will be trusted and respected at all stages in his life, and will be praised by the people. He will have a beneficial and rewarding life.

Least auspicious: He is likely to be dogmatic and pedagogic, stirring up the people with ill-conceived ideas, many of which will be erroneous. He will bring troubles to others, and probably disaster to himself.

In yearly hexagram:

Officer or official	He will be erroneously blamed, and slandered.
Business and professional	His activities will be subject to much undue criticism.
Ordinary people	He will be subjected to, or associate with, propagandists. This will not be beneficial.

KEYNOTES
1. Advance circumspectly.
2. Specialize in something.
3. Strive for independence.
4. Be sincere of heart.
5. Support others carefully. Do not make them feel under obligations.
6. Speak only with depth.

CONDENSATIONS FOR DAILY CYCLES
1. Ideas can be held in the mind. If no actions are taken, the result is neither good nor bad. Ponder further before acting.
2. If one has no control over a situation it is best to keep clear of it. Remain devoted to what is right.

3. Think carefully. Do you want to follow someone else's ideas, or are your own better?
4. Your influence is at its peak. Follow the dictates of your heart.
5. You should not try to influence others if you are not sure within yourself.
6. The influence of mere tongue-wagging is not very successful. Be sure that words are backed by real worth, and that your position is tenable.

Hexagram 32 Héng ☰☷ Constancy (Enduring)

SIMPLE TRANSLATION OF TEXT
Constancy. Success. No error. With righteousness and correctness, firm progress advantageous.

COMMENTARY
Here we have the eldest son, Chên, leading the eldest daughter, Sun. Chên is firm and Sun is yielding. Thus they are in perfect harmony and equilibrium. This signifies constancy and durability, like the motion of the heavenly bodies in the universe. Each has its own orbit; each exerts a constant degree of influence, and each sheds light according to its strength. All exhibit a constancy throughout their existence. They perform their roles with ease, and no errors result from their actions. Those born under this hexagram have the potential to manifest these qualities of the heavenly bodies throughout their lives, through the exercise of righteousness and through making progress in pursuit of their goals. Being human they will probably show weakness and vacillation occasionally, but in the end they will arrive at whatever destination they have set for themselves.

Those born in the first month will be more auspicious.

CONTROLLING LINES (FROM BOTTOM TO TOP)
Line 1 Striving for constancy too hastily results in misfortune. Such a course not advantageous.

Those things in nature which are enduring develop gradually and consistently. Nothing which develops quickly is durable. Consider, for instance, trees growing, in comparison with swamp plants. Furthermore, if one tries to help things grow by stretching them, one soon destroys them. Only proper cultural activities are beneficial. Regrettably, most of these persons will strive for quick results by taking short cuts. These individuals are likely to be egotistical, conceited, opinionated, and impetuous, and thereby, on the whole, unable to make correct and proper evaluations.

Most auspicious: A few will know how to judge actual situations and make appropriate plans before taking action, and will therefore be able to achieve modest results and a good life.

Least auspicious: Most will be too impetuous, and not content with their lives; they will tend to act without due deliberation, and will encounter hindrances in whatever they try.

In yearly hexagram:

Officer or official	He will not be trusted or respected by his ruler or manager, and will experience many trying situations.
Business and professional	It will be difficult for him to find due recognition.
Ordinary people	He will tend to be frequently unreasonable, with bad results. By keeping quiet he can avoid difficulties.

Line 2 Occasion for regret disappears.

This line is the ruler of the hexagram, and is a positive line leading a negative line; it is also supported by its proper correlate, line 5. Therefore these persons are in leading positions and follow the golden mean, exemplifying constancy in all their actions. They base their decisions on sound evaluations using good and wise judgment, and then pursue their aims, both great and small, with a praiseworthy constancy that invariably achieves its purposes.

Most auspicious: He will be a noble and honored person, following the golden mean and cherishing virtue and goodness. He will quickly turn away from erroneous paths and make his reforms permanent. The results will be a blessing and a benefit to many, and he will have a long, rich and rewarding life.

Least auspicious: He will also have a beneficial life without misfortune, but on a lower level or smaller scale. He will be honored locally, and have a good family life and adequate means.

247

In yearly hexagram:

Officer or official	He should be careful and meticulous, and he will have a good year.
Business and professional	He should devote much effort to self-improvement, with beneficial external effects.
Ordinary people	He will have a good year, with no extremes.

Line 3 His constancy wavers and he meets with disgrace. Continuation will lead to regret.

Weak-willed and vacillating individuals are depicted here. They are easily led by others, and change their desires and goals frequently. To them the grass always seems greener on the other side, and they live in day-dreams rather than reality. Prolonged activity of this sort leads nowhere, hence, regrets result.

Most auspicious: He is unable to hold what is right, and hence is constantly criticized and jeered at. His life will be troubled.

Least auspicious: He will be impervious to all that is good, and he will become infamous.

In yearly hexagram:

Officer or official	He will probably be demoted or dismissed.
Business and professional	He will receive reprobation if guilty of using shady methods.
Ordinary people	Disputes and lawsuits are likely.

Line 4 No game in the field.

One cannot find something which is not there to be found. If you want to make money, for example, you must go to where the money is. If you want to go skiing, you must first go and find some snow. These persons are fairly gifted in childhood, but their impracticality keeps them from advancing, and they will possibly also lose whatever advantage they had. They are envious of their neighbors and try to outdo them by wrong means. Their aims and purposes are invariably erroneous.

Most auspicious: He may make money and obtain a favorable position by uncommon means or skills, but his fortune will not last long.

Least auspicious: He will have a humble and mundane existence.

In yearly hexagram:

Officer or official	He will regress a step.
Business and professional	He will fail to make any substantial gains.
Ordinary people	He will expend much effort without deriving any great benefits.

Line 5   Maintaining enduring constancy brings good fortune to a woman but is wrong for a man.

The symbolism is that it is right for a wife to follow the lead of her husband through thick and thin, and brings good fortune to the couple. Conversely, such action on the part of the man, i.e. being an unquestioning follower, an obsequious person or a yes-man, is the wrong procedure to follow for a successful life. To advance this man must be an independent thinker, adjusting to changing circumstances and always ready to take action according to the dictates of the situation, yet keeping his goals constantly in sight. Most auspicious: He will receive help from his wife or a female member of his family which will enable him to establish himself in a moderately good position and circumstances.
Least auspicious: He will let others assume authority and hence will never attain any substantial responsibility. He will not be able to make adequate plans, and those that he does make will never materialize or are of no real importance. He is likely to have a nagging, shrewish wife.
In yearly hexagram:

Officer or official	He will be blamed for making flattering reports rather than presenting actual facts.
Business and professional	If he attempts to advance surreptitiously he will be found out, and blame will accrue.
Ordinary people	He will receive blame for matters that are not entirely his fault.

Line 6   A constancy of nervous agitation results in misfortune.

This line reflects the most extreme state of impatience and agitated behavior. This person cannot wait for a natural sequence of events to take place, and is constantly striving for hasty culminations and foreknowledge of final results instead of relying on proper analysis, good judgment and experience.

Most auspicious: He will be wise and strong enough to curb and overcome his natural propensity towards recklessness and agitation. He will control his impatience to within due limits, and the result will be an average life with few troubles.

Least auspicious: He will be unable to curb his eagerness and recklessness. He will try to do some good occasionally but, on the whole, will accomplish little. Sometimes he will display unseemly behaviour and as a result have trouble with his superiors.

In yearly hexagram:

For everyone	A year of impatient and rash actions, with no truly fruitful results.

KEYNOTES
1. Do not seek lasting results hastily.
2. Follow the golden mean.
3. Vacillations end in disaster.
4. Search only where one's quarry can be found.
5. The creative must lead for success.
6. Indecisiveness is dangerous.

CONDENSATIONS FOR DAILY CYCLES
1. Do not be hasty. Allow things to develop according to their nature.
2. Following the golden mean will produce the results you want.
3. Vacillation and inconsistency lead to humiliation and disgrace.
4. One cannot attain the unattainable, nor that which is not meant for one.
5. Be creative and lead in a superior manner. Constantly following leads only to misfortune.
6. Indecisiveness, especially in a position of authority, will result in nothing worthwhile being accomplished. Sometimes even a wrong decision resulting in some action is better than no decision at all.

Hexagram 33   Tun ☰☷ *Retiring (Withdrawal)*

SIMPLE TRANSLATION OF TEXT
Retiring. Success. Persistence in small matters advantageous.

COMMENTARY

The symbolism is derived from the motion of the two trigrams and the nature of the inner hexagram. The trigram Ch'ien, heaven, which moves upward, is over the trigram Kên, mountain, which stands still. The inner hexagram shows a return of small matters. The Chinese set great store by being wise like Ch'ien, and also by retiring from difficult and inflexible situations like Kên, whereby through their silence or lack of contact both parties can save face. The meaning of such actions is well understood by the persons concerned, and the key to success is the wisdom with which the right moment for retirement is chosen and implemented. Persons exhibiting these traits can be found in all walks of life and at all levels. These persons will have a natural propensity for, or the potential to, retire intuitively when in straits, sometimes to regather strength and subsequently renew the struggle, and at others they will make the withdrawal permanent. Their actions constitute wisdom and not cowardliness. Naturally some cowardice will be found in less auspicious persons and sometimes their withdrawals are endeavors for personal gain rather than for the over-all good of the situation. Strength of will and character are needed as well as wisdom in order to use the retirement most propitiously.

Those born in the sixth month will be more auspicious.

CONTROLLING LINES (FROM BOTTOM TO TOP)

Line 1 Retiring at the tail. The position is dangerous. No goals should be sought.

This line is the foot of the mountain and at the tail end of retirement. The time and position are not right for any advancement, hence goals should not be sought (externally). Being at the tail is obviously a dangerous position in any withdrawal. In addition, the base of the mountain is solid and stodgy. The two symbols combined imply a certain lack of wisdom, judgment and dynamic energy. For the most part, too, these persons will let others do the leading.

Most auspicious: He will have hardships early in life, but will enjoy a good and easy life later. He will start in a humble position, but subsequently will attain and enjoy a respected position.

Least auspicious: He will be full of fears and worry all the time, and have many hardships. He will be unable to establish himself well, even if appropriately helped by others.

In yearly hexagram:

Officer or official	Retreat at the right moment.
Business and professional	Retreat and regroup forces.
Ordinary people	Live peacefully and contentedly, and troubles will be avoided.

Line 2 He holds fast to thongs of yellow oxhide which cannot be parted.

This person is like the center of the mountain, which cannot be torn apart by men. Line 2 is a Yin line, holding fast to its correlate line 5, a Yang. Both lines are in their proper places, and strong in their own way. Small individuals are indicated, who look up to some live person as their idol or guide, or admire and use the biography of some famous individual as a model. Once their minds are made up their beliefs are strong and unshakeable. Those amongst them who are wise, diligent, analytical and discerning will benefit greatly from such strength of mind, and at the same time they will be flexible in adjusting readily to new conditions.

Most auspicious: He will be full of virtues and will follow the golden mean. He will be unshakeable in his purposes, and will choose his associates carefully, staying away from inferiors. He will attain a good administrative position at a national or local level.

Least auspicious: He will be lazy and undiscerning. He will select the wrong characteristics of his superiors and predecessors to emulate, and his accomplishments will be few.

In yearly hexagram:

Officer or official	He will find himself in a position of setting forth policies.
Business and professional	He will make advancements through writings or advertisements.
Ordinary people	He will achieve a modest increase in his personal property. If content with his situation he will have a good year.

Line 3 Retiring under constraint brings ills and dangers.

Maintaining (or supporting) servants and concubines brings good fortune.

The symbolism stems from the hexagram as a whole retiring (from the bottom to the top), and this being the first Yang line, supported and urged forward by the two Yin lines below, while having strong Yang lines above it. Average individuals are indicated, but ones who have the weakness of 'hiding behind their mothers' skirts' or letting someone else protect them, being unable to stand up and defend themselves adequately on their own. However, helping those below them will prove especially beneficial and bring good fortune.

Most auspicious: He will be a clever man, who retreats to avoid troubles and dangers. He will probably be helped frequently by a female (perhaps a member of his family) or by those dependent on him. He will not be very dependable when the going is rough, but he will try to help others occasionally, with moderate success.

Least auspicious: He will be absorbed in trying to live a life of ease, liking to associate with, and frequently supported by, females. He will not adhere to accepted standards, and although he will express some consideration for others, he will not be very effective.

In yearly hexagram:

Officer or official	He will strive for favor or advancement, but not always in the right way.
Business and professional	He will win some support and favors, mainly from those under him.
Ordinary people	His wife will be very helpful, especially when troubles develop. He may be quite ill or in difficult straits for part of the year. He may increase the size of his family.

Line 4   Voluntary retreat. Beneficial to the superior man. Misfortune for the inferior man.

Here in the position of the minister (the fourth line) retreating and withdrawing from situations is a matter of sound judgment, with the interests of the ruler and the people in mind. Acquiescing in such circumstances, while maintaining the dignity and poise befitting one's station, brings good fortune. These knowledgeable and experienced persons will present their points of view in a superior manner, and once a firm decision has been made, will carry out that decision in a distinguished way, from which good fortune accrues.

Most auspicious: He will be a man of high ideals, of broad vision and eminent ability, starting on his chosen career early in life, and advancing rapidly and courageously by his merit. He will keep away from unnecessary difficulties and disasters, and will have a long and good life.

Least auspicious: He will be in a low position, and be obsequious and sycophantic. His abilities will be poor. He may become disgusted over his failure to advance, and retire from worldly activity and vegetate.

In yearly hexagram:

Officer or official	He should retire to avoid troubles.
Business and professional	Circumstances will not be propitious for advancement.
Ordinary people	He may receive help from others which will later prove to be a source of trouble and difficulties.

Line 5 A praiseworthy retreat. Perseverance brings good fortune.

This is the position of the leader or ruler, who, according to the Chinese, should exemplify heavenly and spiritual qualities as well as worldly leadership. The meaning of this line is that a complete withdrawal from worldly influences, in order to follow the will of heaven, is praiseworthy, and that the pursuit of such a course will bring good fortune and should therefore be continued. These are persons who discern, or learn, that there is more to life than mere surface appearances. They study and learn the laws of heaven and earth within their capability, and apply them for the benefit of themselves and others wherever they are.

Most auspicious: He will be a man who upholds virtue, with high morals and correct principles. He will turn away from waywardness to travel the right path, and his life will be an example and a blessing to others.

Least auspicious: He will also follow a just and middle way, resulting in an easy yet beneficial life. He will not be ambitious in a worldly sense, and he will not suffer hardships or insults.

In yearly hexagram:

Officer or official	He can expect promotion in status or responsibility.
Business and professional	He will gain considerably in status and reputation.
Ordinary people	A generally good year.

Line 6   Honorable withdrawal. Everything favorable.

Here, at the top of the hexagram, the withdrawal is complete. All external impediments have been discarded, and the right inner way has been found, from which external good comes by itself. These persons will be found in many walks of life. They will know that the rendering of service to others is a part of the will of the Creator, and they will not strive for gain with selfish or egotistical motives. Their purpose will mainly be to help others, using their own capacities to the maximum.

Most auspicious: He will be fortunate in all aspects of life, having good health, a good position, and adequate wealth. He will follow the golden mean, and will not be concerned about position or esteem; these will come to him automatically. His decisions will always be sound and beneficial.

Least auspicious: He will also have a good life with ample remuneration. He will have no special glory or achievements, yet no great difficulties either. He will be helpful to others.

In yearly hexagram:

Officer or official	He will probably retire.
Business and professional	He should patiently wait for conditions to improve.
Ordinary people	He will gain some profit, and all will go well.

KEYNOTES

1. Patience and calmness are virtues.
2. Cooperate with those both above and below.
3. Renew your courage as and when necessary.
4. Cast out all that is inferior.
5. Be an example of what is right.
6. Render maximum service without depleting oneself.

CONDENSATIONS FOR DAILY CYCLES
1. Remain calm and do not try to do anything at this time.
2. Hold firmly to all that is superior, even though inferior elements are pressing forward. Be persevering.
3. Change your attitude. You appear to be bound and held back by your own thinking. A way out is available.
4. When you are no longer bound by inferior elements you can make your own decisions.
5. You can now retire from a dangerous situation in an amiable way. Continue in what is right.
6. You have the wisdom to proceed correctly. The way is clear. Follow your intuition, and what you know to be right.

Hexagram 34   Ta Chuang ☳☰ *The Power of the Great*

SIMPLE TRANSLATION OF TEXT
The Power of the Great. Persistence in what is right advantageous.

COMMENTARY
The trigram Chên, the energy of spring, is in the realm of heaven, and consequently there is great power generated, hence the name of the hexagram. This is also depicted in the four strong Yang lines rising and about to replace the upper two Yin lines. In its visual appearance the hexagram is like a ram, with the four Yang lines being the body and the two Yin lines the horns. Strength is the main characteristic depicted here. This must be coupled with wisdom to be appropriate and beneficial. Hence the statement that persistence in what is right is advantageous. As will be noted in the commentaries on the individual lines, the degree of auspiciousness is determined by how the power is used. Some of these individuals will be stubborn to an obnoxious degree. Others will merely be adamant in what they think is right. Many will demonstrate their power as persistence in attaining objectives, regardless of whether the objective is right or wrong. A few will use their strength for improving themselves, while even fewer will use it for the benefit of others. The power referred to here is primarily an inner strength, although physical strength and vitality are indicated too.

Those born in the second month will be the most auspicious. Those born in other months when thunder occurs, i.e. the second through the eighth month, will also be auspicious.

CONTROLLING LINES (FROM BOTTOM TO TOP)
Line 1 Power in the toes. It would be unfortunate to try to advance now. Quiet confidence remains.

A man's forward movement commences in the toes. This line is somewhat similar to the first line of hexagram 31. There the dominant trait was influence, while here it is strength. In this lowest position, the strength is likely to be used without adequate preparations, and result in rashness and brashness. To try to advance under such circumstances would lead to misfortune. These persons, however, also have the potential for knowing their limitations, so the wise ones will wait for the most propitious occasions. These persons are likely to be impetuous, headstrong, impulsive, adventurous, indiscreet, ardent and fiery.
Most auspicious: He will be wise and talented, with common sense and good judgment. He will curb his impulses and wait for the right moment to act, and therefore will not become involved in any serious trouble. He will protect his enterprises, family and possessions well.
Least auspicious: He will act rashly, without due preparations or consideration. He will have many hardships, and end up being poor.
In yearly hexagram:

Officer or official	He is likely to be subjected to misrepresentations, to his disadvantage.
Business and professional	He is likely to be too impulsive and hope to gain recognition through luck rather than through diligence and persistence.
Ordinary people	Both great and small disputes are probable, in an adverse year. He may have an injury or contract a foot disease.

Line 2 Maintaining a right course brings good fortune.

This line means exactly what it says. The man who follows a

right course externally is already inwardly correct. This is indicated by this being the central line in the creative trigram Ch'ien, heaven. This person naturally brings blessings and benefits to whatever he engages in. Such persons are supported by heaven and intuitively do what is right and best for the circumstances in which they find themselves. The world is blessed by there being a few such people wherever one goes.

Most auspicious: He will follow the golden mean, and will know how to make corrections and bring about reforms propitiously. He will be in a high and influential position, benefiting a great number of people.

Least auspicious: He will also be a firm and steady leader and administrator, but on a local level. He will have a modest but good life.

In yearly hexagram:

Officer or official	He will be in a position of influence, and given even greater responsibilities and authority.
Business and professional	Progressive actions will lead to benefits and fame.
Ordinary people	His fervent wishes will be fulfilled.

Line 3 The small man uses adverse power. The superior man is reserved. Persistence in the use of strength now would be serious, much like a ram butting against a hedge and getting his horns entangled.

At the top of the trigram Ch'ien, the mentally weak man is inclined to use all his power, without guiding it judiciously, and the result is 'like a ram butting against a hedge and getting his horns entangled.' The hexagram as a whole is symbolic of the ram, so here an inferior man is using every means, both good and bad, to achieve his aims. Naturally a superior man does not act in such a manner. The position of this line is such that the traits of the inferior man predominate.

Most auspicious: He will be a good man, but shallow with respect to worldly conditions and his responsibilities regarding them. Therefore, for the most part, he will be unable to handle matters in a productive and beneficial way, and will have many troubles.

Least auspicious: He will be mentally weak and mean, frequently behaving in an outrageous manner, sometimes violent, sometimes threatening. He will attempt to use intimidating methods on others, and consequently will lose his friends, money and family.

In yearly hexagram:

Officer or official	He will be involved in serious troubles, whether he advances or retreats.
Business and professional	Only with extreme care can difficulties be avoided. It will be hard to advance.
Ordinary people	A generally bad year, with troubles and disputes.

Line 4   Correctness leads to good fortune, and occasion for regret disappears. The hedge parts itself and there is no entanglement. There is great strength in the axle of the cart.

Meticulous and progressive persons who go forward step by step, overcoming difficulties through the use of wide knowledge and correct procedures, are bound to find that troubles disintegrate of their own accord, with good fortune ensuing. The cart is ready to move, so when entanglements are overcome the time is propitious for further advancement. This procedure is obviously a wise one for every stage of one's life's journey. The success of these individuals depends on their starting point, and thereafter on their use of their innate wisdom. Since his line is in the position of the minister, these persons will either support some noble person or some worthy cause.

Most auspicious: He will always follow a righteous and just course, and nothing can prevent his progress. He will help himself, his enterprises, his family, and the general public as well. He will begin to build merit, reputation and wealth in his early youth, and he will have a long and favorable life.

Least auspicious: He will also have a good and beneficial life. His strong desires will be achieved easily, and his household and enterprises will flourish modestly.

In yearly hexagram:

Officer or official	Those in inactive positions will be reassigned to active ones. Advancement is propitious, and one's goals will be achieved.

Business and professional	Forward movement is beneficial, and good results can be expected.
Ordinary people	The year will be favorable for new actions and efforts.

Line 5 He readily sacrifices his ram. No regret.

Broadminded individuals see things from an impersonal point of view, and readily sacrifice their own desires and wishes for the benefit of the greater whole. In the main, these persons are leaders and managers, this being the fifth line, and have the potential for acquiring the requisite knowledge and experience to overcome difficulties and bring about better conditions for others and their enterprises. Regrettably this is a Yin line where it should really be a strong Yang for the best results. Hence, many of these persons will not be the stalwart leaders they ought to be. Most auspicious: He will be a calm and soft-spoken leader, who can readily quell violence and disorders through the implementation of just rules and procedures, which others accept and follow. He will operate mainly on a local level rather than nationally or internationally.
Least auspicious: He will be timid and weak. Although he will know what needs to be done he will be hesitant to put the right course into effect. He will have but few long term gains, and a short life.
In yearly hexagram:

Officer or official	Many will be reprimanded for inadequately carrying out their responsibilities.
Business and professional	His reputation will probably wane.
Ordinary people	He will have many small troubles. He may possibly die.

Line 6 The ram butts against the hedge. Movement in any direction impossible. Recognizing and re-evaluating the situation brings good fortune.

People universally dislike anyone who uses excessive power, regardless of the level on which such a person is operating. These persons have the propensity to use excessive power. The result is that no one wants to support them, cooperate with them, or to come to their aid. Consequently, no matter what they try to do they get nowhere. However, if they recognize this failing, and re-evaluate their situation, they have the potential to change and gradually attain good fortune. This can best be accomplished by their exercising calmness in their activities, by quietly improving their academic knowledge, and through observation and analysis in their profession.

Most auspicious: He will be sufficiently wise and knowledgeable to know when to act and when to remain quiet. The use of this sense of timing will prove advantageous, and substantial gains and advancements will be made.

Least auspicious: He will be over ambitious, with but little talent or wisdom. This is dangerous. He will also be greedy, and will try unsuccessfully to outdo his peers and superiors, creating enmity. He will frequently be in trouble.

In yearly hexagram:

Officer or official	He will probably be dismissed.
Business and professional	His enterprises will require re-assessment and re-evaluation before any success can be expected.
Ordinary people	He is likely to push matters too hard, with adverse results.

KEYNOTES

1. Rashness is dangerous.
2. A right course should always be followed, for advantages.
3. Small-mindedness results in entanglements.
4. Caution is advised when using power.
5. Never be too pushful.
6. An excessive use of power induces adverse reactions.

CONDENSATIONS FOR DAILY CYCLES

1. Using too much power at the beginning of any enterprise is dangerous. Exercise care.
2. The influences are correct. Resistance begins to disappear.
3. You may be trying to use too much strength for your position.
4. Your strength and influence can be used to advantage now, but be careful not to overdo it.
5. Give up using excessive strength. Use only the right amount, duly guided.
6. You may have gone too far. Re-evaluate and redirect your efforts as necessary, and good fortune can still be yours.

Hexagram 35   Chin ☰☰ *Progress (Advance)*

SIMPLE TRANSLATION OF TEXT
Progress. The noble prince is honored with a great many horses.
He is granted audience three times in a day.

COMMENTARY
Light, the trigram Li, is over the earth, the trigram K'un. This
represents the brilliance of the heavenly heart and heavenly mind
of man. Since K'un also represents the people, it indicates that
light is available to guide them. In a ruler or leader it shows
wisdom, knowledge, magnanimity, confidence, and freedom from
jealousy. These are truly kingly persons, in the best meaning of
the word. Lesser men are like noble princes, who support their
ruler with fealty for the good of the country. They are rewarded
generously (horses were scarce in ancient China). These persons
lead in external matters, while in inner wisdom they are an
example to others. Their external lives are a reflection of their
internal worth and greatness. As a ruler or leader one welcomes
such noble princes, is glad to see them frequently, and rewards
them freely for their support and advice. Those who are truly
great reflect the glory and virtue of heaven.

Those born in the second month will be more auspicious.

CONTROLLING LINES (FROM BOTTOM TO TOP)
Line 1   Held back in progress. Perseverance brings good fortune.
Meet lack of confidence in others with liberality towards them.
No error.

In trying to enlighten the lower strata of the people (the bottom
line of the trigram K'un) one often runs into difficulty by such
persons being inadequately prepared, or literally incapable of
receiving the message or teachings. Persevering, as well as being
liberal-minded regarding deficiencies, is the right course. These
persons are likely to be teachers or instructors who deal with a
considerable number of people needing training or illumination.
They will be quite knowledgeable, teaching with calmness,
patience and persistence. They may be, but need not be, professional teachers.
Most auspicious: He will be a person of firm resolve and noble

in character. He will be just, dealing with others without favoritism. He will exercise great self-discipline, and his affairs will always be in good order, and progressive.

Least auspicious: He will try to achieve his goals without proper preparations or cooperation, and will meet with frequent hindrances. He will not accomplish anything great, and is likely to have a short life without much satisfaction.

In yearly hexagram:

Officer or official	He may be stopped in his progress by evil people.
Business and professional	He should hold firm in the present situation.
Ordinary people	Foresight is lacking, so it is difficult to make any progress.

Line 2   Sorrowful in his progress. Righteous persistence brings good fortune. Blessings are bestowed by one's ancestress.

The meaning of this line is quite similar to that of line 1, except that the teaching is on a higher level. The persons depicted here are sorrowful because their own progress does not seem to be what it ought to be, nor does that of others. They instantly recognize the great many things that need to be done, but their helpers are few. Most other people are uncaring. Persistence in what is right will eventually bring good fortune. This line is the correlate of line 5, a Yin line, so one is supported by one's ancestress (a female who has gone before).

Most auspicious: He will be in an influential position, and concerned about the future of his country and its people, if they are not pursuing wise and judicious courses. He will be firm in his goals and strive persistently to fulfil them. He will follow the golden mean. In the end he will be rewarded, and will receive good fortune from an external source, perhaps from a woman.

Least auspicious: He will also be a person striving to follow the right path and achieve that which he knows to be for the good. He will have many changes in his life, some sorrowful and some joyful. He will be auspiciously helped by his mother, or by another woman.

In yearly hexagram:

Officer or official	He will receive public recognition for his efforts.

Business and professional	He will be checked and held back at first; later he will make substantial gains.
Ordinary people	His desires will be fulfilled. Also he will be helped by his mother or his wife, or by their respective families.

Line 3   All are in accord. Remorse vanishes.

Here a man has progressed high on the earthly plane (line 3 of the trigram K'un) and is now ready to investigate the illumination and enlightenment attainable from heaven (the upper trigram Li, clarity, above the earth). The inner light is strong in this man, and attracts others without conscious effort. Through diligence in what is right he maintains his inner strength, and thereby attains successful results for his efforts. His accomplishments will cause any previous occasions for remorse to be forgotten. These persons have magnetic personalities.

Most auspicious: He will have many like-minded friends and associates, who work to improve themselves and to be of benefit to others. Their results are truly successful, and blessings accrue for all concerned.

Least auspicious: He will also be a good man associating with wise and good people. He will have some helpful friends and few enemies, and his life will be quite easy and progressive in a modest way. No great sorrows or worries are anticipated.

In yearly hexagram:

Officer or official	He will experience a happy and invigorating promotion.
Business and professional	He will be successful, and will be recommended by others.
Ordinary people	He will work with friends and achieve his aims.

Line 4   Marmot-like progress. Perseverance is hazardous.

Americans would speak of prairie-dog-like progress, since that animal is the closest American relation of the marmot. The prairie-dog lives within a limited territory, and needs the companionship of others; it acts like an emperor over his domain, yet runs to its burrow when danger threatens, and in general makes little or no progress. People exhibiting such characteristics will find many hazards in the course of their lives, with others taking advantage of these innocuous characteristics. Their progress will be very limited unless they become more dynamic.

Most auspicious: He will be in a high position, but since he does not have the qualities of a true leader, he will be envied by others and disparaged, and will find the maintaining of his status and position difficult.

Least auspicious: He will be a troublesome man with little or no virtue, sometimes even vicious or obnoxious. He will have a difficult life, with few or no achievements.

In yearly hexagram:

Officer or official	His progress and efforts will be constantly thwarted.
Business and professional	He will be stalemated, and unable to find a way to progress.
Ordinary people	He will have many unavoidable disputes.

Line 5 Regrets disappear. No need for concern regarding gains or losses. Keep advancing. All things cooperate favorably.

These persons are truly kingly and noble in character, and everything automatically flows to them, by virtue of their great and righteous inner selves which act as a light for the world. These persons are approaching sainthood in their evolution, and may be found in any walk of life where the Creator feels they will be most useful.

Most auspicious: He will be a man of great virtue, knowledgeable in cultural matters and in the arts. He will be independent but will serve others well if needs be. He will not strive for merit, yet will achieve it; he will not seek profits, yet will make continuous gains. He will not necessarily deliberately work for reforms or to improve the people, but these things will automatically come about wherever he is.

Least auspicious: He will also be a man of good character and wide knowledge. He also will not concern himself with gains or losses, yet everything will go as he wishes, on a modest scale.

In yearly hexagram:

Officer or official	He will advance in status or position.

Business and professional	He will achieve fame or a favorable reputation, and will also make profits.
Ordinary people	He will gain a good profit this year, which will be favorable in general.

Line 6   Advancing with horns. This is right only for punishing one's own cities. Regardless of circumstances he will make no error. Persistence elsewhere will result in occasion for regret.

The time is past being propitious (line 5 was the most propitious) for rapid and smooth advancement. Here, trying to make forceful progress is wrong, except in so far as it concerns correcting and improving oneself in character and knowledge. All self-correction should be made courageously and with thoroughness. Care should be exercised that what is done is right and just. By trying to correct anyone other than oneself one will encounter difficulties. Others must develop and improve their own leadership, for effective results.

Most auspicious: He will be able to make modest gains only. In general, he will be too stern, adamant and inflexible for great responsibilities. He may become the mayor of a small town, or the administrator of an enterprise. His auspiciousness will be meager, yet no great harm will come to him either.

Least auspicious: He will be merciless and cruel, without any natural affection, and will be very touchy and ready to engage in disputes. He may become an officer or an administrator, of low rank.

In yearly hexagram:

Officer or official	He will be assigned to an honored position.
Business and professional	He will make some progress, but will need to bring himself up to date professionally, and to improve himself personally.
Ordinary people	A moderately good year. He may find joy in constructing a house or other building.

KEYNOTES

1. Be magnanimous.
2. Teach slowly for durable results.

3. Proceeding in what is right is advantageous.
4. The possibilities of caution should never be overlooked.
5. Nobleness produces its own rewards.
6. Improve yourself constantly.

CONDENSATIONS FOR DAILY CYCLES
1. You will find yourself held back if you try to proceed single-handed. Meet the situation with love and kindness.
2. Some progress is being made, but it is not happy progress. Blessings and benefits may come from outside, probably from a woman.
3. Now is the time to make progress, both inwardly and externally, with the support of others.
4. You are trying to make progress too quickly, and an adverse reaction will set in.
5. The time is favorable for action. All things should now fall into their proper place.
6. Do not press forward except in the matter of correcting and improving yourself. Deal cautiously with strangers.

Hexagram 36 Ming I ☰☰ Darkening of the Light

SIMPLE TRANSLATION OF TEXT
Darkening of the Light. Persevering despite hindrances or adversity bring rewards.

COMMENTARY
The symbol of the darkening of the light comes from observation of the hexagram itself, where Li, light, is under (within) K'un, the earth. The light is thus hidden and is therefore darkened externally.

The lessons one has to learn during the course of one's evolution are many and varied. Here, potentially strong and good persons are faced with many hindrances and adversities, so that they cannot directly be of benefit to others, just as King Wên was held in captivity before the time was ripe for him to escape and take over the throne of China. People of lesser status often find themselves in situations where all their endeavors seem to be in vain, or something inevitably occurs to keep their desires from materializing. In such times one must veil one's light, and let silent inner strength take over. Eventually good will prevail. Basically, these persons are of good character, and will try to do their best according to the dictates of the circumstances in which they find themselves. Observe how a mother veils her light, and puts herself on the level of the child she is teaching. Superior persons in any position will do well to emulate the mother's good example.

Those born in the eighth month will be more auspicious.

CONTROLLING LINES (FROM BOTTOM TO TOP)

Lines 1 Wounding of the light during flight. He lowers his wings. When pursuing a goal the superior man may go without eating for three days. The master will have something to say about this.

Many birds, in nature's world, will droop their wings and feign injury, even though only slightly hurt, in order to escape danger. Here, at the bottom of the hexagram, the light is only slightly wounded, and attempts to protect itself following nature's example. A man likewise will sometimes withdraw from his struggles and, symbolically, go without food for three days, making others think that he is incapable of fending for himself. The master will verify what he is doing. Others may often speak disparagingly about his actions and apparent weaknesses, yet in reality he follows a wise and fortuitous course. Some of these persons develop themselves so effectively in their quiet way that nearly everyone else is surprised when they are chosen for promotion and positions of responsibility.

Most auspicious: He will be a wise, knowledgeable and experienced man, who knows how to protect himself and others. He will be honest, trustworthy and sincere, and therefore free from blame. In times of peace he will be in a high administrative position. In times of anarchy and disorder he will be in a position of authority to quell the disturbances and restore order. He will have an active life and face many dangers, but will avoid disaster.

Least auspicious: He will be quite ambitious, will meet hindrances often, and he will establish some merit but will never be wealthy. He will feign illnesses, etc., in order to gain sympathy and control over others.

268

In yearly hexagram:

Officer or official	He will find himself in an important position, and close to his leader. He must beware of possible injury through a conspiracy.
Business and professional	He will win some distinction, and make gains.
Ordinary people	He will have some minor troubles, and may receive an injury to his hands or feet. It will be favorable to buy property.

Line 2 Darkening of the light. Wounded in the left thigh. Horses come to his aid. Good fortune.

Line 5, the center line of trigram K'un, earth, and the correlate of line 2, tries to control the latter, being the center line of trigram Li, light, but only succeeds in inflicting a disabling wound in the thigh. Despite the wound the man depicted here can still ride, so he uses horses in effecting deliverance of himself and those dependent on him. Horses represent mobility and flexibility, under the control of wisdom, adjusting to time and circumstances. These persons are likely to be in medical, legal or certain scientific careers, or in the military service as officers.

Most auspicious: He has dignity, power and analytical ability, in both his professional and personal lives. He will try to cultivate the right way and follow it courageously. He will be in charge of an important enterprise whereby evil will be kept away from many people.

Least auspicious: He will have sufficient ability and experience to attain his aims, but at times will exhibit outrageous behavior and treat others cruelly. He is likely to have many troubles.

In yearly hexagram:

Officer or official	He may be assigned to the command of a major enterprise, or a large military unit.
Business and professional	He will achieve outstanding results in matters relating to writing.
Ordinary people	A generally mild year.

Line 3 While hunting in the south the light is wounded. The

rebel leader is captured. Do not expect corrections to be made all at once. Excesses must be avoided.

The trigram Li, light, and south, seeks to rise, in the natural course of events, and in doing so encounters the trigram K'un, which represents the south-west. K'un also signifies a multitude of people. It is only natural that one runs into trouble if one tries to bring light to many people at once. Furthermore, the most difficult thing to impart to people is the need to break away from the old and inject something new. Habit is strong, and overcoming it is no simple task. While these persons know what ought to be done, their position (line 3) is such that it is definitely not right for them to try it in practice. Judiciousness and caution are advised regarding all actions, but this advice quite probably will not be followed.

Most auspicious: He will be a leader and a rabble-rouser, trying to promote change to overcome long-standing ills but without much success. He will have frequent disputes with others. However, his personal life may be quite satisfying.

Least auspicious: He will be a demagogue, with poor judgment, resulting in a life full of constant difficulties in every department.

In yearly hexagram:

Officer or official	He will be assigned to clean up or straighten out some troublesome difficulty.
Business and professional	Written efforts are likely to be misrepresented and ineffective.
Ordinary people	He will have many disputes, yet it is an auspicious year to build or alter one's house.

Line 4   He penetrates the left side of the belly and enters the heart of the darkening of the light. He leaves by the gates of the courtyard.

A period of rest and revitalization is indicated here. The light spirit normally occupies the area above and behind the space between the eyes. During rest it reverts to the liver, i.e. in the area of the belly, so in this line the lower trigram Li is entering the belly of trigram K'un. Furthermore, Li tends to rise while K'un tends to sink, and this also serves to effect a union. After the

light revitalizes itself in the liver it will return to its normal position, leaving the belly 'courtyard' by the gates of returning
consciousness and energy. These persons will be calm and restful
individuals, who quietly bide their time, gathering strength and
waiting for the right moment to act, then being very effective in
achieving whatever they seek when they do take action.

Most auspicious: He will be in a high administrative position,
probably in the government. Will be wise, knowledgeable and
judicious, with a keen sense of timing. He will ably support his
country, his enterprise, and his family.

Least auspicious: He will use his talents for selfish purposes. He
will possess little virtue and be inclined to trickery, cunning and
dishonesty. His activities will be injurious to himself and others.

In yearly hexagram:

Officer or official	He will be assigned to a position of activity. If at the seat of operations, he will be sent elsewhere.
Business and professional	Progressive actions should be initiated.
Ordinary people	He should avoid standstill. Good will come from progressive activity.

Line 5 Prince Chi's light was darkened. Perseverance in
righteous goals advantageous.

Prince Chi was held a prisoner and a slave. He feigned insanity
to avoid being slain, yet inwardly held on firmly to his beliefs.
This is an example for persons born under this line to follow
should they become involved in similar situations. These persons
will work for others throughout their lives, and mainly in conditions where they disagree with the policies and procedures in force.
They must remember that it is not what one does, but rather how
one thinks and feels about one's situation, the way one reacts, and
one's freedom to control one's inner self that are important, not
the fact of being subservient to or dominated by others. External
conditions exist for the lessons one is meant to learn from them,
and for the service one gives by coming to terms with them. There
are many ways to think, and many ways to serve. These persons
have a good number of lessons to learn.

Most auspicious: He will be very knowledgeable, as well as
having the necessary common sense and wisdom to protect

himself and his family from adversities. Worldly possessions will have little or no meaning for him.

Least auspicious: He will have many hardships, frequent changes of job, and lengthy wanderings. His life will be full of sorrows and worries.

In yearly hexagram:

Officer or official	He should cultivate his own virtue while keeping clear of troublesome circumstances.
Business and professional	Hold firm. Recognition will not be forthcoming this year.
Ordinary people	He will have constant family difficulties.

Line 6 Dark and gloomy. He climbed once to heaven and then fell to earth.

This depicts a king or ruler who has it within him to become as a bright light in heaven, but by having no trust or faith in his subordinates and by wounding them at every turn, he meets his fate by being deposed. These persons will rise to positions which they have either not duly earned, or are not appropriately qualified for. They then run into difficulties and find they must start again elsewhere. Some will profit early in life from their experiences, and will take steps to avoid similar difficulties in the future. Some will never learn.

Most auspicious: He will be wise and far-sighted enough to profit from past mistakes and adjust his plans to those which are firm and attainable. He will be in a high position, where he can benefit others by leading properly and propitiously in times of disaster.

Least auspicious: He will be a very selfish wastrel, and he will use or walk over others in his attempts to progress. In later years he will be punished for his earlier mistreatment of others.

In yearly hexagram:

Officer or official	He will probably be demoted or dismissed.
Business and professional	He will make some progress, but the year will end with set-backs.
Ordinary people	The year will be smooth at first, then hindrances will creep in. If old, he may well die.

KEYNOTES
1. Beware of trying to progress too fast.
2. Use nature as an example.
3. Proceed slowly with reforms.
4. Revitalize your energies frequently.
5. Keep your goals to yourself.
6. Learn from past mistakes.

CONDENSATIONS FOR DAILY CYCLES
1. When working for the public good put aside selfish considerations. Move ahead only so far as you can go in safety.
2. Your progress seems impeded. By flexibility you can overcome all hindrances.
3. Meditate and concentrate. Find new ideas and put them into action.
4. You now intuitively know the heart and meaning of your opposition. You can by-pass the situation if you want to.
5. You may be called upon to perform an emergency function. Carry it out to the best of your ability.
6. Implement something new to replace something old. Also, make sure whether or not you have transgressed divine law.

Hexagram 37   Chia Jên ☴☲ *The Family (Proper Relations)*

SIMPLE TRANSLATION OF TEXT
The Family. Advantageous for women to be firm and correct.

COMMENTARY
The trigram Sun, wind, the eldest daughter, is above and leading Li, fire, the middle daughter. Hence the symbolism that it is advantageous for women to be firm and correct. The individual lines depict the family and the proper relations within the family, e.g., line 1 is the youngest son, while line 6 is the patriarch or father. Lines 3 and 5 are symbolic of brothers while the relationship between lines 5 and 2 represents the relations between husband and wife. Lines 2 and 4 (Yin lines) represent women in the family, properly surrounded and protected by their menfolk (the Yang lines). Hence the over-all meaning for the hexagram of

273

the family. Correct family relations are the pillars of Confucianism, especially those depicted above. Quite naturally, too, wind (Sun) rises from fire (Li), reflecting the inner spirit which should pervade family relations. For this spirit to continue there must be substance in which to generate it. This comes from the patriarch, or superior man, who gives duration to the way in which things should be done, through the profundity of his words. Persons born under this hexagram are knowledgeable regarding the customs of their society, and adhere to them instinctively. The superior ones try to establish correct relationships in all activities with which they are associated. They are cautious in their speech, only speaking after due reflection as to the probable consequences of their words. Their character is stable and resolute, and can be relied on by others. They act firmly according to the dictates of whatever circumstances they are in.

Those born in the sixth month will be more auspicious.

CONTROLLING LINES (FROM BOTTOM TO TOP)
Line 1 Firm circumscription within the family. Regrets vanish.

If everyone's position within the family (or any other grouping) is firmly and rightly circumscribed, all cause for regrets vanishes. Everyone then knows his or her responsibility, as well as the limits within which they have freedom to act. All things are then carried out properly, arguments are kept to a minimum, and the feelings of individuals are duly respected. These persons try to emulate the foregoing principles, wherever they are and at all levels of activity. It is a pleasure to be associated with such people, especially because of the harmonious results they attain.
Most auspicious: He will be highly talented in his speciality, and a man of virtue and integrity. He will analyze all matters deeply and initiate appropriate actions, whether these be for himself, his enterprises, his family or his country. He will know how to adapt to any situation and will invariably have favorable results. He will also gain wealth and position.
Least auspicious: He will also be a talented person, on a lesser scale, who is careful and humble. His life will flow smoothly and he will have considerable affluence. He will be happy and contented.

In yearly hexagram:

Officer or official	Those in active positions will be transferred to easier positions, and vice versa.
Business and professional	Small gains will be made.
Ordinary people	A propitious year. Bachelors are likely to marry. An older person may die.

Line 2 She must not assume separate goals. She must attend to household duties. Good fortune.

Line 2 symbolizes the wife. She is admonished not to strive for independence, but rather to carry out her normal duties in the society in which she is living. Such behavior reflects a willingness to serve others (a fundamental precept for all mankind) within the limits of her means and to the best of her ability. These persons will always do the best they can for others, and render the maximum of service within the limits prescribed for them. They will constantly be aware of the needs of others and will try to fill them, as well as carrying out their duties and responsibilities with a minimum of supervision.

Most auspicious: He will be a person who likes people, to be with them and to help them, and who enjoys notable social relations with others. He loves well, and will be loved well in return. He will be prosperous, healthy and happy, with a good family life. Women with this controlling line will make exceptionally good wives and mothers.

Least auspicious: He will have a good life of service; however he will achieve only a modest degree of affluence.

In yearly hexagram:

Officer or official	He will be transferred to the center of activity, or given a rise in salary.
Business and professional	Both input and output will increase substantially.
Ordinary people	He may establish or change the location of his household. He will make gains in his enterprises.

Line 3 Sharpness and severity within the family brings remorse. Good fortune comes from seriousness. If women and children dally and laugh, misfortune.

Those who go to either extreme, i.e. being too severe and domineering on the one hand, or too lax and unconcerned on the other, are bound to have difficulties. This is too evident to need further comment. The right course is a thoughtfulness that respects others as individuals of worth and dignity. Seriousness also includes being kind and forgiving. Persons with this controlling line may vary widely in the traits they display in their relationships, within their families and with others.

Most auspicious: He will be thoughtful, serious and humane in all his relationships. He will be a person of stable character and personal dignity. He will be an example to others, and a leader who can regulate major enterprises and maintain order with ease. He will have a good life in all respects.

Least auspicious: He is likely to be temperamental, with an easily roused temper. He is also likely to be a vehement iconoclast, and indulge in carnal pleasures to extremes. He will ruin his family.

In yearly hexagram:

Officer or official	He is likely to be inflexibly bureaucratic and unforgiving.
Business and professional	He may make a few gains, with difficulty.
Ordinary people	A year with some sorrow and some joy. He should be careful not to become confused.

Line 4 She enriches the household. Great good fortune.

Line 4 is a Yin line in its right place, and hence the picture of the wife enriching the household is suggested. This line reflects the great blessing to any enterprise which the person at one's right hand can be. By keeping everything in proper order this person frees the leader for greater undertakings and endeavors, for expansion, for nobler service, for planning, and for many other activities, all of which would either be neglected or given minimal attention if this freedom were not available. This line teaches that one can be of far-reaching service, no matter what position one is in, and these persons will be among the noble ones who render true and lasting service to mankind.

Most auspicious: He will be in a position akin to that of Cabinet Minister who enriches the country and the people through noble leadership. The economy of his enterprise, or of the country, will flourish. He will have a happy and satisfying life, with much affluence.

Least auspicious: He will have a similar life to the most auspicious, but on a local level.

In yearly hexagram:

Officer or official	He will receive a rise in position or salary.
Business and professional	He will make some major gain, or receive a coveted prize.
Ordinary people	A good year with substantial profit.

Line 5 The king approaches his family. No need for relief. Good fortune.

Noble and wise leadership is depicted here. Despite the power and authority available to this person, he has only good intentions, directed to improving all relationships in his family and work, so there is no basis for any fear arising, nor need for any relief from these conditions to be initiated. Much mutual trust and confidence exists, and is self-sustaining and regenerating, thereby resulting in much good for, and supporting, all concerned.

Most auspicious: His thoughts, speech and behavior will be a model for the people. He will love and respect people as individuals, and will aid them. In return, they will help and support him. Great harmony will exist, and all will be blessed and will benefit.

Least auspicious: He will also be wealthy and influential, and have a harmonious relationship within his family and among his associates. His life will be beneficial and satisfying.

In yearly hexagram:

Officer or official	He will make much progress towards his goals.
Business and professional	He will make progress in his enterprise.
Ordinary people	He will be helped by an influential person and will make gains.

Line 6 Sincerity and nobility. Good fortune in the end.

Sagelike, rather than worldly leadership is indicated here. These are men of great inner development, who express themselves through the media of art, religion, philosophy and literature. The worth of their writings, thoughts and efforts may not be recognized at the time they are produced, but they will eventually result in lasting benefit. Hence 'good fortune in the end.'

Most auspicious: He will have an advancing and refining influence on art and learning. He will be dignified and inspiring; and he will have adequate worldly goods to meet his needs, but these will not be important to him.

Least auspicious: He will also be a man of virtue, producing benefits throughout a good and influential life.

In yearly hexagram:

Officer or official	He will be assigned to a powerful position.
Business and professional	He will make substantial and beneficial progress.
Ordinary people	Strong desires will be fulfilled.

KEYNOTES

1. Define all matters.
2. Attend to assigned duties meticulously.
3. Sharpness and severity in human relations are damaging.
4. All service is beneficial.
5. Noble leadership is propitious.
6. Sageness helps the world.

CONDENSATIONS FOR DAILY CYCLES

1. Establish firm rules and guide lines for whatever you are engaged on, or are now commencing.
2. Be receptive. Carry out your assigned duties well. Do not try to lead now.
3. Beware of using harsh words, or you will lose control of the situation.
4. Carry out your responsibilities well, have others do the same, and you will have good fortune.
5. Be noble and magnanimous in your leadership. Good fortune.
6. Rise above mundane matters today and try to create something of lasting benefit, either within yourself or for others.

278

Hexagram 38   *K'uei* ☲☱ *Opposition (Estrangement)*

SIMPLE TRANSLATION OF TEXT
Opposition. Good fortune in limited matters.

COMMENTARY
The trigram Li, fire, over trigram Tui, lake, definitely indicates opposition, because of their very different natures. They also represent the second daughter and the youngest daughter living in the same household. These belong to different husbands so their tendencies are divergent. The trigrams also stand for beauty (Li) and joy (Tui). Furthermore, the lake is available for nourishment, and fire, in addition, means clarity. Those depicted here have diverse characteristics, some beneficial and some superficial. They are inclined to be dual-natured individuals, presenting their different personalities in different situations and circumstances. They like to be helpful but are inclined to love the limelight more. General salesmen, minor diplomats, and some artists have many of the characteristics of K'uei. Regrettably, they will have good fortune only if they properly define their lives, limit themselves to seeking modest and attainable goals, and unify their divergent interests.

Those born in the second month will be more auspicious.

CONTROLLING LINES (FROM BOTTOM TO TOP)
Line 1   Regrets disappear. When you lose your horses do not run after them. They will return of their own accord. He remains free from blame in relations with evil persons.

Some men's mannerisms are naturally soothing and placating, while others experience difficulties even in minor matters. These persons are advised never to act in haste. They should be careful and wait, since the laws of nature have a tendency to equalize differences without man's interference or wishfulness. Most of these persons will have great patience, and, in general, will be aggressive in an unirritating, yet quite competitive way.
Most auspicious: His nobleness and virtue will cause people to respect him. He will be just, sincere and impartial. His wisdom will be able to eradicate evil from people's minds. He will not be

successful at an early age, but will attain his goals and have his desires fulfilled later in life.

Least auspicious: He will face many difficulties, and will find it hard to establish himself. He will be poor at first, and slowly gain wealth later in life. He will at first work alone, then later associate closely with others.

In yearly hexagram:

Officer or official	He will gain a good position. If previously demoted he will be promoted again.
Business and professional	His efforts, in general, will not receive adequate recognition until later in the year.
Ordinary people	Some losses at first, then gains later.
	Some disputes at first, then harmony later.

Line 2 He meets his lord in a narrow lane. No error.

Line 2 is the center line of trigram Tui, nourishment, so these persons quietly and unassumingly render service to others, avoiding opposition as far as possible. They are blessed with an intuitive foresight, which aids them in steering a safe course. Since the two trigrams are in opposition, line 5 cannot straightforwardly support line 2, hence the picture of an accidental meeting in a narrow lane. This symbolizes the occasional help these persons receive from superior persons. These individuals, in general, will be well versed and effective in whatever they specialize in.

Most auspicious: He will be a loyal statesman, spokesman or negotiator, or even in the legal profession. He will be a man of excellent character, correlating and ameliorating the mistakes of his superiors, as well as improving the morality of the people. He will have a good and worthwhile life.

Least auspicious: He will also render much service, and communicate well with people. He will receive help from friends and associates. Eventually he will probably lead a secluded life, desiring no worldly acclaim. He will have no great ills in his life.

In yearly hexagram:

Officer or official	He will meet a clever superior, and promotion can be expected.

Business and professional	He will meet a knowledgeable individual who will provide beneficial ideas and support.
Ordinary people	With the help of a close friend his strong desires will be fulfilled.

Line 3 His wagon is dragged back. His oxen beaten. His topknot (hair) and nose sliced off. Not a good beginning but a good end.

This man's opposition or estrangement is so intense that the individual is insulted or treated with disrespect in every possible way. His progress is impeded and he is dragged back. His oxen (ideas) are beaten (down), so that further progress will be very slow. His topknot is cut off. This knot was a symbol of status, so his pride is injured. Slicing off the nose was a mild form of punishment for robbing or stealing. There will be much adversity in the lives of these people early on, and they will have many varied handicaps to overcome. Thus progress will be stunted, but their calamities and opposition will bring out the best in them and they will eventually take the challenge, and rise above their initial conditions. This will be very beneficial for them.

Most auspicious: He will be a smart and intelligent person, but too much concerned with details and ramifications. He will examine and criticize everyone and everything too much. Later in life he will, through self-analysis, realize that his earlier methods were erroneous and ineffective, and will change. He will then attain peace, harmony, and the fulfilment of his desires.

Least auspicious: He will be in a low position of menial labor, and have many hardships. He will suffer considerably, but his later life will tend to be smoother and easier.

In yearly hexagram:

Officer or official	He will meet with misrepresentation, and his progress will temporarily be halted.
Business and professional	He will be the second choice at first for an important assignment then selected later.
Ordinary people	He will have many hindrances at first, with an easing off later.

Line 4 Isolated through estrangement. One meets and grows with a companion who is compatible and cooperative. The situation is precarious, but no error.

Since the two trigrams are in opposition, line 4 and line 1 cannot get together without a great deal of difficulty. Once they manage it a very beneficial union ensues. These are analytical persons, who are very knowledgeable of the laws of nature and up to date in their profession, and who apply such intelligence very capably. Their analyses helps them to master any opposition encountered, and to be both an example to and a nourisher of others. A wise use of his knowledge will produce success.

Most auspicious: He will be greatly talented and very diplomatic. He will receive help when needed from good and beneficial friends. He will be a highly capable administrator, and one capable of restoring order if necessary. He will meet with adversity early in his career, but later he will have an auspicious life in all respects.

Least auspicious: He will need to stand alone for much of his life. He will be honorable in his relations, and modest in his living. He also will have unfavorable conditions at first, which then improve later in life.

In yearly hexagram:

Officer or official	He will be respected, recommended and supported by colleagues.
Business and professional	He will meet a superior who will exert influence on his behalf.
Ordinary people	Those seeking marriage will be successful; those in dangerous situations will be saved; those living quiet lives will go on a journey. Those in business will face adversities, and then make good gains later in the year.

Line 5 Regrets vanish. The companion bites through the flesh. Advancing thus, what error can there be?

Whenever these individuals meet with estrangement or opposition some associate or friend joins them. Troubles disappear and there is no regret over their not being able to conquer the difficulties independently. This applies to both the physical and metaphysical realms. Leaders and persons of influence are indicated, but there are times when they too need help and support. Advancing in this manner will be beneficial for them.

Most auspicious: He will be a noble person and a man of talent and virtue, in a high and respected position. His actions and dealings will be sincere and humble. He will be supported and helped by wise and able men, and will render support in return. His attainments will be worthy, and he will have a rich and rewarding life.

Least auspicious: He will receive some help from others, mainly from members of his family. He will have and enjoy inherited wealth. In business matters he will find cooperative associates, but he may have serious disputes with his brothers or sisters.

In yearly hexagram:

Officer or official	He will be promoted.
Business and professional	His writings and other efforts will be quite productive.
Ordinary people	He will receive help and make profits. If a bachelor, he may marry.
	If one of the less auspicious, he will have many difficulties.

Line 6   Solitary and estranged. He envisages a boar covered with mud and a wagon full of fiends. First he draws his bow, then he lays it aside. They are not bandits but relatives through marriage. Proceeding forward, rain falls. Good fortune.

The symbolism comes from the characters and position of, and the effects produced by, lines 6 and 3. At first, line 6 is alone and against much opposition. He looks at those who should help him and imagines that they are dirty pigs, or a wagon full of fiends. He starts on the offensive, but then realizes that they are friends after all. As the situation clears, just as the air is made clear by a fall of rain, good fortune results. In general, these persons are too smart for their own good and for that of others. They see many things that others do not observe. However, by becoming tolerant and able to live with limitations, and by giving others due credit, they can achieve unions, and their work and efforts will then be productive.

Most auspicious: He will be intelligent, sagacious and discerning However, he will be unyielding on many occasions, resulting in solitude until he changes his ways. He will have hardships early in life, and then better fortune as he mellows. He may get married several times.

Least auspicious: He will have much solitude and lonely activity. He will be quite intractable and will cause many disputes. He will have an unstable life.

In yearly hexagram:

Officer or official	Demotion is probable due to mis-representations.
Business and professional	He will have many perplexities at the beginning of the year, but some progress later.
Ordinary people	He will have losses at first, then small gains. He may be falsely accused.

KEYNOTES

1. When confused, let things work themselves out.
2. Intuition and foresight will be very helpful.
3. Rise to meet challenges.
4. Choose cooperative companions.
5. Value all help from others.
6. If you are alone against your wishes it is your own fault.

CONDENSATIONS FOR DAILY CYCLES

1. Should you occasion some loss, do not worry about it. You cannot lose what is rightfully yours. Be cautious when dealing with evil people.
2. Good often comes in unexpected ways. You will unexpectedly meet a person, or intuitively find an idea, beneficial to you.
3. There is a set-back. Do not be misled. Continue to persevere in what is right and just. The result will be good.
4. You feel isolated, but you will find or meet another whom you can cooperate with and trust.
5. Proceeding with current plans will result in blessings, even though there may have been previous doubt about them.
6. Through the law of change your opposition is waning. When this is completed you will have good fortune.

Hexagram 39   Chien ☵☶ Impediments

SIMPLE TRANSLATION OF TEXT

Impediments. The south-west is favorable. The north-east is hostile. Advantageous to see the great man. Perseverance in the right brings good fortune.

COMMENTARY

This hexagram is made up of the two trigrams, K'an, water (chasms), over Kên, mountain. These are both impediments. They are also the north and north-east trigrams in the Sequence of Later Heaven, with Li and K'un being in the south and south-west. Obviously, mountains and chasms are obstacles, whereas clarity and openness are favorable. The strong line in the fifth position leading its proper correlate, a weak second line, makes it advantageous to seek the great man, i.e. a minister from heaven. Perseverance in what is right will result in good fortune in the face of impediments. Those who have their controlling line in one of the first three positions have the potential to be strong, sturdy and steadfast like a mountain, while those with their controlling line in one of the upper three positions will be more inclined to nourish and help others in a step by step manner. All possess a keen awareness of potential dangers as well as an intuitive knowledge of the easier and better courses to follow in any given situation. They will be found where strength of character is advantageous, and will be involved with many other persons. The more auspicious will make good judges and legislators. A number will be aviators. All will spend much time improving themselves inwardly.

Those born in the eighth month will be more auspicious.

CONTROLLING LINES (FROM BOTTOM TO TOP)

Line 1   Advancing leads to difficulties. Quietude brings praise.

Boldly pushing forward against impediments often results in one encountering many unnecessary obstacles or difficulties. At the beginning it is best to quietly ponder, and then lay firm, sound plans which one knows one can carry out. Impetuosity is dangerous. These persons will be planners and administrators, and blessed with a substantial amount of common sense.

Most auspicious: He will be greatly talented and will achieve a worthy and well-earned reputation. He will know how to stop in the face of impending dangers, and how to surmount or circumvent them. He will have a slow and difficult start in his career, but will have a favorable life later.

Least auspicious: He will be reasonably energetic, but unambitious. He will keep clear of difficulties by not charging into them, and will be content to lead a simple and virtuous life.

In yearly hexagram:

Officer or official	Earned praise can be expected.
Business and professional	Hold back from engaging in major projects.
Ordinary people	Be conservative, and stick to proven methods.

Line 2 The king's administrator meets with impediment upon impediment. This is not his fault.

Line 5 represents the king. Line 2 is the proper correlate of line 5, and represents the king's public administrator, who here runs into a great many difficulties. These are due to the situation he is in rather than being self-generated, hence he is not held at fault. Stable and strong persons, who work for the ruler or leader in difficult situations, are indicated. They are able and effective administrators and are supported by their superior or leader. Their work will constantly involve dealing with troublesome matters, both in quantity and quality, but they will be equal to whatever task faces them. Naturally some will be more successful than others.

Most auspicious: He will be patriotic, loyal to his superiors and to his parents, and a noble father to his family. Whatever he does will be well planned and his results will be effective. This applies in both his personal and professional life.

Least auspicious: He will be honest, loyal and sincere, with his family and in his enterprises. Father and son will cooperate in meeting difficulties. Wife will work with husband, but they will not be socially minded. He will be respected in his community.

In yearly hexagram:

Officer or official	Patriotism and loyalty will be displayed with effective results.

| Business and professional | It is not propitious to try to advance this year. |
| Ordinary people | He can expect adversity at first, with things smoothing out later. The less auspicious may die. |

Line 3 Advancing leads to troubles, so he stops and returns.

At the top of the mountain, the third line of the trigram Kên, one is overawed by what one sees. This man does not have the wherewithal to proceed alone (line 6 does not support line 3 here). He is sufficiently wise to be aware of his real situation at all times, and so forgoes dangerous advances, returning instead to his family and friends, where he finds mutual trust, comfort and support.

Most auspicious: He will know the right time to act, and how to get help and support from his friends, peers, and people in general. He may be assigned to a government position, and his life will be peaceful and comfortable.

Least auspicious: He will be in local government or in a business position, where he will assist in making changes and improvements. He will follow accepted mores. Also, he will receive help from his wife or her family.

In yearly hexagram:

Officer or official	He will be transferred to the seat of government, and promoted.
Business and professional	Being more competitive will produce favorable results.
Ordinary people	He may marry or have a child. Those less auspicious may be injured.

Line 4 Advancing leads to troubles. Returning brings union.

Line 4 is at the brink of the chasm, and thus serious impediments are faced. Since this is the position of the minister it is right for this man to pause and unite the divergent elements in every situation so that a successful advance can be made when the time is propitious. These persons will become factory managers, union organizers, psychologists, and in all similar activities where coordination of divergent activities or ideas is involved.

Most auspicious: He will associate with leaders and intellectuals and he himself will be well versed in their concerns. His knowledge and character will naturally attract others to him, and he will be of benefit to his country and his business. He will receive a substantial inheritance, and will have a good family, with several children.

Least auspicious: He will also have a good and productive life, and will receive help from others.

In yearly hexagram:

Officer or official	He will receive a promotion of some sort.
Business and professional	Efforts in the direction of fame and profit will be successful.
Ordinary people	The more auspicious will make gains. The less auspicious will have many disputes.

Line 5 In the midst of great impediments, friends come.

This line is the ruler, and is proper in all respects. It is, however, in the chasm, so this man faces impediments, but by virtue of the line's correctness, friends come and he receives all the help and support he needs to overcome or circumvent the impediments, and achieve his aims.

Most auspicious: He will be a wise, able and respected leader or manager, who follows the golden mean, and carries out what is right and just at all times. He is trusted and respected by his juniors and seniors alike, and will always receive whatever support he needs. He will contribute to the welfare of the world, his country, and his community. He will have a good and rewarding life.

Least auspicious: He will come from a poor family, but because he always does things correctly and has a good character, he will be helped by others, and will gradually improve and increase his status, influence and affluence.

In yearly hexagram:

For everyone	It will be an auspicious year. He will be supported by good people, and will achieve his goals and a profit.

Line 6 Advancing leads to impediments. Remaining brings great good fortune. It is advantageous to see the great man.

The top line has gone as far as it can. These persons have learned how to overcome impediments, so proceeding further would not be beneficial. Instead, it brings great blessings to them if they stay where they are in life, and support, help and bring along those under them. Seeing the great man here means turning inward to find the guidance and inspiration for the actions they should take in their magnanimity. They will be great teachers and leaders, whether in the employ of others or acting independently.

Most auspicious: He will be greatly talented, and a man of strong virtue, who works unselfishly to serve his ruler and the people, directly or indirectly. His efforts will be effective and he will establish great merit. He will have a favorable reputation and will probably become famous. He will exert much influence, and will have a good family and personal life.

Least auspicious: He will also lead a good and influential life at a fairly high level. He will receive much support from others.

In yearly hexagram:

Officer or official	If in the mainstream of activity, he will be promoted.
Business and professional	Altruistic efforts will be productive.
Ordinary people	He will associate with good people and gain profit.

KEYNOTES

1. Impetuousness and haste results in opposition.
2. Always proceed step by step.
3. Help your own family first.
4. Unite divergent elements.
5. Always use whatever leadership ability you have.
6. Always help others when you can.

CONDENSATIONS FOR DAILY CYCLES

1. Stop, look, and listen. Forging ahead rashly will only lead to difficulties.
2. Often when working for someone else one meets with impediments that are not one's own fault. Cope with these as best you can.
3. When great dangers are being faced, fall back on your known support. Do not plunge recklessly ahead alone.
4. Unite divergent elements, and seek outside strength and influence as necessary, to overcome your obstacles.

5. The difficulties are truly great. Through continued progress and right actions you will automatically receive the help you need. 6. Rely on your intuition, or on the advice of a great and good leader, and you will conquer your difficulties.

Hexagram 40   Hsieh ☰☰ *Deliverance (Release, Clarification)*

SIMPLE TRANSLATION OF TEXT
Deliverance. The south-west is favorable. When going forward is not productive, going back brings good fortune. When going forward is a necessity, early action will bring good fortune.

COMMENTARY
This hexagram is made up of the trigrams Chên, thunder, over K'an, rain. The name Hsieh implies untying something difficult. The air is always clear and smells fresh again after thunder and rain, hence the names Deliverance, Release, and Clarification. K'an includes step by step progress, and Chên signifies the renewal of life in the springtime. Thus these persons will be inwardly tenacious, persevering, progressive, purposeful and resolute individuals. They will take their time reaching decisions, but once their mind is made up they will do everything possible to achieve their goals expeditiously. Some may be criticized for being too laborious, but on the whole most will be noble, understanding and considerate, forgiving freely, and being lenient yet just regarding crimes and wrongdoings. The south-west is symbolic of where the people are to be found, so these persons should work in public or concern themselves with public matters.

Those born in the twelfth month will be more auspicious.

CONTROLLING LINES (FROM BOTTOM TO TOP)
Line 1   No error.

These persons possess the basic traits described in the commentary above, but since this is the first line of the hexagram they are not as strong nor as deeply ingrained as they could be. In general, the actions of these persons will be innocent rather than conniving or devious, and their lives will tend to be free from major error, especially in the area of their character development.

Most auspicious: He will have a well-balanced character, combining toughness with gentleness in his leadership and in the division of family duties and responsibilities. He will know the right times to use severity or gentleness, and his leadership will produce lasting benefits. He will be free from serious troubles and will have an auspicious life.

Least auspicious: He will also be persistent, stable and calm, acting correctly and leading in the right manner. Others will readily cooperate with him, and he will have a good life.

In yearly hexagram:

Officer or official	He will make favorable progress. Promotion can be expected.
Business and professional	All written efforts will be especially productive and beneficial.
Ordinary people	If a bachelor, he may get married, and it will be an auspicious event. Business enterprises will flourish.

Line 2　He slays three foxes in the field and receives a golden arrow. Righteousness will bring good fortune.

The 'three foxes' are, according to ancient symbolism, greed, ignorance and fear. And a golden arrow was a highly prized award received only when something truly great had been done. Persons capable of eliminating these three 'foxes' within themselves, and in others, are exceptional. If they succeed, they definitely merit a substantial reward. These individuals will have inherent leadership qualities, and their lives will be favored, by the localities in which they live and the education that they receive. They will develop into moral and spiritual leaders (some may even become religious leaders) wherever they are and irrespective of their worldly careers.

Most auspicious: He will follow the golden mean and will be a just and impartial person. He will have good morals, personal integrity, and a favorable reputation. He will be able to inspire others, promote good, and expel evil. His life will be beneficial and favorable on many levels.

Least auspicious: He will also associate with, and help, good people. He will have wise persons as close friends, and he will avoid evil. He will always have ample wealth and, may get married two or more times.

In yearly hexagram:

Officer or official	He will be assigned to a central position of influence.
Business and professional	He will be recommended highly, and his efforts will be readily accepted.
Ordinary people	He will increase his property holdings. It will be propitious to start something new.

Line 3 Luggage bearers ride in the carriage. This attracts robbers. Continuing in such a way leads to blame.

This line shows that pretending to be something that one is not leads to dangers and difficulties. On the other hand, it is auspicious for those for whom pretense is a requirement, such as actors and actresses, or those connected with advertising and careers of a similar nature. Regrettably this trait will have a tendency to enter into their private lives, and this can result in difficulties.

Most auspicious: He may rise to a high position and income, in a well chosen and appropriate field, but it will have much artificiality associated with it.

Least auspicious: He will tend to be cunning, vicious, mean, corrupt, ugly and unsociable. His life will be one of hardships.

In yearly hexagram:

Officer or official	He may be demoted unless he is extremely careful.
Business and professional	Defamations and handicaps are likely.
Ordinary people	He is likely to be robbed, and suffer losses. Disputes are probable.

Line 4 Emancipate yourself from your big toe. A friend then comes. Put your trust in him.

Some inferior internal elements, or some external weaknesses (in associates, career, position, ideas or situation) are impeding rapid progress, as would happen with an individual suffering from an ailing big toe. Advancements can be made, but they will not be easy or without suffering until the big toe is well. But, since like attracts like, a friend will come, in whom you can and should put your trust. These persons have great potential, but they must find themselves first before it can be developed and be of beneficial use to them. Their degree of success will depend on correct self-analysis, and on the extent to which they are willing to be of service to others (the fourth line is the position of the minister). Most auspicious: He will find the right path early in life, and will then have a good career, with many friends and associates. He will eventually rise to a position of influence and affluence.

Least auspicious: He will not find the right path, and will fumble and stumble through life. His talents, efforts and perseverance will be minimal, resulting in a poor life.

In yearly hexagram:

Officer or official	Do not let yourself be drawn into an evil clique.
Business and professional	There is a possibility of malpractices and malfeasance.
Ordinary people	Beware of trouble from mean and conniving people.

Line 5 The superior man achieves release. Good fortune ensues. He receives the confidence of inferior persons.

No human being is perfect, but these individuals develop themselves to such an extent that inferior elements are automatically repelled, and good fortune consequently results for these superior persons. Their greatness brings respect and confidence, without any jealousy, even from inferiors, whatever their position. The function of those born under this line demands great self-sacrifice and only a few people can attain such a high degree of evolution. The potential for doing so, of course, exists in others as well.

Most auspicious: He will be a sage and sagacious person, with a keen insight into, and understanding of, human nature. He will correct evil and evil persons, and will help all people. He will select individuals wisely when meeting needs, and will be in an influential position benefiting many people.

Least auspicious: He will also attract people through his sincerity and honesty, and will have a favorable and locally influential life.

In yearly hexagram:

Officer or official	He will be assigned to a highly important position.
Business and professional	He will achieve fame.

Ordinary people	A year of benefits and profits. Troubles will tend to correct themselves.

Line 6   The prince shot an arrow and killed a hawk on a high wall. Everything is favorable.

The highest degree of effecting deliverance or release is depicted here. The prince is a truly noble person. The hawk is symbolic of evil or inferior elements, which the prince eliminates with the proper weapon, i.e. an arrow. These are, or will be, persons who are highly developed, and who will leave the normal mundane manner of existence behind them and devote themselves to higher causes and spiritual matters. They are to be found in several different spheres of activity, and will usually be quite successful.

Most auspicious: He will be greatly talented, and enthusiastic in his efforts to achieve results. He will be a man of influence and favorable reputation, courageous, brave and effective, with sword, tongue or pen. He will make great contributions to his country and to the world, as well as having a good personal life, especially with his family.

Least auspicious: He will also be a fortunate and influential individual, highly respected, and with a favorable life, in a modest way.

In yearly hexagram:

Officer or official	An auspicious year, with a beneficial transfer or promotion.
Business and professional	A year of unusual effectiveness.
Ordinary people	A favorable year with considerable gain.

KEYNOTES

1. Calmness is propitious.
2. Conquer yourself before trying to conquer others.
3. Avoid false pretenses.
4. Overcome your pushfulness.
5. Self-confidence is ever desirable.
6. Be helpful to others.

CONDENSATIONS FOR DAILY CYCLES

1. Relax and rest. Remain calm and peaceful today.

2. Eliminate greed, ignorance and fear from considerations, and the results will be favorable.

3. People readily discern false pretenses. Be yourself.

4. Stop driving so hard externally, and refine yourself inwardly. Cooperate with a companion.

5. Have faith, confidence, and respect for yourself and your subordinates, and you can accomplish great things.

6. Continue perfecting yourself; then help others.

Hexagram 41   Sun ☶ *Decrease (Loss)*

SIMPLE TRANSLATION OF TEXT

Decrease. If there is sincerity, sublime good fortune. No error. Firmness and correctness in one's goals make all actions taken advantageous. How shall this be demonstrated? By sincere sacrifice, even with just two small bowls.

COMMENTARY

When a mountain (Kên) sits over a lake (Tui) part of the lake is absorbed into the mountain, and part of the mountain is immersed in the lake, so there is a decrease in each. These are persons who present a stern, strong front, who need to soften their natures and traits inwardly for maximum effectiveness. Some will be stubborn, fixed, and set in their ways. Others will have different faults which need to be decreased. The lower trigram is a lake, which indicates that they have the potential to nourish others. These people will develop this potential more and more as they sincerely rid themselves of harmful attributes, especially anger and irritability, and increasingly adopt more beneficial characteristics. They should be particularly wary of their tendency to try and live in the past. Being humble, reverent, and thankful for all the blessings bestowed by the Creator will be helpful, both to these persons and to those whom they are helping.

Those born in the seventh month will be more auspicious.

CONTROLLING LINES (FROM BOTTOM TO TOP)

Line 1   It is not wrong to depart quickly when one's work is done. First he should reflect how much he can help others without harming them.

Normally it is the best policy to move on quickly without fuss to a new task when the previous one is completed. The world, however, is based on people helping and supporting each other, directly or indirectly. So, when this person's task is finished he should help any others who need it. He is cautioned that being too helpful and doing too much for others may be just as harmful as not doing enough. He must give help only after due thought, and only to the extent that it does not place the other under an oppressive obligation. These persons will continually help themselves and then help others, no matter what position they may hold. Most auspicious: He will be in a high position, serving his ruler or leader unselfishly. He will adapt quickly to changing circumstances and handle matters in such a way as to bring praise. He will discern the true needs of others and will assist them judiciously when necessary. He will become wealthy and famous. Least auspicious: He will be a man of virtue, but lacking in common sense, so that he neither helps himself nor others advantageously; therefore he will have a hard life and will be very busy. Unfortunately he will remain poor.

In yearly hexagram:

Officer or official	He will place duty ahead of his family and will win praise from his superiors.
Business and professional	His chances of selection to receive an award or distinction are very good.
Ordinary people	A good year for gains and profit.

Line 2 Maintain correctness. Undertakings bring misfortune. He increases others without decreasing himself.

All life is a matter of service in one form or another, and there are an almost limitless number of ways one can serve. Those depicted here will fare best if they pursue only established ways, and do not try to take that one extra step into the unknown. Also, the more service they render to others, the greater their own advantage. Hence, 'he increases others without decreasing himself.' The gifts of the universe are unlimited, and the more one gives the more one receives. The basic principle here is to find needs and then fill them, within due limits and in accordance with existing mores.

Most auspicious: He will be upright in character and diligent in the pursuit of benevolence. He will continuously make beneficial contributions to his country, his work and his family, as well as uplifting many others. He will have a rich and rewarding life.

Least auspicious: He also will be largely unselfish. He will make conscientious efforts to be of service to others, and will have ample means for a modest life.

In yearly hexagram:

Officer or official	Hold firm. One can expect no advancement this year.
Business and professional	Maintain conformity to the standard laid down. There will be real progress this year.
Ordinary people	Stick to accepted and normal ways. A routine year.

Line 3   When three people set forth together, their number decreases by one. When one sets forth alone, he finds a companion.

This reflects a balanced pattern in keeping with the balance between Yin and Yang. These persons will be good arbiters and administrators, who equalize matters for the maximum benefit of all concerned. Their private lives will be as well balanced as their professional lives. This holds true in all spheres, mental, physical and spiritual.

Most auspicious: He will have excellent associates, with whose cooperation much can be achieved. He will be virtuous, judicious and benevolent. His deeds and accomplishments will merit praise, and will have the approval of both his juniors and his seniors. He will have a good life.

Least auspicious: He will also be successful in cooperation and social activity, with his desires and actions readily accepted by others. He will have an easy life, with ample material possessions.

In yearly hexagram:

Officer or official	He will work in harmony with others and produce effective results.
Business and professional	He will study extensively, and/or have a successful enterprise in conjunction with a friend.

| Ordinary people | He will receive help with his plans and desires, and will profit. If a bachelor, he may marry. |

Line 4   He reduces the troubles besetting him. Others then come and are glad to help him. No error.

To correct external conditions one must first correct oneself inwardly. To reduce one's troubles one must first overcome one's faults. When this is done others (under the aegis of line 1) are glad to come and help. This brings happiness and freedom from error. These persons will be in positions where they can render service to others, and will have the intuitive understanding that by constantly improving themselves they will gradually become of greater benefit to themselves and to others. This will bring happiness to all those concerned. Some will make much more rapid progress than others.

Most auspicious: He will forge ahead and try to do what is right at all times. He will gladly correct his own faults, and judiciously point out faults in others. He will attain much knowledge and experience which he will use to advantage by establishing something truly worthwhile. He will be favored.

Least auspicious: He also will correct his own faults rapidly. He will have many hardships during his early years and in middle age. His senior years will be easier and more effective.

In yearly hexagram:

| For everyone | Those who are in the midst of troubles or disasters will overcome them. Those who are sick will be healed. Those who are worried will have a joyous year. Those who have been inactive will be active. All will experience some unusual joy. All will make gains. |

Line 5   One is enriched by ten pairs of tortoise shells. It cannot be opposed. Great good fortune.

The changing of this line into a Yang results in hexagram 61, Chung Fu, Inner Truth. When inner truth is great, no external force can prevent good fortune from materializing. It is like receiving the good fortune of ten pairs of tortoise shells (tortoise shells were used for divination in ancient times) all giving auspicious omens. Thus, when one truly decreases one's faults nothing can prevent one's good fortune. These people are leaders and managers who have learned a lesson similar to that expressed by Napoleon when he said, 'If I could keep my anger beneath my chin I could rule the world.' These persons achieve great control over other faults as well, and are examples for others to emulate.

Most auspicious: He will be a strong, open-minded administrator for, and supporter of, the leader in his enterprise. He will be in a high position, and helped by wise and able associates. He will be respected by his juniors and seniors alike, and will attain wealth and fame.

Least auspicious: He will be respected and well known locally. He will have a favorable life and a good family.

In yearly hexagram:

Officer or official	He will find himself in or be assigned to a high position, as a planner for and advisor to his leader.
Business and professional	He will achieve some special merit or award.
Ordinary people	He will make money. It will be a good year in other ways as well.

Line 6 He increases others without depriving himself. No error. Right actions will produce good fortune. Firm goals advantageous. He obtains followers but no longer has a home.

Unselfish devotion to duty for the benefit of others results in directly helping others, and indirectly helping oneself as well. Naturally this is not erroneous. Furthermore, the more correct one's actions are, the better the good fortune produced. Since this man has firm goals he will attract followers. The demand for his services will be so great that he will have to sacrifice his home life to devote his energies to the public good. Men of great strength of character, coupled with deep wisdom and able leadership, will be the most successful.

Most auspicious: He will establish universal goals for himself, designed to benefit the masses, and will work unselfishly to achieve these goals. Indirectly he will attract wealth and satisfaction for himself. What he establishes will be lasting and worthwhile.

Least auspicious: He will set higher than average goals for himself, but will not be ambitious. He will tend to talk rather than act, and hence his accomplishments will not be great. His travels will bring him in contact with the upper classes, and he will be moderately successful in most of his activities. He may even become a religious leader or a monk.

In yearly hexagram:

Officer or official	He will attract the masses to his leader and will be rewarded.
Business and professional	Strong desires and persistent efforts will achieve favorable results.
Ordinary people	He will receive help from superiors. He will gain profit, and will also go on a journey.

KEYNOTES
1. Follow the golden mean when helping others.
2. Serve others well.
3. Strive for balance in all matters.
4. Correct internal conditions first.
5. Inner truth is the key to all success.
6. Have a universal goal to work on.

CONDENSATIONS FOR DAILY CYCLES
1. Help others after you have finished your own work, but do not help them unnecessarily.
2. There is a time for giving and a time for receiving. Be correct in all the actions you take.
3. One is too lonely. Three is a crowd. Strive for proper balance.
4. Before being critical of others, first correct your own faults.
5. Inner greatness automatically brings external reward. Develop your inner self.
6. If you look at matters from a broad rather than from a selfish point of view, then others will help you in your efforts.

Hexagram 42   I ☴ *Increase (Gain)*

SIMPLE TRANSLATION OF TEXT
Increase. It is propitious to have a goal and to engage in undertakings (cross the great stream).

COMMENTARY
The Image associated with this hexagram symbolizes increase. It advises the superior man when he sees good to imitate it, and when he sees faults to correct them. The action of the wind driving clouds together, producing thunder and rain, clears the air and nourishes others. That is the action of the two trigrams in this hexagram. Hence, this is a time for rendering service to others. Through service one gains control of one's life, which increases others and oneself as well. These persons will be men of vision, with beneficial ideas. They will be wise and energetic, and have a strong liking for people as well as a pleasing personality. Their worth will become obvious to others early in their lives, and the more auspicious will rise quickly in their careers. They will never stop learning, nor will they ever cease rendering service.

Those born in the seventh month will be the most auspicious. Those born between the second and eighth months will be more auspicious than those born from the ninth to the first month, inclusive.

CONTROLLING LINES (FROM BOTTOM TO TOP)
Line 1 It is advantageous to undertake great deeds. Sublime good fortune. No blame.

This line is the ruling line of the trigram Chên, arousing, and, since it is in the right place, it is a time for deeds of great quality. There is no blame, whether they be great or small in scope. The important thing is that they should be noble of purpose. These individuals will have a strong vitality, imagination and enthusiasm. They will analyze their possible actions thoroughly in advance, formulate feasible plans, and then execute them precisely. Rarely, if ever, will they do anything on the spur of the moment without a purpose.
Most auspicious: He will become capable of undertaking great works, of a nature that will establish long term benefits, and be considered meritable. He will intuitively know and support those things which are durable or worthy of duration. He will serve the Creator, his country, his family and his work well, and will have an auspicious life.

Least auspicious: He will be a man of worthwhile character and much ability. He will not be over ambitious, and not inclined to undertake deeds of great magnitude, but he will manage his household affairs ably and successfully.

In yearly hexagram:

Officer or official	Promotion is probable.
Business and professional	Advancements are favored.
Ordinary people	Strong desires will be fulfilled.

Line 2 One is enriched by ten pairs of tortoise shells. It cannot be opposed. Righteous persistence brings good fortune. The Creator is served by the king. Supreme good fortune.

As with line 5 of Hexagram 41, through change in this line the hexagram turns into Hexagram 61, Chung Fu, or inner truth, from which all external conditions stem. The force of inner truth cannot be opposed. Here, too, this person is primarily in a supporting role, in keeping with the general character of the hexagram, i.e., being of service to others. He who renders service here is commended by the king to the Creator during worship and sacrifice. In ancient times this was a very great honor, since it implied being included in the king's own family. The result of mutual support and service from persons so ably qualified, and in their proper positions, is truly great good fortune for the king, the masses, and for the individuals themselves. The maxim to be drawn from all this is that to serve is to rule.

Most auspicious: He will be a well-qualified person of noble character, possessing noteworthy traits, and a strong inner desire to render service. He will be humble and open-minded, associating with good friends in proper places. He will be in a high position, respected by those in authority, by his peers and by the people. He will have a long, favorable and prosperous life.

Least auspicious: He also will be of noble character, but not too intelligent nor too ambitious. He will have a modest life, with ample wealth. His few accomplishments will be beneficial ones.

In yearly hexagram:

Officer or official	Promotion may be anticipated.
Business and professional	His efforts will favorably enhance his reputation.
Ordinary people	He will gain profits, and his property may increase.

Line 3 He gains through unfortunate circumstances not of his own making. Walking in the middle he announces himself to his prince by the emblem of his office.

Here at the top of the trigram Chên, arousing, one is very ambitious but one's position (line 3) is precarious and insecure. Divine manifestations are not always in keeping with man's ideas. These persons will be able and sincere, devoted in their efforts to be of service to their leaders and their country, but they will often find themselves in difficult situations. In many dire circumstances there will be an unexpected turn of events which will be enriching and rewarding. Such matters are controlled by the Creator, who knows far better than man what should truly be and why. These persons do not seek fame or glory for themselves, yet will find themselves well known and sought after, as a result of their ever increasing reputation. Any hardships and worries are due to their karma, which they are in process of coming to terms with. Most auspicious: He will be loyal, upright and diligent in his service to his leader, and will serve equally well in times of peace or war. He will be dynamic and courageous, and will seek opportunities to be of ever greater service to his country, his work, and his family. He will establish himself in a high position, socially, professionally and financially.
Least auspicious: He will have considerable knowledge and much common sense, and will know how to deal with almost any situation that is not too difficult. He will be trusted and respected, and his senior years will be very favorable.
In yearly hexagram:

Officer or official	He will establish merit, or undertake a great work.
Business and professional	He should be high-minded and energetic, and thereby achieve good results.
Ordinary people	He will gain profit, and have a good ending to the year.

Line 4 He walks in the middle and the prince follows his advice. His fealty is such that he can be entrusted with removing the capital.

Noble, capable and trustworthy individuals are depicted here. Full

303

confidence can be reposed in them to do whatever needs to be done, great or small. They will carry through all duties and responsibilities laid upon them. They will work for, and close to, great leaders.

Most auspicious: He will be in a high position in the government, working for the ruler. His efforts will be fair and just, for the people as well as for the ruler. He will make contributions of lasting benefit, and will gain fame and wealth and have a rewarding life.

Least auspicious: He will also be an effective administrator, but in a business or other enterprise. His ideas and efforts will have much merit, and will be readily accepted. He will have a good life.

In yearly hexagram:

Officer or official	He will be in a high and influential advisory position.
Business and professional	He will gain a favorable reputation.
Ordinary people	He will build or alter his house, or move to a new one. His affairs will go well.

Line 5   When you have a truly sincere heart you need not ask questions. Supreme good fortune. Your unswerving virtue will be recognized.

The highest degree of rendering service to increase others is depicted here. It stems from a deep inner desire so strong that it moves everything externally in the desired direction. One's actions are right and just, and consequently these persons have no need to ask the oracle for advice or guidance. The right answers are already there inside, merely waiting for the opportunity to be made manifest. These individuals will be a blessing and benefit wherever they are.

Most auspicious: His talents and abilities will be great enough to control his country if necessary. He will love people and will do his best for them. They, in turn, will respect him. He will achieve well-deserved fame and wealth.

Least auspicious: He will also have a great love for people and will want to do the best he can for them, but in a quieter and more private way than the most auspicious. He may control an enterprise of benefit to others, or be a minister or a monk.

In yearly hexagram:

Officer or official	He will be assigned to the support of a high official.
Business and professional	His efforts at advancement will bring beneficial gains.
Ordinary people	Strong desires will be fulfilled. He will associate with several good friends.

Line 6 He who does not strive to increase others will be attacked. Inconsistency of heart brings misfortune.

Moral, physical, intellectual and spiritual atrophy are depicted here. These are persons who have talents and knowledge but fail to use them. The result is a retrogression leading to misfortune. One should strive to the best of one's ability to keep one's talents active through use, and especially through service to others. Neglect is a waste and a failure to carry out a part of one's responsibility to one's fellow men. Lack of ambition, laziness, selfishness, egoism, and a generally negative attitude are indicated. Most auspicious: He will be grasping, and covetous of fame and profits. He will tend to use others callously, and walk over those in his path in order to attain his desires. He may obtain considerable wealth, but there will be neither happiness nor friendship associated with it.
Least auspicious: He will be a vicious, treacherous, lecherous and evil person, hurting all with whom he comes in contact. He will have a harmful life.
In yearly hexagram:

Officer or official	He will be blamed for greed.
Business and professional	He will be blamed for over extending his enterprise.
Ordinary people	He will have difficulties due to greediness, and he may even get seriously hurt.

KEYNOTES
1. Great deeds should be done only when they are timely.
2. Inner truth overcomes external difficulties.
3. Insincerity reaps its own reward.
4. Trustworthiness is ever essential.
5. True sincerity is unquestioned.
6. Selfishness is self-destructive.

CONDENSATIONS FOR DAILY CYCLES
1. The time is favorable for action. Do not hesitate any longer.
2. When your inner nature is truly good, external benefits will automatically come to you. Examine your character.
3. You will probably be enriched by seemingly dire or adverse circumstances.
4. Serve others well, and you will be serving yourself well.
5. With unselfish and noble motives you can achieve fulfilment of your desires.
6. Any display of selfishness or egotism will harm your efforts. Do not be lazy or greedy either.

Hexagram 43   Kuai ☰ *Resoluteness (Removal)*

SIMPLE TRANSLATION OF TEXT
Resoluteness. One must make the matter known truthfully in court. Also one must announce it in one's own city to avert a resort to arms. Advancing is advantageous.

COMMENTARY
The last weakness or evil (that you possess) must be removed (from the top of the hexagram) in order that the perfection of the Creative may be achieved. This must be done with determination, openly and in public. There is always the danger of evil trying to fight its way back to regain its former place. Hence not only is an open confession required, but one's inner self must know and accept the change, and carry it through in a peaceful manner. Fighting will give the evil strength. Advancing, and removing the weeds one by one, in a just way, will be advantageous. The trigram Tui, lake, is above Ch'ien, heaven. Heaven indicates heavenly nourishment, i.e. the improvement of morals and character in some, and the enhancement of spiritual development in others. These individuals have the potential to be superior persons, able to help other individuals to improve themselves. They will be found in all walks of life and at various levels, always at the stations where destiny decrees they can serve the divine purpose best. Their inner strength and ability is great if

they choose to use it. Through use it will grow and thus be of ever greater value.

Those born in the third month will be more auspicious.

CONTROLLING LINES (FROM BOTTOM TO TOP)
Line 1 Power in the toes. Advance. No success. He is blameworthy.

This line, in the bottom position, does not have sufficient strength to advance and attain success by itself. Hence, any boastfulness or show of power is erroneous since this will not accomplish results. If one acts thus, one truly deserves blame. Primarily, it indicates that those with this controlling line should be cautious in their lives, and only try to advance at any given time as far as they know they can safely go, yet they should always strive for advance. All will have great inner strength, but some will use it for purposes of good and some will not.

Most auspicious: He will know when, in which direction, and how far to advance. He will be wise, and capable of avoiding danger. He will be wise inwardly; his external circumstances will be such, however, that he will not be able to use all his knowledge effectively. He will have a good life.

Least auspicious: He will be a man of no virtue, who will use his powers for gain and self-satisfaction. He will be boastful and will exaggerate. He will always try to be the leader, but will lack the basic intelligence to carry matters through effectively. He will have many hardships, and may bring disaster upon himself and his associates.

In yearly hexagram:

Officer or official	He will be blamed for a rash decision.
Business and professional	Efforts to advance will be repelled by others.
Ordinary people	He will make many mistakes, due to rashness and impetuosity.

Line 2 Cries of alarm at night. He who is prepared (armed) need have no fear.

He who is alert and prepared can cope with any situation. These persons are strong, energetic and diligent in their efforts, and in correcting and improving. They have the innate intelligence to know what needs to be done, and how to do it. They then have the necessary strength of character, and a sufficiently propitious personality, to carry it through to completion. They also know how to protect themselves against even the most artful people.

Most auspicious: He will be wise and thoughtful. He will take logical precautions against calamities, and will help save the nation from imminent dangers. He will follow the golden mean; people will readily submit to him; and he will achieve fame in literary and/or military matters.

Least auspicious: He will also be good at planning and in strategic matters. He will like to be active. Sometimes he will have joy, and sometimes sorrow. He may establish merit and gain a favorable reputation in the government or military, but not to such a high degree as the more auspicious.

In yearly hexagram:

Officer or official	He will be assigned to a position of great authority.
Business and professional	He will make gains through written or literary efforts.
Ordinary people	He will probably suffer from worries, shocks, attempted burglaries, insurance losses, etc.

Line 3 Being powerful in the cheek-bones brings misfortune. The superior man is firmly resolved. Walks alone. Encounters rain. Gets bespattered by mud. The people speak against him. No blame.

These persons are quite strong and intelligent, but unfortunately over eager. They like to talk, but if their efforts are primarily talk with nothing concrete behind it, or if they are injudicious and inadvertently make their plans known in advance to the wrong persons, then misfortune will result. Their eagerness will make them hasty, and, in general, they will not be able to wait for, or cooperate with, slower thinking and acting people. So they will set forth to attain their goals on their own. The rain symbolizes that they will tend to achieve their purpose, but if they are muddied on the way people will think adversely of them. Since their purposes, in general, are correct, they should not be blamed even if they go about trying to attain their goals in the wrong way.

Most auspicious: He will be greatly talented and knowledgeable, and possess toughness and fortitude. He will thoroughly think matters through before acting. He will be able to destroy separatist cliques and help remove the troubles of the country, for the benefit of the government and the people. He will achieve great merit.

Least auspicious: He will be smart yet hawkish, liking to fight, and generally troublesome. He will enjoy solitude, and will have few friends. He will be very critical and will worry frequently.

In yearly hexagram:

Officer or official	He will try to remove evil persons, but will probably fail and be punished by the evil person's followers.
Business and professional	He will tend to be critical and complain that the world does not recognize him appropriately.
Ordinary people	If he follows the right path, a generally favorable year. If one of the less auspicious, he will have hardships, and encounter much evil.

Line 4 There is no skin on his haunches and he walks with difficulty. If he allowed himself to be led like a sheep, occasion for remorse would disappear. Even hearing these words he will not believe them.

Normally the fourth line depicts the minister and the actions appropriate for him. In this case it speaks of an intelligent culprit who has been punished for not listening or not following the advice given him. If he would accept the suggestions made, as a sheep will allow itself to be led, then his troubles and irate feelings would disappear. But he will tend to remain stubborn and not listen to this advice either, but follow his own way, adamantly and defensively. However, if he is wise, as a minister should be, he will use this advice as a guide for removing mean people and evil influences. Some will take this action and some will not.

Most auspicious: He will be a knowledgeable and experienced man of virtue, working for the maximum good. He will work unobtrusively, and will readily accept valuable advice from others.

In general, he will make correct decisions and do what is right, and thereby attain fame.
Least auspicious: He will hold to wrong beliefs obstinately, and his plans will fail. He may become crippled or deaf. He may become a cowboy, a shepherd or a zoo-keeper.
In yearly hexagram:

Officer or official	He will have difficulties due to being considered inadequately qualified for his assignment.
Business and professional	Proposals of a new type will fail.
Ordinary people	He will have disputes, be punished, or have ear or foot trouble.

Line 5   In eliminating undesired vegetation, firm action is necessary. Following the middle course leads to no blame.

The elimination of persistent and insidious evil is depicted here. In the USA the analogy would be to the difficulty in removing crab grass, which establishes roots wherever its tentacles touch the ground, as well as having long and hidden roots in all directions underground. These persons will be leaders, but in difficult and dangerous positions. They must be indomitable in spirit and strong of purpose. They must analyze each situation correctly, and then unrelentingly and persistently pursue the best action possible. If they can do this, following a middle course will help, and not be wrong. The task is great.
Most auspicious: He will be intelligent, perspicacious and quick-witted. He will follow the golden mean, and will correct many evils for the benefit of his country. He will improve the morality of the people, and will curb evil, and evil persons. He will have a rich and rewarding life.
Least auspicious: He will be cowardly and lackadaisical, and will shrink from taking necessary corrective actions. He will lack determination but will try to compensate by being stubbornly biased. He will not be easily accessible; he will be unpredictable, subject to flattery and favors, and will have many difficulties and serious troubles in his life.
In yearly hexagram:

Officer or official	Beware of insidious evils and corruption.
Business and professional	He will make small gains, if diligent.

Ordinary people	Strong wishes will be fulfilled. He will win lawsuits; his health will be good.

Line 6 No support. In the end, misfortune.

Line 6 receives no support, either from line 3 or line 5, so this man is alone. He has arrived at a high place through his own hard effort, and feels himself superior to others, not hesitating to show it in many ways. This becomes damaging to his long term development.

Most auspicious: He will attain wealth and status, but will develop arrogance with it. He will tend to abuse his power by taking advantage of others and harming those with lesser power. He will receive constant sniping at his wealth, and will not find happiness. Least auspicious: He will be extremely jealous, with an acrid disposition. He will have few friends, if any. Misfortunes of one sort or another will be associated with all his efforts.

In yearly hexagram:

Officer or official	Find a way to retreat gracefully from a difficult situation.
Business and professional	It would be best to spend this year improving yourself, personally and professionally.
Ordinary people	Plans will not materialize readily; stick to proven methods. There will be difficulties in the family. An older person may die.

KEYNOTES

1. Stay within your limits.
2. Always be prepared.
3. Back your words with deeds.
4. Accept sound advice, regardless of its source.
5. Be thorough.
6. Never lose the support of others.

CONDENSATIONS FOR DAILY CYCLES

1. It would be a mistake to try to force results today. Proceed only as far as you can safely go.
2. Check your preparations. If you are well prepared, have no fear.

3. Try to be well balanced. Do not try to influence others by words alone. Support words with strength.
4. You are being stubborn. Be willing to listen to, and accept, the advice of others, including this advice.
5. Utmost determination must be used to root out and eliminate adverse influences. With forthrightness it can be done.
6. If you find yourself isolated you have overstepped the mark. Re-assess and redirect your efforts at once.

Hexagram 44   Kou ☰ *Contact (Relationships)*

SIMPLE TRANSLATION OF TEXT
Contact. The maiden is bold and powerful. One should not marry her.

COMMENTARY
A double symbolism is contained in this hexagram. The first is given by the Yin line, which is bold and powerful, and has entered at the bottom of the otherwise all Yang hexagram. Such a maiden, consorting with five men, is not the type one should marry. The other symbolism is given by the trigram Sun, wind, below trigram Ch'ien, heaven. Heavenly matters are thus made known and their influence is felt everywhere. Conversely, whatever things are happening on earth will be known by those above. The controlling lines determine the nature of the meetings and relationships, for all those affected by them. In the adverse lines, inferior individuals are trying to rise primarily, while in the auspicious lines great personages are exercising commendable leadership.

Those born in the fifth month will be more auspicious.

CONTROLLING LINES (FROM BOTTOM TO TOP)
Line 1   The carriage is held back by a metal brake. Righteous courses bring good fortune. Movement permitted in any direction brings misfortune, like when a lean pig rages about.

When inferiors or evil forces try to enter, they must be held in check properly through the pursuit of righteous courses. This keeps everyone and everything in their right places, and brings good fortune. The evil or inferior man, given an inch will take an ell, and will be obstreperous like a lean pig. If permitted, his actions will not be in keeping with the customs, and he will go around fighting and scraping for advantages or gain. Strong persons must be in control.

Most auspicious: He will try to do what is right but will have insufficient talent and strength to accomplish anything truly great. However, he will provide for himself and his family adequately.

Least auspicious: He will possess very little talent or experience, and limited abilities. He will tend to act rashly or recklessly in his efforts to succeed, but this will only produce more difficulties.

In yearly hexagram:

Officer or official	He may be demoted.
Business and professional	He will have grave concern about maintaining his position.
Ordinary people	He will meet a noble person whom he can trust, and who will help him make gains. Women will probably bear a child. The least auspicious may become seriously ill or have disputes.

Line 2 There is a hamper of fish. No error. No advantage to the guests.

The 'hamper of fish' represents line 1, which this line, being immediately above it and one of the rulers of the hexagram, has to hold in check and repel so that it does not mingle with 'the guests,' the remaining four lines above. Individuals of strong character, capable of controlling difficult situations, are depicted here. These persons can be found in nearly all walks of life, and they will be protectors of good government and good ethics.

Most auspicious: He will be greatly talented, experienced, open-minded, open-hearted and benign, with a deep love of people and a willingness to cooperate. He will automatically attract people and be helped by them, and he will have a favorable life.

Least auspicious: He will become a rich person by the wrong means, and will be niggardly, miserly, narrow-minded and obstinate. He will not like people, and will try to make gains at the expense of others. He will not have an enjoyable life.

In yearly hexagram:

Officer or official	He will be promoted.
Business and professional	He will have a chance to be selected for a favorable position.
Ordinary people	He will gain profits, and his personal property may increase. Women are likely to become pregnant.

Line 3 There is no skin on his haunches and he walks with difficulty. The position is dangerous. No great error.

This image refers to what would happen if this line (the third line is normally unfavorable, as it is here) were to try to meet half way, and have a relationship with, line 1. Line 3 does not here receive help from line 6, which normally does assist it, so the position of this man is dangerous. Since he decides to strive upwards he will fare reasonably well and make no great mistakes, even though, for the most part, he must work alone. This will develop a toughness of character which will be both a blessing, keeping him on the right path, and a handicap when dealing with others.

Most auspicious: He will not be sufficiently skilled or gifted to accomplish anything truly great, but he will attain enough affluence to keep his household and have a good family life. His later years will be more fruitful than his earlier life.

Least auspicious: He will work and strive in solitude, and receive no assistance. He will face many hardships, including illnesses. His feet may give particular trouble.

In yearly hexagram:

Officer or official	He will be reprimanded or demoted.
Business and professional	His progress will seem impeded in every direction.
Ordinary people	He will have troubles, and probable business losses.

Line 4 No fish in the hamper. Misfortune imminent.

The 'hamper of fish' is line 1, which correlates with line 2 and hence is not available to this line, its normal partner, thus 'no fish.' The world is designed on a basis of interdependence, mutual support and service, so if one remains alone, as line 4 does here, misfortune will eventually result. These persons are somewhat more auspicious than those in line 3, but not a great deal more, even though the possibility of rising higher is present.

Most auspicious: He will be an individual of noble character, but will not have a position or substantial base from which to operate. People will not be naturally attracted to him, and he will not have followers. He will, however, have a gift of timing and an intuitiveness, which will keep him from having great difficulties. He will have modest means, but not a particularly happy life.

Least auspicious: He will not receive cooperation, and so will not have the benefits that come from associations with good friends and able peers. He will have a generally unhappy life.

In yearly hexagram:

Officer or official	He will be dismissed or demoted.
Business and professional	He will have difficulty maintaining his position.
Ordinary people	He will be plagued by lawsuits and disputes. If old, he may die.

Line 5 The medlar tree leaves hide the fruit. It drops as if from heaven.

This line refers to the kind of person who quietly and unassumingly goes about his business, and at the same time is always improving himself. No one pays particular attention to such persons, and, in general, they are not well known, until suddenly the time is propitious and they reap their reward as if it came from heaven. These persons reflect great wisdom and common sense, since their rising in this unobtrusive manner creates no opposition or enemies. This is very beneficial.

Most auspicious: He will be very wise and open-minded. He will love people and be able to treat all, the good and the bad alike, impartially. He will be an exceptional speaker and writer, by the means of which, with his learning and innate intelligence, he will gain fame and fortune.

Least auspicious: He will also be diligent in learning as well as being practical, with a love of people; but he will not rise as high nor gain as much as the most auspicious.

In yearly hexagram:

Officer or official	He will be appreciated and promoted.

| Business and professional | His efforts will be duly rewarded. |
| Ordinary people | He will meet a noble person who will help him make gains. Women may become pregnant. The least auspicious may die. |

Line 6 He meets others with his horns. Some regrets. No errors.

These persons are inclined to be impractical and reject the world. They fail to realize that there is a right place for everything, and will tend to withdraw from what they consider to be worldly matters. When such matters encroach on them they will try to guard themselves as if meeting them with horns. For these persons such conduct brings few regrets and results in no great error. Regrettably, they will be of little benefit to others.

Most auspicious: He will be lofty and upright, and have a strong personality. His thoughts, actions and advice will be more moral than practical, and evil persons will strive to harm him. His life will be unstable, but adequate financially.

Least auspicious: He will be strong-minded, indomitable, and unreasonable, and for the most part will disregard other people's rights and feelings. Will tend to arouse ill will through his dislike of people. He will be very busy, but to no great avail. Will have many hardships.

In yearly hexagram:

Officer or official	He will be reproached by his peers and juniors for being in too high a position.
Business and professional	All written efforts will be quite effective.
Ordinary people	He will receive no help from others and will have a difficult year.

KEYNOTES

1. Curb evil at its inception.
2. Check and control evil whenever and wherever found.
3. Being a loner is erroneous.
4. Friends are necessities.
5. Quiet development is most propitious.
6. Too much good can be harmful if not properly protected.

CONDENSATIONS FOR DAILY CYCLES
1. Something wrong or evil is trying to enter your life. Check and correct the situation immediately.
2. You are close to evil influences. Do not let them infect you.
3. Are you fully qualified to cope with the situation facing you? Get help if necessary.
4. No man is an island. Cooperate with others and solicit their support.
5. When what one wills is consonant with the will of heaven, it will come to one like ripe fruit dropping from a tree.
6. Do not adopt a 'holier than thou' attitude. If you do, it will be injurious.

Hexagram 45   Ts'ui ☷ *Gathering Together (Assembling)*

SIMPLE TRANSLATION OF TEXT
Gathering Together. Success. The king approaches his temple. Advantageous to see the great man; then there will be success. Great sacrifices generate good fortune. It is advantageous to strive for a goal.

COMMENTARY
The gathering together is symbolized by the two trigrams forming the hexagram, i.e. the lake over the earth. Waters gather from all directions to form the lake, and thus assembled in one area are available for nourishment. The upper trigram also denotes joy, which reflects the pleasure of engaging in the enterprise depicted. Only great leaders can bring about true assembling. Such persons will do whatever duties are required, just as the king carries out the rituals. Naturally, strength of character and singleness of purpose are needed, along with a knowledge of what is right and how to achieve it (symbolized by 'seeing the great man'), and the offering of sacrifices. People instinctively adhere to what they know to be right, so a proper goal is a necessity as well. Few are the individuals who can truly carry out the full import of this hexagram as a whole. Many will face these demands but will have short-comings, as reflected in the individual controlling lines.
   Those born in the sixth month will be more auspicious.

CONTROLLING LINES (FROM BOTTOM TO TOP)
Line 1 If sincerity for union wavers, there will sometimes be dispersal, sometimes gathering. If he cries out, then with one grasp of the hand he can laugh again. No need for remorse. Advancing will be without error.

These persons will not be capable of meeting all the demands imposed upon them without personal improvement and reforms. People want strong leadership which provides acceptable guidance. They will vacillate if the leadership wavers. The fourth line normally helps the first, but the two intervening weak lines which would also like support make this difficult. Help only comes to these persons if they reach out and ask for it. Since this line is weak where it should be strong, the help is not adequate to overcome innate deficiencies. Cooperation, sociability and support from friends and peers will not be readily forthcoming, so these persons will not automatically fare well in life.
Most auspicious: He will be in a leading position, but stubborn, and will stick to his own opinions despite facts and good advice; frequently he will accept the wrong advice. His gathering and assembling will not be very beneficial to himself or to others unless he reforms.
Least auspicious: He will lack in ability and moral character, and will vacillate frequently between good and evil. His life will be one of hardship, with no real accomplishments.
In yearly hexagram:

Officer or official	He will be dismissed, or at least demoted.
Business and professional	He will tend to be set in his ways and opinions. He will have difficulties if he opposes progress.
Ordinary people	There will be troubles early in the year, with things improving later.

Line 2 Letting oneself be drawn brings good fortune. No error. With sincerity, even small offerings are acceptable.

Lines 2 and 5 are each of the proper nature for their positions, hence line 2 is led by line 5. Permitting this brings good fortune and is not wrong. Even though this line is in a secondary position, it has the sincerity to support line 5. The results and efforts of these persons will not be as great as those of a ruler, but nevertheless they will be deemed quite acceptable because of their inner sincerity. Gathering together the varied requirements of a ruler or leader calls for many specialized individuals in many walks of life. All these persons will have a goal or noble purpose higher than themselves, which they will be striving for and serving well with deep sincerity.

Most auspicious: He will have a broad viewpoint, coupled with practicality, common sense and energy. He will be loyal and honest, and will be a good administrator, choosing the right people for the right positions, and assigning them appropriate duties within their capabilities. Thus work will be effectively and efficiently accomplished. He will set a high personal standard, which will be emulated readily by others. He will be above reproach, and will have a highly favorable and long life; he will become known internationally.

Least auspicious: He will also be a good administrator who can communicate well. He will easily obtain help from his juniors and favorable life.

seniors alike. He will fulfill his strongest desires, and have a

In yearly hexagram:

Officer or official	He will be recommended, and promoted.
Business and professional	He will be recommended, and will advance.
Ordinary people	A favorable year, with reasonable profits.

Line 3 Striving for gathering together, with longing, but nowhere finding it advantageous. Advancing is not erroneous. Slight humiliation.

Line 3 is held back from joining with, and being supported by, line 6, through the deterrence of the two Yang lines, 4 and 5. It cannot join with lines 4 or 2 either, since these are already correlated with their counterparts. Line 3 is thus alone, yet longing for union and to be a part of a group. Fate decrees that this man must travel alone and try to find someone with influence, who can help him gain admission to the group of his choice. There is some humiliation in having to act this way, but it is not wrong.

Most auspicious: He will be a man of many talents, capable of achieving great things through his own thoughts and efforts. He will use the services available efficiently and effectively, but will not need to associate directly with others. Many people will be willing to assist him; he will be healthy, jovial and content, and later he will become wealthy as well.

Least auspicious: Cold feelings will exist among his relatives. His family business will decline. He will have to leave the clan and make his own way alone, which he will do reasonably well, despite many hardships and handicaps.

In yearly hexagram:

Officer or official	He will be assigned to a distant place.
Business and professional	Personal development will be propitious, but business will be stagnant.
Ordinary people	It will not be a pleasant year in general. He will probably suffer the loss of a close relative. If old he may die.

Line 4 Great good fortune. No blame.

Great good fortune comes about because this is a strong line, representing the minister, whose duty it is to gather matters together for prosperity and peace. It is also the beginning of the trigram Tui, joy, the function of which is nourishment. K'un, the lower trigram, amongst its several meanings, stands for the people. Line 4 is below line 5, the primary ruler of the hexagram. Thus we find the minister appropriately supporting the ruler or leader, and nourishing the people as well. This is a fortunate combination, producing great good fortune. Line 4 is strong, whereas normally it should be weak, but in view of the accomplishments attained, this engenders no blame. The masses will flock to this man naturally. Regrettably, he may lose a proper perspective and let himself be swayed from his course by the adulation.

Most auspicious: He will be an extremely able administrator, who will establish beneficial programs and methods which will be effective and of value to the country, to its leader, and to the people. His efforts will bring prosperity and peace. He will have a very satisfying life, with many friends, a good family, and wealth.

Least auspicious: He will also be talented, and ambitious, but as he rises he will become vainglorious, and thereby lose his worth. He will eventually bring harm to his enterprise and his family.

In yearly hexagram:

Officer or official	Jealousies and misrepresentations will be evident, and could be damaging. Exercise care.
Business and professional	Beware of unethical practices or procedures.
Ordinary people	If one does not follow the golden mean a disaster is inevitable.

Line 5 Gathering together through favorable position. No error. If the confidence of the people is not present, it must be gained through persistent correctness and exemplification of virtue. Then regrets disappear.

Line 5 is a Yang, thus is a strong line in the right place, and in a favorable position for gathering together. Those depicted here always have the potential to be leaders, but are not always assigned to leading positions (owing to the strong influence of line 4). Therefore, when they do take over, if people do not already have confidence in them, this must be earned by exemplary virtue of conduct and persistent correctness. This will overcome all opposition, and any occasion for remorse will disappear.

Most auspicious: He will be humble, modest and sage in the exercise of true leadership. He will attain a high position and a large salary, but he will not regard this as a glory. People will be naturally attracted to him, and he will have a large following which he will hold in respect rather than accept as an honor. He will work persistently and diligently for the good of others. He will have a long, rich and noble life.

Least auspicious: He will be a good leader in a minor capacity, and will provide well for his family and himself while rendering service to others.

In yearly hexagram:

| Officer or official | He will not attract others readily, making his work difficult to accomplish. |

Business and professional	A situation will develop in which he will find cause for regret in having not kept up to date professionally.
Ordinary people	He will experience much disharmony in relationships. Plans will not go smoothly.

Line 6   Lamenting and weeping. No error.

Line 6 is isolated, and has no line with which to unite. That makes this man sad, and he will tend to bemoan his fate. However, being in this high position, he will turn his gaze inward. Externally, he will not accomplish a great deal, but he will find satisfaction in making inner improvements. Thus, at the top of the hexagram, the gathering together is internal rather than external.

Most auspicious: Whenever things are peaceful he will remember that disaster can strike, and hence he will prepare himself as best he can, and will avoid troubles. He will not rise high in worldly status, but through self-development he will find peace in his soul, and with his family.

Least auspicious: He will be timid and weak in the external world. He will not have many friends or associates to help him, and will achieve little. He will not help himself to any great extent either.

In yearly hexagram:

Officer or official	He will have a year of troubles and worries until he adopts the correct inner attitude.
Business and professional	He will experience uneasiness in business matters. Professional improvement will help overcome the adverse conditions.
Ordinary people	He will have troubles and sorrows. It will be an active year, but his efforts will mainly be in vain. He may die.

KEYNOTES

1. Avoid stubbornness and accept advice.
2. Specialization will help you. Have a goal.
3. Sometimes one must work alone.

4. Render service, following the golden mean.
5. Position alone is not enough to achieve success.
6. Inner improvement brings satisfaction.

CONDENSATIONS FOR DAILY CYCLES

1. You are indecisive. Keep searching for the right guidance. You will find it.
2. Be receptive to spiritual impulses and let yourself be drawn into what you ought to do, rather than try and select for yourself.
3. You are trying vainly to find people who will cooperate with you. Try their leaders instead.
4. In work of an impersonal nature you will make great strides forward, and find favor.
5. You need the confidence of others to attain your aims. Make a special effort to achieve it.
6. It will not be a good day from an external point of view. Work hard to improve yourself inwardly instead. With better foundations you can achieve more.

Hexagram 46   Shêng ☷☴ *Rising (Ascending)*

SIMPLE TRANSLATION OF TEXT

Rising. Supreme success. Seeking the great man eliminates apprehension. Advancing towards the south brings good fortune.

COMMENTARY

The lower trigram is Sun, wood, which moves upward into the upper trigram K'un, earth. Thus rising vertically is symbolized. This is a step by step process, and produces supreme success. One must strive for and follow what is right in order for one's path to be correct, and to eliminate the apprehension and anxieties that would otherwise enter in. The upper trigram represents the south-west in the Sequence of Later Heaven, and stands for the place where work is done and where matters should be brought to completion. It also signifies the people. Thus, constantly progressing, working with people, and helping bring matters to fruition produces good fortune. Like the tree which grows slowly, this man's progress will come through patient, persistent and

323

diligent effort, and the results will be beneficial and lasting. His accumulations by the end of his lifetime will be great. He will be a strong, capable, intelligent, stable and persistent individual, who will achieve success upon success. Furthermore, the south represents clarity, so striving to increase one's clarity helps bring good fortune as well.

Those born in the eighth month will be more auspicious.

CONTROLLING LINES (FROM BOTTOM TO TOP)
Line 1   Ascending brings great good fortune.

This is the lowest line of the trigram Sun, wood, and indicates that seeds are sprouting and trees beginning to rise. This is welcomed by those above. Thus we have the right work and effort going on below, with the support and cooperation of those above. This working together produces great good fortune. These individuals will naturally attract others by their pleasing personality, their stability and character, and their serious intentions and diligent efforts.

Most auspicious: He will be sincere, humble and modest, yet also wise, talented and communicative. He will instinctively draw people to him, and will often be offered unsolicited yet beneficial assistance. He will rise quite rapidly, but in a strong and stable manner. He will gain fame and fortune, and will also have a good family life.

Least auspicious: He also will be liked by others and frequently assisted. He will cooperate and communicate well, his enterprises will prosper, and his household will be favored.

In yearly hexagram:

Officer or official	Promotion can be expected.
Business and professional	He will receive promotion, or make gains in his enterprises.
Ordinary people	Strong and persistent desires will be fulfilled.

Line 2   With sincerity, even a small sacrifice is acceptable. No error.

A strong officer, the Yang line in position 2, is supported by a weak ruler, the Yin line in position 5. The sincerity of the officer is deeply rooted, and exemplified in all that he does. Even where minimal support is required it is freely and sincerely given. No errors are committed in such a relationship. Persons of ability and loyalty, serving their ruler or a cause, as well as themselves, are depicted here. Such persons are sought after, and are highly esteemed in any organization.

Most auspicious: He will be a man of great virtue and strong character, and greatly talented. He will be honest, just and forthright, and will follow the golden mean. He will accomplish great and worthwhile tasks, for others and for himself, and will generate a rich and rewarding life.

Least auspicious: He will be similar to the most auspicious, but his achievements will be on a lesser scale and at a lower level.

In yearly hexagram:

Officer or official	He will be promoted.
Business and professional	He will receive fame or recognition.
Ordinary people	A happy year. Matters will go smoothly, and those who are ill will be cured.

Line 3   Rising as if into an empty city.

Line 3 is a strong line, at the top of the trigram Sun, wood, and has only weak lines above it, so progress is easy, like taking over an empty city. Its rising is unobstructed and it can be expected to proceed far. One should bear in mind, however, that this line is symbolically a part of the tree, and therefore its progress will be by gradual growth. Also, no mention is made of good fortune, and this should be taken as a warning to be wary of too easy progress. One should always remain true to one's purposes, and to the goals and mores which one knows to be right. What is easily gained can likewise be easily lost.

Most auspicious: He will rise to an important position and govern part of the country, or become the president of a large organization and lead well. He will have a good life with adequate means.

Least auspicious: He will also be a good administrator, publicly and privately. He may have a strong gambling instinct. Eventually he may choose a life of greater or lesser seclusion.

In yearly hexagram:

Officer or official	He will face selection, and probable promotion.

Business and professional   He will achieve fame and recognition.

Ordinary people   Strong desires will be fulfilled.

Line 4 The king sacrifices at Mount Ch'i. Good fortune. No error.

Mount Ch'i was the place of worship for King Wên. Line 4 is the 'Minister,' so the implication is that the minister was invited to join in the sacrifice. To be invited to participate was a great honor, indicative of being accepted and favored by the king. Thus this line symbolizes a time when the individual finds that he can attain his goals as well as rendering much service to the ruler and the people. These are truly remarkable persons, both in character and ability. They set a fine example, which others would do well to emulate, with good fortune and no error resulting.

Most auspicious: He will be a minister by nature, and he will lead by example. He will be kind, considerate and yielding (like water), yet will remain true. He will approach the acme of sincerity, and will be favored by those in authority. His work will be beneficial and of lasting quality, and he will be fortunate in all aspects of his life.

Least auspicious: He also will strongly influence people through his ability and integrity. He will obtain a moderately high position and adequate wealth, and will have a good family.

In yearly hexagram:

Officer or official   He will be appreciated by his seniors and respected by juniors. Promotion is probable.

Business and professional   Enterprises will be fostered by those in authority, and supported by the people.

Ordinary people   Some will make favorable gains in minerals or forestry (or wood products). All will benefit from going to a mountainous region. All should be godfearing, and most will be.

Line 5 Correct advancement step by step. Good fortune.

Able leaders, who administer their duties and responsibilities in an efficient and effective manner, in keeping with the golden mean, are depicted here. They will be natural leaders, and will develop their leadership potential through learning and the wisdom of experience. They will be a blessing wherever they are.

Most auspicious: He will be recognized for his leadership and abilities early in his career. He will be a man of broad vision, a capable communicator who will promote and consummate large and worthwhile undertakings. His desires will be fulfilled and he will have a long, rich and rewarding life.

Least auspicious: His life will be similar to the most auspicious, but in a lesser degree.

In yearly hexagram:

Officer or official	He will receive a well-earned promotion.
Business and professional	He will be personally recommended, as well as having his efforts supported or sponsored.
Ordinary people	Strong desires will be fulfilled.

Line 6 Ascending blindly. Unremitting correctness advantageous.

Some individuals have a compulsive drive to constantly keep moving forward. They never truly stop to rest and relax, or to reassess their situation. It is a blind inner urge that keeps them trying to move ahead, without adequate plans and preparations, or knowledge of possible support. That no man is an island is one of the basic tenets of *I Ching*, and forging ahead alone here will lead to difficulties and disasters, unless actions are unremittingly correct.

Most auspicious: He will overcome compulsive urges and cultivate himself personally and professionally to the point where his inner being will create a successful life for him, both in his work and with his family.

Least auspicious: He will be greedy, mean inconsiderate, and constantly pushing in his efforts to gain status and profit. His actions will bring much unavoidable opposition and ill will. He will have a hard life.

In yearly hexagram:

Officer or official	He will probably retire this year.
Business and professional	If he cultivates himself, personally and professionally, he can retain his position.

Ordinary people   Greediness will create opposition.
                         Less auspicious persons may die.

KEYNOTES
1. It is beneficial to become a good communicator.
2. Services sincerely rendered will be duly rewarded.
3. Beware of seemingly easy situations.
4. Righteous development brings its own rewards.
5. Service to others is always beneficial.
6. Constant pushing forward is damaging.

CONDENSATIONS FOR DAILY CYCLES
1. The seeds are sprouting. Forward progress and good fortune are assured. Those above are in accord.
2. Be filled with faith gained from ancient wisdom, and further progress will be assured.
3. The course of action taken will cause no doubts to rise in the minds of others. Even though things seem easy, check again that no mistakes have been made.
4. Now you will start to attain your goals. Do not forget reverence to God and adherence to duty and tradition.
5. It is only through righteousness, persistently and correctly made a part of one's life, that full success can be achieved. Be guided accordingly.
6. Constant advance today may be dangerous. Reassess your situation. Learn what is the right thing to do before proceeding; blind impulses can be dangerous.

Hexagram 47   K'un ☱☵ *Adversity (Exhaustion)*

SIMPLE TRANSLATION OF TEXT
Adversity. Success through perseverance. Actions of the great man advantageous. No error. Though he speaks words they are not convincing.

COMMENTARY
The hexagram is composed of the trigram Tui, lake, over K'an, water, indicating that the water has seeped out of the lake. This symbolizes adversity because the lake is dry and exhausted, no water being available for nourishment. These persons have the

potential to be beneficial. If they do not use it, or fail to develop it properly, they can expect adversity. By a similar token, if they do not let themselves be overcome by adverse conditions they can still achieve success through indomitable will-power, perseverance in right courses, and by cultivating the inner optimism and faith of a great man. In this way they free themselves from error. Regrettably, the factors influencing this man's life are largely negative, since both trigrams have a downward trend. Therefore his accomplishments will not be great and he will be hampered by conditions beyond his control, unless he heeds the warnings and advice given. Actions, and not words, are required.

Those born in the fifth month will be more auspicious.

CONTROLLING LINES (FROM BOTTOM TO TOP)
Line 1   He sits in adversity under a bare tree. He wanders in a gloomy valley. For three years he remains in darkness.

The words used here present the picture of a person at the lowest point of adversity. Everything is dark and dismal around him. He sees nothing, and takes no action. Also he has no protection, like a man sitting under a bare tree. If he lets adversity conquer him, he must resign himself to failure. If he is strong and wise enough to continue in what is right, he will eventually find a way out of his situation. Becoming exhausted is dangerous, for chance will then take over. However, through rebuilding and application, good fortune will return.

Most auspicious: He will be a man of noble character and virtue but will have little or no opportunity to be useful. His sphere of activity will be limited, and he will gain neither fame nor fortune. On the other hand, life will not be particularly bad either.

Least auspicious: He will be muddle-headed and lacking in common sense. He will not see things clearly. He will find himself in financial or other straits, and not know how to, or be able to, work his way out of them.

In yearly hexagram:

Officer or official	He will have to retreat or withdraw from otherwise favorable situations.
Business and professional	A time of waiting. One should revitalize one's professional knowledge.

| Ordinary people | Some major worries or fears are imminent. |

Line 2 Adversity during food and drink. The wearer of a scarlet knee cover arrives. Engaging in sincere sacrifice advantageous. Actions lead to misfortune but no errors.

Some people rise in spite of themselves rather than because of themselves. This is the result of their karma, or destiny. These persons are sincere in their attitude to the universe and life, and are helped by persons with greater authority. (In ancient times princes wore scarlet knee covers.) However, if these persons try to lead or to strike out on their own, misfortune will result. Cooperating with others, and accepting help, is the best way for them.

Most auspicious: He will be a very personable man, with much knowledge and a good character, who will attain a high position as a result of help from others (perhaps through inheritance) rather than through his own merit. He will enjoy a large salary, and will avoid troubles and let others make decisions.

Least auspicious: He will be ostentatious, biased, aloof, sensuous, and self-indulgent. He will have sufficient means for food and drink. He will not accomplish anything lasting.

In yearly hexagram:

Officer or official	He can expect promotion, and activity if previously inactive.
Business and professional	His activities will be rewarded in some unusual way.
Ordinary people	He will be helped by someone in authority. He will make gains and profits. It would be best not to start anything new.

Line 3 Adversity like being trapped in rock. He leans on thorns and thistles. He enters his home and does not see his wife. Misfortune.

As this is the topmost line of the trigram K'an, danger, there is virtually complete exhaustion here. These persons will be restless and indecisive, with a tendency to fail to see things as they really are. The result is that only menial tasks are able to be performed successfully, and then only under specific guidance and direction.

Most auspicious: He will become a doorman, waiter, or butler, or have some similar job, or else he will live in the mountains and forests and largely idle his time away. He will most likely never marry, or if he does it will not last. He will remain generally healthy throughout his life.

Least auspicious: He will have no character, talent or ambition, and will lead a solitary life plagued by many hardships and troubles.
In yearly hexagram:

Officer or official	He will be demoted, dismissed, or arrested.
Business and professional	Unexpected troubles from closely related sources will arise.
Ordinary people	He can expect family difficulties, and perhaps some serious trouble generated by his wife. Loss of reputation and death are also possible.

Line 4 Journeying slowly. He faces adversity in a golden carriage. He is reproached. Good ending.

Anyone who is riding in a carriage, even though he may be in authority, is relying on inferiors. Line 4 should receive support from its inferior, line 1, but that line's efforts are diverted by, the strong line (2) above it. Since line 2 is symbolic of a metal carriage, the adversity of line 4 is blamed upon it. Thus this person will find himself advancing slowly, and often relying on inferiors who do not render the proper support. He will be reproached as he is not wise enough to choose better helpers. Noting his mistakes as a result of analyzing his slow progress, he can make corrective changes. The results will be good.

Most auspicious: He will rise very slowly in his career but eventually will reach a high and respected position. He will receive little help along the way, and his achievements will be the result of constant self-improvement, both personally and professionally. Apart from his slowness, and having to work largely alone, he will have a good life.

Least auspicious: He will have many hardships at first. Later he will be helped by a rich or powerful person, and will have achievements, but always under the control and guidance of this person. In his senior years his life will become easier and he will be more independent.

In yearly hexagram:

Officer or official	He will have many troubles to cope with.
Business and professional	His efforts will be curtailed by outside influences, e.g. the economy or the state of national affairs.
Ordinary people	He will have many minor troubles, but these will all be overcome.

Line 5 His nose and feet are cut off. Adversity generated by the man with a scarlet knee cover. Joy comes slowly. It is advantageous to offer sacrifices.

Having the nose and feet cut off was a mild form of punishment in earlier days. The judgment was, of course, rendered by those in authority, i.e. the persons wearing scarlet knee covers. Through persistent and righteous actions, and appropriate reverence, a reprieve will be granted to these persons and joy will gradually enter into their lives. They have character traits that will handicap them early on in life, and their efforts and intentions will often be misunderstood, as they do not conform to the customs and mores of their society. Eventually their value and usefulness will be recognized, and, since this is the fifth line, they have the potential to rise to high positions.

Most auspicious: He will be diligent in the learning of ancient wisdom, and will courageously carry out what he believes is right. His actions will not always conform to present practices, so he will at first have many difficulties in his profession. Eventually he will rise to a high position, and have a good life.

Least auspicious: He will have hardships at first, but an acceptable life later. He may have serious health problems, or his close friends or relatives may be jailed.

In yearly hexagram:

For everyone	There will be hindrances and troubles early in the year, with things smoothing out later.

Line 6 Encumbered by creeping vines. Indecisive, he thinks, 'If I move I shall regret it.' With repentance, advancing will be productive of good fortune.

The adversity is coming to an end, and one has only a few creeping vines to remove. This can easily be done by repentance. Proceeding forward will bring good fortune. These persons will start out in life with many hindrances, both externally and those resulting from their own attitudes. These can all be easily overcome. It will be through a deep introspection, analysis and reassessment conducted at some point in their lives that they will see truly the errors of the past, and set forth on a new and highly successful course. Most auspicious: He will learn, and discover how to reform early in life, and will then cultivate and follow the golden mean. He will gain sound professional knowledge and experience, and this will permit him to overcome adversities.

Least auspicious: He will be weak-minded and unambitious. He will always be the scapegoat for troubles and adversity. Later in life, and after much loneliness, he will begin through great personal effort to establish himself.

In yearly hexagram:

Officer or official	He may be reprimanded, punished, demoted or even dismissed.
Business and professional	His efforts will be misunderstood early in the year, but there will be some improvement later on.
Ordinary people	He will face many worries, and probably an unexpected event which will alter circumstances later in the year.

KEYNOTES

1. Never let adversity conquer you.
2. Sincerity will often bring unexpected help.
3. Restlessness and indecisiveness blur one's vision.
4. Be certain of your support at all times.
5. If you are misunderstood, analyze to determine why.
6. Periodically reassess your situation honestly.

CONDENSATIONS FOR DAILY CYCLES

1. It is not the situation but what you think about it that counts. Do not let gloom take charge.
2. One must give before one can receive. This applies in all realms, mental, material and spiritual. Give as necessary.
3. You are faced with adversity and have put your trust in the wrong things. Search out and use those things which will help you.

333

4. Your faith and trust in one higher than you is not well founded. However, you will get some help and achieve part of your aims.
5. You seem to be oppressed from all sides, but since it is not entirely your own fault the situation will gradually clear.
6. You are oppressed by your own attitude and character. Change for the better and you will start achieving good results.

Hexagram 48   Ching ☵☴ *The Well*

SIMPLE TRANSLATION OF TEXT
The Well. The town may be moved but the well remains unchanged. The water never increases nor decreases, and those who come and go can draw from it. If the rope is too short or the bucket broken before reaching the water—misfortune.

COMMENTARY
The well is symbolized in the upper trigram, K'an, water, and the lower trigram Sun, wood, giving the picture of water in a bucket being lifted from a well. It indicates that nourishment is permanently available for all who come and go, regardless of where they live. Those depicted here will have the potential for doing good deeds and rendering beneficial service, and for teaching the right things to others. All men, by the nature of earthly existence, are both salesmen and teachers. One is a salesman in that one is constantly selling oneself to others, consciously or unconsciously. Similarly, one is a teacher through the words one speaks or writes, the acts one performs, and by the example one sets whenever and wherever one is observed. Those depicted here will have a well above average tendency to influence others. They should be aware of this, so that their speech and actions may be as beneficial as possible. Regrettably, this power will sometimes remain unconscious, or else be forgotten.

Those born in the third month will be more auspicious.

CONTROLLING LINES (FROM BOTTOM TO TOP)
Line 1   The muddy water at the well bottom is unfit to drink. Even animals will not drink from an old well.

The bottom of the well is so muddy that neither humans nor

animals will drink from its waters. The way that a well becomes muddy is through agitation, or else through need of renewal. Wise persons do not cause agitation. Hence persons with little knowledge or common sense are depicted. Many will be rabble rousers, with extreme ideas which people in general will not want to accept. They will have little of true value to offer.

Most auspicious: He will have some talent and knowledge, but will not have the common sense to use it properly, and so his life will be ruled by chance. He will not accomplish anything worthwhile, and will have difficulty earning a modest living and providing for himself and his family.

Least auspicious: He will live in poverty in a ghetto or evil surroundings. He will be unambitious, a drifter, an idler and a wastrel.

In yearly hexagram:

Officer or official	A year of retreat.
Business and professional	He will be opposed at every turn.
Ordinary people	Those seeking to advance will fail. Hold back. The least auspicious may die.

Line 2 The fish dart at the wellhole. Water leaks from the broken bucket.

Both of these sentences indicate that very little nourishment is available. When fish dart out from a wellhole it means that the water has nearly all leaked away. The implication is that this man can nourish himself adequately but will never be qualified nor in a position to nourish, and truly be of benefit to, others.

Most auspicious: He will refine and cultivate himself by studying the humanities and the arts. His work will never come to the attention of anyone of influence or real importance. He will lead a modest life and find contentment in his studies rather than through accomplishments.

Least auspicious: He will also study, but will not learn much, and in general he will be impractical. He may have a serious illness or injury, or long-standing troubles. He will barely be able to support himself and his family.

In yearly hexagram:

Officer or official	Relax or retreat and enjoy your own life.

Business and professional	Bide your time. Do only what needs to be done.
Ordinary people	Do not attempt anything new, or troubles will develop.

Line 3 The well has been cleaned but is not yet used. Men's hearts sorrow over this, for the water might be drawn and used. If the king were wise, mutual good fortune might result.

Line 3 is the top of the bucket. This is the point from which nourishment should be drawn. It is a strong line in a strong place so its potential is great, and the people wish that the king would make use of this asset. But, having no correlate, the line remains isolated, and no one gains any real value from the situation. Fate or destiny often prevents persons from rendering valuable service to others, even though they may be excellent, well-qualified individuals. Such is the case here.

Most auspicious: He will have a noble character, and be a man of vision and knowledge. He could be useful to the government and the ruler, but he will remain relatively unknown. He will render service to the poor and the needy, and will gain a favorable reputation over a limited area. He will also gain wealth through good investment.

Least auspicious: He also will be a man of good character who will accumulate some money. His efforts to be of use will always be frustrated by outside influences or an unexpected turn of events. He will have many worries and few friends.

In yearly hexagram:

Officer or official	Retreat and cultivate yourself.
Business and professional	Hold back, and bring yourself up to date in your profession.
Ordinary people	Be content with where you are and what you have.

Line 4 The well is being lined. No error.

The general message of this hexagram is that one should nourish (and teach) others, but only when one is duly prepared. As this is the lowest line of trigram K'an, water, these persons are not yet fully ready to teach and guide others. Their destiny is primarily to cultivate themselves; then, when due progress has been made, they can turn to external matters beneficially. In the meantime it behoves them to learn every possible lesson, wherever they are and whatever they are doing. They should be perpetual students, both in and out of school.

Most auspicious: He will be mild and cautious, and will obey customs, mores, and laws rigorously. He will be reverent. However, he will be indecisive and will lack the courage to take a firm stand or make major decisions. He will provide modestly for himself and his family.

Least auspicious: He will always have ideas as to what should be done, but he will never get others to accept them, nor will he carry them through himself. He will accomplish virtually nothing.

In yearly hexagram:

Officer or official	It will be beneficial to initiate practical innovations and to curb what is harmful.
Business and professional	A good year to hold back and bring oneself up to date in one's profession.
Ordinary people	It will be propitious to engage in constructing a building or a bridge, or to till the land, mine, or sink a well.

Line 5 The well is fed by a clear, cool spring from which everyone can drink freely.

Great leaders are depicted here, who have the welfare of others at heart and lead primarily through service. The more they give the more they have to give. They are like a clear, cool spring, giving inexhaustible nourishment. Line 5 is the ruler, and as it is a strong line in the right place, much good is presaged for all concerned.

Most auspicious: He will have the talent to become the leader of a nation, and also a world leader. He will be a man of vision and strong character, virtuous and decisive, with a great love of people. His work and efforts will be beneficial to many and will have far-reaching effects. He will be famous, rich and noble.

Least auspicious: He also will be a good man like the most auspicious, but at a lower level, with only modest accomplishments. He will have a very satisfactory and satisfying life.

In yearly hexagram:

Officer or official	He will be assigned to a high position and will perform his tasks meritoriously.
Business and professional	He will achieve an increased reputation and will make gains as well.
Ordinary people	He will have good gains in his business or enterprises.

Line 6   The well is not concealed and the rope is available. It is dependable. Great good fortune.

In ancient times, in times of drought, wells were often concealed, or protected against unauthorized use. Here the well is freely visible, and the means for obtaining the water are readily available. Consequently this line represents sage persons who freely and impartially dispense blessings, through their teachings, writings or advice. This brings many benefits and great good fortune.

Most auspicious: He will be a great humanitarian, in thought, word and deed, showering many blessings on others, and helping them to develop and prosper. He will also make gains personally and professionally.

Least auspicious: He will be in a consultant, research, teaching or artistic position where his work will have much influence on others. He will have a modestly affluent and smooth life.

In yearly hexagram:

Officer or official	He will be promoted, because of special merit.
Business and professional	He will enhance his reputation and render much beneficial service.
Ordinary people	He will have enough for his needs, and some extra for special purposes.

KEYNOTES

1. Unnecessary agitation is damaging.
2. Never waste energy if it can be avoided.
3. Occasionally stop and see of how much benefit you are being to others.
4. Renew your energies periodically.
5. A humanitarian outlook is well worth while.

6. Never fail to help others when you reasonably can.

CONDENSATIONS FOR DAILY CYCLES
1. No one is sought who has nothing of value to offer. What have you to offer? Are you being sought?
2. You may be associating with the wrong people for the achievement of the success you desire. Be careful in everything you do.
3. Opportunities are beginning to open up. Take advantage of them.
4. A delay will probably occur. Continue to improve yourself inwardly.
5. You can help others wisely and well today. However, it must be accepted as a blessing. You may receive some help too.
6. Some achievement is presaged. Continue to be sincere and dependable, and you will have good fortune.

Hexagram 49   Ko ☱☲ *Change (Revolution)*

SIMPLE TRANSLATION OF TEXT
Change. When change has been completed then it is believed. Supreme success. Determined perseverance in correctness advantageous. Regrets vanish.

COMMENTARY
Fire is below water, and therefore a change is inevitable. Either the fire will boil away the water, or the water will extinguish the fire. Li, summer, is below Tui, fall, another symbolism that indicates change. Also, Li is the sun and Tui is the west, and the sun in the west denotes the change from day to night. In a personal sense, the hexagram shows clarity within and the lake without. Thus the potential for nourishing others with clarity is depicted; and this is achieved through change. No action in this respect should be taken unless it is a definite necessity and the time is ripe, and only by one who is duly qualified and called to the task. People tend to view change with suspicion. It is only after changes have been successfully implemented that faith and belief develop in them, through the perseverance and determined correctness of the leaders. Those with this natal hexagram will be leaders, and able to make beneficial changes, when the time is ripe,

throughout their lives. They are also able to regulate matters for the benefit of others. The nature of their actions, however, will be governed by their controlling line.

Those born in the second month will be more auspicious.

CONTROLLING LINES (FROM BOTTOM TO TOP)
Line 1　Bound by yellow oxhide.

In this hexagram, line 1 is not only the lowest point of the evolution but is also without a correlate or outside help, so this man is limited in his actions, as if bound by yellow oxhide. Yellow is the symbol of the mean, and the ox represents docility. These persons see many things which need to be changed or corrected, but recognize that change should only be initiated when no other alternative is available. They will follow the golden mean and have a calm existence, but fate and destiny will not place these persons in a position to take action. Thus they seem bound.
Most auspicious:　He will have much knowledge and ability, and will find satisfactory positions, but never the ones best suited to him. He will be content, however, since he will have a modest life free from major difficulties.
Least auspicious:　He will live in lowly surroundings and perform menial or difficult tasks. He will be quite poor, but he also will have no major difficulties.
In yearly hexagram:

Officer or official	Hold back, and do not attempt change or advance.
Business and professional	All plans and proposals should be built on firm and proven foundations. Anything new will bring misfortune.
Ordinary people	Learn to be content with where you are and what you have this year, and you will avoid serious troubles.

Line 2　When the time is ripe, make changes. Advancing then brings good fortune. No error.

Line 2 is the center of the trigram Li, clarity, which is in the inner position. These persons possess therefore an inner clarity, and the ability to analyze, to lay strategic plans and to understand cause and effect; in addition they have a keen sense of timing as to when changes should take place. They are strong individuals, who will support their ruler or leader through thorough staff work, and in the execution of approved plans; they are knowledgeable persons of firm character and broad vision.

Most auspicious: He will be an exceptional person who is able to correctly analyze situations, determine the seeds of the future in present conditions, and wait for the seeds to ripen. He will be trusted by the ruler and respected by the people. He will be assigned heavy responsibilities, and will carry out his duties efficiently, effectively and beneficially. He will have a favorable life.

Least auspicious: He also will be broadminded and kind-hearted, handling matters in a proper and useful manner. He will replace the old with something new at propitious times. He too will have a favorable life.

In yearly hexagram:

Officer or official	He can expect a change in position.
Business and professional	He will gain a favorable reputation.
Ordinary people	He will have several joyous occurrences.

Line 3   Advancing precipitously brings misfortune. Persistence leads to danger. When change has been thrice discussed one may act and will be believed.

Line 3 is a strong line in the right place. Hence this man is inclined to pursue courses of action, but as this line represents clarity on the wane his actions will tend to be made in haste, and without due consideration. If this were persisted in, danger would result. On the other hand, where matters have been fully and carefully deliberated, actions can be commenced with the acceptance and confidence of others assured. Throughout their lives, these individuals must beware of the danger of acting hastily in matters facing them, even though there will be a strong natural tendency to do so. They should train themselves to act deliberately and only after due consideration, and, as far as possible, obtain strong support in advance.

Most auspicious: He will always act in a calm, leisurely and deliberate manner. He will understand the laws of cause and effect, especially relating to people as individuals and as members of a group. He will act in a careful, thorough and timely manner, and the results will be beneficial. He will gain fame and fortune. Least auspicious: He will act rashly and hastily most of the time, and as a result will have many hardships, face frequent difficulties, and fail to establish himself adequately.

In yearly hexagram:

Officer or official	He may make one or more hasty major decision, with unfavorable results.
Business and professional	It will take an extra effort to attain one's aims this year.
Ordinary people	He will have many disputes, within and without the family circle.

Line 4 Regrets disappear. There is confidence. Changing the ordinances brings good fortune.

The total upward effect of the trigram Li, clarity, is first felt here in line 4, the position of the minister. These persons will first prepare themselves adequately for the high positions which they know intuitively they will attain, and subsequently participate in some major change of grave importance. They will be responsible for turning the old into the new, and their renovations and changes will bring good fortune, as a result both of the new rules and their just and beneficial administration of them.

Most auspicious: He will be a highly developed person of strong and good character, with a love of what is right and just. He will prepare himself constantly and at some time will participate in a major renovation of the administration. This will be welcomed by the people and appreciated by the ruler. He will always be a capable administrator, in both his personal and professional life. Least auspicious: He will also be knowledgeable and magnanimous, and a successful administrator at a lower level. He will have hardships at first, then a good and easy life. He will travel considerably.

In yearly hexagram:

Officer or official	He will be promoted.
Business and professional	All his efforts will receive favorable consideration, and benefits will accrue.

Ordinary people   A change, or changes, will result in
                         good fortune.
Line 5 The great man changes like a tiger. He does not need to
use divination. Others repose faith in him.

Line 5 is the ruler of the hexagram, and the changes that this
man makes are as dynamic and clear as the stripes of a tiger. He
is so highly developed, both personally and professionally, and
possessing such a degree of innate widom and perception, that he
does not need to employ divination in order to know what to
correct, how and when to make the corrections, and how to obtain
the necessary support. He acts, and faith is reposed in all he does.
Everyone will have confidence in him. He will be a very strong
leader and a highly efficient, effective administrator.
Most auspicious: He will be a man of rare talents. Great
responsibilities will be placed upon him. He will be outstanding,
personally and professionally, and his work will be of great and
lasting benefit. He will achieve fame and fortune, and will have a
very favorable life.
Least auspicious: He will be favored by destiny, and will also
have a good life. He will be a good administrator, making reforms
as needed. He will accomplish his desires.
In yearly hexagram:
    Officer or official   He will be promoted and assigned
                                 to a more responsible position.
    Business and professional He will enjoy advancement in his
                                 efforts, and additional recompense.
    Ordinary people   Life will be enjoyable this year.
Line 6 The superior man changes like a leopard. The inferior
man changes his face. Advancing now brings misfortune. Being
persevering and constant brings good fortune.

Here, as is often the case with the sixth line, the time for propitious action has passed. In this case this relates to making changes.
If they are made, the superior man will make them with the
detailed clarity of a leopard's spots, but the inferior man will
merely change his allegiance. In general, it is best for these
persons not to initiate any changes, but rather to follow through
those changes which have already been directed or implemented,
in order to derive the maximum benefit. These persons will be

potentially good administrators, but on the whole as technicians rather than planners or strategists.

Most auspicious: He will be a man of strong executive ability, communicative and decisive. He will gain a favorable reputation and have a high salary. He will have a reasonably good life.

Least auspicious: He will often act rashly, and pretend to be an expert or to have more knowledge than he actually does; this will result in extensive troubles unless he changes his ways.

In yearly hexagram:

Officer or official	Those in power should retreat. Those not in power will advance.
Business and professional	A good year, but only if major changes are avoided.
Ordinary people	He should obey laws and keep out of trouble.

KEYNOTES
1. All changes must be timely.
2. Changes must be well thought out.
3. Changes must be agreed to by others.
4. Be in the right position before trying to carry out reforms.
5. Strong leadership is vital for major changes.
6. After changes have been initiated, work persistently to make them effective.

CONDENSATIONS FOR DAILY CYCLES
1. Reflect. The time is too early for change. You are still limited in your possible actions, and you are alone.
2. There is now great potentiality for actions that will bring success. One knows the right time to move forward, and should maintain a correct inner attitude.
3. Only thoroughly discussed changes, and those having the support of others, should be made. Work for the support of others.
4. The time is right for making such changes as have been duly prepared. Act, and success will be yours.
5. You intuitively know what to do, and will spontaneously win the support of others.
6. A superior man can take action, but an inferior man should remain firm. Each in his own way should be satisfied with what is attainable.

Hexagram 50   Ting $\equiv\!\equiv$ *The Cauldron (Sacrificial Vessel)*

SIMPLE TRANSLATION OF TEXT
The Cauldron. Supreme success.

COMMENTARY
The *ting* was a tripodal vessel of bronze with two handles, used in ancient times primarily for sacrificial rituals. It is a symbol of spiritual power and an emblem of imperial power. The hexagram, being composed of fire over wood, signifies purification of the self and an unlimited spiritual nourishing of others. The highest earthly values are sacrificed in the support and the fostering of divine purposes, and this is what these individuals should strive to emulate. The controlling lines begin with the emptying of oneself to make room for the good, and progress to the apex where the good is dispensed with the blessing of heaven. The sixty-four hexagrams cover all aspects of life, and this one primarily deals with the mental and spiritual development of oneself and others, and is considered one of the more important hexagrams from the point of view of acting in accordance with the plan of heaven. This is not a separate career, *per se*, but a seven days a week, twenty-four hours a day activity. Those who have this as their natal hexagram will have a special purpose in connection with matters of spiritual development. Some will be involved visibly and others will be active behind the scenes. They may be found in almost any worldly career.

Those born in the twelfth month will be more auspicious.

CONTROLLING LINES (FROM BOTTOM TO TOP)
Line 1   The *ting* is overturned, feet up. Advantageous to get rid of spoiled meat. One takes a concubine for the sake of bearing sons. No error.

The two images have different meanings but are equally applicable. In the first instance, that which is old and useless must be removed in order to make room for something new and more beneficial to enter in. A man's mind will not accept two divergent ideas simultaneously. In the second instance, it is set forth that if the motive for an action is right then the action itself will be right. A vital part of a man's immortality, according to the Chinese, is the continuation of his lineage, which can only be achieved by having sons. Thus, taking a concubine for the sake of having a son is not wrong. While the previous hexagram dealt primarily with changes in the physical realm, this one is concerned more with the mental realm. Teachers, artists and *literati* are depicted here.

Most auspicious: He will cultivate virtue, learning and techniques of communication. He will rise early in his career and establish a favorable, influential reputation. His later life will be very beneficial and fruitful.

Least auspicious: He will face hardships early in life, with conditions slowly improving. He will leave home and travel considerably, and will gain some wealth but will fail to achieve fame. He may marry several times in order to have an heir.

In yearly hexagram:

Officer or official	He will achieve success out of apparent failure, and be promoted.
Business and professional	He will revitalize something that has become stale, and gain in reputation and recompense.
Ordinary people	He will gain profits with the help of others. Any adverse condition will improve.

Line 2 There is sacrificial food in the *ting*. Believing my enemies cannot harm me; they will not. Good fortune.

Another law of mental life is expressed here, i.e. that when a man is full of faith, that which he believes will tend to be realized. This is the next step in personal mental cultivation after the old has been removed. This line implies great determination, positive hope, and a true ability to concentrate, which are three attributes common to all great men.

Most auspicious: He will have positive goals, strong determination, and great powers of concentration. He will have a noble character and will work for the betterment of himself and others. He will be in a high position, with heavy and far-reaching responsibilities, and will be an important figure in his nation and the world. He will have an active and rewarding life.

Least auspicious: He will also be a magnanimous, sincere,

honest and upright person, with keen mental faculties. He will serve others well, and will have a more than ample income for himself and his family. He will be envied by others.

In yearly hexagram:

Officer or official	It is recommended that he act strictly according to the rules; he should be wary of misrepresentation.
Business and professional	Only strong, concentrated efforts will meet with recognition.
Ordinary people	He will make gains but is likely to be at the receiving end of some unpleasantness. He may become seriously ill.

Line 3 The ears (handles) of the *ting* have been altered. Progress is hampered. The fat of the pheasant is not eaten. Rain falls, and regrets disappear. In the end, good fortune.

Line 3, a part of the body of the *ting*, does not receive help from line 5, the ears, so it is as if the ears have been altered. Consequently, the sacrificial food is not available for eating. Gradually line 6 gains the strength to overcome line 5, and help line 3. Once this is done the situation clears, as after rain, and regrets disappear. Thus good fortune comes in the end. The concepts involved in this line are, first that, in the mental realm as in the physical, to every action there is a reaction, and, second, that every thought or idea brings about a corresponding physical reaction. This person is confused and hampered in his progress by erroneous thinking. Through continued effort his mind will gradually clear, and his life and development will then become stable, beneficial and rewarding.

Most auspicious: He will devote much energy in his early life to self-development and self-improvement without having a specific external goal, and hence will not have a basis from which to grow until he sees his error and makes the necessary changes in his life, which will then improve.

Least auspicious: His life will be full of hardships and difficulties. He may even use immoral means to attain his aims. Later he will reform, and with his altered attitude begin to achieve something worthwhile.

In yearly hexagram:

Officer or official	The actions of a wicked official will hamper one's efforts, until the evil is overcome.
Business and professional	Matters will move only with difficulty until late in the year.
Ordinary people	An auspicious year for older people. Young people will face troubles and hardships.

Line 4   The legs of the *ting* are broken. The prince's meal is spoiled and his person soiled. Misfortune.

The fourth line is the position of the minister, who ought to disseminate nourishment to the people and support the ruler. In this case he does not receive the support of line 1, as indicated by the legs of the *ting* being broken. In serving alone, the minister is inept, and spills the food in the *ting* over the prince. As far as mental activity is concerned, this implies that ideas must have a sound foundation in order to be useful, and also that the longer an idea remains in the mind the more opposition there will be to its replacement. The minister's actions are ill considered, and since the actions are wrong, the attitude of mind behind them is wrong also. He is using old ideas and methods which ought to be replaced. If this person does not exercise due forethought, misfortune will result.

Most auspicious: He will hold a high position, but will employ obsolete ideas and/or unsuitable persons for the advancement of his country. This will result in opposition, much bickering, and other troubles. While having ample means to meet his personal needs, he will not be happy or satisfied with his life.

Least auspicious: He will be in a high administrative position and will use his mental powers for evil purposes and personal gains. He will frequently rely on force rather than persuasion, and will have an unstable personal and professional life.

In yearly hexagram:

Officer or official	He will be dismissed or demoted.
Business and professional	Opportunities for gain will come to nothing.
Ordinary people	He will have a substantial loss and/

or foot trouble. The less auspicious
may die.
Line 5   The *ting* has yellow handles, with golden rings. Firm
correctness advantageous.

Line 5 is correctly placed and duly supported. Yellow implies
following the golden mean; the golden rings imply that one's
actions are particularly effective. From the point of view of mental
activity, this line points to the fact that imagination is more
powerful than knowledge when dealing with one's own mind or
with the minds of others. Firm correctness is essential in order for
good and not evil to result, especially when influencing the minds
of others, as is done by leaders.
Most auspicious: He will be a man of noble character and great
virtue, and wise in the ways to handle men. He may be employed
in the government of his country or to negotiate for his country,
and he will be an example well worth emulating. He will be
trusted by the leaders, and respected by his associates and by the
people. He will have a rich and rewarding life.
Least auspicious: He also will be an honest, noble person, good
at communicating with people, and of benefit to any enterprise
with which he associates. He will have a good and prosperous
household and business, and will have much good fortune.
In yearly hexagram:

Officer or official	A very good year. He will be assigned to a high position, or will win a prize.
Business and professional	Written efforts will be especially effective. He will reap gains and win a coveted award.
Ordinary people	A favorable year in many respects, with substantial gains.

Line 6   The *ting* has rings of jade. Great good fortune. Everything is beneficial now.

A truly wise person renders service to his leader and nourishes the
people, just as the rings serve a *ting*. Jade is hard, pure and valuable,
and possesses a soft luster, thus signifying that this person possesses
an exceptionally beneficial quality of leadership in what is desirable and right. This is enhanced by a love of people, which shows

itself in penetrating consideration and tolerance. On the mental plane, this line indicates that the finest actions spring naturally from a perfected, conscious inner self. Those depicted here will be among the most highly developed individuals in the world, and will exert a beneficial influence wherever they are.

Most auspicious: He will be exceptionally wise in leading, guiding, and understanding people. He will be a man of great virtue, thoughtful and communicative. Everything will go his way, and he will be of great benefit to others. He will have a rich and rewarding life.

Least auspicious: He also will be fine and noble, but will live in seclusion, helping others indirectly, through ideas, writings and philanthropy. He also will have a highly satisfying life.

In yearly hexagram:

Officer or official	Those in active positions will retreat; those in inactive positions will advance. All will exert much influence.
Business and professional	His actions and efforts will be supported and promoted by others.
Ordinary people	A good, stable year, with gains.

KEYNOTES

1. Get rid of useless material.
2. Be full of positive faith and thoughts.
3. One's every thought produces a reaction.
4. One must have foundations to be useful.
5. Imagination is more powerful than knowledge.
6. All external influences begin within.

CONDENSATIONS FOR DAILY CYCLES

1. Anyone with good ideas can achieve success. Get rid of any that have not been helpful to you, and replace them with new ideas.
2. You can be of benefit to others today and it is right that you should, even though it may create some envy.
3. You are not getting the recognition and support you need. Reassess your ideas. Something a little better will bring you good fortune.
4. Beware of negligence today, so that an opportunity for progress is not lost.

5. You are free from the mistakes and errors of the past few days, and are now on a beneficial course.
6. The circumstances are entirely favorable, and the work being done is in accordance with the will of heaven. Good fortune.

Hexagram 51   Chên ☳☳ *Thunder (Arousing)*

SIMPLE TRANSLATION OF TEXT

Thunder generates success. Thunder comes amid gaiety and glee. It terrifies people for a hundred miles. He does not let the sacrificial spoon spill its spirits.

COMMENTARY

The name of the hexagram derives from it being the trigram Chên doubled. Chên also represents springtime, when the renewal of life becomes evident and the earth restores its bounty. This brings joy and success. The manifestations of the divine also bring renewed hope and cheer to those capable of understanding them, while they induce great fear in the hearts of others. Anyone who is highly developed, and full of virtue and understanding, will be so calm under all circumstances that even if thunder occurs during sacrificial rites it will not disturb him. From a personal point of view, this is a time for renewal and for coming out from within oneself to develop and to be of benefit to others. These persons will be innovators, instigators, and prime movers in progressive movements. Their actions will be mainly impartial rather than for gain, although some will use these traits for selfish purposes.

Those born in the tenth month will be more auspicious than the rest, of which those born between the second and the eighth month will be the more auspicious.

CONTROLLING LINES (FROM BOTTOM TO TOP)

Line 1   Apprehension when thunder comes. Afterwards gaiety, laughing and glee. Good fortune.

There is a movement stirring within the society, and much apprehension regarding its possible success. Since this is a time for growing and advancing, the movement will be productive and

351

followed by happiness and good fortune. Since this line is correct and in its right place, the leadership of this individual will be strong, dynamic and progressive, and he will bear a reverence for divine manifestations.

Most auspicious: He will be a man of uncommon personal and professional brilliance, dignified, awe-inspiring and deep thinking. He will be in a high position, and influential in revitalizing the spirit and enthusiasm of the nation. He will establish great merit, and his life will be rich and rewarding.

Least auspicious: He also will be aware of the pitfalls of life, as they relate to the nation, to corporate enterprises, and to his own personal affairs, and he will be able to make the necessary corrections when needed. He will have hardships early in life, but things will gradually smoooth out later.

In yearly hexagram:

Officer or official	He will have a surprise, or an unexpected turn of events, with much joy later.
Business and professional	There is the possibility of becoming well-known as the result of a sudden development or occurrence.
Ordinary people	There is the possibility of something alarming occurring early in the year, with an occasion for celebration later.

Line 2 Thunder approaches. He relinquishes his valuables and ascends the nine hills. He should not search for them. In seven days he will regain them.

It is as if the thunder has left a flood in its wake and one has to flee, leaving one's possessions and valuables behind, while one ascends some high hills away from danger. But there is no need for alarm. One will regain the valuables in time, and there is no need to go in pursuit of them. The words 'seven days' represent a cycle of events based on this hexagram. In the process of renewal many strange seeming events take place, which are a reaction to the new attitudes being generated. One must not resist or fight evil coming to the fore, but flee to safety, since evil gains strength from being resisted. When a man has fully renewed himself, i.e. at the completion of the cycle, he will regain all his losses and much more besides. Persons capable of achieving this are unusually gifted.

Most auspicious: He will have great innate intelligence and wisdom, and will follow the golden mean. He will plan ahead and avoid many troubles, and he will be a capable negotiator and mediator. He will not start a new enterprise, but will materially assist in promoting and elevating an existing one. He will be amply rewarded.

Least auspicious: He will not possess foresight and will often be encompassed by dangers which could have been avoided. He will also be greedy, which will add to his difficulties. He will be a wanderer and philanderer, and his life will be full of worries.

In yearly hexagram:

Officer or official	He will experience troubles through cunning officials and associates.
Business and professional	He will be perplexed much of the time, with gains towards the end of the year.
Ordinary people	He will have disputes and troubles which will clear up satisfactorily later.

Line 3 Thunder frightens. If he is excited into action, no mistakes.

The third line is the 'lower line of man' in any hexagram, and is often considered the representative of the common man. (Lines 5 and 6 represent heaven, lines 3 and 4, man, and lines 1 and 2, the earth.) Hence the dilemma of the ordinary man is here shown, regarding his self-development. He is awestruck and fearful of the wonderful manifestations of the divine, which he is beginning to understand. If these inspire him, and stir him to try and make further progress, then he will slowly advance and make no grave mistakes. These persons are beginning to become aware of the laws of nature, and of how to apply them in the world of man.

Most auspicious: He will be an intelligent and cautious individual, advancing modestly and safely. He will not forget the possibility of danger in times of safety, or of disorder in times of peace. He will not be single-minded, and so will not accomplish anything very great. He will, however, lead a moral, virtuous life, meeting his commitments, and having a modest yet contented existence.

Least auspicious: He will be intelligent but very timid, which will result in an unstable life, with no accomplishments and only minimal reward.

In yearly hexagram:

Officer or official	He will be blamed for the inactivity of those under him.
Business and professional	He will tend to do only that which is demanded of him.
Ordinary people	A year for caution. Troubles, disputes and lawsuits are imminent.

Line 4 Thunder descends into the mud.

This Yang line, with a pair of Yin lines on either side of it (in part forming the nuclear trigram K'an, danger, water), symbolizes the thunder sinking into the mud. It is as if a man is surrounded by sensuality and desire (Yin lines are female) and lets himself be overcome by them. In another sense, it indicates that the mind is inert and cannot see clearly the things which would help it. These things keep this person from having the auspicious life, position and accomplishments that one born under the fourth line can normally expect.

Most auspicious: Unless he proceeds slowly and carefully he will frequently let his personal wishes and desires override his good judgment, even though he will know how to control them. He will gradually lessen his faults by striving to improve himself. He will not have a business of his own, but he will prove useful to others, will keep out of trouble, and will have a moderately comfortable life.

Least auspicious: He will not rise to a very high position, and will live in poor surroundings. He occasionally will make an effort to improve himself, but in general he will have a miserable life.

In yearly hexagram:

Officer or official	He will be dismissed or demoted.
Business and professional	He will encounter a depression or retrogression in his affairs.
Ordinary people	An unstable year. He will find himself without support. The less auspicious may be jailed.

Line 5 Going hither and thither amid thunder. Danger. Exercising care will avert loss, yet things need to be done.

The difficulties of self-improvement without a guide are truly great. There are many times when one is perplexed as to the best direction in which to proceed. This man is in the position of the ruler or leader (line 5), but even so, auspiciousness is not presaged. It is true, however, that exercising care will avert losses or retrogressions. In such cirumstances it is highly desirable to have a firm goal. These persons will, generally speaking, try to do their best with what they have.

Most auspicious: He will be a man of high morals and virtue, but will not be highly qualified professionally unless guided. He will be of benefit, to an average degree, in whatever enterprises he is associated with. His home life, too, will be averagely beneficial.

Least auspicious: He also will be an honest person, wandering in his early years, and travelling considerably all his life. Matters will turn out quite favorably in his later years.

In yearly hexagram:

Officer or official	He will keep his present position.
Business and professional	Business will be as usual, with little fluctuation.
Ordinary people	He will have many worries.

Line 6 Thunder brings devastation. People gaze with apprehension and terror. Advancing brings misfortune. If it has not affected us but only our neighbors, no error. Like with a marriage, there is cause for comment.

Those depicted here will misguidedly try to emulate great spiritual leaders, martyrs, or leaders in the material world, without having the necessary development or qualifications. They will believe that they can absorb some of the greatness through physical imitation of actions or appearances, rather than strive consistently to achieve the same mental or spiritual qualities. Religion of one sort or another is invariably associated with such actions. Their lives will be so unusual that they will become the source of much comment. However, if one strives to emulate greatness in the right way, no error will result, regardless of what one's neighbors or others may do.

Most auspicious: He will constantly strive for improvement in his personal development. He will take precautions against possible calamities, and will nip troubles in the bud. His character and dignity will earn the respect of his neighbors. His family life will be modest but good.

Least auspicious: He will be self-centered, egotistical and misguided. His only concern will be himself, and he will have little or no regard for others. He will be a disturbing influence whereever he is, and if married will have much family discord.

In yearly hexagram:

Officer or official	He will face the possibility of demotion for erroneous blame.
Business and professional	There will be a decline in his enterprise, or diminished results.
Ordinary people	Only with extreme caution can troubles be avoided.

KEYNOTES

1. The inner self must be developed, as well as the external self.
2. New thoughts will produce new conditions if implemented.
3. Too rapid progress is dangerous.
4. Eliminate fears and erroneous desires, one at a time.
5. Perplexities are to be expected during any self-development.
6. Never overdo anything, even self-development.

CONDENSATIONS FOR DAILY CYCLES

1. Some unusual thought or event will occur, which may spur you to either change or revitalize something.
2. There is evil at hand, and you may suffer a loss. Do not try to force its return. Later you will regain your losses.
3. Are you being lethargic? Search for new opportunities, or take corrective measures as necessary.
4. You will be inert or muddled in your thinking today.
5. Repeated dangers often threaten one's activity, but if you devote care and consideration to your work, no loss will be occasioned.
6. Remain calm today, even if things seem dire. Any action you take may only make matters worse.

Hexagram 52   Kên ☶ *Keeping Still (Mountain)*

SIMPLE TRANSLATION OF TEXT
Keeping the back still, so that he is insensitive. Walking in the courtyard without seeing people. No error.

COMMENTARY
The hexagram is the trigram Kên, mountain, doubled, which bespeaks a stillness, calmness and imperturbability. The spinal column is the center of the nervous system. When it is so calm as to be insensitive the individual has attained a state of perfection where the body is of no great consequence other than to be a vehicle. When one's eyes notice no one, one has an inner security from which fears and vanity have been eliminated. Vanity is the hardest of all traits to be free from. These persons have the potential to become persons of such a free nature, and the controlling lines provide guidance for such development. In the end one can rise to the grandeur of a mountain. Keeping still does not mean inactivity. Rather it is the taking of propitious actions at the right time, and using the expedient of tranquility to attain freedom from selfish thoughts and yearnings, when appropriate. No errors are committed when one has fully attained this freedom.

Those born in the fourth month will be more auspicious.

CONTROLLING LINES (FROM BOTTOM TO TOP)
Line 1 Keeping the toes still. No blame. Firm correctness advantageous.

As in other hexagrams, this lowest line symbolizes the toes, in which originate physical progress forward by a man. This line is the base of both mountains, and therefore represents firmness and immobility. Hence these persons should be firm, and anxious to do what is right at all times. At the beginning of matters they will usually be quite unsullied by external influences. If they maintain firm correctness, the right direction to proceed will become known when needed, and progress can be made. Knowledgeable and just, yet cautious and conservative individuals are depicted here.

Most auspicious: He will follow the golden mean, and will therefore be free from the harms that attend following an evil path. His conservatism will keep him from rising high or making great gains, but he will have a personally satisfying and easy life, with no major troubles.

Least auspicious: He also will be modest and sincere, but not as knowledgeable as the most auspicious. He will have a good family, and a humble life, with no major difficulties.

In yearly hexagram:

Officer or official	There will be no mistakes this year.
Business and professional	An average year, without much progress.
Ordinary people	He will be contented with his existence, and free from envy or harmful desires; hence he will avoid troubles.

Line 2   Keeping the calves still. He cannot help whom he follows. He is not happy.

The calves are not an independent part of the body, nor do they control movement. This man must follow a stronger leader. Since line 2 is a Yin line in its proper place, he will try to do what is right and just, and try to halt if on a path of wrongdoing. As he is not in control he will be unable to help the one above him (line 3). For the most part these persons will pick the wrong careers, and consequently will hamper their own progress somewhat, while being relatively ineffective in the helping of, and rendering service to, others.

Most auspicious: He will be talented and ambitious, but will be in the wrong situations to be truly effective. His personal character will improve through the conquest of obstacles, but as he is impeded in helping others he will not rise high. He will work diligently for what is right, and his reputation will become favorable after his death.

Least auspicious: He will be quite knowledgeable and have a good character, but will be timid, shy and wavering. Consequently, his achievements will be quite limited, professionally and with regard to his family and himself. Regrettably, he will be an inveterate worrier.

In yearly hexagram:

Officer or official	Routine matters will be satisfactorily handled, but he will be inept in emergencies.
Business and professional	New ideas will not be accepted this year.
Ordinary people	Desires, in general, will not be accomplished, and gains will not be made. He may also have leg trouble, or family difficulties.

Line 3 Keeping the loins still. No movement of the pelvis. Perilous. His heart suffocates.

This is the top line of the first mountain, but held still by the base of the mountain above it. This is a perilous position, and many talents and worthy attributes are seemingly immobilized by virtue of the situation. If one tries to use force before the situation becomes pliant, irritation, dissatisfaction and danger will result. This is a time for preparation and development, in both personal and external affairs. One should avoid artificiality and insincerity, and let things develop naturally. Calmness must come from within. One should also be cautious regarding the enforcement of stillness before one is ready for it.

Most auspicious: He will be quite wise and will eventually be assigned to a high position. But if he is envious and greedy, he will be unable to exercise a stabilizing influence and help keep good people in office. He is then likely to be blamed severely for not being adequate to the demands of his position.

Least auspicious: He is likely to be a man of considerable means, using his assets for selfish or evil purposes, which will result in great difficulties and a troublesome life.

In yearly hexagram:

Officer or official	He will probably be transferred.
Business and professional	His written efforts will be quite effective.
Ordinary people	An unstable and tough year.

Line 4 Keeping the torso still. No error.

When the trunk (in particular the spine, central nervous system, and heart) is still, one achieves a calmness of spirit and the elimination of impulsive and egoistic drives. When this has been achieved one becomes free from error. It is a worthy goal to strive for, but few are the persons who can truly achieve it. They will be individuals of noble character, full of wisdom and confidence, who think, speak and act in a cool, calm and deliberate manner. Most auspicious: He will be knowledgeable, sincere, stable and composed, but a man whose value will be recognized only to a very limited degree. He will not be in a position to be valuable to his nation, but he will be a pillar of strength in his enterprise. He will be highly respected for his dignity and virtue, and will have a good, modest life.

Least auspicious: He also will have a good character, but his main interests will be his own goals. He may become a monk or a priest.

In yearly hexagram:

Officer or official	He should stay in his present position, and try not to change.
Business and professional	Use proven methods only. Trying to advance matters surreptitiously will result in failure.
Ordinary people	Keep within duly circumscribed limits and things will go well.

Line 5 Keeping the jaws still. His words are well ordered. Cause for regret disappears.

All great leaders have quick, clear and incisive minds, and the ability to communicate readily with others. By not indulging in idle chatter, and speaking only when one has something worthwhile to say, using only well chosen words, one's communication is highly effective and every occasion for regret disappears. Not only can the influence of these persons be great, but their personal development will be considerably enhanced as well.

Most auspicious: He will be a man of knowledge, wisdom and experience, who can speak effectively for the ruler of his country and its people. He can also be a valuable advisor. His own life will be highly favorable in all aspects.

Least auspicious: He will be a person who communicates and influences others through singing, acting, public speaking, etc. He will be gifted at telling stories. He will be helped considerably by friends or relatives, and will have modest success.

In yearly hexagram:

Officer or official	He will be assigned to a high staff, advisory, or consultant position.
Business and professional	He will achieve effective results, primarily by written material.
Ordinary people	He should be communicative and cooperative, and he will receive help. Consequently, things will go smoothly. The less auspicious may have oral disputes.

Line 6   Keeping still eminently. Good fortune.

This line is the ruler of the hexagram, and signifies persons who have achieved an inner development of an exceptionally high order. Their tranquility and acceptance of divine manifestations results in singular blessings, wherever they are and irrespective of their pursuits. They possess the majestic dignity and towering strength of a mountain. Their lives will be peaceful and they will be at ease regardless of circumstances. They will bring benefits to all matters in which they engage.

Most auspicious: He will be a tranquil man of noble character, dignified and respected, and full of wisdom. He will lead an exemplary life, filled with rewards, health and happiness.

Least auspicious: He also will lead a beneficial life, but on a lesser scale. He will also have a long life, and will acquire much property.

In yearly hexagram:

Officer or official	He can expect promotion.
Business and professional	He will achieve gains and fame.
Ordinary people	A good year with substantial profit.

KEYNOTES
1. Think before acting.
2. 'This above all: to thine own self be true.'
3. Never force a situation before the time is ripe.
4. Eliminate egoistic and impulsive drives.
5. Always choose words carefully.
6. Tranquility comes from inner development.

CONDENSATIONS FOR DAILY CYCLES

1. Be unwavering in what is right. Then you can advance.
2. There is a possibility that you have begun an activity when you should have remained quiet. Reassess your situation.
3. It is dangerous for you to forcibly try and curb your thoughts and actions from the heart, before you are ready to do so. Take care.
4. Stillness of the mind and body leads to higher personal development. Strive to achieve it.
5. If you choose carefully what you say, and avoid thoughtless remarks, any occasion for remorse will disappear.
6. Tranquility of the highest degree can be yours today through the exercise of stillness.

Hexagram 53   Chien ☰☶ *Gradual Development (Progress)*

SIMPLE TRANSLATION OF TEXT
Gradual Development. The marriage of a maiden. Good fortune. Firm correctness brings rewards.

COMMENTARY
The hexagram is composed of the trigram Sun, wood, above Kên, mountain. A tree (Sun) grows slowly. Likewise, the preparations for the marriage of a maiden, according to Chinese custom, proceed gradually, with due deliberation and consideration. If these are carried out fully and correctly, good fortune results. In this hexagram, progress leads to a commanding position, i.e. a tree on the top of a mountain, visible for a great distance. The symbolism of the lines concerns the wild goose, which according to Chinese legend flies towards the sun. In the Western hemisphere one could find a parallel in the snow goose, which often flies to the mountains from out at sea. These persons will acquire ever increasing knowledge, influence and power, especially if a path of self-development is undertaken.

Those born in the first month will be more auspicious.

CONTROLLING LINES (FROM BOTTOM TO TOP)
Line 1   The wild goose gradually approaches the shore. The young son is in danger. There is talk, but no error.

This line is a weak line in a strong place, and without a proper correlate. Being thus alone is dangerous, just as if a young son were to try to make his way alone in life. In flying towards the shore it is necessary for the goose to pick out landmarks and orient itself before doing anything else. This is a position of initial doubt and uncertainty, which will cause talk, but no grave errors will be made if this person keeps his long term goals constantly in mind, and devotes his efforts to achieving them.

Most auspicious: He will be clever, talented and virtuous. Early in his career he will enter a position of leadership, and will continue to make gradual progress. He will be alert for opportunities, but will never act in haste. He will always be progressive in his thinking and deliberate in his actions. Destiny will favor him with a rich and rewarding life.

Least auspicious: He will have many hardships early in life, but will make slow, steady progress. He will establish himself, personally and professionally, late in life.

In yearly hexagram:

Officer or official	He will be involved adversely in internal and external politics.
Business and professional	Changes in rules and requirements will limit results.
Ordinary people	There will be many difficulties early in the year, with matters easing off later.

Line 2 The wild goose gradually approaches the cliffs. Eating and drinking sociably. Good fortune.

The second line is the position of an official, and as line 2 is here a Yin line in its proper place he will receive the support of the strong ruler (line 5). This line depicts a person who has found a safe place in which to live, with plenty to eat and drink. In the material world, most gains are achieved in a setting of conviviality. The wild goose is said to share its good fortune, and a man likewise will benefit from sharing his. One must give in order to receive, and the value of sociability as a means of giving and receiving is well established.

Most auspicious: He will be in a high position, supporting the nation and its ruler, and helping to stabilize conditions and bring about improvements. His efforts will be effective, and he will be respected at all levels and duly rewarded. He will have an interesting and highly satisfactory life in all respects.

Least auspicious: He also will be a leader in an influential position, with ample means, and enjoying a generally easy life. Later he may live in seclusion or travel abroad considerably.

In yearly hexagram:

Officer or official	A very good year.
Business and professional	He will make considerable gains.
Ordinary people	A year of contentment, with plenty of money and good food.

Line 3 The wild goose gradually approaches the plateau. The husband goes forth and does not return. The wife is pregnant, but does not nourish the child. Misfortune. Resisting plunderers is advantageous.

Here, as in some other hexagrams, line 3 is a strong line without a proper correlate. This signifies that this person is in a difficult position, as the goose would be, if lost on an arid plateau. The next two statements imply that he is like a husband who does not care for his wife, or like a wife who does not care for her child. These both are conditions that lead to misfortune. This man will have a tendency to act alone, to try to force the culmination of projects and activities, and to be reckless in his efforts at advancement. If he is wise he will see these potential pitfalls and avoid them. He is also likely to be subjected to unjustified accusations, and he will have to defend his position frequently, through right words and actions.

Most auspicious: He will be courageous and erudite, and, with experience, will be able to contribute much of benefit to his country and to the world. He will have ample material means, but will meet with opposition professionally and will face trouble with his wife at home.

Least auspicious: He will enter a career where travelling and being away from home much of the time are involved. He will not be noted for his sociability, and he may separate from his wife and children. He will not have a desirable life.

In yearly hexagram:

Officer or official	He may be blamed erroneously, or else demoted.
Business and professional	A stagnant year.

| Ordinary people | The year will lack in harmony and cooperation. He may be robbed, or suffer a heavy loss. |

Line 4 The wild goose gradually approaches the tree. There he may land on a branch. No error.

The upper trigram is symbolized by the tree, and the goose has now arrived there. Since the goose's feet are flat it will have much difficulty in trying to perch on a branch. The lesson to be drawn is that this man must be sprightly and nimble, but even so he will be subject to danger. This trigram also represents humility, so if he can combine humility with these other traits there will be no error. A weak fourth line does not suggest auspiciousness, but these individuals will be able to develop themselves, personally and professionally, so that they can render valuable service for the benefit of many.

Most auspicious: He will be a man of exemplary morals and strength of character. He will be well qualified, and in a high position. He will make an excellent diplomat or negotiator. He will achieve much merit, and will have a good, satisfying and uncomplicated life.

Least auspicious: He will find it hard early in life to make a living and to establish himself. By being circumspect reverent and frugal, he will gradually improve himself and his life, and in later years he will reap the rewards of his diligent and persistent efforts.

In yearly hexagram:

Officer or official	Many matters will be in a state of delicate balance, but if correct methods are followed they will end favorably.
Business and professional	He will not start having any real success until late in the year.
Ordinary people	He will have ample funds and few worries. A good year to build or alter one's house.

Line 5 The wild goose gradually approaches the summit. The woman does not become pregnant for three years, but in the end it cannot be prevented. Good fortune.

Having a child and heir is symbolic of achieving one's desires. The summit is a high place, and as one approaches high positions in life one often meets with envy, slanders, malicious gossip and opposition. It is only by having firm goals and concentrating on them perspicaciously, and by making oneself worthy of the higher position, that one can achieve it. This man will have the qualities and character necessary to attain his aims and purposes, but they will only materialize later in life, after much diligent persistence. Most auspicious: In his youth he will be exuberant, ambitious, energetic and relentless in pursuit of his desires and goals. He will be ready to set the world on fire. After much experience, which he will refine into wisdom, he will achieve his purposes and be highly successful, personally and professionally.

Least auspicious: He will choose the path of devotion to self-development, rather than work for the improvement of others. He will possess, or will attain, modest means, and will later live a secluded life. He may marry late in life, but will have few children.

In yearly hexagram:

Officer or official	Beware of misrepresentations, and erroneous information when making decisions.
Business and professional	Much hard work early in the year put into advancements will be productive late in the year.
Ordinary people	Those born in the first month will be very auspicious. Otherwise, a year with early difficulties smoothing out later. Older persons may die. Children may have health problems.

Line 6 The wild goose advances beyond the summit. Its feathers can be used in the sacred rituals. Good fortune.

These are persons who will become intellectual leaders, as their mentality will be developed beyond the material realm. They will be noted writers, orators, educators, spiritual leaders, and eminent artists, etc., who give of themselves for the benefit of others. The sacred rituals in ancient China were a means of reminding persons to perform their duties and follow the right paths for progress in life. Hence the work and efforts of these persons will be of (greater or lesser) benefit to mankind.

Most auspicious: He will be a man of noble character and great virtue, with a magnificent ability to communicate. He will have a deep love for people, and will be respected by them in turn. His work will be of great benefit to mankind. He will have a good life, with many friends and ample wealth.

Least auspicious: He will not be concerned about fame or fortune. He will live a secluded life, or become a monk or priest and work for the benefit of mankind in that way. He will be beneficent but will have no wealth.

In yearly hexagram:

Officer or official	His behavior would make a good model for the entire nation.
Business and professional	He will have excellent results in literary or artistic efforts.
Ordinary people	A very good year, with desires and wishes attained. He will enjoy good cooperation with others.

KEYNOTES

1. At the start of any enterprise have long term goals.
2. Appropriate sociability is an effective tool.
3. Never lose faith, even during dire difficulties.
4. Personal and professional development will overcome handicaps.
5. Recognize that opposition is a natural part of advancement.
6. Never cease rendering service to others.

CONDENSATIONS FOR DAILY CYCLES

1. There is gossip about the union you are striving for. If you are aware of it you can make progress.
2. A path of activity is opening up. Follow it, and good fortune will be yours.
3. Analyze your situation. Learn the lessons indicated by your recent mistakes.
4. Cooperate and act in good faith with good, intellectual friends.
5. Remain steadfast through today's early difficulties. They will clear up later.
6. Be thankful for the blessings you have received. Share them with others.

Hexagram *54   Kuei Mei* ☳☱ *The Marrying Maiden*

SIMPLE TRANSLATION OF TEXT
The Marrying Maiden. Enterprises bring misfortune. Attempted progress disadvantageous.

COMMENTARY
The hexagram is composed of the eldest son, Chên, leading the youngest daughter, Tui. This is unfavorable in two ways, firstly because of the wide disparity between the ages of the partners in the marriage, and secondly, because the bride comes to the groom's home, rather than he coming to her home. Hence, the omens for the hexagram are not very good. As is well appreciated, situations are often not what they seem, and that is true in this case. There will be frequent miscalculations and misrepresentations. Extreme caution is recommended, especially at the beginning of anything new. Those depicted here will be enthusiastic, and would like to be progressive. However, circumstances will circumscribe their potential and their usefulness. The inner hexagram shows that matters, on the whole, have already reached a state of completion, and that advancing further would bring about a state of decline rather than progress. Due circumspection can result in a satisfying life.

Those born in the seventh month will be more auspicious.

CONTROLLING LINES (FROM BOTTOM TO TOP)
Line 1   The marrying maiden becomes a concubine. A lame man can still walk. Advancing portends good fortune.

Line 1, although a strong line in the right place, is held back by the strength of Yang lines 2 and 4. Thus its effectiveness is likened to a concubine who serves as a secondary wife, and to a lame man, who can still walk but not as effectively as others. Hence these persons will be limited by external conditions beyond their control, e.g. the situation into which they were born, obligations they must fulfil to their families or to creditors, or contractual commitments. A desire to serve and to rise in the world will be there, but only a few will break through and overcome the limitations that bind them.

Most auspicious: He will be quite well educated and virtuous, but he will not have the opportunities to demonstrate his abilities or his usefulness. He will follow matters through to completion, but will receive no help or support from outside. He will have only small accomplishments in life.

Least auspicious: He also will carry undertakings through to completion, and will finish everything he begins, but he will have severe hardships and impediments along the way.

In yearly hexagram:

Officer or official	He will support a superior who accomplishes something worthwhile.
Business and professional	He will face many difficulties, but will still be able to make small gains.
Ordinary people	He will lead a useful existence and make small gains. He may receive help from an influential person.

Line 2   A one-eyed man can see. The firm correctness of a recluse advantageous.

Unflinching loyalty and singleness of purpose are symbolized here. It is like a widow who resists all further offers of marriage, preferring to die rather than be disloyal to her late husband. A one-eyed man can see and can concentrate on one thing at a time, but has no depth perception. Ancillary matters will not be properly taken care of by these persons, and therefore they will not rise high. This is because this is a strong line in a weak place, and supported by a weak line 5. A break-through from these limitations can be made if appropriate partners and associates are found.

Most auspicious: He will cultivate himself, personally and professionally, but his personality will limit his effectiveness. He will be ambitious and will work diligently. He will be faithful and true to all his commitments, and will have a comfortable life, despite not rising very high by worldly standards. He will be respected by his family and by others as well.

Least auspicious: He also will have sufficient, or even abundant, means, and consequently will have a reasonable standard of living. He will be of benefit to others, but never to the extent of receiving acclaim or a great reputation.

In yearly hexagram:

Officer or official	There will be no change in his circumstances.
Business and professional	As above.
Ordinary people	He will find contentment and have no troubles, if he follows established patterns and methods.

Line 3 The marrying maiden in servitude. She returns and becomes a concubine.

Line 3 is weak where it should be strong, and at the top of the trigram Tui, joy, but without a proper correlate. Therefore, this person will have a tendency to seek and to obtain pleasure in other than right and honorable ways. The result is that the maiden will not have the right background to become the principal wife, but with a change in her ways she may find a position as a concubine. Sensuality and sexuality will tend to hold sway over this person's life. He will have many periods of irritability, as well as fleeting periods of pleasure and joy. Without proper associates and goals, little progress, if any, will be made.

Most auspicious: He will have limited talent, will be modestly well educated, and will possess a knowledge of, and training in, virtue, but he will have an effete conscience. He will be able to accomplish small things with much effort, but all attempts towards major accomplishments will be blocked.

Least auspicious: He will have erroneous ideas, and will direct his energies towards the wrong goals. Fortune will not favor him. He may have to be supported by a rich wife or another wealthy person. He will have a difficult life.

In yearly hexagram:

Officer or official	He will be dismissed or demoted.
Business and professional	He will have difficulty in maintaining his status.
Ordinary people	He will have many hardships, and may be involved in a publicized illicit affair, or divorced.

Line 4 The maiden protracts the time of her marriage, but eventually she is wed.

These individuals will have firm goals, and will carry out correctly what is required of them while waiting for their aims to material-ize. They will never use improper methods, preferring always to be honest, forthright and trustworthy. They will be calm and patient, but by no means placid. They will be constantly involved in improving themselves, personally and professionally, and will know where they want to go.

Most auspicious: He will be a knowledgeable person of high intelligence, who follows proper methods and the golden mean. His development in early life will be slow, but in his later years his goals will be fulfilled and he will have a very favorable exist-ence in all respects.

Least auspicious: He will be quite well educated, but will only have modest talents. He will encounter numerous impediments and difficulties. He will probably marry or have children, late in life. His life will become easier in his later years.

In yearly hexagram:

For everyone   Difficulties at the beginning of the year will smooth out later. Be calm, and exercise patience. Matters will work out propitiously. Those seek-ing marriage will probably not be successful.

Line 5   The emperor's younger sister wore garments at her wedding less regal than her bridesmaid's. The moon is nearly full. There will be good fortune.

The subordination of characteristics and abilities is sometimes necessary in order to achieve one's aims and purposes. However, once such a course has been decided upon, it is vital to carry it through precisely. One will not be eclipsed by so doing, and in the end good fortune will arise, both for oneself and for what one is endeavoring to accomplish. Only knowledgeable and wise persons with strong characters can successfully act in this manner.

Most auspicious: He will have great innate intelligence, wisdom and strength, together with virtue and broad-mindedness. He will follow such courses as are known to be successful, and he will be free from vanity. He will accomplish many worthwhile projects, and will receive fame and rewards. His life will be highly favored in all respects.

Least auspicious: He will be similar to the most auspicious, but not as daring, nor will his accomplishments be of such great scope or value. He will be modest and frugal, and will have a good life.

In yearly hexagram:

Officer or official	He can expect promotion.
Business and professional	He can expect an increased reputation and profits.
Ordinary people	He will experience an exceptionally joyful event. Strong desires will be fulfilled. He may make money through his marriage.

Line 6 A woman holds a basket, but there is nothing in it. A man slaughters a sheep, but no blood flows. Nothing favorable now.

The marriage contract is broken, and the man and the woman both go to the temple to offer a sacrifice. However, there is evidently great insincerity, as the offerings are a pretence, i.e. an empty basket and a sheep that is already dead. The right attitude and correct attributes are not available for union, unless this person undergoes a change of character. These persons have certain lessons to learn, including that of trying to find satisfaction wherever they are, since fate prevents them from accomplishing anything great.

Most auspicious: Although he will have many talents he will gain neither high position nor fame. Although he will be noble his salary will not be of comparable stature. He will marry, but will have few children.

Least auspicious: He will have many periods of solitude and many hardships in life. The more he tries in the external world, the worse he will fail, until he changes inwardly.

In yearly hexagram:

Officer or official	He will have a position in title, but with no real power; his salary will be limited.
Business and professional	His previous favorable reputation will have little or no value this year.
Ordinary people	He will find no satisfaction in his accomplishments; they will seem empty once concluded. Older persons may die.

KEYNOTES

1. When in a secondary position still try to do your best.
2. Have unflinching loyalty and singleness of purpose.
3. Beware of the dangers of trying to obtain things by improper methods.
4. When delays occur maintain firm correctness.
5. Do whatever is required, regardless of circumstances.
6. Insincerity bodes evil.

CONDENSATIONS FOR DAILY CYCLES

1. You are in a secondary role regarding some important matter. Nevertheless, good results can be obtained by doing whatever is required.
2. Normally you ought to work with and support your superior. Here you are faced with a matter you must handle alone.
3. Hold back. Wait for a more propitious occasion.
4. If you are too servile and ingratiating, your advice will only be given secondary consideration.
5. Guard against ostentation. Even be subservient today if necessary, but not ingratiating.
6. Your thoughts are likely to be insincere today. Do not act.

Hexagram 55   Fêng ☰ ☰ *Abundance*

SIMPLE TRANSLATION OF TEXT

Abundance. Success. The king has attained abundance. Be not sad. Be like the sun at noon.

COMMENTARY

The trigram Chên, movement, is above, and leading the trigram Li, clarity, below and within. This combination is bound to produce abundance. This abundance can be for good or for bad, depending on how it is obtained and the attitude associated with it. Every rise is followed by a decline, according to the law of change (unless something new is injected to replace the old). One should not be sad, since every day and every cycle of events serves its intended purpose. One should maintain an attitude like the sun at its zenith, cheering, sustaining and helping to enlighten all.

One's individual position, given by the controlling line, is important, since this determines one's relationship to the abundance and its nature. All persons born under this hexagram will have good minds and will tend to be active and energetic, irrespective of their circumstances. All will strive to perpetuate abundance.

Those born in the ninth month will be more auspicious.

CONTROLLING LINES (FROM BOTTOM TO TOP)
Line 1 A man meets his destined partner. Though they be together for ten days, no error. Progress meets with approval.

Here, because of the nature of the hexagram, i.e. clarity combined with action, we have an exception to the normal rule regarding line correlates, and even though lines 1 and 4 are both strong, they are said to be destined for each other. Therefore, even though they may work together for a complete cycle of activity, signified by the expression 'ten days,' there will be no error; the progress made will meet with approval. Wisdom is being supported and helped by appropriate action. The persons depicted here will have characteristics and abilities that are recognized by their superiors. They will receive help and support from those above them, as if being specially favored or tutored. This help will be very beneficial if properly accepted.

Most auspicious: He will be talented, magnanimous, wise and just, and living in a period of prosperity. He will be drawn to, and work with, persons of like mind, character and ability, and will achieve major accomplishments. He will have a good and beneficial life.

Least auspicious: He will know that his talents and abilities are above average, but he will become arrogant and selfish. He will disdain help when proffered, and will frequently have disputes with others. He will have an unhappy life.

In yearly hexagram:

Officer or official	He will be brought into contact with a high superior, who will enable him to be promoted.
Business and professional	He will come into contact with good peers and associates, and he will gain fame and profits.

Ordinary people He will be helped by his superiors, and will achieve positive results this year.

Line 2 The curtain is so dense that the pole-star can be seen at noon. His advancing now will be viewed with suspicion and distrust. Through sincerity, confidence is regained. Good fortune.

Men of clarity, vision and ambition are depicted here, but their fate is to be subjugated by jealous or envious leaders. It is only through long, diligent, often frustrating, and single-minded effort, carried out with absolute sincerity, that they can eventually overcome fate and rise to a level appropriate for their character and ability.

Most auspicious: He will rise to a high position, but will face many difficulties and hardships, due to a muddle-headed, jealous leader who believes he is trying to be usurped. Through consistent virtuousness and sincerity, the handicaps will finally be overcome, and his later life will be rich and rewarding.

Least auspicious: He will not be able to sustain himself adequately against suspicious and bullying leaders, and will be subject to misrepresentation and defamation. Eventually he will find his right position, and life thereafter will go smoothly.

In yearly hexagram:

Officer or official His loyal advice will either not be passed on or not accepted, until late in the year.

Business and professional An opportunity for advancement will present itself, but this will not culminate until late in the year.

Ordinary people Those with past troubles or illnesses will have them solved and healed. The later part of the year will pass smoothly.

Line 3 The obscurity is so great that he can see the small brilliant stars at noon. He breaks his right arm. No error.

By virtue of past karma, destiny will prevent these able persons from rising to great heights and being successful, or even from being able to render any degree of useful service to others. They will always seem to be in the wrong place, subject to incompatible

375

rules and regulations, and to be under those who deliberately or unknowingly fail to see their potential. They will also often fail to communicate properly, and their intentions will thus be misunderstood. These persons almost never rise far above these conditions. It is as if they are perpetually functioning with a broken arm.

Most auspicious: He will be knowledgeable, clear thinking and honorable, but will be placed under muddle-headed leaders. Any effort towards major gains in status or conditions will be thwarted and obstructed by leaders and colleagues. He will have no major accomplishments.

Least auspicious: He will have ability but will use it thoughtlessly, thereby harming himself professionally and frequently hurting the feelings of his family. He will make a few successful but small gains. In general, his life will be unsatisfactory.

In yearly hexagram:

Officer or official	He will be retired, or should consider retiring.
Business and professional	He will make great efforts but will achieve very little progress.
Ordinary people	Obtaining one's goals will be difficult. He may have trouble with his hands and/or feet.

Line 4 The curtain is so dense that the pole-star can be seen at noon. He meets his partner of like kind. Good fortune.

Lines 1 and 4 are proper correlates in this hexagram (see commentary under Line 1) and join their forces together. This is a union of clarity and action and is very propitious, even though it will frequently act independently of the ruler. Since guide lines are correctly followed, there will be good fortune. Such independence needs to be frequently exercised by persons working for muddled or inadequately qualified leaders. Those depicted here will have the ability and attributes necessary for success in such a course of action. On the whole, they will be men of action, supported by the wisdom of others.

Most auspicious: He will have a bright and constant virtue, which will shine forth, as through a veil, like a gentle light. His thoughts, ideas and actions will all be meritable, but he will always need the support and help of others to bring them to fruition. In this manner he will have many worthwhile achievements, for which he will be duly rewarded. His family life will be enviable, with much cooperation between all the members.

Least auspicious: He will leave his family and their enterprises to establish himself on his own merit, but will find that he needs cooperation from others, which will be difficult for him to obtain. He will have many hardships at first, with things becoming smoother later. He is likely to be involved in financial matters in his career.

In yearly hexagram:

Officer or official — The leader will be jealous and suspicious. Not a good year.

Business and professional — He will be helped by a superior.

Ordinary people — Expansion of areas of endeavor can be successful. However, he may have difficulties on a journey.

Line 5 Men of brilliant ability appear. Blessings and fame come forth. Good fortune.

Here the unusualness of this hexagram is again depicted, in that line 5, the ruler, although weak, has not only the strong support of the minister, line 4, but that of the complete lower trigram as well. These latter lines are the 'men of brilliant ability.' Combined, their actions presage blessings and fame. The persons depicted here will have a natural propensity to surround themselves with intelligent and brilliant people. They will, of course, be highly qualified themselves, as well as being natural leaders. In this way great accomplishments can result.

Most auspicious: He will be a well-educated man, with great common sense and a noble character, rising from relatively obscure status to become a man of renown. He will eventually be in an important position, and responsible for many beneficial accomplishments. He will have a well-earned, favorable reputation, and a good life in all aspects.

Least auspicious: His life will be similar to that of the most auspicious, but on a much smaller scale.

In yearly hexagram:

Officer or official — A prosperous and influential year.

Business and professional — He will be advanced and rewarded.

377

Ordinary people	He will be aided favorably. A special blessing will be granted to older people.

Line 6 His dwelling reflects abundance. It screens his household. Peering through the door, he sees no one for three years. Misfortune.

Here, at the top of the hexagram, the value of abundance is rapidly waning. It is like trying to keep up a castle or a mansion when times have changed and they are no longer appropriate. These persons will have a misguided sense of values, and will try to hang on to the past instead of keeping up to date. The harder they try the worse they will fail, and they will become isolated from their own families for long periods of time. They will even misinterpret and misuse their education and experience. There will be but little hope for them.

Most auspicious: He may inherit an ancestral estate or property, but will not have the ability to keep it. He will be helped occasionally, but will not benefit by it, and he will later become isolated through arrogance. He will always believe himself to be in the right, and will act rashly. He will not reform, and his life will end in disaster.

Least auspicious: He will be talented, but will become so arrogant that he isolates himself from his relatives and friends. He will vacillate in his occupations, and will experience many difficulties in all phases of his life.

In yearly hexagram:

Officer or official	He will find himself in difficulties and danger.
Business and professional	Unless he exercises extreme care he may lose the favorableness of his position.
Ordinary people	He will have disputes with his relations, and he may leave his family and home. He may be involved in a lawsuit.

KEYNOTES

1. Cooperate with fate and destiny.
2. Always beware of jealous or envious leaders.

3. Even the best of intentions can be misunderstood.
4. Combine wisdom with action for effective results.
5. Choose the best qualified associates at all times.
6. Arrogance breeds isolation.

CONDENSATIONS FOR DAILY CYCLES

1. You will find yourself associating with a person of like mind. Work with him closely.
2. You are nearly cut off from the help you need. If you use your intelligence fully you will find a correct way to proceed.
3. You are cut off from the help of others. Be patient, like a man with a broken arm.
4. If you unite wisdom and action today you can expect good results.
5. Employ your helpers to the maximum. If you do, the results will be most rewarding.
6. Share blessings with others, or else you will become isolated.

Hexagram 56   Lü ☰ *The Traveller*

SIMPLE TRANSLATION OF TEXT

The Traveller. Small success and progress. Firm correctness brings good fortune.

COMMENTARY

The hexagram represents fire, the trigram Li, on the mountain, the trigram Kên, hence the idea of something or someone that travels. Since fire on a mountain can be seen over great distances, those depicted here will be persons of importance whose actions carry weight and influence, but, just like fire, they will shift and stray from one place to another. What is important is the clarity with which they can handle matters. This will be particularly true in situations that should be handled quickly, wisely and effectively, such as disputes, lawsuits and disciplinary matters. As Hsun Tzu, an ancient Chinese philosopher said, in essence, about travellers: one should select only the proper means of conveyance, go to proper communities, seek out only the proper scholars and officials, and stay away from the heretical and depraved. In the lines of the hexagram one is shown how to comport oneself under various circumstances. Since action does not play a dominant part in either trigram, only small successes are presaged. The advice given here can be used by anyone whose life and work involve travelling. Furthermore, stability within and clarity without are desirable traits in any circumstances; and these are the dominant traits of those persons born under this hexagram.

Those born in the fifth month will be more auspicious.

CONTROLLING LINES (FROM BOTTOM TO TOP)
Line 1   If the traveller engages in trivial matters, he brings misfortune upon himself.

Deporting himself in an undignified manner, and at the same time dealing only in inferior matters, creates disdain for the travelling stranger, and he draws misfortune down upon himself. This also applies to those who treat life scornfully and playfully, no matter where they are. As far as possible one should try to follow the manners and customs of the country one is in. This respect for manners applies to other situations as well.

Most auspicious: He may be quite knowledgeable, but will be able to attain small positions only. This will be due to his lack of conformity. He will be in difficulties frequently because of diffidence. He will not establish merit for himself, at home or in his profession.

Least auspicious: He will start life in poor and appalling conditions. Through education he will improve his lot, but as soon as things start to go well he will become arrogant and high-handed, and he will lose what he has gained. He will be greatly distressed about his adverse conditions, but will never realize that he must change inwardly. Eventually he will give up struggling and will succumb to calamity.

In yearly hexagram:

Officer or official	He will regret his insufficient talent for handling his work.
Business and professional	He will act parsimoniously and will encounter losses.
Ordinary people	He will tend to be very narrow-minded, and limited in his activity, resulting in adverse conditions.

Line 2 The traveller arrives at an inn. He has his resources with him. He gains the loyalty of a young servant.

Line 2 is a Yin line in its proper position, and so depicts a traveller who is at a safe and proper place. He has had a safe journey and still possesses his resources. As he is dignified, modest and reserved, he wins the loyalty of a young servant. All in all, the traveller has everything he requires. Only able, far-sighted, wise, practical and courageous persons can achieve such a circumstance.

Most auspicious: He will be in a high position, involving national and international activity. He will love people and will take an interest in them. He will work for, and obtain many benefits for, others. His accomplishments will be a blessing to all people everywhere. He will be supported and respected by many, and will have a rich, fruitful and rewarding life.

Least auspicious: He will be in a high civilian position, and will have control of much wealth. He will live in a large apartment building, hotel or mansion. His life will be moderately advantageous in all respects.

In yearly hexagram:

Officer or official	A bright year with many successes.
Business and professional	He will make good progress, and will achieve a favorable reputation or fame.
Ordinary people	A good year to build, alter, or expand one's property. Personal wealth should increase.

Line 3 The traveller's inn burns down, and he loses his loyal servant. Persistence leads to danger.

Line 3 has the whole of trigram Li, fire, above it, and so depicts the burning down of the lodgings, and, at the same time, the losing of the servant, i.e. the support of line 1. In general, those at the top of the mountain (Ken) tend to be stubborn, headstrong, opinionated and contumacious, to a greater or lesser degree. In their travelling, these persons do not adapt to the customs and mores of the people around them, but arrogantly hold to their own beliefs and behaviour. This leads to trouble and danger.

Most auspicious: He will be a tough and determined man, but

will not have the social practicality and common sense to use his gifts properly, and so will not gain a high position. He will love to talk and to act big, which will frequently get him into difficulties. He may make some profit from investments, but his home life and career will be unsatisfactory.

Least auspicious: He will constantly imagine that life is better somewhere other than where he happens to be, and he will wander a lot. He will never truly establish himself, as he will be handicapped by adverse personality traits.

In yearly hexagram:

Officer or official	He may lose his job or be demoted.
Business and professional	He may lose his status, position or investments.
Ordinary people	He will perhaps face an unexpected emergency which results in disaster. Someone in the family may die.

Line 4 The traveller has reached a resting place. He has his resources and an axe. His mind is restless.

Only lines 2 and 3 are correctly positioned, so they have lodgings; others only have shelters. These persons will have ample means to carry out their mission, and will know how to protect themselves against adversities they may face. This line is at the beginning of the trigram Li, clarity, so they are learning to comport themselves in the right way under new and varying conditions.

Most auspicious: He will be a talented and able person who will frequently be advanced or assigned to new localities or activities. He may be in industry, business, or the diplomatic or military services. He will establish himself firmly wherever he is, and will enjoy a favorable reputation. He will know how to protect himself and his responsibilities, and will have a good life.

Least auspicious: He is likely to be a wandering merchant or salesman, and always believing that there are better conditions to be found elsewhere. His achievements will be minimal, and his family life will be limited and not very satisfying.

In yearly hexagram:

Officer or official	He will be transferred or promoted, and will gain mastery over his new situation.

Business and professional · He will successfully establish something new.

Ordinary people · He will gain profits or other benefits, and he may travel considerably. However, something unhappy may occur.

Line 5 · He shoots a pheasant with the flight of a single arrow. In the end he wins praise and office.

Line 5 is the center of trigram Li and the acme of clarity, so these persons will know exactly the right thing to do at all times. In olden days, foreigners, especially statesmen, introduced themselves by offering a pheasant. To have shot it personally, with but one arrow, was commendable. This image also symbolizes persons of exceptional ability, who use what they have to the best advantage, as suggested by the attaining of an office.

Most auspicious: He will be an outstanding individual, personally and professionally. He will begin his career early on, and will win fame quickly. He will have high academic degrees and will win other honors readily as well. He will accumulate much wealth, as well as establishing merit for himself and his enterprises. He will have an exceptionally favorable life.

Least auspicious: He also will be a man of skill and diligence, with a magnetic personality and excellent powers of communication. He will hold an important local position, and will have a good life.

In yearly hexagram:

Officer or official · He will be in a position of high status, without much responsibility.

Business and professional · He will increase his responsibilities and make gains.

Ordinary people · A very good year.

Line 6 · The bird burns its nest. The traveller laughs, and then later cries out. Through carelessness the cow is lost. Misfortune.

Persons who go to extremes are depicted here. It would be extremely rare for a bird to burn its nest. Good, kind people would not laugh. Losing one's cow symbolizes losing one's docility. These persons will be antagonizing, irksome and even perhaps malicious, and will be only interested in themselves.

They are individuals who have not learned that to help others is also to help oneself.

Most auspicious: He will be a person possessing considerable knowledge, but tough, stubborn, unyielding and unmanageable. He will be arrogant and full of false pride and vanity. He may gain a high position through artifice, but will lose it. He may also lose his family.

Least auspicious: He will be a wanderer, perhaps even a vagrant. He will lose his job frequently, and will eventually lose his household and family. He will have hardships all his life.

In yearly hexagram:

Officer or official	He will find it hard to keep his position. He will gain and then lose what he has gained.
Business and professional	Efforts to advance will be obstructed.
Ordinary people	A year with some good and some bad. He may move or make alterations to his house. He may have losses through fire, or contract an eye disease.

KEYNOTES
1. Never deport yourself in an undignified manner.
2. Being modest and reserved wins praise.
3. Adapt yourself to your circumstances.
4. Always try to prepare against calamities.
5. Always introduce yourself properly.
6. Going to extremes is dangerous.

CONDENSATIONS FOR DAILY CYCLES
1. Beware of dealing in trivia, and of having no firm will of your own. These could cause trouble.
2. Check that your position is firmly established and that you are meeting all requirements fully.
3. If you are offensive and follow wrong courses you must suffer the consequences.
4. You are beginning to achieve some success, and would like to progress more rapidly. Be cautious and move slowly.
5. You know intuitively what needs to be done and how to act today in order to progress and achieve success.

6. Ineptness or immodesty will lead to severe difficulties. Make the necessary corrections.

Hexagram 57   Sun ☴ *The Penetrating Wind*

SIMPLE TRANSLATION OF TEXT
The Penetrating Wind. Small efforts achieve success. It is advantageous to have firm goals and to see the great man.

COMMENTARY
This hexagram is made up of the trigram Sun, signifying wind, doubled, and symbolizes achieving one's purposes through constancy. The wind acts in invisible ways, and attains results even though it is not seen. So this man, by using the powers of his mind, can develop thoughts which, if constantly reinforced will achieve his purposes. He should meditate and concentrate repeatedly on whatever he wishes to attain. By so doing, even small strength will, over an extended period of time, achieve its goals. Meditation and concentration are among the tools of all great men. Since the nature of what one thinks about influences what takes place, it is advantageous to have firm goals, as well as to follow the examples of great and wise men. The quantity and quality of one's mental influence is governed by one's controlling line.

Those born in the fourth month will be more auspicious.

CONTROLLING LINES (FROM BOTTOM TO TOP)
Line 1 Advancing and retreating. The steadfastness of a warrior is advantageous.

Line 1 is weak, when it should be strong, hence the image of vacillation and indecisiveness. The advice here is to be like an ancient warrior, i.e. to have a singleness of purpose coupled with persistency. Thus one eliminates doubt in one's own mind, and one's intentions become firm. This is excellent for the development of the will.
Most auspicious: He will be a calm and thoughtful person. Regrettably, he will be very slow to make up his mind. This will be a definite handicap. He will begin to establish his career in a

foreign land. He will have periods of hardship and periods of ease. He may gain a favorable reputation as an author in his professional field.

Least auspicious: He will start life in a position of low status, and will never rise much above it. He will be indecisive and vacillating. He will do well in a small business, but any efforts put into a large enterprise will end in failure. He will be quite narrow-minded, and he will do well in any activity where attention to small detail is needed. On occasion he will be helped by his peers and subordinates.

In yearly hexagram:

Officer or official	A year with some advance and some regression. He may be assigned two jobs at once.
Business and professional	He will have some successes and some failures. He should try to pursue a firm goal.
Ordinary people	He will have some gains and some losses. Difficulties early in the year will smooth out later.

Line 2 Penetrating wind beneath the couch. Many diviners and exorcists are employed. Good fortune. No error.

The trigram Sun also represents wood. In ancient times couches were made of wood. Looking beneath a couch signifies searching out hidden motives, intangible influences and erroneous thoughts. In those days this was the task of diviners and exorcists. Today it is the task of knowledgeable men who possess common sense, sound judgment, discernment and penetration. Their decisions can influence the rise or fall of a particular matter, or even determine the success or failure of an important enterprise. The auspices here are favorable, and no error will result.

Most auspicious: He will be a clever man, with much virtue and ability. He will have a love of people, and will deal respectfully with all. He will be beneficial to whatever enterprises he is engaged in, and will rise to a high position, accomplishing worthwhile projects and achieving fame. He will have a rich and rewarding life.

Least auspicious: He will be a knowledgeable person, but will have the weakness of trying to engage in too many different activities at once. He will be in a position where many facets of his ability will be involved, and he may be a doctor, a psychologist or a religious leader. He will have an average life, with modest success.

In yearly hexagram:

Officer or official	He may be promoted. In any event he will be involved with rules and regulations.
Business and professional	He will earn a highly favorable reputation.
Ordinary people	If he is honest and reliable he will win support and achieve his desires, along with gains and profits.

Line 3 Repeated penetration. Opprobrium.

The third line is the lower line of man, in the six lines of a hexagram. This man will repeatedly seek to ascertain the results he can expect, rather than being courageous and making a firm decision, sticking to it, and carrying it through to completion. His actions will be shameful and disgraceful, and not worthy of a man of nobleness and distinction. These persons will have but little faith in themselves or in others. Consequently, they will make poor leaders and ineffective administrators.

Most auspicious: He will be educated, but inflexible and adamant externally, while lacking courage inwardly. He will be unable to yield or accept sound advice. He will be proud and vain, and will easily exhaust his will-power. His methods will alienate him from others, including his family.

Least auspicious: He will be extremely selfish, egotistical, and opinionated, with an inward lack of courage. He will be very disappointed because people do not like him. This results from his false attitude of superiority. He will become hardened later in life, to his own detriment. He will never have wealth.

In yearly hexagram:

Officer or official	He will be demoted.
Business and professional	He will be subjected to a substantial demotion or loss.
Ordinary people	He will maybe have some gains, maybe some losses. He is likely to suffer disdain and ill will from others.

Line 4 Regrets disappear. Game for three purposes is caught in the field.

These persons will be in responsible positions as a result of their ability, practicality, ambition, energy and ready experience, which they will weld into a well-balanced and useful life. The three purposes for which game was caught were religious sacrifice, the feeding of guests, and household requirements. This signifies that one should always do what is required, in all circumstances, and hold right thoughts.

Most auspicious: He will be a well-educated individual of great intelligence and common sense, yet gentle and modest. He will have a highly favorable reputation, and will do much of benefit for his country and its people. He is likely to be the head of a large enterprise, possibly the governor of a state. In war, if in command, he will win battles.

Least auspicious: He will have hardships early in life, easing later on. He will be a very capable individual, who will accumulate wealth through service, and who will follow the principle that it is necessary to give in order to receive. He will have an enjoyable life.

In yearly hexagram:

Officer or official	A prosperous year, with promotion likely.
Business and professional	A prosperous year, with many benefits accruing.
Ordinary people	A prosperous year, with good profits.

Line 5 Persistent correctness advantageous. Regrets vanish. Undertakings are favorable. A poor beginning, but a good end. Three days before the change; three days after the change. Good fortune.

As this is line 5, the advice here is directed to leaders and rulers. It would appear that these persons have not yet perfected themselves for the positions they hold. They are cautioned to exercise persistent correctness for the maximum success in advancement. This they will naturally and intuitively do, and so their results will be favorable. They are also warned to be deliberate in their actions, analyzing them thoroughly in advance, and then noting the reactions and effects later, in order to be sure that their rules, ordinances and administration are what they should be. Since they will tend to take all the right actions the results are favorably presaged.

Most auspicious: He will be a personable, far-sighted and knowledgeable individual, following a middle path. He will plan matters in great detail, and will carry them through effectively. He will be too cautious to be highly successful early in life, but he will amend this fault as he progresses and will have a highly successful and good life in all respects later.

Least auspicious: He will be exploratory by nature, advancing from one enterprise to another until he finds the one which completely satisfies him. In the end he will be successful, and will have a good life with ample mental and material rewards.

In yearly hexagram:

Officer or official	He will experience some vacillation early on regarding the course he should follow. Later he will reach a firm decision and will be successful. He may be promoted, or transferred to a more important position.
Business and professional	Writings and well-presented plans will be effective. He will add to his reputation.
Ordinary people	A good year, with all things ending favorably.

Line 6 Penetration under the couch. He loses his possessions and his axe. Perseverance unfavorable.

This man is shown to be using his powers unreasonably, with unfortunate results. He will have little confidence or faith in himself or in others, and will try to ferret out possible secret motives in everything. By so doing he will lose the power to make decisions or take decisive action. Consequently, he will not be successful in any enterprise. He will be able to use his mind for personal development, but in view of his impracticality cannot expect great achievements in his career.

Most auspicious: He will be calm, placid, and reasonably content with what is available to him. He will be able to accept hardships and violence, and will know how to protect himself. He will have a very modest life, but will be unconcerned about the fact that his achievements are not great.

Least auspicious: He will be a person of mean disposition, constantly questioning and suspicious, with shallow views regarding the material world. Misfortunes will be unavoidable.

In yearly hexagram:

Officer or official	He will resign, or be demoted or dismissed.
Business and professional	There will be no possibilities for advance this year.
Ordinary people	He may suffer a loss, or an illness. But also, he may have unexpected good fortune.

KEYNOTES

1. Display singleness of purpose.
2. Be discerning and penetrating. Let your thoughts be your friends.
3. Avoid seeking to ascertain results before the time is ripe.
4. Inspiration coupled with action is advantageous.
5. Be analytical and deliberate.
6. Be strongly decisive, not excessively indecisive.

CONDENSATIONS FOR DAILY CYCLES

1. Do not vacillate like the wind. Make your decision and then stick to it, with singleness of purpose.
2. Look out for hidden motives, yet take the lead in establishing influence. Let your thoughts be your friends.
3. You are seeking to discover what results you can expect. Change your mental attitude. Be persistent and consistent.
4. Energetic action, following meditation and concentration, is what is required here.
5. Exercise care. Anything that is new must be properly nurtured. The beginning may be weak, but the end will be strong.
6. You have gone too far by trying to ferret out all the possibilities. Do not waste energy needlessly.

Hexagram 58   Tui ☱☱ *Joy*

SIMPLE TRANSLATION OF TEXT
Joy. Success. Progress in firm correctness favorable.

COMMENTARY
The hexagram is made up of the trigram Tui, the youngest daughter, lake, doubled. The trigram Tui by itself signifies joyousness, and when doubled the joy becomes pleasure. Joy comes in many forms, and it is the deep desire of most people to attain it. Some joys are only superficial, while others stem from deep within. Joy also comes from doing things well, and when people are properly led. At such times people forget their troubles and burdens, something all people wish for. Only pure joys provide lasting satisfaction. That is why 'firm correctness' is favorable. This hexagram also signifies the beneficial nature of discussion and the practice of truth and learning. Some of the persons with this natal hexagram will be talented in such a way as to bring joy through leadership, some through cooperation and companionship, some through personal accomplishments, and some will be given over to, or at least strongly tempted by, worldly pleasures. These persons will be found in nearly all walks of life.

Those born in the tenth month will be more auspicious.

CONTROLLING LINES (FROM BOTTOM TO TOP)
Line 1   Harmonious joy. Good fortune.

Two forms of joy are depicted here, namely, that which automatically springs from inner harmony, and the pure and spontaneous joy that occurs when a pleasure is first felt. These persons bring harmony to others, by example or through advice and guidance. They will have a natural ability and propensity to say joyous and ameliorative things, as the occasion dictates. They will have a natural attraction, and others will enjoy being in their presence, or participating with them in social or professional activities.

Most auspicious: He will be a calm, clear-thinking individual, with a remarkable ability to communicate. He will be a scholar as well as a professional person, serving and working in harmony with others. He will establish himself early in life, and will accomplish many worthwhile things. He will have a favorable life in all respects.

Least auspicious: He will be kind, considerate, gentle, and at peace with himself. Although quite capable of entering a profession, he will prefer nature and a rural existence, finding contentment and happiness with the simple things in life.

In yearly hexagram:

Officer or official	He will be helped and supported, and will earn praise.
Business and professional	A harmonious year, with cooperation and progress.
Ordinary people	A harmonious year, with much domestic felicity.

Line 2 Sincere joy. Good fortune. Absence of regrets.

The joy in the hexagram as a whole is brought about by the strong Yang lines, 1 and 2. Even though a Yang line in this position is not correct, this person acts in a genuine way, and conforms to what is right, hence the very favorable auspices for this line. Capable men of broad vision, who understand to an appreciable degree the workings of the universe, the world they live in, their fellow men and themselves, are depicted here. They will use their wisdom effectively and sincerely at all times, within the limits of their understanding.

Most auspicious: He will be a man of brilliant talent and virtue, knowledgeable with regard to the important aspects of life, and dealing sincerely with everyone. He will be trusted, supported and respected by his leader, and by all others as well, and will accomplish a number of worthwhile and beneficial projects. He will have a good life, and will become famous.

Least auspicious: He also will be a well-educated and wise individual, who can communicate well with others and will handle matters with sincerity. He will bring about harmony, wherever he is. He will have no serious troubles or regrets in his life.

In yearly hexagram:

Officer or official	Promotion is probable.
Business and professional	He can expect advancement and gains.

Ordinary people   A harmonious year. Previous troubles and difficulties will be solved.

Line 3   Coming joy. Misfortune.

Attraction to worldly joys and pleasures is depicted here as this is a weak line in a strong place, and line 5. The attraction to, and experience of, fleeting joys results in misfortune. This line also represents persons who try to gain wealth, position or influence through offering worldly pleasures, or who use fawning, ingratiating methods in their efforts to achieve their aims.

Most auspicious: He will be able to communicate with powerful and wealthy persons, and to get some help by this means. He will not be able to use this help properly, so his advances will be fleeting, and he will never accomplish anything truly worthwhile. He will be able, however, to keep himself employed.

Least auspicious: He will have a fawning, ingratiating personality, which he will use to excess; reactions will set in, with the result that he gets into trouble for his efforts. He will have an unhappy and unsatisfactory life.

In yearly hexagram:

Officer or official   He is likely to lose his honor through fawning.

Business and professional   He will be constantly worried about gains and losses.

Ordinary people   He will tend to follow blindly, or to go against his principles, with resultant misfortune.

Line 4   While weighing joys he is restless. He verges on the injurious, but there is still cause for joy.

When one ponders over the kinds of joy one should strive for or accept one is restless until one rids oneself of seductive pleasures, thereby finding true inner peace. These persons will be beset by allurements, but will have the strength to forgo temporary pleasure and rise above them if they so desire. By so doing, they are able to obtain some of the blessings of pure joy. These will be knowledgeable persons, serving in supporting roles and positions, in which they will frequently face the choice between a seemingly easy path and the slower, more deliberate, and eventually more correct way.

Most auspicious: He will associate with wise and able persons, and keep away from heretical and debasing persons. He will act with sound judgment in all matters. He will also take timely and propitious actions, resulting in highly beneficial achievements. He will also be a good communicator.

Least auspicious: He will vacillate between what is good and what is bad. He will be unstable and will change his mind frequently, but he will also frequently be stubborn and inflexible. He will be a generally difficult person, and he will find it hard to support himself and his family.

In yearly hexagram:

Officer or official	He will be in an important position, but pestered by obsequious persons. Promotion is likely.
Business and professional	He will win a well-deserved award or distinction.
Ordinary people	The size of his family will increase. Business will flourish. For the least auspicious: Illnesses will not cure easily, and he may have mental difficulties.

Line 5   Misplaced trust in disintegrating matters is dangerous.

This person will tend to trust the weak man above him (line 6) rather than the strong man below (line 4), since he is envious of the latter being nearly his equal. Leaders and rulers will place their faith and trust in the wrong people, which will lead to many mistakes and embarrassments, and perhaps even to serious troubles. In general, these persons will be very knowledgeable, but will be lacking in the innate qualities necessary for good leadership, and in practicality. Their sense of values will be distorted to a greater or lesser degree.

Most auspicious: He will rise to an honorable position by consistent virtuousness, but will put his trust in mean persons. This will tend to destroy his effectiveness and profitability, and will occasionally even threaten his position. He will have a modestly favorable private life.

Least auspicious: He will follow no firm or set goals, either privately or professionally, and hence will vacillate, to the detriment of himself and those associated with him. Sometimes he will act in an unrestrained manner, and this will usually lead to trouble. He will have some gains and some losses.

In yearly hexagram:

Officer or official	He will have troubles due to misrepresentation.
Business and professional	Set-backs are likely.
Ordinary people	He will be disturbed by evil forces. A difficult year.

Line 6   Alluring joy.

The idea behind the image is that this line, a weak Yin in its proper place, is trying to draw the strong lines, 4 and 5, with it on the path of worldly joy. For the more auspicious the direction will be towards good, but the less auspicious will be seduced by their own vanity. The persons depicted here will truly exemplify the principle that like attracts like.

Most auspicious: He will be a well-educated and noble person, who will give others a feeling of harmony, and will lead and guide them along the right paths. He will have an effective and rewarding life.

Least auspicious: He will be confused by evil and often seduced. He will envy the world, and he will not be respected by others. His wishes will fail, and he will be unfortunate in life.

In yearly hexagram:

Officer or official	He will be pleased with and helped by, a colleague.
Business and professional	He will be recommended, but will make little advancement.
Ordinary people	He will have very few gains, if any. He may be injured, or have eye trouble or infections.

KEYNOTES

1. Heartfelt joyousness brings good fortune.
2. Inner harmony creates joy externally.
3. Being attracted to worldly pleasures is dangerous.
4. Weighing pleasures shows a lack of stability.

5. Misplaced trust leads to sorrows.
6. Remember that like attracts like.

CONDENSATIONS FOR DAILY CYCLES
1. You are free from doubt today. Relax and be contented.
2. Confident joyousness achieves its goals. You need have no regrets over the course you have chosen.
3. Indulging in worldly pleasures will bring misfortune. Be selective in what you seek.
4. Stop weighing matters in detail. Be more spontaneous and intuitive.
5. Be very selective in your choice of companions and subordinates, and in your goals. It is easy for you to put your faith in the wrong persons and ideas. Be very careful.
6. Like attracts like. Be watchful of your thoughts, feelings and inner affinities.

Hexagram 59   Huan ☴☵ *Dispersion (Disintegration)*

SIMPLE TRANSLATION OF TEXT
Dispersion. Success. The king goes to his ancestral temple. Advantageous to cross the great waters. Firm correctness brings rewards.

COMMENTARY
The hexagram is composed of the trigram Sun, wind, over trigram K'an, water. Strong winds blowing over water create dispersion and scattering. The upper trigram also represents wood, which provides a means to ride over troubled waters. In another sense, it is mental penetration, by means of which troubles can be corrected or averted. Line 5 is of the right polarity, and the ruler will find it best to gain enlightenment at his family temple. Having received guidance, it is necessary for him to take action, which, if it is firm and correct, will bring rewards. Those depicted here will be involved in overcoming estrangements and conditions of disorders, and will be agents of law enforcement, legislators, counselors, etc. Much mental activity is predicted here, and for the most part it will be ably and effectively performed, as well as the use of devices to promote unity, such as

music, ceremony, religious rites and festivals, etc. Persistence and constancy are important qualities to be developed. Admittedly, the greater their intelligence and training, the better will be their achievements. Those born in the third month will be more auspicious.

CONTROLLING LINES (FROM BOTTOM TO TOP)
Line 1 Helping others with the strength of a horse. There will be good fortune.

Line 1 is weak, and should be strong. Also, it has no correlate in line 4, so it has to seek support from the strong line 2 above it, the 'horse' in the image. As a horse can roam anywhere, so the help here can be limitless. This is useful in dealing with incipient dispersion or disintegration, which can be corrected fairly easily before it gets out of hand. Since rendering service to one's fellow men is one of the fundamental principles of our world, those depicted here will, in general, have good lives.
Most auspicious: He will be a knowledgeable and noble individual, setting a good example to others. He will be courageous in carrying out what is right. He will accomplish his purposes and achieve some things of lasting benefit. He will have the respect and support of the people, and he will help stabilize his country. His professional and personal lives will be rewarding.
Least auspicious: He also will establish himself easily, accomplish worthwhile projects, be beneficial to others, and have a nice home and a good life.
In yearly hexagram:

Officer or official	He will enjoy quicker progress than usual.
Business and professional	He will receive a boost, in both finances and status.
Ordinary people	He will be helped by his superiors. Strong desires will be fulfilled.

Line 2 Amid dispersion he hurries to that which supports him. Regrets vanish.

Line 2, a strong line, is in the middle of the dispersion caused by lines 1 and 3, as if placed in a valley or gorge, and is the center line of the trigram K'an peril. This man will either have disintegration and alienation all around him, or else he will perceive the beginnings of such within himself. By adopting a positive attitude, and initiating corrective action, he will be able to overcome dangers. Strong, noble, penetrating, courageous and dynamic persons are indicated. Such persons are vital to every agency and activity; the nature of their work will depend on their own natural bent.

Most auspicious: He will be a good man, with much common sense and practicality, following a middle way. He will know the value of, and will use, a positive attitude. He will be analytical, and will observe changes in people, with time and will take rectifying actions as necessary. He will have hardships early in life, but circumstances will ease later, giving a good life.

Least auspicious: He will have to go out into the world on his own, early in life. He will have much work and many hardships, but his efforts will be more effective later in life, and he will then enjoy a quiet and moderately wealthy existence.

In yearly hexagram:

Officer or official	He will be assigned to a high and powerful position.
Business and professional	He will achieve fame or a favorable reputation.
Ordinary people	Strong desires will be fulfilled and household matters will improve. The least auspicious may wander into, or escape from, danger.

Line 3 Dispersion of self. No regrets.

Those persons are destined to serve others. They will be of little value to the world except through renunciation of self and possessions. This means getting rid of everything that might prove a barrier to working with, and understanding, others. Their goals must be completely altruistic, and as universal as possible, for the best results. Their accomplishments will be so satisfying that these persons will have no regrets over the life they lead.

Most auspicious: He will work for his community or country, correcting any major mistakes that occur. He will serve both his leader and the people well. He will spend much time away from home, but otherwise will have a very good home life.

Least auspicious: He will go out into the world on his own, early in life, and will establish himself in a foreign land. He will have a middling life, with neither great achievements nor major difficulties. He will have a good life, and may turn to the cultivation of himself as his mode of existence.

In yearly hexagram:

Officer or official	He will be transferred to an outside position.
Business and professional	He should consider the possibility of changing his location for the rendering greater service to others.
Ordinary people	Enterprises will be profitable, and troubles will dissolve.

Line 4 He dissolves established bonds. Sublime good fortune. Dispersion leads to accumulation, but ordinary people do not understand this.

The necessity to give before one can receive has been understood and applied by leaders at all levels throughout the ages. These persons must forget themselves in the interests of their public, rising above man-made rules, party factions and exclusive associations in their efforts at impartial service. By so doing they will truly give, and from their actions attain sublime good fortune. Only truly dedicated persons, in high and influential positions, can successfully work for the benefit of many.

Most auspicious: He will be a man of vision and insight. He will establish himself early on in a noble manner, and will achieve fame for his meritorious accomplishments. He will abolish separatist activities and quell selfish cliques. He will be trusted by his leader, and will unify the people through his own leadership. He will have a very favorable life.

Least auspicious: He also will be a brilliant and successful leader. He will make gains and benefit from every enterprise in which he engages. He will enjoy a variety of activity, and will change his job several times in his life. He will have a modestly beneficial and successful life.

In yearly hexagram:

Officer or official	He will be in a high position, and exercising command.
Business and professional	New proposals will be successful.

Ordinary people	Troubles will dissolve, and plans materialize. Wishes will be fulfilled.

Line 5 Amid dispersion he issues commands, with much perspiration. The king dispenses his treasures. No error.

Two symbolisms are expressed here. Just as sweating breaks a fever, so will the king's proclamations disperse and cure rebellious thoughts and actions. The second image shows the king employing the principle that to give is to receive. By giving to the people he will receive much more in return. Wise and able leadership is depicted here. These persons will be called upon to correct unhealthy conditions, some of which will have been brought about by their own mistakes, and some of which will be the fault of others. In the end no grave errors will occur.

Most auspicious: He will be in an important and influential position, carrying out his duties with a deep love of people and an innate respect for what is right and just. He will establish much of benefit to others, and will be duly rewarded in return. He will merit a highly favorable reputation.

Least auspicious: He will be ambitious and knowledgeable. He will always aim high, and will enjoy winning others over. He will rise from a position of low status to modest fame and honors.

In yearly hexagram:

Officer or official	He will be promoted.
Business and professional	He will make favorable advancement.
Ordinary people	He will gain profits. If sick he will be healed.

Line 6 Dispersing the blood. Going out, and separating himself from it, is without blame.

This line will, on occasion, suffer problems, owing to its correlate being line 3, which is at the top of the trigram K'an, peril. These persons must disperse those matters and situations which might lead to bloodshed and wounds. This applies in his personal life, and in his dealings with his associates, his work, and his country. He must act in such a manner as will keep danger away, or take appropriate action to dissolve and disperse danger when encountered. Only strong, courageous and wise persons will be successful in this.

400

Most auspicious: He will be very knowledgeable, talented, practical, intelligent and quick thinking. He will be loyal and patriotic, for the well-being of the people. He will know how to overcome difficulties and will do so. He will be in a high position, and will achieve much of lasting benefit. He will have a rich and rewarding life.

Least auspicious: He will know when is the right time to initiate change, when to advance, and when to retreat. He will travel considerably, and will establish himself a long way from his place of birth. He will overcome troubles and dangers, and be of benefit to others, on a modest scale.

In yearly hexagram:

Officer or official	If a civilian, he will be transferred away from the home area. If in the military, he will establish merit through conquering.
Business and professional	It will be auspicious to expand or start something new.
Ordinary people	Troubles will be solved; disputes and lawsuits will be settled. Everything will change for the better.

KEYNOTES

1. Deal with incipient disintegration quickly.
2. A positive attitude is always beneficial.
3. Break down barriers between yourself and others.
4. One must give before one can receive.
5. Make corrections with the changing times and changing circumstances.
6. Never allow disintegration to become severe.

CONDENSATIONS FOR DAILY CYCLES

1. An estrangement is beginning. Deal with it now while it is still manageable, with the help of friends or new ideas.
2. You are in a somewhat dangerous situation. Deal with it spiritually, and work with like-minded associates.
3. Cast out or disperse evil thoughts and keep only the good, within and without.
4. Dissolve one-sided factions so that gains can be made. One must give before one can receive.

5. Dispense your inner resources and external treasures, and you will break the deadlock that is hampering you.
6. Take whatever steps are necessary to overcome danger, for your own protection and the protection of those dependent on you.

Hexagram 60   Chieh ䷻ *Restraint (Limitations)*

SIMPLE TRANSLATION OF TEXT
Restraint. Success. Harsh restraints will not endure.

COMMENTARY
This hexagram is composed of the trigram K'an, water, over trigram Tui, lake. A lake is limited in size, while water is unlimited. Therefore restraints must be imposed on the water to keep the lake from overflowing. Primarily, this hexagram is a symbol of correct government through wise rules for the guidance and control of the people. Proper restraints will produce proper success. Harsh restraints will not be adhered to, and consequently will not endure. As stated before, *I Ching* is designed principally for superior persons. The persons born under this hexagram are advised how best they can circumscribe themselves and their lives for the most satisfactory relations with others. This is vital, so that all partners can know what to expect and how to act properly. Broadly speaking, the restraints are brought about by the upper three lines and imposed on the lower three. Restraint is necessary at all levels of society and in every activity. These persons will be intimately connected, either with the developing of restraints, or with their application and execution. These are worthwhile and vital functions, since true freedom can only be exercised within duly circumscribed limits.

Those born in the eleventh month will be more auspicious.

CONTROLLING LINES (FROM BOTTOM TO TOP)
Line 1   Remaining within the courtyard outside the door. No error.

These persons will know their prescribed limits, and will keep within them. Line 1 is strong in the right place, and hence would exercise power and go its own way. Because this line has its correlate in line 4, the first line of the trigram K'an, peril, this man will realize that it is wisest for him to keep calm and tranquil and not try to exceed due limits in any way. Since he will do this of his own free will, he will be exercising proper restraint, conforming to customs and mores, and will be perfecting his own conduct.

Most auspicious: He will have great knowledge, both academically and practically, and will truly understand the nature and laws of change. His actions and proposals will affect the laws of his country. He will be well known for his works and efforts, and will have a good life in all respects.

Least auspicious: He will have much common sense, and will follow accepted ways and means. He will not be envious, nor unduly competitive. He will hold his own professionally, but will resist change. His life will be free from major troubles.

In yearly hexagram:

Officer or official	No changes are predicted.
Business and professional	It will be best for him to remain within accepted limits.
Ordinary people	Be conservative, and avoid major changes.

Line 2 Not going out from the inner gate and courtyard. Misfortune.

Line 2 is a strong line in a weak place and so cannot exert its strength properly. It is also held back by the strong line 5. These restraints will definitely limit the potential of these persons, and give them the characteristic of holding back when they ought to be taking action. Even though inwardly they will have the potential to be leaders, destiny will restrain them and limit their effectiveness.

Most auspicious: Although he will be talented, either he will not know how to display his abilities properly, or else situations and circumstances will be such that his abilities will not be recognized or cannot be used. His progress likewise will be limited and restrained. He is advised to look inward and improve himself, rather than contest his destiny unsuccessfully in the external world. His personal life will be modest yet satisfactory.

Least auspicious: He will be moderately well educated, but dull-witted and bound by conventions. He will be a poor communicator, and will not look for ways to progress but will stick instead to old and obsolete methods. He will accomplish nothing worthwhile, and his family life will lack felicity.

In yearly hexagram:

Officer or official	Following old methods will lead to difficulties. He should innovate, and initiate activity.
Business and professional	As above.
Ordinary people	He may miss a favorable opportunity by sticking to old ideas.

Line 3 By not observing due restraint he will have cause to lament. No blame.

Here at the top of trigram Tui, the water from above, i.e. the upper trigram, is filling the lake to the point of overflowing, indicating that restraints are not being observed. This will obviously bring cause for lament. Here, 'no blame' signifies that he has had no one to blame but himself, line 3 being weak and having no proper correlate.

Most auspicious: He will attain a high position and a large salary, but will not be frugal, spending gains quickly and never establishing himself on a sound financial basis. He will also be careless with the financial state of his business, and will face many worries and uncertainties.

Least auspicious: He will be envious of others, and servile, always trying to gain something for little or nothing. He will quite likely miss his footing in his haste for gain, and will seldom make a real profit. He will have means enough for food and shelter, but he will never be truly happy.

In yearly hexagram:

Officer or official	He is likely to go to extremes of extravagance.
Business and professional	He is likely to use unethical practices, with resultant difficulties.
Ordinary people	He will worry constantly about money and the cost of living.

Line 4 Contentment with restraint. Success.

Line 4 is weak, as it should be, and subject to the good, strong leadership of line 5. Hence, these persons will be content with the restraints imposed upon them, and will abide within their limitations. Loyal and obedient persons are depicted, who are ideally suited for their supporting positions, and, under the guidance of strong leaders, will effectively and efficiently carry out all that is expected of them. This will give great pleasure and satisfaction to their leaders. This mutual cooperation will be productive of many accomplishments and much success.

Most auspicious: He will help the ruler or leader successfully, and will follow the golden mean. He will accomplish many worthwhile projects, and will maintain his positions with ease. His advice will be sought by both his juniors and his seniors. He will have a rich and rewarding life.

Least auspicious: He will be moderately talented, and well qualified for the positions he will hold. These may not be very high, but they will provide him with an easy, generally trouble-free life.

In yearly hexagram:

Officer or official	He will become the favorite of his leader or manager.
Business and professional	He will achieve a highly favorable reputation.
Ordinary people	If he is law-abiding and godfearing he will have a favorable year.

Line 5 Employing acceptable restrain. Good fortune. Advancing brings success.

Line 5 is strong in the right position, but without a correlate. Hence it signifies persons who regulate their lives well, with restraint, as well as imposing restraints that are acceptable to others. Many leaders impose rules and regulations, which, instead of correcting and curbing evil, merely bring additional hardships to those who are good anyway. Truly wise, noble and virtuous leadership is depicted here. It will be coupled with a great love and deep understanding of people. Consequently, the actions of these leaders will be beneficial to all, and will result in good fortune.

Most auspicious: He will be in a high position, and his efforts will result in beneficial and acceptable systems and regulations. He will be respected by nearly everyone, and he will place his country or his enterprise in a sound financial position. He will gain well-earned fame, and his life will be highly beneficial and rewarding, for himself, his family and his country.

Least auspicious: He will regulate his life within acceptable limits, and will demand and receive the like from others. He will be content with modest accomplishments, and will have a good life, with sufficient funds, frugally managed, but never luxury.

In yearly hexagram:

Officer or official	He can expect promotion.
Business and professional	He will advance in all spheres.
Ordinary people	Strong desires will be fulfilled.

Line 6 Irritating restraint. Persistent enforcement brings misfortune. Later, remorse disappears.

Idealism has replaced practicality here, as is often the case with the sixth line. The vast majority of people are not sufficiently advanced for idealistic rules and regulations, and will rebel, feeling them to be unjust. Efforts to try and enforce irritating restraints will only lead to further difficulties and increased violations. This will bring misfortune, for all concerned. Sometimes, however, it is only through strict self-discipline that lasting corrections can be made. In such cases, if the leaders willingly impose self-restraint and set a good example themselves, others will gradually follow and the occasion for sternness will pass.

Most auspicious: He will be in a high position, yet modest, reverent, incorruptible, honest and plain-spoken. He may be quite idealistic, and probably exceedingly frugal. He will deal with situations as they come, and will never complain.

Least auspicious: He will be a difficult person, austere and stingy. He will have many impractical ideas, and have difficulty adapting himself to life. He will have few friends, many regrets, and perhaps even some serious misfortune.

In yearly hexagram:

Officer or official	He will be wrong to hold stubbornly to his own ideas.
Business and professional	He will be suspicious of his associates and peers.
Ordinary people	He will try to accomplish something that is beyond his ability. If old, he may die.

KEYNOTES
1. Keeping within prescribed limits has value.
2. When you possess a potential you should use it.
3. Lack of restraint is invariably damaging.
4. Loyalty and obedience are valuable assets.
5. Wise leadership prescribes only acceptable restraints.
6. Irritating restraints will not be heeded.

CONDENSATIONS FOR DAILY CYCLES
1. Be careful. Keep within the limits set for you, and you will remain free from blame.
2. A blessing will present itself. It would be remiss of you not to take advantage of your good fortune.
3. If you do not observe due restraint, you must suffer the consequences. If you realize your errors and correct them, you will enhance your responsibility.
4. You adhere to restraint, as you should. This concentration of energy will be productive of success.
5. Laying down constraints and rules, in an impartial manner, will bring good fortune, whether it be in connection with oneself, one's family, or one's profession.
6. Examine your situation, and see if stricter adherence to rules may not be what you need at this time, for your own benefit.

Hexagram 61   Chung Fu ☲ *Inner Sincerity* (*Truth*)

SIMPLE TRANSLATION OF TEXT
Inner Sincerity. Pigs and dolphins. Good fortune. Advantageous to cross the great water; beneficial to be firm and correct.

COMMENTARY
The hexagram is composed of the trigram Sun, wind, over trigram Tui, lake. The invisible action of the wind manifests in its visible effect on water. The hexagram is open within (lines 3 and 4), with two strong lines at each end. On the whole, the pig is considered to be one of the least intelligent animals, and the dolphin among the most intelligent. A man's inner strength, therefore, must be truly great for him to be able to influence all

animals. Such a power is bound to bring good fortune. This hexagram also signifies inner sincerity that can influence, unsuspected by the recipient. Persons born under this hexagram are specifically enjoined to use whatever abilities they have, and not leave any dormant. This should be an important precept in anyone's life. Since a man's external influence stems from within, one must be careful regarding the nature of one's thoughts and meditations. Maximum effectiveness will be achieved when mental barriers have been removed and doors opened. Establishing a rapport with others will be exceptionally helpful. These persons will have such inner strength of character that they will influence many others, both near and far. In general, they will do this with an open heart (the hexagram being open in the middle) and without guile. The degree of their influence will be determined by their controlling line, and by their karmic level and their intelligence. Since their influence will often be unconscious and great, they should periodically check the effects they are having on others, and make adjustments as necessary.

Those born in the eighth month will be more auspicious.

CONTROLLING LINES (FROM BOTTOM TO TOP)
Line 1 Quietly developing inner sincerity. Good fortune. Any insincerity is disquieting.

This line is very difficult to translate precisely, but the meaning is clear, namely, that following a path of moderation, developing oneself constantly and maintaining sincerity, is bound to bring good fortune. Those who have the persistence and tenacity to carry out such a course will have highly favorable lives. Inner strength and sincerity are always keys to success in life; this is especially true for those who try to develop these qualities deliberately.

Most auspicious: He will be a noble person, gentle and obedient, who follows the golden mean. He will be a clever and intelligent individual, constantly striving to improve himself and those with whom he comes into contact. He will help his leader establish merit, and will be duly recompensed. He will have a good family life.

Least auspicious: He will vacillate in his aims and intentions, and hence will be generally unstable. He will frequently consider changes, seeking to ascertain his purpose in life. He will probably achieve clarity of purpose too late in life to be very effective.

In yearly hexagram:

Officer or official	He will be recommended for a higher position.
Business and professional	He will be recommended by others.
Ordinary people	He will receive help from his superiors, but will have some personal sorrow or worry. If he follows the golden mean, he will have reasonable success. Following an easy, care-free life will lead to failures.

Line 2 The crane calls in seclusion. The young respond to her. I have a fine goblet, and will share it with you.

A crane's young can hear and recognize their mother's call at a great distance, even when she is hidden. This indicates two things, namely, that one's heartfelt desires will meet with a response from those of like mind, and that one's thoughts are able to transcend the limitations of space. Sharing a goblet of wine symbolizes a willingness to respond to persons of a kindred nature to oneself, especially those of corresponding virtue. Events will come to pass as an echo of that which is within, and as the effects of concentrated thought. This man's thoughts will travel to all parts of the world. Hence, he must be very careful about the attitudes that he holds, and his desires. He will be knowledgeable in the uses and powers of the mind, and will employ what he knows, according to his ability. His thoughts, in general, will serve mankind well.

Most auspicious: He will be a contemplative and learned person, with excellent powers of communication. He will follow the golden mean, in thought, word and deed, to the best of his ability. His influence will be natural and of great magnitude, and he will accomplish many worthwhile projects. He will have a highly satisfactory life in all respects.

Least auspicious: He also will be a man of virtue and excellent behaviour. He will be highly respected and well loved. He will be versed in literature, and professionally capable. He will be aided through wealth, or by superior persons, and will have a son who one day will be outstanding. His life will be moderately good in all respects, with no major troubles.

In yearly hexagram:

Officer or official	He can expect promotion.
Business and professional	He will advance and have gains.
Ordinary people	He will gain profits, and may have a child. Strong desires will be fulfilled.

Line 3 He meets an enemy. Now he beats a drum. Now he stops. Now he weeps. Now he sings.

Line 6 is the proper correlate of line 3, and, being a Yang line, is stronger than the Yin of line 3. Regrettably, both are incorrect for their positions, so the influence of line 6 will not be consistent nor always correct. This signifies that these are persons who will find their source of strength in others. Unfortunately, others are not always around to help, guide or direct them, so they will frequently vacillate. Some solo efforts will be made, but many of these will result in mistakes. Their situation will alternate rapidly between good and bad.

Most auspicious: He will have no wise or clever father or brother to help rear and guide him. Furthermore, he will fail to find the right teachers and friends to support him. His goals will not be firm and he will frequently waver. He will work hard, and may gain considerable wealth, but he will have difficulty keeping it. His irresolution will be reflected in his personal life.

Least auspicious: He will be a weak person, possessing little sincerity, who will frequently be deceitful, and will often pose as something other than what he is. He will also vacillate repeatedly. Eventually he will be reduced to a solitary existence.

In yearly hexagram:

Officer or official	He will not be in harmony with his colleagues. He may be advanced, only to subsequently resign.
Business and professional	Joys and gains will be fleeting.
Ordinary people	He will experience alternate periods of joy and sadness, gains and losses.

Line 4 The moon is nearly full. The composition of the team of horses is altered. No error.

In the ancient days, chariots were drawn by four horses. In a hexagram these are represented by lines 1 and 4 and 2 and 5. Here, line 1 is not the proper correlate of line 4 and goes astray. Line 4 then seeks support from line 5. Since both lines 4 and 5 are in their proper places, no error occurs. Inner sincerity and truth are deepened through the guidance and leadership of superior persons, or by their words, just as the moon receives its light from the sun. To receive additional enlightenment from a superior person requires, first, a strong desire, second, a proper attitude, and third, the establishment of a true rapport. Few there are who can achieve this with the necessary humility and wisdom to be able to learn from a true sage. Great selflessness and dedication are demanded.

Most auspicious: He will work for the good of his country, for its leader and for the people. He will dissolve cliques and factions that try to tear down and replace existing controls. He will have an influential position and will be respected by the various leaders of the nation. He will have a richly endowed mind, and his entire family will repose trust in him.

Least auspicious: He will be quickwitted and clever, but lacking in fundamental wisdom. He will have difficulty achieving long term gains and benefits. He may have financial, marital or parental difficulties.

In yearly hexagram:

Officer or official	He will receive a well-deserved advancement.
Business and professional	He will have professional gains and much satisfaction.
Ordinary people	He will probably be helped by a superior person. He may lose a valued possession.

Line 5 Perfect sincerity. Uniting closely. No error.

This line is the position of the leader, and in this case he will be a sage, whose deep sincerity will go forth and bind all together. These persons will be truth-loving, just, honorable and ingenuous. They will possess great knowledge, practicality and a deep love of people. They will also be able communicators.

Most auspicious: He will possess sincerity in the highest degree, together with nobleness and virtue. He will know how to govern the country and his own enterprises. His leadership will automatically unite the people, who will follow him with devotion. He will accomplish much of lasting benefit, and will have a favorable life in all respects.

Least auspicious: He also will be a knowledgeable and practical man of virtue, leading others capably. He will be respected by his juniors and his seniors alike. He will have an abundance of enjoyments, and a long and satisfying life.

In yearly hexagram:

Officer or official	He will be highly trusted, and assigned to an important position.
Business and professional	He will advance and achieve renown.
Ordinary people	A year of harmony, with all things proceeding smoothly.

Line 6 The cock's crow strives to reach heaven. Persistence brings misfortune.

Line 6 is strong, and ought to be weak. After the great strength and auspiciousness of line 5, here there is a natural decline. Admittedly, the cock is dependable in its crowing, but by attempting to reach heaven it is trying to do the impossible, and persistence in such efforts will lead to misfortune. Many of these persons will strive to be thorough, with confidence and sincerity, and will be modestly successful. Others will be impractical or deceptive and will try to perform tasks beyond their abilities, with unfortunate results.

Most auspicious: He will achieve fame in his youth, and will rise to a high position. He will retire from public life in his senior years, as a result of not being able to adapt and keep up to date.

Least auspicious: He will rise to a moderately high position early in life. He will be stubborn, headstrong and intractable, and will not be able to maintain his position or status. By living in seclusion he will be able to have a favorable existence.

In yearly hexagram:

Officer or official	He will have the satisfaction of being close to the leader or ruler.
Business and professional	He will advance in all aspects of his profession.
Ordinary people	He will find himself competing

with others for supremacy. He
will have disputes, and will probably lose money.

KEYNOTES
1. Deep sincerity is bound to bring good fortune.
2. Inner strength is echoed externally.
3. Avoid being dependent on others.
4. Never cease deepening your sincerity.
5. Leaders must be sincere and ingenuous.
6. Sincerity must be combined with adaptability.

CONDENSATIONS FOR DAILY CYCLES
1. You have now learned which is the right direction, and are
beginning to follow it. Be as self-reliant as possible.
2. Your heartfelt desires will find a response in those attuned to
you. Remember that it is divine will that one should render
service to others. Do so.
3. You are finding that some of the lessons you have to learn are
tough. Do not make the same mistakes twice.
4. You are now well ahead, and are still advancing. Follow your
course without deviating.
5. Remember that the power of inner truth binds all together,
and results in good.
6. Being over-confident, and bragging about your capabilities
and good fortune, is selfish, and destroys the power of inner
truth. Check yourself.

Hexagram 62   Hsiao Kuo ☳☶ *Outer Preponderance*

SIMPLE TRANSLATION OF TEXT
Outer Preponderance. Success. Persistence furthers. Small
things should be done, but not great things. The flying bird
means that it is better to remain low than to strive too high.
Great good fortune.

COMMENTARY
External extravagances and excessive displays of emotion should
not be indulged in. There will be success in small matters, but

not in big ones. The humble will be favored. The mighty should bide their time. These statements have their basis in the visual appearance of the hexagram, with its preponderance of weak lines, and the two strong lines in the center. The shape also suggests a soaring bird (cf. hexagram 28). These persons will have a tendency to do everything to excess, e.g. being miserly instead of thrifty, imposing on others when helping them instead of merely providing support and doing good, and making a display of sorrow in bereavement instead of keeping one's grief within the bounds of good manners. Birds that fly too high get into difficulties. A man who strives too high for his abilities will likewise experience troubles. Great good fortune will come from remaining where one ought to be, and from doing whatever is expected of one in one's position. Naturally, it is right to strive upward, but the goals should be reasonably attainable. Some of these persons will learn from bitter experience the value of modesty, humility, and proceeding one step at a time. Regrettably, others will never learn.

Those born in the second month will be more auspicious.

CONTROLLING LINES (FROM BOTTOM TO TOP)
Line 1 The ascending bird meets with misfortune.

When anyone tries to act in a manner for which he is not duly prepared or qualified, misfortune is bound to be the result. Those who are born under this line will have a propensity to step forward without looking, to act with but little understanding, and to talk when they should be listening. They should remember that in the hands of the Great Architect no material is useless, and that they too serve a purpose, even though it will not seem as important as that of many others.
Most auspicious: He will receive a good education, and will establish himself early in life. He will rise to a high position, in his prime. He will then be favored by the leader and much sought-after by the people which will make him arrogant, proud and vain, resulting in his downfall. His home life will be affected likewise.
Least auspicious: He will constantly make efforts to rise, relying mainly on his own strength. Through making some good gains early on, he too will become arrogant and vain, resulting

in many troubles and a disruption of his household and family life.

In yearly hexagram:

Officer or official	He will tend to advance too fast, and run into difficulties.
Business and professional	Steering a middle course will keep him from trouble.
Ordinary people	If he tries to rise in position, he is likely to get into difficulties. He will fare well if he remains modest and humble.

Line 2 Passing his ancestor he meets his ancestress. He does not meet the ruler but the minister. No error.

Line 5 is the normal correlate of line 2, but here it is weak, so line 2 receives help instead from line 4, bypassing the strong third line. Since line 2 is of the correct polarity, no error is made. This person will stick to whatever work he is best suited for, and will do whatever is right for the circumstances in which he finds himself. The help from line 4 is not as great as that he would have received from a strong ruler, but is sufficient to be quite favorable. These persons will be helped throughout their lives by others higher than themselves, but not by those in the top positions.

Most auspicious: He will be modest in his outward relations, serving his ruler and leader well. He will be famous for his writings and philosophy. His principal desire will be to be useful and serve his country and his fellow men well, which he will do to a high degree. In return he will be helped and supported by others. His family life will be of substance, yet frugal.

Least auspicious: He will be modest, and will possess singleness of purpose. His friends and superiors will help him, and he will serve his community, his business and his family well.

In yearly hexagram:

Officer or official	If he does a good job he will be promoted.
Business and professional	He will be helped by persons with superior knowledge or wealth.
Ordinary people	He will be helped in an unexpected way, perhaps by a woman.

Line 3 Taking no precautions against danger provides others with the opportunity to attack him from behind. Misfortune.

This image derives from the unprotected top of the mountain (Kên) being subjected to thunder (Chên), and the symbolism being applied to human life. Wise persons will heed the warning and will exercise prudence, whereas others will believe themselves to be stronger than a mountain and will act in a disdainful manner. Good judgment and common sense demand that appropriate precautions be taken in all circumstances, not only for one's own sake, but also for the sake of those whom one is serving and those who are dependent on one.

Most auspicious: He will be born wise, and will know how to prepare in advance against calamities, mental and physical. He will have a strong and noble character, and will be able to subdue people when necessary. He will protect himself and his family well, and will have a good life.

Least auspicious: He will be disdainful of precautions, and will rely on his own strength and ability. Since no man is an island, this will result in frequent troubles.

In yearly hexagram:

Officer or official	Evil will arise. Be careful.
Business and professional	Progress will appear blocked.
Ordinary people	Only extreme care will avert troubles.

Line 4 No error. He meets his situation without exceeding it. Proceeding brings danger. Exercise care. Nothing demands unceasing firmness.

This line symbolizes the exercise of moderation. One should never go to extremes, and at the same time it is equally wrong to always remain absolutely central. Here, a strong line is held in check by its weak position, so this man will tend to avoid extremes of behaviour. Hence, 'no error.' However, if he tries to exceed his position, or do that for which he is not duly qualified, he will be going to an extreme, and this will bring danger in its wake. He should also remember that no situation is ever such that perpetual obduracy is the right course. One should be flexible, to the degree that the situation demands.

Most auspicious: He will rise to a high position, yet will remain humble. He will have due pride but will never be arrogant. He will show an interest in serving others, and will be careful to maintain correctness, tempered by good judgment. He will establish sound rules and will be flexible in their execution. He will have a highly favorable and beneficial life.

Least auspicious: He also will be a man of sincerity, with a love of people. He will lead a well-planned, circumspect life, comfortably and quietly, seeking no great wealth or glory.

In yearly hexagram:

Officer or official	He will have nothing to fear. A good year.
Business and professional	He will have many opportunities for small gains.
Ordinary people	A year of contentedness, with no losses.

Line 5 Dense clouds, but no rain from the western regions. The prince shoots an arrow and hits him who is in the cave.

For the most part, in China, rain comes from the east, the direction of the ocean. Clouds from the west are without sufficient moisture to produce rain. This (cf. hexagram 9) signifies a time for preparations. The line is weak, so a prince is depicted here, rather than a king as is normal in this position. His ability is not too great, since he shoots a bird in a cave rather than one on the wing. These persons will be leaders of small enterprises, given to much planning and preparing rather then executing or supervising. They will be competitive and aspiring.

Most auspicious: He will be quite talented and very ambitious, but circumstances will not favor him and he will be limited to modest achievements. He will be restless and forceful, wasting much of his energy. This will be reflected in his home life as well.

Least auspicious: He will imagine that he is cleverer than he actually is, and will be vain and arrogant, believing himself always to be in the right. He will engender disharmony, which is likely to result in him living in isolation. Very few of his wishes will be accomplished.

In yearly hexagram:

Officer or official	It would be better to retreat voluntarily than be forced to retreat.

417

| Business and professional | He is likely to be aided by an outside sponsor. |
| Ordinary people | It would be best to stick to old ways. Big plans and radical changes should be avoided. Not an auspicious year for older persons or those who are sick. |

Line 6 He exceeds his situation rather than just meeting it. The flying bird passes him by. Misfortune.

These persons will have difficulty exercising proper restraint, as they have a natural propensity to excesses and for overshooting the mark. Constantly striving higher and higher, never knowing or establishing acceptable limits, is detrimental to oneself and others. The grass will never seem greenest, wherever they are.

Most auspicious: He will become unduly proud and arrogant, through a false opinion of himself and his ability. He will never see himself as others see him. He will be continually striving, and ambitious, but by using wrong methods and by not correcting his faults, that which he accomplishes will give empty satisfaction, and any gains will later be lost.

Least auspicious: He will be insatiably covetous, and envious of others. He will use his strength indiscriminately, and act rashly, trying to force situations before they are ripe. His accomplishments will be few and small, and he will have many troubles, including frequent family difficulties.

In yearly hexagram:

Officer or official	There is a danger that he will be too rigid in his resolution, thereby destroying fundamentally stable conditions.
Business and professional	Only written work will be advantageous.
Ordinary people	He will experience difficulties if he often goes beyond what is proper.

KEYNOTES

1. Make sure that you are prepared and qualified before acting.
2. Stick to what you are suited for.
3. Observe appropriate caution always.

4. Be flexible, as necessary.
5. Set acceptable and attainable goals.
6. Avoid overstepping the mark.

CONDENSATIONS FOR DAILY CYCLES

1. A bird should not try to fly until fully fledged. If you take action now you will probably encounter a danger which cannot be averted.
2. Take one step at a time. Contact the right people, in the right order.
3. Remain humble, even when dealing with small matters, otherwise danger or harm may result.
4. Do not force issues, even though you may have more than enough strength to win.
5. Your leadership is not as strong as it ought to be. Results are not being achieved. Seek appropriate help (through thought or from people).
6. Are you striving too high? Are you exercising proper self-control? You should keep within the limits of your abilities.

Hexagram 63   Chi Chi ☵☲ *After Completion*

SIMPLE TRANSLATION OF TEXT
After Completion. Success in small matters. Good fortune at the beginning. Disorder likely at the end.

COMMENTARY
Every line in this hexagram is in the right place, signifying that matters have been brought to completion. With this completion comes success. The good fortune comes at the beginning, when the process of completion is still effective. A hexagram, however, is not static, so by the time the top of the hexagram is reached, and the lines are tending to change to their opposite, disorders are likely to occur. This need not necessarily happen, if new ideas or actions are injected to replace the old. This is what is implied by 'success in small matters,' i.e. when major accomplishments are complete there invariably remain small matters to be taken care of, and timely replacement of outworn details can keep a project stabilized and successful. This naturally requires continual

planning and forethought. In human affairs this should be done with firmness and correctness, in great and small matters alike, and in all realms, mental, physical and spiritual. One must bear in mind the law of change: nothing ever remains stationary; all things are either progressing or retrogressing, however slowly. Those with this natal hexagram will exercise much thought, and, in general, will plan well and know the right things to do.

Those born in the first month will be more auspicious.

CONTROLLING LINES (FROM BOTTOM TO TOP)
Line 1   He brakes his wheels. His tail becomes wet. No error.

This line expresses the conditions at the completion of an enterprise. In *I Ching*, an important enterprise is usually signified by the expression 'crossing the great water' (or 'stream'). Braking one's wheels and slowing down keeps one from getting needlessly wet when fording the great water. However, it seems that this person is like a fox who gets his tail wet, and consequently has no desire to cross the water again. With matters being completed, it is right to rest and restrict one's activities. However, continued analysis of one's situation is required to keep matters appropriately in hand.
Most auspicious: He will be knowledgeable and wise, and in a high position. He will take adequate precautions against possible calamities, nipping them in the bud whenever possible, or helping to repair such conditions as may occur after natural disasters. He may be in the legislative branch of government, or associated with an insurance business. He will help keep his country free from troubles. He will have a well-earned reputation and a highly favorable life, and will be loved by many.
Least auspicious: He will be clever, but lacking in common sense and wisdom. He will often accomplish the wrong things. He will vacillate frequently, and will have few achievements and little lasting profit.
In yearly hexagram:
Officer or official   He will be recommended for a responsible position.
Business and professional   A good year for planning and for regrouping one's forces and assets.

| Ordinary people | By taking appropriate precautions and keeping within normal limits, he will have a reasonable year. |

Line 2 The lady loses her carriage-window curtain. She should not go in pursuit of it. It will return in seven days.

Modesty and reserve are indicated here. This is proper (the line is weak in the correct place) as the period after completion has not progressed very far as yet. When this period has served its purpose, i.e. completed *its* cycle, as indicated by the words 'in seven days,' then it will be time to recommence action. It is part of this person's destiny that circumstances will not be propitious for great achievements until late in life.

Most auspicious: He will be knowledgeable, wise and virtuous, and will follow the golden mean. His ability and goodness will not be appreciated, and consequently will remain unused. He will persevere along the right path, and his diligence and patience will in time be duly rewarded. In his senior years he will reap the benefits that he could not attain earlier, and he will establish much of merit, as well as achieving fame and wealth.

Least auspicious: He also will have wide and sound knowledge, and will be stable and reliable in whatever he does. He will have many hardships early in life, but will have modest yet sufficient affluence in his old age.

In yearly hexagram:

Officer or official	The year will be adverse at first, but easing later.
Business and professional	He can expect losses or set-backs at first, then gains later.
Ordinary people	He will have difficulties at first, but things will be easy later. Those less auspicious may die.

Line 3 The Illustrious Ancestor carries out an attack on the Devil's Region, and conquers it after three years. Inferior men must not take part in such an undertaking.

Although the principal gains have already been made, many problems of detail still remain to be overcome and set right. This will be done. However, those in power are cautioned to use only duly qualified and reliable people if they expect to receive continuing satisfaction. Furthermore, they must be properly led, by giving the right guidance and by allotting appropriate duties and responsibilities. Maintaining successful operations is not easy. Basically, this line relates to the way people are employed by others once a major enterprise has been completed. Those depicted here will, by and large, be the employers.

Most auspicious: He will be well educated and brilliant, but lacking to a degree in common sense, and hence he will take a long time to truly establish himself. He is likely to become a military commander, or be in charge of a law enforcement agency. He will have a good family and household, but will not enjoy an extended family life.

Least auspicious: He will possess and express resentment about not being given the jobs he believes himself capable of. He will exercise cunning to try to get his way, and he may become acrimonious and arrogant. He will often spend more money than he has, and thus will frequently be in financial difficulty. He will have many troubles and disputes with his own family.

In yearly hexagram:

Officer or official	If in the military, he may be sent into combat. If a diplomat, he may be sent overseas. Other officials will be assigned to trouble areas.
Business and professional	Progress will be very slow, in all matters.
Ordinary people	He should proceed slowly in all matters, to avoid troubles and lawsuits. If taken to court, he will probably lose.

Line 4 The finest clothes, torn to rags. Be mindful all day long.

Making repairs is indicated here. This is an essential part of any activity or enterprise. These persons will be in high and important positions, as indicated by their having the finest of clothes. They will be forced to disperse their knowledge and personal wealth to protect themselves and those dependent on them, as if they were making rags out of their clothing and were stuffing them into a crack to stop a leak in a boat. These persons will be considerate, observant, forthright, magnanimous, noble and chivalrous. Their lives will benefit many.

Most auspicious: He will have great strength of character and courage, and will employ them judiciously. He will be able to achieve peace in times of danger, and likewise prevent calamities in times of peace. His inner strength will be great, and he will support others very ably at all times. He will have a very favorable life, serving well his country, his family, his enterprises and himself.

Least auspicious: He also will be a man of innate wisdom, exercising caution and sound judgment. He will quell troubles and disorders at their inception. He will achieve sufficient, but not abundant, affluence.

In yearly hexagram:

Officer or official	He will maintain his status, despite the troubles surrounding him.
Business and professional	He will be well prepared for whatever is in store for him, and he will not fail.
Ordinary people	By being careful, troubles can be avoided. When travelling by water, he should beware of possible leaks.

Line 5 The neighbor in the east merits less benefit from his sacrifice of an ox than does the neighbor in the west with his simple yet sincere spring sacrifice.

Thankfulness for blessings received (in this case, when matters have been brought to completion) was shown in ancient times by performing sacrificial rites. Two very different modes of sacrifice are depicted here, one person making a grandiose display by slaughtering a valuable ox, while the other makes a simple yet sincere offering in the spring ceremony (when the offerings should be small, according to custom). Since God sees what is in a man's heart, the simple offering sincerely rendered is much more desirable than the elegant offering presented mainly for show.

Most auspicious: He will be careful and thorough, attentive to detail yet far-seeing, broadminded and considerate. He will act only after thorough deliberation, and then with singleness of purpose. He will make many gains and reap the benefits of his efforts, and he will always be of service to others. He will have a highly satisfactory and rewarding life.

Least auspicious: He will be cunning and clever, and without much honesty. He will seek luxury out of vanity, and will harm many persons in his path, including his own family and household. He will have difficulty in all interpersonal relationships. Only if he lives in seclusion will he truly enjoy life.

In yearly hexagram:

Officer or official	He may commit a grave mistake in carrying out rules and regulations.
Business and professional	He is likely to face a number of minor set-backs.
Ordinary people	Large scale plans will fail. Small schemes can be successfully accomplished. It would be auspicious to move to or work in the west, but unfavorable towards the east.

Line 6 His head gets immersed. Danger.

Returning to the idea that 'crossing the great water' means carrying out some great enterprise, here we find a person trying to accomplish something great on his own, and getting his head wet. Obviously this indicates a dangerous situation. It is a basic principle of human life that everyone should serve others in one or more ways. Mutual support and cooperation are vital to success. Regrettably, some, who are otherwise quite intelligent and capable, will believe that they can accomplish major enterprises best single-handed. They have lost sight of what it means to be be a true leader.

Most auspicious: He will have great talent and a love of people. Through exercising constant reverence and care he will accomplish major achievements. At the same time, he will consider and be wary of potential dangers and calamities. He will be slow to make gains, but he will keep and protect what he attains, and will look after his family.

Least auspicious: He will be talented and ambitious, but he will also be vain and will regard himself highly. This will incur the wrath of heaven and the opposition of man. Difficulty upon difficulty will pile up, and he may die young.

In yearly hexagram:

Officer or official	He will destroy himself professionally if he tries to rise too high this year.

Business and professional	He will meet frequent opposition, and it will be difficult to progress.
Ordinary people	He may associate with a mean person, get into trouble, or grow mean himself.

KEYNOTES

1. You must continually analyze situations to keep them in hand.
2. Modesty and reserve bring their own rewards.
3. Use only qualified people and suitable ideas.
4. Be prepared to give of yourself whenever necessary.
5. Quality is more to be desired than quantity.
6. For major efforts seek out the cooperation of others.

CONDENSATIONS FOR DAILY CYCLES

1. Joyousness is great when an enterprise is complete. Beware of becoming heedless, and proceed with caution.
2. Act with restraint, and do not force activity. Matters will commence at the right time.
3. Only that which is right should be attempted, and with strong support, since considerable time will be required for its consummation.
4. People will test everyone and everything new. Watch out for possible evil.
5. Actions taken with sincerity are ultimately more rewarding than those done for show. Good fortune is on its way.
6. Do not glory in the past, or rest on your laurels; it is the present that counts. Keep moving ahead.

Hexagram 64   Wei Chi ☰☰ *Before Completion*

SIMPLE TRANSLATION OF TEXT

Before Completion. Success. The little fox gets his tail wet just before the completion of his crossing. Nothing advantageous.

COMMENTARY

This hexagram is the exact opposite of hexagram 63, and every line is in the wrong place. Success is augured by virtue of the potential of each line to change, and thereby, through action, bring matters to a successful conclusion. The fox has always been considered a wily and wary animal. When crossing a frozen stream a fox will proceed carefully, listening for possible cracks. Depicted here is a little fox, therefore one that is young and inexperienced. Hence he is not sufficiently wary, and, just before completing the crossing, in his hurry to get across, gets his tail wet. The foregoing shows the possible courses of action before completion. By being correct, by exercising care and prudence, and by using one's potential wisely, success can be attained, and is presaged. However, if one is like the young fox, then nothing will be advantageous, no matter how carefully planned in advance. The three lower lines, on the whole, relate to inadequate experience or insufficient inner worth to produce great success, while the three upper lines bespeak favorableness, and great things about to be accomplished.

Those born in the seventh month will be more auspicious.

CONTROLLING LINES (FROM BOTTOM TO TOP)
Line 1   His tail gets wet. Humiliation.

Line 1 is a weak line, and implies a lack of experience, inner strength, wisdom and prudence. These qualities, however, are precisely those that are needed at the commencement of great enterprises. Those persons who are innately good will be able to sustain themselves moderately well, but those without any strength of character will suffer appreciably. Their destiny is not very favorable, and hence their timing will always seem to be wrong whenever they try to accomplish something. In general, it will be hard for them to achieve anything.
Most auspicious: He will possess considerable knowledge, but he will be unable to accomplish worthwhile projects. He will be what might be termed 'a dumb *savant*,' i.e. he will possess much knowledge, but little practicality with which to put it to use. He will find circumstances opposing his efforts to advance so often that he will give up his ambitions and settle down to a simple life, in which he will find contentment.
Least auspicious: He will have a generally unfavorable life, from beginning to end. He will tend to quit everything he begins, whether it be higher education, learning a trade, establishing a friendship, developing family relationships, or whatever. He will

never be contented, and will always be searching, and he will have many troubles.

In yearly hexagram:

Officer or official	There will be impediments and difficulties ahead, and he will be unable to advance.
Business and professional	He will have small gains only, if any.
Ordinary people	There will be troubles in the family business. He should be alert to the possibility of drowning.

Line 2 He brakes his wheels. Firmness and correctness bring good fortune.

Line 2 is strong, but since it is in the wrong place this person should proceed slowly and carefully, following the right courses and thereby bringing matters gradually to completion. Thus he will attain good fortune. The results that these individuals achieve will be by no means outstanding, yet they will be capable and intelligent persons, respected in their chosen professions and in their personal lives.

Most auspicious: He will be genteel, sincere and reverent in all his thoughts, words and deeds. Fate will circumscribe his activities and his achievements, but he will be respected by others and will have many friends. He will be content with modest accomplishments in both his profession and his personal life.

Least auspicious: He also will be a reverent, harmonious and likeable person, who follows the golden mean. He will avoid arguments whenever possible. He will have only modest achievements, but no shortage of material essentials.

In yearly hexagram:

Officer or official	He will overcome a major handicap or difficulty, and will win favor.
Business and professional	Efforts towards advancement will largely be blocked.
Ordinary people	He should follow established patterns for the best results, and wait for a better time to try and progress. Troubles will readily develop if he succumbs to rash ideas.

Line 3   The situation has not been fully and correctly prepared. Advancing brings misfortune. Advantageous to cross the great stream.

The position of line 3 is such that although matters have partially developed, an incorrect start has been made. Continuing on the present path would lead to misfortune. It would be better, and definitely advantageous, to start again, following the correct principles and with adequate and worthy cooperation from others, by the means of which any enterprise can be accomplished. A few of these individuals will learn exactly what needs to be done for success, but they will be hesitant to put their new-found theories into practice. The rest will continually make mistakes.

Most auspicious: He will enjoy being led rather than leading. He will avoid decisions as much as possible, and this quality will keep him from progressing far intellectually. He would find it an undesirable burden if he were assigned to a high position, but he will gladly follow others, feeling that this is the path to harmony.

Least auspicious: He will be cunning and deceitful, and will be in constant trouble with others. As it will be arduous for him to advance, he will not try with any persistence. His home life will be inharmonious, and he will have very few gains.

In yearly hexagram:

Officer or official	He will possess inadequate ability for his position, but if he receives help he will be able to muddle through.
Business and professional	Some proposals and attempts at progress will fail.
Ordinary people	He will have several difficulties. Overseas business ventures should be gainful, but home undertakings will barely break even.

Line 4   Persistence brings good fortune. Regrets disappear. He energizes his resources against the Devil's Country. After three years, rewards are bestowed.

Line 4 is at the bottom of the trigram Li, clarity, and persons born under this line see what needs to be done and begin to do it.

The experience of line 3 enables them to follow correct principles and this brings good fortune. Hence, any regrets over the course they have chosen will disappear. These persons are more advanced (in terms of karma) than those born under line 3. Consequently, they must carry out corrective measures as well as progressive ones. This is never simple, and requires great personal courage, impartiality and persistence. In due course, their efforts will be successful, and rewards will be bestowed on them.

Most auspicious: He will start life in modest circumstances. He will obtain a good education, and will strive constantly to improve himself, both personally and professionally. His persistence will be rewarded by appointment to a high and influential position late in life. He will then be favored by the leader. His home life will be the envy of others.

Least auspicious: He will be in a position where he is responsible for making corrections and reforms. He will cherish what is right and good. He will receive help from his superiors, and his strongest desires will eventually be fulfilled.

In yearly hexagram:

Officer or official	He will be placed in a high position, and will receive a coveted award. If in the military, he will be in charge of a campaign.
Business and professional	New proposals and progressive moves will be favored.
Ordinary people	To profit this year one must gain the help and cooperation of good people.

Line 5 Persisting in firmness brings good fortune. No regrets. The light of the superior man is true. Good fortune.

Even though line 5 is weak, there are several aspects favoring it. It is the ruler of the hexagram, and the center of the trigram Li, clarity (light). The inner hexagram is 'After Completion,' where all the lines are in their proper places. In that hexagram the ruler is line 2, because it is the proper correlate of the strong line 5. Line 2 of the inner hexagram is also the center line of trigram Li. Thus, even though line 5 here is weak, this man has support and can advance persistently, making no major errors. Being the heart of Clarity above, and supported by the heart of

Clarity inwardly, makes his light lustrous and true. When a man's inner light is true, external blessings follow; and that is what transpires here.

Most auspicious: He will be a great administrator, selecting highly qualified people to support his enterprises, and assigning appropriate responsibilities within just and acceptable limits. He will win the confidence and support of the people. He will achieve a reputation through his ordinances and writings, and will have a highly favorable life in all respects.

Least auspicious: He also will be a person of noble character and shining virtue. The omens are highly favorable for a business or professional career. He will be able to make large profits as well as promote and develop his enterprise. He will have a good family life as well.

In yearly hexagram:

Officer or official	He will be promoted.
Business and professional	He will make good gains. Written work will receive special acclaim.
Ordinary people	He will make good profits, and strong desires will be fulfilled.

Line 6 Confidence reposed in him. Feasting without excessive indulgence. If he allows his head to get wet, he forfeits this trust.

This being line 6 indicates that something great is about to be undertaken. Confidence and trust are reposed in the one who will undertake the task. The people are gay and festive within due limits, while waiting for the new situation to come into being. If he gets his head wet, i.e. if he does not exercise inner strength, wisdom and prudence, and follow the right courses, then he is bound to forfeit the trust reposed in him. Some of these persons will have the ability and strength of character to carry out their responsibilities, while others will be weak and will succumb to the temptations present in high positions.

Most auspicious: He will be knowledgeable, talented, wise, courageous and practical, and will even possess the ability to save his country from disaster if necessary. His path and activities will be ordained and blessed by heaven, and he will attain merited fame and fortune.

Least auspicious: He will rise to a high position, but will be morally and spiritually weak. He will be self-seeking, and will over-indulge in sensual pleasures. He may even become totally degenerate, and he will gradually be shunned by his peers, his friends and his family.

In yearly hexagram:

Officer or official	He will be promoted.
Business and professional	He will be advanced, and will make gains.
Ordinary people	Difficulties will be smoothed out, and the year will be good. Older people will reap some special reward, relating to food.

KEYNOTES

1. Fortune does not smile on weak characters.
2. Adjust the speed of your actions to the demands of the times.
3. If your course is wrong, begin again.
4. When you see something which needs to be done, do it.
5. Develop clarity, and let your inner light shine forth.
6. Life is what you make it.

CONDENSATIONS FOR DAILY CYCLES

1. Do not be over enthusiastic, with but little knowledge. Be thoughtful and conservative.
2. Stop to contemplate your situation. Proceed with caution at first; then advance with conviction and do what is right.
3. Make necessary corrections and repairs before proceeding. Start again from scratch, if necessary.
4. What you desire will come about, if you pursue your goal humbly and with righteous persistence.
5. Your intuition will tell you what is right for you today. Follow your hunches.
6. Whenever a task has been satisfactorily completed it is right to enjoy the accomplishment within due limits. Be careful not to go to excesses.

4 | Compatibility

The selection of partners and companions

The basic principles of *I Ching* are as applicable to human relationships as they are to philosophy, medicine, astrology and other aspects of life. A man, as we have seen previously, can be given certain trigrams that represent his character. The nature of the year of birth also colours the character. Certain major influences exist during any one year, and determine the general nature of persons born in that year. The compatibility or non-compatibility of their respective yearly trigrams determines how well two individuals are likely to get along with each other. Hence, the selection of marriage (and other) partners, and companions, will benefit from consideration of the trigrams involved.

For the purpose of determining compatibility, the Later Heaven Sequence of trigrams and the Magic Square of Three (Figures 2 and 3, p. 10) are used as the base. The trigrams are numbered as if the Later Heaven Sequence were superimposed on the Magic Square. Since there is no trigram in the center of the Later Heaven Sequence corresponding to the number five, special studies had to be made regarding this number. From an extensive collection of data, the ancient scholars found that for a man the trigram K'un, ☷, would be the most representative, while the trigram Ken, ☶, would best apply to woman. Thus we obtain the information shown in Table 21.

Table 21 *Trigrams for determining compatibility*

1 = ☳		4 = ☴		7 = ☱	
2 = ☷		5 = *		8 = ☶	
3 = ☲		6 = ☰		9 = ☵	

* For a man, the trigram for 5 is ☷, which is the same as for 2. For a woman, the trigram for 5 is ☶, which is the same as for 8.

432

Additional studies by the ancient scholars showed that compatibility is influenced by groupings of the trigrams. They considered K'an, ☵; Chên, ☳; Sun, ☴, and Li, ☲, representatives of water, wood and fire, as the East natal group, and K'un, ☷; Tui, ☱; Ch'ien, ☰, and Kên, ☶, representatives of earth and metal, as the West natal group. In another sense, the groupings are: father, mother, youngest son and youngest daughter in the West, and eldest son, eldest daughter, middle son and middle daughter in the East. The effects of the groupings in terms of compatibility are shown in the tables below.

It must be remembered, however, that as with the other portents in *I Ching*, the auspices here can be challenged by the use of one's free will, in thought and action. Consequently, from observations, some matchings in life may not appear to agree with the tables given below. The reality may be either better or worse than the prediction, depending on the spiritual development and attitude of the individuals concerned. The tables, therefore, should only be considered as a general guide.

On looking at the yearly number tables below, it will be noticed that for the first year of the Upper Sexagenary Cycle, 1864, the man's number is one, and the woman's is five. Five is midway between one and nine. Furthermore, in the fixed magic square, five works equally with all the other numbers. Man is assigned the number one, because the male initiates action.

Compatibility tables are given below the yearly number tables. The rationale behind them can be ascertained by anyone desiring to do so from the information given above. (See also pp. 11–15.)

Table 22   *Yearly number tables*

Year	Man	Woman	Year	Man	Woman	Year	Man	Woman
1864	1	5	1871	3	3	1878	5	1
1865	9	6	1872	2	4	1879	4	2
1866	8	7	1873	1	5	1880	3	3
1867	7	8	1874	9	6	1881	2	4
1868	6	9	1875	8	7	1882	1	5
1869	5	1	1876	7	8	1883	9	6
1870	4	2	1877	6	9	1884	8	7

Table 22 (*contd*)

Year	Man	Woman	Year	Man	Woman	Year	Man	Woman
1885	7	8	1918	1	5	1951	4	2
1886	6	9	1919	9	6	1952	3	3
1887	5	1	1920	8	7	1953	2	4
1888	4	2	1921	7	8	1954	1	5
1889	3	3	1922	6	9	1955	9	6
1890	2	4	1923	5	1	1956	8	7
1891	1	5	1924	4	2	1957	7	8
1892	9	6	1925	3	3	1958	6	9
1893	8	7	1926	2	4	1959	5	1
1894	7	8	1927	1	5	1960	4	2
1895	6	9	1928	9	6	1961	3	3
1896	5	1	1929	8	7	1962	2	4
1897	4	2	1930	7	8	1963	1	5
1898	3	3	1931	6	9	1964	9	6
1899	2	4	1932	5	1	1965	8	7
1900	1	5	1933	4	2	1966	7	8
1901	9	6	1934	3	3	1967	6	9
1902	8	7	1935	2	4	1968	5	1
1903	7	8	1936	1	5	1969	4	2
1904	6	9	1937	9	6	1970	3	3
1905	5	1	1938	8	7	1971	2	4
1906	4	2	1939	7	8	1972	1	5
1907	3	3	1940	6	9	1973	9	6
1908	2	4	1941	5	1	1974	8	7
1909	1	5	1942	4	2	1975	7	8
1910	9	6	1943	3	3	1976	6	9
1911	8	7	1944	2	4	1977	5	1
1912	7	8	1945	1	5	1978	4	2
1913	6	9	1946	9	6	1979	3	3
1914	5	1	1947	8	7	1980	2	4
1915	4	2	1948	7	8	1981	1	5
1916	3	3	1949	6	9	1982	9	6
1917	2	4	1950	5	1	1983	8	7

The most auspicious combinations are:

6 – 2	4 – 3
2 – 6	1 – 9
7 – 8	9 – 1
8 – 7	1 – 4
6 – 7	4 – 1
7 – 6	3 – 9
3 – 4	9 – 3

The moderately auspicious combinations are:

2 – 7	8 – 2
7 – 2	4 – 9
6 – 8	9 – 4
8 – 6	1 – 3
2 – 8	3 – 1

More or less neutral combinations are:

1 – 1	6 – 6
2 – 2	7 – 7
3 – 3	8 – 8
4 – 4	9 – 9
5 – 5	

Moderately bad combinations are:

1 – 6	6 – 3
6 – 1	3 – 6
3 – 8	8 – 1
8 – 3	1 – 8
7 – 4	4 – 2
4 – 7	2 – 4
9 – 2	7 – 9
2 – 9	9 – 7

The least auspicious combinations are:

1 – 2	6 – 4
2 – 1	4 – 6
6 – 9	1 – 7
9 – 6	7 – 1
3 – 7	3 – 2
7 – 3	2 – 3
4 – 8	9 – 8
8 – 4	8 – 9

For those wishing to examine the degree of compatibility further, a comparison of the natal hexagrams should be made. Lines which are of opposite polarity between the two hexagrams enhance the potential compatibility. There can be from nought to six such correspondences, and the higher the number, the more favorable the omens. For example, consider Hexagrams 1 and 2. All the lines are opposite in character, so this situation would be most favorable. However, if both individuals were born under Hexagram 1, there would be no opposites, and little compatibility. As another example, if the two natal hexagrams are numbers 11 and 12 there is likely to be great compatibility, because the Yangs and Yins are all in opposite places. The most favorable pairings of hexagrams are given in Table 23. The comparison of other natal hexagrams should be done on an individual basis, comparing line 1 with line 1, line 2 with line 2, etc., determining how many are of the opposite polarity, and hence the degree of favorability.

Table 23   *Most favorable pairings of hexagrams*

1 − 2	17 − 18	33 − 19	49 − 4
2 − 1	18 − 17	34 − 20	50 − 3
3 − 50	19 − 33	35 − 5	51 − 57
4 − 49	20 − 34	36 − 6	52 − 58
5 − 35	21 − 48	37 − 40	53 − 54
6 − 36	22 − 47	38 − 39	54 − 53
7 − 13	23 − 43	39 − 38	55 − 59
8 − 14	24 − 44	40 − 37	56 − 60
9 − 16	25 − 46	41 − 31	57 − 51
10 − 15	26 − 45	42 − 32	58 − 52
11 − 12	27 − 28	43 − 23	59 − 55
12 − 11	28 − 27	44 − 24	60 − 56
13 − 7	29 − 30	45 − 26	61 − 62
14 − 8	30 − 29	46 − 25	62 − 61
15 − 10	31 − 41	47 − 22	63 − 64
16 − 9	32 − 42	48 − 21	64 − 63

As stated above, these various tables are used primarily for determining partners. It should be mentioned that there are several other methods for this purpose in Chinese astrologies.

However, the method described here is the only one relating to *I Ching*. It should always be remembered that, as in other uses of *I Ching*, the auspices of fate can be overcome by man's free will, and the actions he takes.

Appendix A | Table of winter solstices*
1884–1976

Year	Day	Hour	Minute	Year	Day	Hour	Minute
1884	20	17	—	1906	22	01	—
1885	20	22	—	1907	22	07	—
1886	21	04	—	1908	21	13	—
1887	21	10	—	1909	21	18	—
1888	20	16	—	1910	22	00	—
1889	20	21	52	1911	22	06	—
1890	21	03	18	1912	21	11	37
1891	21	10	43	1913	21	17	27
1892	20	15	11	1914	21	23	15
1893	21	20	45	1915	22	05	08
1894	21	03	01	1916	21	15	59
1895	21	08	—	1917	21	21	46
1896	20	14	—	1918	22	03	42
1897	20	20	—	1919	22	09	27
1898	21	02	—	1920	21	15	17
1899	21	08	—	1921	21	21	08
1900	21	13	—	1922	22	02	57
1901	21	19	—	1923	22	08	54
1902	22	01	—	1924	21	14	46
1903	22	07	—	1925	22	08	37
1904	21	13	—	1926	22	14	34
1905	21	19	—	1927	22	20	18

* According to US Nautical Almanacs. Time given is Greenwich Mean Time.

Year	Day	Hour	Minute	Year	Day	Hour	Minute
1928	22	02	04	1953	22	03	32
1929	22	07	53	1954	22	09	25
1930	22	13	40	1955	22	15	12
1931	22	19	30	1956	21	21	00
1932	22	01	15	1957	22	02	49
1933	22	06	58	1958	22	08	40
1934	22	12	50	1959	22	14	35
1935	22	18	37	1960	21	20	27
1936	22	00	27	1961	22	02	20
1937	22	06	22	1962	22	08	15
1938	22	12	14	1963	22	14	02
1939	22	18	06	1964	21	19	50
1940	21	23	55	1965	22	01	41
1941	22	05	45	1966	22	07	29
1942	22	11	40	1967	22	13	17
1943	22	17	30	1968	21	19	00
1944	21	23	15	1969	22	00	44
1945	22	05	04	1970	22	06	36
1946	22	10	54	1971	22	12	24
1947	22	16	43	1972	21	18	13
1948	21	22	34	1973	22	00	08
1949	22	04	24	1974	22	05	57
1950	22	10	14	1975	22	11	46
1951	22	16	01	1976	21	17	36
1952	21	21	44				

Appendix B / *Squares*

	4	9	2
Fixed Magic Square	3	5	7
	8	1	6

Nine Star Circulating Squares:

	9	5	7			1	6	8
(1)	8	1	3		(2)	9	2	4
	4	6	2			5	7	3

	2	7	9			3	8	1
(3)	1	3	5		(4)	2	4	6
	6	8	4			7	9	5

	4	9	2			5	1	3
(5)	3	5	7		(6)	4	6	8
	8	1	6			9	2	7

	6	2	4			7	3	5
(7)	5	7	9		(8)	6	8	1
	1	3	8			2	4	9

	8	4	6
(9)	7	9	2
	3	5	1

Note: The center number of each circulating square relates to the number for a man; consequently each square can be related to a specific year, e.g. square (1) above would relate to 1972, or any other year for which the man's number is one (see Chapter 4).

440

Appendix C / Applicability in the Southern hemisphere

At the time of writing the *Astrology of I Ching* the authors recognized that it was not directly applicable to the Southern hemisphere (see footnote, p. 23). Nothing in the Ho Map Lo Map Rational Number manuscript revealed any firm statements as to how it would be applied elsewhere than China. This, of course, was natural since the word China in Chinese means Central Country. Apparently this meaning was accepted quite literally by many. Thus little or no consideration was given to those outside of China and especially not to those in the Southern hemisphere. Recognition of these facts led Dr Chu to do extensive research into the matter and his results are set forth below.

Everyone knows that the Southern hemisphere is the counterpart of the Northern hemisphere, i.e. when it's summer in the north it's winter in the south; the circulation of the ocean and windstorm currents are reversed, indicating different influences acting on each area. While the applicable earthly hours remain the same for the same longitude, the point of reference for calculations in the Southern hemisphere must be a point diametrically opposed to the point used in the Northern hemisphere. One of the first things this does is to offset the astrological year by six months from that in the Northern hemisphere, i.e. from what we call Summer Solstice to Summer Solstice in the Northern Hemisphere to what is known as Winter Solstice to Winter Solstice in the Southern hemisphere, roughly June 22 to June 21.

> e.g. 1929 astrologically is from June 22, 1929 to June 21, 1930 approximately in the Southern hemisphere. Similarly, 1978 is from June 22, 1978 to June 21, 1979 approximately.

It will be noted too that the sexagenary* subcycles shown in Table 24

---

* See p. 16 for the origin of the sexagenary cycles.

commence 'five' years later than those of the Northern hemisphere. In actuality it is five and one-half years, as the astrological years start six months apart.

Since the Southern hemisphere is the counterpart of the Northern we must use opposites when considering the time and location in the Southern hemisphere. Now the astrological year in the north is from December 22 to December 21 approximately whereas in the south it is June 22 to June 21 approximately, with the year in the south commencing six months later than the corresponding year in the north (astrologically). In actuality then, for an 'A' year in the north the first half will be an 'E' half-year in the south and the last half-year an 'F' half-year in the south. By progression we see that the next 'A' year for the south will be the astrological year 1929 or from June 22, 1929 to June 21, 1930. Further, the opposite of the Horary Branch symbol 'a' is 'g' so an 'a' day in the Northern hemisphere is a 'g' day in the Southern. These differences form the basis of the values in Table 24. The months are calculated the same way in both hemispheres but their effect is opposite (see Tables 5 and 25). The sidereal times are the same in both hemispheres for the same longitude but the horary symbols may vary according to the Celestial Stem used in entering Table 7.

The method of calculation for obtaining the natal hexagram is the same in both hemispheres. It is in the table values wherein a difference occurs. The following steps will illustrate the appropriate methods:

1.   Enter Table 24 with the appropriate astrological year (June 22 to June 21 approx.) and determine the yearly and daily cycle values.
2.   Enter Table 2 and determine the sexagenary cycle value.
3.   Enter Table 1 and determine the numerical values for the yearly cycle.
4.   Enter Table 26 with the yearly Celestial Stem and determine the monthly symbols.
5.   Enter Table 1 and determine the values for the monthly symbols.
6.   Add the daily value from Table 24 to the daily value from Table 6.
7.   Enter Table 2 and determine alphabetical symbols for the numbers obtained in step 6.
8.   Enter Table 1 and determine the numerical values for the daily value symbols.
9.   Enter Table 7 with the Celestial Stem for the daily value and select the symbols for the sidereal time of birth, i.e. time corrected for longitude, daylight savings, etc.

10. Enter Table 1 and determine the numerical value for the time of birth.

11. etc. Proceed as described in the main section of the book (p. 28, step 15 and subsequent).

The sexagenary subcycles in the Southern hemisphere

Table 24a   *Middle cycle* (1869–1928)

year	yearly cycle	daily cycle	year	yearly cycle	daily cycle	year	yearly cycle	daily cycle
1869	1	23	1870	2	28	1871	3	33
1872	4	38	1873	5	44	1874	6	46
1875	7	54	1876	8	59	1877	9	5
1878	10	10	1879	11	15	1880	12	20
1881	13	26	1882	14	31	1883	15	36
1884	16	41	1885	17	47	1886	18	52
1887	19	57	1888	20	2	1889	21	8
1890	22	13	1891	23	18	1892	24	23
1893	25	29	1894	26	34	1895	27	39
1896	28	44	1897	29	50	1898	30	55
1899	31	60	1900	32	5	1901	33	10
1902	34	15	1903	35	20	1904	36	25
1905	37	31	1906	38	36	1907	39	41
1908	40	46	1909	41	52	1910	42	57
1911	43	2	1912	44	7	1913	45	13
1914	46	18	1915	47	23	1916	48	28
1917	49	34	1918	50	39	1919	51	44
1920	52	49	1921	53	55	1922	54	60
1923	55	5	1924	56	10	1925	57	16
1926	58	21	1927	59	26	1928	60	31

Table 24b *Lower cycle* (1929–1988)

year	yearly cycle	daily cycle	year	yearly cycle	daily cycle	year	yearly cycle	daily cycle
1929	1	37	1930	2	42	1931	3	47
1932	4	52	1933	5	58	1934	6	3
1935	7	8	1936	8	13	1937	9	19
1938	10	24	1939	11	29	1940	12	34
1941	13	40	1942	14	45	1943	15	50
1944	16	55	1945	17	1	1946	18	6
1947	19	11	1948	20	16	1949	21	22
1950	22	27	1951	23	32	1952	24	37
1953	25	43	1954	26	48	1955	27	53
1956	28	58	1957	29	4	1958	30	9
1959	31	14	1960	32	19	1961	33	25
1962	34	30	1963	35	35	1964	36	40
1965	37	46	1966	38	51	1967	39	56
1968	40	1	1969	41	7	1970	42	12
1971	43	17	1972	44	22	1973	45	28
1974	46	33	1975	47	38	1976	48	43
1977	49	49	1978	50	54	1979	51	59
1980	52	4	1981	53	10	1982	54	15
1983	55	20	1984	56	25	1985	57	31
1986	58	36	1987	59	41	1988	60	46

Table 24c *Upper cycle* (1989–2048)

year	yearly cycle	daily cycle	year	yearly cycle	daily cycle	year	yearly cycle	daily cycle
1989	1	52	1990	2	57	1991	3	2
1992	4	7	1993	5	13	1994	6	18
1995	7	23	1996	8	28	1997	9	34
1998	10	39	1999	11	44	2000	12	49
2001	13	55	2002	14	60	2003	15	5
2004	16	10	2005	17	16	2006	18	21
2007	19	26	2008	20	31	2009	21	37
2010	22	42	2011	23	47	2012	24	52
2013	25	58	2014	26	3	2015	27	8
2016	28	13	2017	29	19	2018	30	24
2019	31	29	2020	32	34	2021	33	40
2022	34	45	2023	35	50	2024	36	55
2025	37	1	2026	38	6	2027	39	11
2028	40	16	2029	41	22	2030	42	27
2031	43	32	2032	44	37	2033	45	43
2034	46	48	2035	47	53	2036	48	58
2037	49	4	2038	50	9	2039	51	14
2040	52	19	2041	53	25	2042	54	30
2043	55	35	2044	56	40	2045	57	46
2046	58	51	2047	59	56	2048	60	1

Table 25 *The twenty-four seasons in the Southern hemisphere*

Name	Month	Hexagram	Date (1975)	Time (GMT)*	C.L.S.†
Slight Heat		䷗	1–05–75	23:18	285
	(−)6th				
Great Heat			1–20–75	16:37	300
Autumn Begins		䷒	2–04–75	10:59	315
	(+)7th				
Limit of Heat			2–19–75	6:50	330
White Dew		䷊	3–06–75	5:06	345
	(−)8th				
Autumnal Equinox			3–21–75	5:57	360
Cold Dew		䷡	4–05–75	10:02	15
	(+)9th				
Hoar Frost Descends			4–20–75	17:07	30
Winter Begins		䷪	5–06–75	3:27	45
	(−)10th				
Little Snow			5–21–75	16:24	60
Heavy Snow		䷀	6–06–75	7:42	75
	(+)11th				
Winter Solstice			6–22–75	0:26	90
Little Cold		䷫	7–07–75	17:59	105
	(−)12th				
Severe Cold			7–23–75	11:20	120
Spring Begins		䷠	8–08–75	3:45	135
	(+)1st				
Rain Water			8–23–75	18:24	150
Excited Insects		䷋	9–08–75	6:33	165
	(−)2nd				
Vernal Equinox			9–23–75	15:55	180

Clear and Bright		10-08-75	22:02	195
	(+)3rd			
Grain Rains		10-24-75	1:06	· 210
Summer Begins		11-08-75	1:03	225
	(—)4th			
Grain Fills		11-22-75	22:31	240
Grain in Ear		12-07-75	17:47	255
	(+)5th			
Summer Solstice		12-22-75	11:46	270

* GMT: Greenwich Mean Time   † C.L.S.: Celestial longitude of the sun.

Table 26 *Monthly Celestial Stems and Horary Branches
in the Southern hemisphere*

Month	Season	Applicable years				
		A and F	B and G	C and H	D and I	E and J
January	— { Slight Heat / Great Heat	Hh	Jh	Bh	Dh	Fh
February	+ { Autumn Begins / Limit of Heat	Ii	Ai	Ci	Ei	Gi
March	— { White Dew / Autumnal Equinox	Jj	Bj	Dj	Fj	Hj
April	+ { Cold Dew / Hoar Frost Descends	Ak	Ck	Ek	Gk	Ik

447

Table 26 contd.

Month	Season		Applicable years				
			A and F	B and G	C and H	D and I	E and J
May	−	Winter Begins / Little Snow	Bl	Dl	Fl	Hl	Jl
June	+	Heavy Snow / Winter Solstice	Ca	Ea	Ga	Ia	Aa
July	−	Little Cold / Severe Cold	Bb	Db	Fb	Hb	Jb
August	+	Spring Begins / Rain Water	Cc	Ec	Gc	Ic	Ac
September	−	Excited Insects / Vernal Equinox	Dd	Fd	Hd	Jd	Bd
October	+	Clear and Bright / Grain Rains	Ee	Ge	Ie	Ae	Ce
November	−	Summer Begins / Grain Fills	Ff	Hf	Jf	Bf	Df
December	+	Grain in Ears / Summer Solstice	Gg	Ig	Ag	Cg	Eg

Index